D1666676

# Experimental Political Science

*Research Methods Series*

General Editors: **Bernhard Kittel**, Professor of Economic Sociology, Faculty of Business, Economics and Statistics, University of Vienna, Austria, and **Benoît Rihoux**, Professor of Political Science, Université catholique de Louvain (UCL), Belgium.

In association with the European Consortium for Political Research (ECPR), Palgrave Macmillan is delighted to announce the launch of a new book series dedicated to producing cutting-edge titles in Research Methods. While political science currently tends to import methods developed in neighbouring disciplines, the series contributes to developing a methodological apparatus focusing on those methods which are appropriate in dealing with the specific research problems of the discipline.

The series provides students and scholars with state-of-the-art scholarship on methodology, methods and techniques. It comprises innovative and intellectually rigorous monographs and edited collections which bridge schools of thought and cross the boundaries of conventional approaches. The series covers both empirical-analytical and interpretive approaches, micro and macro studies, and quantitative and qualitative methods.

*Titles include*:

Alexander Bogner, Beate Littig and Wolfgang Menz (*editors*)
INTERVIEWING EXPERTS

Bernhard Kittel, Wolfgang J. Luhan and Rebecca B. Morton (*editors*)
EXPERIMENTAL POLITICAL SCIENCE
Principles and Practices

Lane Kenworthy and Alexander Hicks (*editors*)
METHOD AND SUBSTANCE IN MACROCOMPARATIVE ANALYSIS

Audie Klotz and Deepa Prakash (*editors*)
QUALITATIVE METHODS IN INTERNATIONAL RELATIONS
A Pluralist Guide

**Research Methods Series**
**Series Standing Order ISBN 978–0230–20679–3–hardcover**
**Series Standing Order ISBN 978–0230–20680–9–paperback**
(*outside North America only*)

You can receive future titles in this series as they are published by placing a standing order. Please contact your bookseller or, in case of difficulty, write to us at the address below with your name and address, the title of the series and one of the ISBNs quoted above.

Customer Services Department, Macmillan Distribution Ltd, Houndmills, Basingstoke, Hampshire RG21 6XS, England

# Experimental Political Science

## Principles and Practices

Edited by

**Bernhard Kittel**
*Professor of Economic Sociology,*
*University of Vienna, Austria*

**Wolfgang J. Luhan**
*Assistant Professor*
*Ruhr University Bochum, Germany*

and

**Rebecca B. Morton**
*Professor of Politics*
*New York University, USA*

Editorial matter and selection © Bernhard Kittel, Wolfgang J. Luhan and Rebecca B. Morton 2012
All remaining chapters © respective authors 2012

All rights reserved. No reproduction, copy or transmission of this publication may be made without written permission.

No portion of this publication may be reproduced, copied or transmitted save with written permission or in accordance with the provisions of the Copyright, Designs and Patents Act 1988, or under the terms of any licence permitting limited copying issued by the Copyright Licensing Agency, Saffron House, 6–10 Kirby Street, London EC1N 8TS.

Any person who does any unauthorized act in relation to this publication may be liable to criminal prosecution and civil claims for damages.

The authors have asserted their rights to be identified as the authors of this work in accordance with the Copyright, Designs and Patents Act 1988.

First published 2012 by
PALGRAVE MACMILLAN

Palgrave Macmillan in the UK is an imprint of Macmillan Publishers Limited, registered in England, company number 785998, of Houndmills, Basingstoke, Hampshire RG21 6XS.

Palgrave Macmillan in the US is a division of St Martin's Press LLC, 175 Fifth Avenue, New York, NY 10010.

Palgrave Macmillan is the global academic imprint of the above companies and has companies and representatives throughout the world.

Palgrave® and Macmillan® are registered trademarks in the United States, the United Kingdom, Europe and other countries

ISBN: 978–0–230–30085–9

This book is printed on paper suitable for recycling and made from fully managed and sustained forest sources. Logging, pulping and manufacturing processes are expected to conform to the environmental regulations of the country of origin.

A catalogue record for this book is available from the British Library.

A catalog record for this book is available from the Library of Congress.

10  9  8  7  6  5  4  3  2  1
21  20  19  18  17  16  15  14  13  12

Printed and bound in Great Britain by
CPI Antony Rowe, Chippenham and Eastbourne

# Contents

v

Univ.-Bibl. UB Bamberg
Bamberg ausgeschieden

Univ.-Bibl.
Bamberg

# Figures

# Tables

# Preface and Acknowledgments

This book is one of the tangible results of Rebecca B. Morton's fellowship at the Hanse Wissenschaftskolleg (HWK) in Delmenhorst, situated in north-western Germany between Bremen and Oldenburg, in the fall of 2008, where she had been invited to stay by Bernhard Kittel and Wolfgang J. Luhan for some joint experiments on voting behavior.

In December 2008, a group of German and American experimentalists in political science met at the HWK to discuss some recent work. Though the group was rather small, among the participants was a large share of all political scientists doing experimental work in Germany at that time. During the discussions, the idea came up to compile a book that aims beyond a handbook-style overview of the field and the explanation of the principles of experimental work. This book should cover the issues that have been the topic of the discussions during the workshop: Why did we do it this way and not in a different way? What practical restrictions did we encounter and how did we deal with them? How did we circumvent that specific challenge to inferential leverage or validity? Hence, the aim of the book would be to discuss the confrontation of scientific principles with actual practices. The book in your hands is the final result of this collective endeavor. We hope that it meets these aims and that it will become a useful addition to the existing literature on experimental political science.

We thank the rector of the HWK, Reto Weiler, for making Rebecca B. Morton's stay and the workshop possible as well as for his famous Swiss hospitality; the scientific advisory board of the HWK, for supporting the application; and Wolfgang Stenzel, research manager at the HWK, for his invaluable support in preparation of and during the stay. We also thank Tanja Sluiter for copyediting the manuscript and Liz Holwell, our editor at Palgrave Macmillan, for her continuing and patient support. Benoît Rihoux, Bernhard Kittel's co-editor of the ECPR Research Methods Series, has been encouraging and supportive of this project from the very beginning. In particular, we thank the anonymous reviewer for his or her critical and invaluable comments on the initial proposal as well as on the final outline that have helped to push the project forward.

The workshop has been co-sponsored by HWK and the Center for Social Science Methodology (MSW) at the University of Oldenburg, partly investing funds that have been allocated to the MSW by the Ministry of Science and Culture of Lower Saxony in the framework of the 'Niedersachsen Vorab' of the Volkswagen Foundation. We thank all of these institutions for their support.

Last but not least, our families had to endure evenings and weekends spent behind the computer instead of engaging in family life. It is part of the current academic tragedy that the work-life balance is out of balance. We thank them for their understanding, and hope that they take part in our pride of having the project finished.

# Contributors

**André Blais** is Professor in the Department of Political Science at the Université de Montréal, a research fellow with the Centre interuniversitaire de recherche en économie quantitative (CIREQ) and the Canada Research Chair in Electoral Studies. His research interests are voting and elections, electoral systems, public opinion and research methodology.

**Ted A. Brader** is Associate Professor of Political Science at the University of Michigan, author of *Campaigning for Hearts and Minds*, and associate principal investigator on both the American National Election Studies and Timesharing Experiments for the Social Sciences. He received the 2009 Emerging Scholar Award in Elections, Public Opinion, and Voting Behavior.

**Thomas Bräuninger** is Professor of Political Economy and Academic Director of the Graduate School of Social and Behavioral Sciences at the University of Mannheim. His research interests are in political economy, comparative politics and analytical politics. His articles have appeared in the *British Journal of Political Science, Journal of Theoretical Politics, European Journal of Political Research, European Union Politics, Journal of Conflict Resolution*, among others.

**Thomas Gschwend** is Professor and Chair of the Department of Political Sciences, University of Mannheim. His research has been published in *Political Analysis*, the *British Journal of Political Science* and the *European Journal of Political Research*, among others.

**Jens Großer** is Assistant Professor of Political Science at Florida State University and he was previously a research associate/lecturer at Princeton University, Department of Economics, and a research assistant at the University of Cologne, Department of Economics. He holds a PhD in Economics from the University of Amsterdam and Tinbergen Institute, the Netherlands. Some of his work has been published in the *American Political Science Review* and the *American Journal of Political Science*.

**Marc Hooghe** is Professor of Political Science at the University of Leuven in Belgium, and a visiting professor at the Universities of Mannheim in Germany and Lille, France. He publishes mainly on issues like social capital, political participation, political socialization and electoral behavior.

**Thomas Kalwitzki** is a junior lecturer and PhD candidate at the Carl von Ossietzky University Oldenburg.

**Jana Keller** is Professor of Economic Sociology at the University of Vienna since March 2012. Before, he has been an MA student in Social Sciences at the Carl von Ossietzky University Oldenburg.

**Bernhard Kittel** is Professor of Economic Sociology at the University of Vienna since March 2012. Before, he has been Professor of Social Science Methodology at the Carl von Ossietzky University Oldenburg. He is interested in collective decision making and comparative political economy. His work has appeared in *Social Choice and Welfare*, the *European Political Science Review*, the *European Sociological Review*, the *Socio-Economic Review*, and *Work and Occupations*, among others.

**Jean-François Laslier** is a senior member of the French National Center of Scientific Research. He is an economist and a mathematician, working in the fields of normative economics, social choice, game theory, formal political science, and experimental economics. He teaches at Ecole Polytechnique in Palaiseau in France.

**Wolfgang J. Luhan** is Assistant Professor and Head of the Experimental Lab (RUBec) at the Ruhr-University of Bochum's Department of Economics. His work has appeared in *Experimental Economics* and *Social Choice and Welfare*.

**Kamil Marcinkiewicz** is a postdoctoral researcher at the Center for Social Science Methodology at the University of Oldenburg in Germany. His main fields of interest include quantitative text analysis, party politics and elections in Germany and countries of Central and Eastern Europe.

**Sofie Marien** is a postdoctoral researcher of the Research Foundation Flanders (FWO) at the University of Leuven. She is a visiting scholar at Åbo Akademi University and a member of the PARTIREP project. Her work on political trust and political participation has appeared in *Electoral Studies, European Journal of Political Research* and *Political Studies*.

**Michael F. Meffert** is Assistant Professor in Political Psychology and Political Communication in the Department of Political Science at Leiden University. His research has been published in journals such as the *American Political Science Review* and the *European Journal of Political Research*.

**Rebecca B. Morton** is Professor of Politics in the Wilf Family Department of Politics at New York University. She is the author of *Experimental Political Science and the Study of Causality: From Nature to the Lab* (with Kenneth C. Williams, 2010) and *Methods and Models: A Guide to the Empirical Analysis of Formal Models in Political Science* (1999). Her research has also appeared in leading political science and economics journals.

**Heiko Rauhut** holds a Master's in Social Research Methods, London School of Economics (2003) and a PhD in Sociology, University of Leipzig (2008).

Since 2012 he has had a full position (equivalent to Assistant Professor) at the University of Zurich. He received a best paper award of the German Sociological Association (2010). His work has been published in *Social Forces, Proceedings of the National Academy of Sciences, Rationality & Society,* and elsewhere.

**Nicolas Sauger** is a senior research fellow at the Centre for European Studies in Sciences Po, Paris. He is the principal investigator of the French national election study in 2012. His fields of research focus on the analysis of changes in structures of political competition in France and Europe. His work has been published in *Social Choice and Welfare, Political Research Quarterly, French Politics* and *West European Politics.*

**Susumu Shikano** is Professor of Political Methodology at the University of Konstanz and former fellow of the Hanse Institute for Advanced Study in Delmenhorst. His research areas are electoral politics and coalition formation. His work has appeared in *Party Politics, Public Choice* and *West European Politics.*

**Michael Stoffel** is a researcher in the project 'Pork Barrel Politics in Germany' at the Mannheim Centre for European Social Research (MZES) and doctoral candidate at the University of Mannheim. His research interests lie in the areas of comparative politics, political economy and quantitative methods of the social sciences.

**Karine van der Straeten** is IDEI Researcher and member of the Toulouse School of Economics (TSE), as well as a researcher at Centre national de la recherche scientifique (CNRS) and Groupe de Recherche en Economie Mathématique et Quantitative (GREMAQ). She is interested in political economy and public economics. Her work has appeared in *Experimental Economics, Social Choice and Welfare* and *The Economic Journal.*

**Joshua A. Tucker** is Professor of Politics at New York University (NYU), and the author of *Regional Economic Voting: Russia, Poland, Hungary, Slovakia, and the Czech Republic, 1990–99* (2006). He is a past recipient of the Emerging Scholar Award for the top scholar in the field of elections, public opinion and voting behavior.

**Fabian Winter** received his Magister Artium in Sociology, Philosophy and Formal Logic at the University of Leipzig. He is a member of the Strategic Interaction Group of the Max-Planck Institute of Economics in Jena. He has submitted his PhD thesis on 'Social Conflict and the Evolution of Norms' in June of 2011. He received a best paper award from the German Sociological Association in 2010. His work has appeared in *Social Forces, Social Science Research* and elsewhere.

**Jonathan Woon** is Assistant Professor of Political Science at the University of Pittsburgh. His research tests the predictions of theoretical models using experimental and observational methods to study how uncertainty, reputations and agenda power influence elections and policy outcomes in a representative democracy. His work has been published in the *American Journal of Political Science,* the *Journal of Politics* and *Legislative Studies Quarterly.*

# 1
# Introduction: Experimental Political Science in Perspective

*Bernhard Kittel and Rebecca B. Morton*

## 1.1 Experiments in political science

After a long incubating phase, experimental political science has experienced a rapid growth from the mid-1990s onwards and has now been established as a respected approach to research in the discipline (Druckman et al., 2006; McDermott, 2002). Recently, the state of the art has been summarized and organized in handbooks covering laboratory experiments in the social sciences in general (Webster Jr. and Sell, 2007), and the whole breadth of experimental research in political science more specifically (Druckman et al., 2011). The American Political Science Association established the Organized Section on Experimental Research in 2010, which, among other activities, has started to publish biannually the newsletter *The Experimental Political Scientist*. Novices are now introduced to the methodology of laboratory experiments by a full-length textbook that not only covers a course into the techniques, but also extensively discusses underlying fundamental questions such as the problem of causality (Morton and Williams, 2010). Another new textbook covers the methodology of survey experiments (Mutz, 2011).

Experimental work has contributed to many substantive areas in political science, and it is differentiated into a variety of subareas, research streams and experimental designs. Among the subdisciplines of political science, experimental work has its stronghold in political economy and political psychology. Political economy has maintained its strong connection to economics. While the early phase of experimental political science has been characterized by the exploration of traditional rational choice models on the institutional factors that are at the core of political economy, the surge of behavioural and experimental economics has also spurred interest in the effect of bounded rationality and social preferences on political decisions. Political psychology, on the other hand, has strong links to psychology, a discipline that has a long tradition in experimental work on the determinants of individual and collective decision-making. In addition, the approach is rapidly gaining momentum in adjacent fields such as political behaviour, political sociology and political communication.

The two main sources of inspiration – economics and psychology – have also had their impact on the ideas of what constitutes correct experimentation. For example, political science is positioned somewhere in the middle between economics and psychology on the issues of deception and payment (Dickson, 2011). Accepting from psychology the relevance of deception for research questions that focus on attitudes and values, the importance of inducing value through monetary rewards for certain types of actions has become the backbone for research on voting, spatial politics and collective decisions.

With regard to research streams, the agenda of experimental political research has been marked by two approaches for a long time. On the one hand, in a predominantly theory-driven, deductive mode of science using formal mathematical representations of models, the phenomena explored by the founders of the rational choice approach to political science have determined the questions that were asked. Problems such as the impossibility theorem (Arrow, 1963), the median voter theorem (Black, 1958), the party convergence model (Downs, 1957) and the effect of voting rules (Buchanan and Tullock, 1962), from which a variety of theoretical puzzles such as the voting paradox (Riker and Ordeshook, 1968) or the indeterminacy of majority rule in two-dimensional space (McKelvey, 1976) have been derived from first principles and have set the scene for experimental work testing the implications of the models.

On the other hand, a major concern guiding experimental work has been the widespread lack of motivation among citizens to participate in politics, which was felt to endanger the democratic achievements. This enlightened perspective with an ambition to educate and develop better citizens has spurred both field and survey experiments exploring both the effects of particular measures to 'get out the vote' and the impact of different forms of mass communication in politics on voting behaviour (Eldersveld, 1956; Green and Gerber, 2008).

These two perspectives have some 'elective affinities' (Weber, 1978) with the distinction between forward- and backward-looking perspectives on causal thinking (Scharpf, 1997: 24–6), or, put otherwise, causes of effects versus effects of causes (Morton and Williams, 2010: 33–5). In the effects-of-causes perspective, based on the Rubin causal model, a causal effect is observed if the difference in outcomes that can be attributed to the manipulation of one particular factor is statistically significant (King, Keohane and Verba, 1994: 76–85). This is the approach underlying the classical experimental design focusing on a single variable of interest. Through random assignment of subjects to either the treatment or the control group, the difference in outcomes can be interpreted as the effect of the cause. In the causes-of-effects perspective, in contrast, a formal model is evaluated as a whole, and predictions are derived and compared to the experimental results (Morton and Williams, 2010: 202–50). However, can we really clearly differentiate between the two perspectives? Anytime we run a regression analysis – the typical strategy for analysing experimental results – without specifying a formal theoretical model, we implicitly assume a certain specification of the formal model (Taagepera, 2008), by default the linear additive one. But the whole logic of regression analysis, building on the attempt to account for variation in the dependent variable, rests on a causes-of-effects framework. Instead, significance testing of coefficients is equivalent to evaluating one aspect of the model in an effects-of-causes framework embedded in an explicit or implicit causes-of-effects framework. While the distinction is clear, it is not clear at all whether the two approaches can be dealt with as two different, but equal ways of doing experimental research. The effects-of-causes perspective can point to relevant variables, but unless predictions from a theoretical model incorporating these variables in the structural way of the causes-of-effects perspective have been tested against experimental evidence, we cannot say how these variables add to the cumulative understanding of the phenomenon studied.

## 1.2   Experimental approaches

Experimental approaches are usually classified into three categories: laboratory, survey and field experiments. As with many classifications, the classes are not crisp and the only limit of possible combinations is academic creativity. For example, a survey treatment can be part of a laboratory experiment, or it can be part of a field intervention which has an experimental treatment embedded. However, there is variation in the usage and relevance of different experimental approaches that can be linked to the research field, the relative role of concerns for internal and external validity and the specific research question asked. We will briefly elaborate on each of these issues.

In line with the specific subdisciplinary research interest, different experimental approaches have dominated different fields. In the field of political economy, laboratory experiments have become the major approach. Partly because of the strong influence from experimental economics (Wilson, 2011), and partly due to the nature of the factors studied, such as institutional rules that tend to vary only across nation states or have only rarely been implemented in practice, researchers have designed experiments in the laboratory (Iyengar, 2011; Palfrey, 2006, 2009). In contrast, field experiments have been considerably more popular in political psychology and political behaviour (De Rooij, Green and Gerber, 2009; Gerber, 2011), as well as, perhaps somewhat surprisingly, in International Relations (Hyde, 2010). They are gaining a foothold also in economics (Harrison and List, 2004).

Survey experiments, finally, have their stronghold in political sociology and political communication, including topics such as campaign or personality effects on voting behaviour (Sniderman, 2011). Substantive topics studied experimentally will be explored in more detail in the next chapter.

Another factor affecting the choice between laboratory, field and survey experiments is the extent to which a researcher has a target population or environment that is beyond that represented in a laboratory experiment. If the sample of subjects that can be recruited to the laboratory is not representative of the researcher's target population, then the experiment may not have statistical validity, and if the environment in the laboratory is not representative of the target environment, then the experiment may not have ecological validity.

Laboratory experiments have the largest control over the experimental conditions, the behavioural incentives and the treatment specification, and thus score high on construct and causal validity, two major dimensions of internal validity (Morton and Williams, 2010). However, they may score low on statistical validity, in the sense of limitations with regard to the generalizability to the experimenter's desired target population, and ecological validity, or mundane experimental realism, in the sense of similarity to some target environment. Most notorious in this respect is the debate about the generalizability of results from convenience samples of students, which may (Hooghe et al., 2010), or may not (Druckman and Kam, 2011), be consequential for inferences beyond the student population. Perhaps less prominent but also relevant is the usually fairly small size of the samples, typically due to restrictions in the size of the budget or the subject pool, which sometimes puts heavy strains on the inferential statistics used for testing the statistical significance of differences in outcome across treatments.

Survey experiments definitely improve the representativeness of the sample with regard to some populations which cannot be recruited to the laboratory, typically the citizens of a country, because they are embedded in a national survey covering a large number of respondents selected by a careful sampling procedure (Mutz, 2011). Thus, survey experiments score high on the two main methodological objections against laboratory experiments. However, given that the treatment conditions depend on the way in which the survey is administered, there is only limited control of incentives, yielding a lower degree of insulation of the experimental treatment from potentially confounding factors, and thus both construct and causal validity may be questionable.

Finally, field experiments, being set in the natural world of the experimental subjects, who may or – more often – may not be aware of the fact that they are taking part in an experiment, certainly have reason to claim mundane realism and, to the extent that the subject selection has been the result of some reasonable sampling procedure, statistical validity for some target populations (Levitt and List, 2009). However, the lack of control of the experimental conditions makes definite statements about the causal claims that they are meant to test rather difficult.

While these arguments certainly raise important points, we believe that they effectively propagate a ranking in the level of scientific value as they are often interpreted as implying a continuum between laboratory and field in terms of internal and external validity – with the view that at one end, laboratory experiments are argued to have high internal validity but low external validity, and at the other end, field and survey are argued to be low on internal validity but have high external validity. However, statistical validity and ecological validity are distinctive and not equivalent to external validity. External validity has to do with whether an empirical result generalizes to other target populations, environments and research questions beyond that examined in the empirical research. Just because an experiment has an arguably random sample from a given target population, say citizens of Berlin, and thus has high statistical validity, does not necessarily generalize it to other target populations such as citizens of Sao Paulo, Brazil. Similarly, a voting experiment that is extremely realistic to voters in Berlin, using actual voting equipment, party labels and other naturally occurring aspects, and thus has high ecological validity, does not necessarily generalize it to voting in other target environments such as in Sao Paulo.

Furthermore, 'external validity can only be established for results that have been demonstrated to be internally valid' (Morton and Williams, 2010: 275). Thus, if the claim that field and survey experiments are of questionable internal validity should be maintained, their supposedly high scores on statistical and ecological validity, even if that did imply higher external validity, do not matter. Given that the literature has clearly demonstrated that survey and field experiments have yielded important and replicable results, this way of introducing the distinction, in our view, does not do justice to these designs. Instead, we should describe the differences in terms of the most important factor, which is that the choice of design is driven by the properties of the main treatment variables.

In the choice of design, the substantive interest of the researcher and the possibility to produce experimental variation on the crucial variables will thus in practice be much more important than the consideration of purported trade-offs between different dimensions of validity. The criteria are: What is the variable of interest, which variation is relevant and by which design can that variable best be isolated while holding constant all other potentially relevant variables (Falk and Heckman, 2009)?

For example, many theories of voting behaviour base their predictions on institutional properties such as voting rules. While an ingenious research design for a field experiment might profit from 'natural' variation in voting rules, such as different quora in the first and second chamber of a parliament, or differences across the voting procedures in associations or clubs, finding all the constellations in the field that are necessary for making valid inferences may be a question of luck. Moreover, the impact of unapplied or even newly invented voting rules, in principle, cannot be studied observationally. Laboratory experiments, instead, allow for the systematic manipulation of these rules in an otherwise highly controlled context. The question is, does the specific difference in institutional conditions produce incentives for differences in individual behaviour that lead to predictable differences in outcomes? In such situations, the laboratory is the only place where counterfactual conditions can be generated which allow for a test of the treatment condition. In contrast, varying items in a survey experiment will either not be helpful at all or be only marginally relevant for studying institution-driven differences in voting behaviour.

The strengths of survey experiments in the analysis of voting behaviour play out in other research settings. One is eliciting the disclosure of specific attitudes in public opinion that may be hidden or severely underestimated in nonexperimental survey designs because of bias due to social expectancy and political correctness. In a laboratory experiment, the expression of such attitudes may be suppressed or attenuated by monetary incentives. Another possible field in which survey experiments may be the design of choice is the exploration of the effect of specific kinds of information on voter attitudes and preferences, such as party policy positions or pre-election coalition signals.

Put in a different way, the distinction between laboratory and survey experiments can be described with regard to the role of individual preferences. If the focus is on the effect of institutions on aggregate voting or policy outcomes, idiosyncratic individual preferences are marginal to the research question. The provision of a strong, manipulable motivation should elicit the behaviour described in the model. This is most effectively done by incentivizing preferences through monetary rewards. If, in contrast, the research interest is in the conditions of individual preference formation, then monetary incentives might interfere with and wipe out the sources of variation of interest. Instead, respondents are expected to be influenced by cues provided in vignettes, and inferential leverage is generated by an experimental design that systematically varies those cues. Naturally, such techniques can also be used in the laboratory for research designs that focus on the joint impact of institutions and information on voting behaviour.

Field experiments, in contrast, relate in a different way to laboratory and survey experiments. Actually, laboratory experiments can be seen as field experiments in a rather artificial, and thus least naturalistic, setting (Harrison and List, 2004). However, some issues cannot be studied in the laboratory but need to be explored in the natural environment of experimental subjects. Take the question asked by the 'get-out-the-vote' literature (Eldersveld, 1956; Gosnell, 1927; Green and Gerber, 2008): What effects do different canvassing techniques have on actual turnout in an election?

The laboratory does not provide an environment in which turnout decisions can be related to persuasion techniques because behaviour needs to be incentivized by much stronger inducements such as monetary payments. A survey can only address effects of cues on intentions to vote, not actual voting behaviour. In addition, a survey is not designed to cover different canvassing techniques. Hence, given that the research question cannot be answered by other experimental designs, a field experiment is the only way of systematically varying the core variables of interest. Hence, again it is the research interest that drives the choice of design, not validity considerations. Comparing the validity problems of different designs is irrelevant because there is no choice to make. As compared to observational studies, the field experiment definitely improves inferential statements on the validity criterion.

## 1.3   Aims of the volume

Whereas experimental research has become an established approach in the United States, most prominently observable in the surge of articles employing experimental methodology in the large American political science journals, the approach has hardly reached a foothold in Europe or other parts of the world. For example, the *Cambridge Handbook of Experimental Political Science* (Druckman et al., 2011) does not list a single author that is not based in the United States. Likewise, *Laboratory Experiments in the Social Sciences* (Webster Jr. and Sell, 2007) lists two European contributors among 24 North Americans. Although this state of affairs is only marginally different from handbooks for other fields in political science organized by American editors,[1] this concentration is striking if it is compared with experimental economics. For example, the *Handbook of Experimental Economics Results* (Plott and Smith, 2008) lists 26 per cent Europe-based and three per cent Asia-based authors, which, though, still leaves 71 per cent North-American-based contributors. Moreover, European economists and political economists have made important contributions to the experimental study of topics that are also considered to be part of the core of political science, such as group decision-making, lobbying and contributions to public goods (van Winden, 2002) or voter behaviour (Großer and Schram, 2010; Sonnemans and Schram, 2008), to name a few prominent examples.

However, this distribution of authorship cannot be merely attributed to an alleged parochialism of American political science. It is true that European political scientists have only recently realized the potentials of experimentation and that the discipline as a whole has been even more reluctant to accept the approach than their American peers. While the number of articles based on experimental research has risen dramatically in the large American journals since the early 1990s, articles based on an experimental research design still are a rare bird in European journals. In German-language journals, experimental research has been close to nonexistent during the last decade (Faas and Huber, 2010). A full-text search based on the word stem 'experiment' for the period from January 2000 until August 2011 produced three survey experiments and one laboratory experiment in the *European Journal of Political Research*, two survey experiments and one field experiment in the *British Journal of Political Science*, two survey experiments and a laboratory experiment in *Scandinavian Political Studies*, two laboratory experiments and one field experiment in the *European Political Science Review* (since its first volume in 2009) and no experimental articles in the *Revue Française de Science Politique*. Ten out of these 13 articles were published in 2007 or later.

While an occasional experimental paper has been presented at one of the larger European conferences such as the ECPR Joint Sessions or the ECPR General Conference, it was only at the ECPR General Conference in Potsdam 2009 that a panel was organized by Leif Helland (Norwegian School of Management) and Jon Hovi (University of Oslo), which explicitly brought together experimental research. At the ECPR Joint Sessions in St. Gallen 2011, the slot of the ECPR Standing Group on Political Methodology had been assigned to a session on voting experiments organized by Michael Meffert (Leiden University) and Nicolas Sauger (Sciences Po, Paris).

The present volume is the result of a more circumscribed workshop on experimental political science organized by the editors in December 2008 at the Hanse Wissenschaftskolleg in Delmenhorst, Germany, with the aim of bringing together a group of German and American scholars who engage in experimental work. During the workshop, in which papers were presented that have been in submission processes at various journals, the idea emerged to collectively write a book that provides some insight into those aspects of experimental research that are not routinely reported in the format of a journal article – in other words, to provide a look behind the screen of political science experimentation. Hence, the chapters can be considered 'companion papers' to the original articles in which the authors reflect on design decisions taken or rejected, and the analytical pathways chosen or slid into, that eventually led to the outcome presented in the original paper.

Hence, this volume claims that a nascent community of experimental political scientists does indeed exist in Europe. It aims for a modest contribution to the field by providing a complement to the handbooks and textbook in offering more in-depth insight into the actual practices of experimental political science. It also reveals the extent to which experimentalists evaluate their own approach with caution and a considerable dose of self-criticism. This may be a consequence of having been exposed to a set of alternative 'ways of knowing' (Moses and Knutsen, 2007), such as critical theory, interpretive methodology and qualitative methods, which is to a larger extent an integral and respected part of the European political science community than in the United States (Moses, Rihoux and Kittel, 2005). The style of the contributions is more narrative than formal in order to accommodate the focus on experiences and practices of experimentation.

## 1.4 Overview of the chapters

In the first part of the book, three cuts are made to shed light on experimental political science. Chapter 2 discusses the substantive contribution of experimental work in important areas of political science. Chapter 3, concentrating on the problem of causality, elaborates on the potential for generating inferential leverage for causal statements. Chapter 4, highlighting the importance of experimental manipulation of conditions, explores the potential of experimental work in supporting the development of voting rules through mechanism design by providing experimental evidence for the consequences of particular rules.

Chapter 2, written by Bernhard Kittel and Kamil Marcinkiewicz, presents a bird's eye view of some of the main questions studied in political science by experimental work. They focus on three large literatures: Firstly, they address the debate on voting behaviour that has been spurred by the paradox of voting and the problem of strategic voting. Secondly, they explore the analysis of institutional factors determining voting outcomes that has been fueled by the chaos theorem. And thirdly, they study the work discussing the effect of communication and deliberation on voting behaviour and outcomes. This chapter is intended to set the scene and put into context the other chapters of the book, each discussing in more detail specific aspects of experimental political science.

In Chapter 3, Jonathan Woon presents a framework for inferences in experimental political science. He differentiates a formal model into three components: the model of the social situation, the model of preferences and the model of behaviour. The complete formal model describes how the three components interact to produce outcomes, empirical implications, which can be tested. He then explains how experimental designs can ensure a precise match between the three components of the formal model, thereby providing inferential leverage for the theory predicting the empirical implications. The argument is then illustrated by an example from the field of democratic accountability which investigates whether subjects sanction previous performance or select promising candidates in elections. Thereby, he shows that the perfect Bayesian equilibrium used for deriving conclusions does not adequately describe actual behaviour of subjects.

Chapter 4, contributed by Jens Großer, explores the potential of political engineering by explicitly varying the rules under which voting takes place. This approach, also called mechanism design, allows studying the impact of specific manipulations of institutional constraints to elicit behaviour in a predictable way. He first outlines the impact that experimental

work has had on formal theory by discussing the examples of social preferences and quantal response equilibria. Discussing four of his own studies,
he then shows how the understanding of specific aspects of voting can be
improved in a systematic way that approaches the core problem of interest
from various angles, thereby gradually building up a clearer picture of the
mechanisms at work.

Part II, consisting of three chapters, deals with different aspects of practical design issues. While Chapter 5 discusses laboratory experiments, and
Chapter 6 elaborates on survey experiments, Chapter 7 presents a way of
profiting from both perspectives by methodological triangulation within
one and the same paradigm.

Chapter 5, co-authored by Nicolas Sauger, André Blais, Jean-François Laslier
and Karine van der Straeten, focuses on the development of the experimental protocol in a laboratory experiment conducted in a cross-national
research project with multiple research interests. While being ubiquitous in
cooperative research projects, the variation in subject pools introduced is a
challenge to validity of inferences because it adds potentially uncontrolled
systematic factors. They describe the gradual evolution of the protocol from
a simple question to an elaborate design with multiple additional treatments
controlling for specific concerns that have been raised in the research team
or that were the result of the cooperation across different institutions and
countries.

In Chapter 6, Ted A. Brader and Joshua A.Tucker reflect on the design of a
survey experiment on the effect of partisan cues on voting behaviour which
they have conducted in Russia. They elaborate on the problems associated
with finding adequate cues that sufficiently differentiate between parties
and that are plausible with regard to the expectations about the parties' relative positions. Furthermore, they discuss the effect of specific constraints
due to the structure of the Russian party system. Finally, they raise some
concerns about the role of deception in the context of survey experiments,
which is necessary because of the nature of the research question, but still
questionable from an ethical perspective.

Chapter 7, written by Michael F. Meffert and Thomas Gschwend, shows
the advantages of triangulation using different experimental designs, where
one and the same research question is approached from different perspectives in order to maximally profit from the relative advantages and disadvantages of different designs. In a series of experiments on the effects of
coalition signals on strategic voting, the authors have undertaken a laboratory experiment in the classical economic tradition with monetary induced
preferences, a laboratory experiment in the psychological tradition that
studied the effect of different vignettes on voting intentions, and a survey
experiment embedded in an opinion poll. In the chapter, the authors discuss
the relative contributions of the three experiments to the understanding of
the effects of coalition signals.

Part III of the book is devoted to data analysis. Whereas Chapter 8 deals with traditional quantitative techniques, thereby highlighting the relevance of multilevel analysis, Chapter 9 introduces a technique for taking advantage of qualitative data generated as byproducts of experimental protocols.

In Chapter 8, Susumu Shikano, Thomas Bräuninger and Michael Stoffel argue that the reliance on rather simple statistical tools may be delusive because of remaining uncontrolled variation across treatments and sessions. Instead, they propose to use a Bayesian multilevel approach which allows controlling for remaining heterogeneity and they exemplify their approach through an experiment on decision costs in voting.

Chapter 9, written by Thomas Kalwitzki, Wolfgang J. Luhan and Bernhard Kittel, takes a different perspective by exploring the information on individual preferences, intentions and behaviour provided by the chat protocols in experiments with unconstrained communication. Given that this sort of material calls for qualitative research methods, they propose a combined experimental-qualitative approach in which individual statements are classified into different categories and which allows an extension of the number and depth of inferences about the effect of deliberation on voting than a simple quantitative, outcome-oriented analysis might reveal.

Part IV highlights some important potential challenges to inferences from experimental studies. Chapter 10 addresses the core potential problem of the validity of experimental results. Chapter 11 focuses on problems of causal validity that may be generated in the collection of counterfactual evidence, which is crucial for the generation of scientific inferences. Finally, Chapter 12 addresses the advantages and disadvantages of using time and sequence in laboratory experiments in order to make better causal inferences.

In Chapter 10, Heiko Rauhut and Fabian Winter discuss four dimensions of validity and the challenges to these which they encountered in their experiment on crime and punishment. They also show how specific design decisions – for example, which variables are tested in a within- and which variables are tested in a between-subjects design – can help to contain the impact of validity challenges, and how additional information collected via ex-post interviews can help to assess the size of the impact of potential validity problems.

Chapter 11, co-authored by Marc Hooghe, Sofie Marien and Thomas Gschwend, reports on a survey experiment among first-year students which aims to uncover the effect of pre-election coalition signals on voting intentions. Following up on the topics discussed in Chapter 7, they first discuss the challenges posed by the use of a student sample and a within-subject design, and then elaborate on the effect of pre-election signals, including likely and unlikely coalitions.

Chapter 12, contributed by Rebecca B. Morton, discusses how researchers use time and sequence in laboratory experiments. She focuses on three main uses of time: (1) to facilitate within-subjects' designs, which provide researchers with better control over unobservable variables; (2) to better evaluate game theoretic predictions; and (3) to consider particular hypotheses that require choices be made over time. Potential problems such as sequencing, selection, wealth and repeated game effects are also addressed and suggestions are made on how to deal with these problems.

Part V concludes the volume. Chapter 13, contributed by Bernhard Kittel and Wolfgang J. Luhan, summarizes some lessons from the chapters and reflects on further potential trajectories of experimental political science. In the Appendix, we offer of a brief overview of tools for experimental research.

Jointly, the chapters introduce the reader into the latent tension between the principles guiding experimental political science, and the practices of actual experimental work, that is characteristic of all scientific work but that has very specific faces in political science. We hope that the volume both contributes to advancing the understanding of experimental work in political science and gives readers some orientation in the sometimes-bewildering multitude of possibilities for developing experimental research designs.

## Note

1. For example, *The Oxford Handbook of Political Methodology* (Box-Steffensmeier, Brady and Collier, 2008) lists, among 47 North Americans, five at least partly Europe-based authors, four of whom are in the United Kingdom, and no authors based in other continents.

## References

Arrow, Kenneth Joseph (1963) *Social Choice and Individual Values* (New Haven: Yale University Press).

Black, Duncan (1958) *The Theory of Committees and Election* (New York: Cambridge University Press).

Box-Steffensmeier, Janet, Henry E. Brady and David Collier (2008) *The Oxford Handbook of Political Methodology* (Oxford: Oxford University Press).

Buchanan, James M. and Gordon Tullock (1962) *The Calculus of Consent. Logical Foundations of Constitutional Democracy* (Ann Arbor: University of Michigan Press).

De Rooij, Eline A., Donald P. Green and Alan S. Gerber (2009) 'Field Experiments on Political Behavior and Collective Action', *Annual Review of Political Science*, 12, 389–95.

Dickson, Eric S. (2011) 'Economics versus Psychology Experiments. Stylization, Incentives, and Deception' in James N. Druckman, Donald P. Green, James H. Kuklinski and Arthur Lupia (eds) *Cambridge Handbook of Experimental Political Science* (Cambridge: Cambridge University Press).

Downs, Anthony (1957) *An Economic Theory of Democracy* (New York: Harper and Row).

Druckman, James N., Donald P. Green, James H. Kuklinski and Arthur Lupia (2006) 'The Growth and Development of Experimental Research in Political Science', *American Political Science Review*, 100, 627–35.

Druckman, James N., Donald P. Green, James H. Kuklinski and Arthur Lupia (2011) *Cambridge Handbook of Experimental Political Science* (Cambridge: Cambridge University Press).

Druckman, James N. and Cindy D. Kam (2011) 'Students as Experimental Participants: A Defense of the Narrow Data Base' in James N. Druckman, Donald P. Green, James H. Kuklinski and Arthur Lupia (eds) *Cambridge Handbook of Experimental Political Science* (Cambridge: Cambridge University Press).

Eldersveld, Samuel J. (1956) 'Experimental Propaganda Techniques and Voting Behavior', *American Political Science Review*, 50, 154–65.

Faas, Thorsten and Sasha Huber (2010) 'Experimente in der Politikwissenschaft: Vom Mauerblümchen zum Mainstream', *Politische Vierteljahresschrift*, 51, 721–49.

Falk, Armin and James J. Heckman (2009) 'Lab Experiments Are a Major Source of Knowledge in the Social Sciences', *Science*, 326, 535–8.

Gerber, Alan S. (2011) 'Field Experiments in Political Science' in James N. Druckman, Donald P. Green, James H. Kuklinski and Arthur Lupia (eds) *Cambridge Handbook of Experimental Political Science* (Cambridge: Cambridge University Press).

Gosnell, Harold F. (1927) *Getting out the Vote: An Experiment in the Stimulation of Voting* (Chicago: University of Chicago Press).

Green, Donald P. and Alan S. Gerber (2008) *Get Out the Vote: How to Increase Voter Turnout* (Washington D.C.: Brooking's Institution).

Großer, Jens and Arthur Schram (2010) 'Public Opinion Polls, Voter Turnout, and Welfare: An Experimental Study', *American Journal of Political Science*, 54, 700–17.

Harrison, Glenn W. and John A. List (2004) 'Field Experiments', *Journal of Economic Literature*, 42, 1009–55.

Hooghe, Marc, Dietlind Stolle, Valérie-Anne Mahéo and Sara Vissers (2010) 'Why Can't a Student Be More Like an Average Person? Sampling and Attrition Effects in Social Science Field and Laboratory Experiments', *The Annals of the American Academy of Political and Social Science*, 628, 85–96.

Hyde, Susan D. (2010) 'The Future of Field Experiments in International Relations', *The Annals of the American Academy of Political and Social Science*, 628, 72–84.

Iyengar, Shanto (2011) 'Laboratory Experiments in Political Science' in James N. Druckman, Donald P. Green, James H. Kuklinski and Arthur Lupia (eds) *Cambridge Handbook of Experimental Political Science* (Cambridge: Cambridge University Press).

King, Gary, Robert Keohane and Sidney Verba (1994) *Designing Social Inquiry. Scientific Inference in Qualitative Research* (Princeton: Princeton University Press).

Levitt, Steven D. and John A. List (2009) 'Field Experiments in Economics: The Past, the Present, and the Future', *European Economic Review*, 53, 1–18.

McDermott, Rose (2002) 'Experimental Methodology in Political Science', *Political Analysis*, 10, 325–42.

McKelvey, Richard (1976) 'Intransitivities in Multidimensional Voting Models and Some Implications for Agenda Control', *Journal of Economic Theory*, 12, 472–82.

Morton, Rebecca B. and Kenneth Williams (2010) *Experimental Political Science and the Study of Causality. From Nature to the Lab* (Cambridge: Cambridge University Press).

Moses, Jonathan W. and Torbjørn Knutsen (2007) *Ways of Knowing. Competing Methodologies in Social and Political Research* (Basingstoke: Palgrave-Macmillan).

Moses, Jonathon W., Benoît Rihoux and Bernhard Kittel (2005) 'Mapping Political Methodology: Reflections on a European Perspective', *European Political Science* 4, 1–14.

Mutz, Diana C. (2011) *Population-based Survey Experiments* (Princeton: Princeton University Press).

Palfrey, Thomas R. (2006) 'Laboratory Experiments' in Barry R. Weingast and Donald A. Wittman (eds) *The Oxford Handbook of Political Economy* (Oxford: Oxford University Press).

Palfrey, Thomas R. (2009) 'Laboratory Experiments in Political Economy', *Annual Review of Political Science*, 12, 379–88.

Plott, Charles A. and Vernon Smith (2008) *Handbook of Experimental Economics Results. Volume I* (Amsterdam: North-Holland).

Riker, William and Peter Ordeshook (1968) 'A Theory of the Calculus of Voting', *American Political Science Review*, 62, 25–42.

Scharpf, Fritz W. (1997) *Games Real Actors Play. Actor-centered Institutionalism in Policy Research* (Boulder: Westview Press).

Sniderman, Paul M. (2011) 'The Logic and Design of the Survey Experiment: An Autobiography of a Methodological Innovation' in James N. Druckman, Donald P. Green, James H. Kuklinski and Arthur Lupia (eds) *Cambridge Handbook of Experimental Political Science* (Cambridge: Cambridge University Press).

Sonnemans, Joep and Arthur Schram (2008) 'Participation Game Experiments: Explaining Voter Turnout' in Charles R. Plott and Vernon Smith (eds) *Handbook of Experimental Economics Results, Volume 1* (Amsterdam: North-Holland).

Taagepera, Rein (2008) *Making Social Sciences More Scientific: The Need for Predictive Models* (Oxford: Oxford University Press).

van Winden, Frans (2002) 'Experimental Investigation of Collective Action' in Stephen L. Winer and Hirofumi Shibata (eds) *Political Economy and Public Finance: The Role of Political Economy in the Theory and Practice of Public Economics* (Cheltenham: Edward Elgar).

Weber, Max (1978) *Economy and Society. An Outline of Interpretive Sociology* (Berkeley: University of California Press).

Webster Jr., Murray and Jane Sell (eds) (2007) *Laboratory Experiments in the Social Sciences* (Amsterdam: Academic Press).

Wilson, Rick K. (2011) 'The Contribution of Behavioral Economics to Political Science', *Annual Review of Political Science*, 14, 201–23.

# Part I
# Overview

# 2
# Voting Behavior and Political Institutions: An Overview of Challenging Questions in Theory and Experimental Research

*Bernhard Kittel and Kamil Marcinkiewicz*

## 2.1 Introduction[1]

Voting and committee decisions can be considered the two core elements of the democratic political process. By voting, the members of a constituency determine whom they entrust as representatives with the right to decide on their behalf. By voting, the members of a committee decide which course of action they will take collectively. Hence, voting determines both the input and the output of politics, or in other words, the way in which individuals contribute to a collective outcome. We cannot, however, infer policy from the distribution of individual preferences but in very simple constellations because the chosen policy depends on the interaction between different voters who may have heterogeneous preferences and form different coalitions. These issues have been the main topic of the spatial theory of politics. The role of this chapter in this volume is to give readers some understanding of the broader context of the experiments described in subsequent chapters. Even if we restrict the focus on the theoretical and experimental literature on voting and committee decisions, we are confronted with a wide and differentiated field that is too large to present in all details in a single chapter. Our aim is thus more modest and twofold. First, we summarize and organize the main lines of discussion, evaluate the extent to which the theoretical arguments have been supported by experimental evidence and identify, to the extent that this seems possible at this stage of development, some stylized facts. Second, we aim to suggest to the reader some useful places to start further investigations into specific areas of voting behavior. We systematize the literature in three steps, loosely following the logic of thesis, antithesis and synthesis. We start by discussing individual voting behavior, then move to political institutions as the rules guiding individual behavior and finally explore the interaction processes leading to collective decisions as the synthesis of individual behavior and institutional frameworks. Thus, in the second section, we focus on the micro-level of individual voting behavior. There are basically two sequential, though not necessarily independent, decisions that voters have to take. First, voters have to decide whether to take part in the collective decision, which may be an election of representatives or a vote on a policy proposal. Second, voters have to choose one of the options. This may either be a sincere vote for the preferred outcome or a strategic vote for a lesser preference in order to avoid an even less preferred outcome. Studies exploring the factors influencing these two decisions are paramount, although they tend to deal with them separately.

In the third section, we move to questions related to the institutional determinants of interaction among voters and to the way in which institutions condition voting behavior. Mostly, these issues are conceptualized in the context of committee voting. This research area is interested in the way in which electoral institutions such as voting rules, vote aggregation mechanisms and agenda control allow the researcher to predict voting outcomes.

The fourth section focuses in more detail on the process of collective decision making itself. We discuss bargaining, communication and deliberation processes. Although even more difficult to capture in a formal model, the impact of communication on voting behavior and collective decision making is considerable and has recently become a major area of investigation. In the fifth section we draw some conclusions.

Focusing on voting behavior and spatial theory, we omit large research areas of significant interest to political scientists, such as social dilemmas in general (Sell, 2007), and public goods problems (Chan, Mestelman and Muller, 2008; Laury and Holt, 2008) as well as common goods problems and the interaction mechanisms fostering their solution (Ostrom 2005; Ostrom and Walker, 2003; Sell, 2007) in particular. We also do not discuss network formation and the distributional implications of group structures (Galeotti et al., 2010; Goyal, 2007; Keser, Ehrhart and Berninghaus, 1998; Kittel and Luhan, 2011; Kosfeld, 2004; Siegel, 2009). The economic and psychological literature on group effects in decision making is extensive (Bornstein and Yaniv, 1998; Bosman, Hennig-Schmidt and van Winden, 2006; Cason and Mui, 1997; Kerr and Tindale, 2004; Luhan, Kocher and Sutter, 2009) but, although we acknowledge that it is highly relevant, because of space restrictions we only refer to those parts of this literature that explicitly relate to voting behavior. Moreover, we exclude observational studies on voting based on surveys from this overview.

## 2.2   Individual voting behavior

In this section, we present work that looks at voting behavior from the perspective of individual behavior. While macro outcomes such as election results are certainly considered important and reported in these studies, the literature we focus on here puts the analysis of individual decisions at center stage. The question of why people vote in elections has been among the first topics extensively studied in formal political theory. Spurred by the paradoxical finding that voting in large electorates seems irrational, given the assumption of selfish utility maximizing behavior, much work has attempted to reconcile theory with the undeniable fact that voters do vote in practice. Important topics in this area are information asymmetries and the extension of two-party to multiparty elections, which adds the moment of strategic voting to the turnout problem. Further steps in the debate are heuristics and adaptive learning processes. While all this work can be conceptualized within the framework of utility maximization, partly in the bounded-rationality variant, new work departs from this assumption by extending the model through the inclusion of norm-guided behavior and social preferences. Finally, building on the idea of norm-guided voting behavior, field and survey experiments focus on the impact of mobilization efforts on voter turnout.

### 2.2.1 Rational choice and turnout: the voting paradox

From a rational-choice perspective, voting in large electorates appears irrational. Turnout models usually assume elections with two candidates, which may be politicians running for office or parties seeking seats in parliament. Theoretical results in a decision-theoretic framework (Ferejohn and Fiorina, 1974; Riker and Ordeshook, 1968) suggest that individuals maximizing subjective expected utility should abstain because the probability of being pivotal is too low to produce a positive outcome in the cost-benefit balance. The basic formulation (Riker and Ordeshook, 1968) equates utility from voting ($R$) to the differential benefit incurred by the voter in case of a victory by her preferred candidate ($B$), weighted by her probability of being pivotal ($P$) minus the cost of voting ($C$): $R = PB - C$. Since in large elections $P$ is approaching zero, $R$ is most likely negative and voting is irrational. Given that this result is clearly at odds with the empirical observation of substantial turnout, a term capturing various aspects of civic duty ($D$) has been included which provides a counterweight to $C$, yielding $R = PB - C + D$. Assuming $C > D \geq 0$, voting is rational if $PB > C - D$. Given that the ad-hoc inclusion of a vague civic duty term has been rather unsatisfying theoretically, this "paradox of voting" became an extensively studied topic of theoretical work that eventually spurred experimental examinations.

A first take at the problem was made by focusing on the individuals' assessment of the probability of being pivotal and by shifting from a decision-theoretic to a game-theoretic framework, conceptualizing voting as a participation game in the context of two-candidate elections (Palfrey and Rosenthal, 1983; 1985). Individuals are assumed to use a mixed voting strategy that is based on their probability of being pivotal. Abstention by all voters turned out to be just one of two types of mixed strategy equilibria. Instead, Palfrey and Rosenthal show that under certain conditions turnout can approach 100% even in large elections. However, introducing uncertainty regarding relative costs is sufficient to reinstall the voting paradox (Palfrey and Rosenthal, 1985). Somewhat surprisingly, given its salience, the topic was not among the earliest contributions to experimental political science (Kinder and Palfrey, 1993; McKelvey and Ordeshook, 1990). Direct experimental tests of the Palfrey-Rosenthal model were performed in the 1990s (Sonnemans and Schram, 2008). Initial turnout was substantial but declined over time (Schram and Sonnemans, 1996a). Moreover, turnout is inversely associated with the size of the electorate and positively associated with the closeness of the election, and it is higher among supporters of the less popular candidate (Levine and Palfrey, 2007). In an experiment directly measuring subjective beliefs of the probability of being pivotal, turnout rates turned out to be close to the theoretical expectations, but individuals systematically overestimated their probability of being pivotal (Duffy and Tavits, 2008).

Although these experiments have supported comparative statics derived from the model, the fundamental theoretical problem of the voting paradox has remained puzzling within the Palfrey-Rosenthal framework. In consequence, several extensions and variants of the model have been proposed (see, e.g., Feddersen, 2004). We will discuss, in turn, arguments that refer to voter mobilization, the amount of information available, extensions to multicandidate elections, heuristics and framing, and learning processes.

### 2.2.2 Voter mobilization

Voter turnout has been aptly represented as a participation game (Schram and Sonnemans, 1996a). Hence, research on voter mobilization is closely related to the study of turnout. Laboratory experiments normally induce preferences through monetary incentives (Smith, 1976). In consequence, there is a manifest association between individual behavior, collective outcome and individual payoffs, and individual decisions can be clearly related to the incentive structure. This relation is much more intricate in real-life elections. In contrast to the laboratory approach, turnout has been studied by field and survey experiments in terms of conditions spurring participation in elections from a perspective inspired by sociology. The tradition of field and survey experiments studying the impact of mobilization effort on turnout goes back to the 1920s (Gosnell, 1927) and the 1950s (Eldersveld, 1956), although in its modern form it has been revived only in the late 1990s (Gerber and Green, 2000). Viewed from the perspective of the initial Riker-Ordeshook model, this work can be considered to have focused on the civic duty term, instead of the pivotal probability. Hence, instead of exploring the strategic interaction involved in the decision to vote, it targets one of the substantive terms in the equation. Couched within the political participation and voting literature developed in the fields of political behavior and political sociology that studies the socio-economic and structural determinants of voting behavior (Duch and Stevenson, 2008; Manza, Brooks and Sauder, 2005; van der Eijk and Franklin, 2009), its focus is much more practical in ambition than laboratory work and foremost aims at testing the effect of stimuli to participate in elections. The basic treatment in these experiments involves some appeal to vote or other incentive for participation that is administered to subsets of the sample covered by a campaign (De Rooij, Green and Gerber, 2009).

Generally, field experiments have suggested that the content of the appeal hardly affects the mobilization potential of voters. Extensive studies could not detect any effect of neutral information supply, impersonal appeals to civic duty or solidarity or partisan messages (De Rooij, Green and Gerber 2009). However, a clear impact of the mode of message conveyance could be observed. Personal door-to-door canvassing, calls from volunteer phone banks and conversational calls from professional phone banks do seem to increase turnout (Arceneaux and Nickerson, 2009; Green and Gerber, 2008). In line with this result, an important factor appears to be social pressure such as the publication of information on individual turnout (Gerber, Green and Larimer, 2008) or contagion from other household members (Nickerson, 2008), whereby eliciting shame seems to be more effective than pride (Panagopoulos, 2010). Given that shaming strategies might lead to reactance that would be harmful for democracy, less heavy-handed social pressure strategies have been explored and found effective, at least for some populations (Mann, 2010).

Another issue in field experiments in the get-out-the-vote tradition are divergent mobilization levels among different ethnic and racial communities. A get-out-the-vote campaign among African-American voters during the 2000 presidential election resulted in moderate mobilizing effects of direct mail and phone calls when subjects were already exposed to abundant mobilization messages from other sources (Green, 2004). These findings are confirmed for Asian voters (Wong, 2005). The impact of a mobilization message transmitted either by mail or by phone is moderate, however. A study focusing on voters of Latino heritage in the rural area of Central California suggests that the success of canvassing efforts depends on face-to-face contact and a sense of common preferences between a canvasser and a subject (Michelson, 2003). Furthermore, appealing to ethnic identity instead of civic duty does not significantly augment the effect (Trivedi, 2005).

Mobilization has also been studied in the laboratory in the context of voluntary contribution to public goods (Laury and Holt, 2008; Schram and Sonnemans, 1996a; Sonnemans and Schram, 2008). For example, the contagion effect through networks has been confirmed in the laboratory (Großer and Schram, 2006). Also, the success of mobilization depends on high stakes in the common good on the part of potential contributors, while people in a low-stakes context seem to respond to mobilization efforts from experts outside the group, but not from within (Aroopala, 2011).

### 2.2.3   Asymmetric information and strategic turnout

Early models assumed that candidates have full knowledge of the electorate's preferences, and voters know the positions of those running for office. However, the assumption of perfect symmetrical information underlying the Palfrey-Rosenthal framework has long been considered a weak point of the rational theory of voting in general (Collier, Ordeshook and Williams, 1989; McKelvey and Ordeshook, 1985). Full information is considered a precondition for efficient functioning of democratic institutions (McKelvey and Ordeshook, 1986), but it contrasts with empirical evidence showing that the average citizen knows little about the candidates between whom she has to choose (Delli, Carpini and Keeter, 1996; Gordon and Segura, 1997; Luskin, 1990). The effect of asymmetric information on participation in elections is explored in the two-candidate situation (Feddersen and Pesendorfer, 1996; 1999). The model builds on the assumptions that the electorate can be divided into partisans, who always vote for their candidate, and independents, who vote for the candidate that they believe to be the best given the state of the world, and that the world can adopt two states, about which a fraction of the independents is informed while the others are ignorant. Under these conditions, there exists an equilibrium, dubbed the 'swing voters' curse' (Feddersen and Pesendorfer, 1996), in which uninformed voters abstain with some probability, while the others vote. The logic is that an uninformed independent voter will reason that the party to be preferred in the actual state of the world is more likely to win if she does not interfere in the election because she might vote for the wrong party. In an experimental study that closely follows the model (Battaglini, Morton and Palfrey, 2010), the predictions have been corroborated. Independent voters without access to information tend to abstain and thus delegate the decision to independents with richer knowledge. The presence of partisans, however, induces uninformed voters to vote, thereby balancing out the bias in favor of the partisans' preferred candidate.

### 2.2.4   Multicandidate elections and strategic voting

With the introduction of a third candidate, the voting decision becomes more complex. Rational, selfish voters may have an incentive not to vote sincerely for their most preferred candidate if they do not expect her to win the election, but to give their vote to their second preference in order to avoid a majority for an outcome that is even worse from their perspective (Cox, 1997; Riker, 1982). In other words, they vote for their most preferred candidate given their expectations about attainable outcomes. Hence, strategic voting is rational because voters still maximize their expected utility.

The complexity of the voting decision is substantially increased because voters must not only identify the candidates' positions in relation to their own position, but also assess their viability in the election in order to avoid wasting their vote. Given that voters have to build expectations about attainable outcomes, information is a crucial precondition of the ability of an electorate to coordinate on the Condorcet winner and thus reach a voting equilibrium (Myerson and Weber, 1993). Experimental evidence has shown that polling information about the relative support of candidates available to all voters and information on election histories indeed foster strategic voting by those preferring a trailing candidate and thereby generate a bandwagon effect (Forsythe et al., 1993; Rietz, 1993). Concomitantly, uncertainty about the opinions held by others reduces the propensity to vote strategically because voters might suspect they are following a bandwagon in the wrong direction (Myatt and Fisher, 2002). Experimental evidence corroborates this hypothesis and – as a rather consequential side result – also shows that a decision-theoretic conceptualization of strategic voting fits the data better than game theoretic alternatives (Fisher and Myatt, 2002). An experimental exploration of one- and two-round plurality elections shows that strategic voting indeed occurs, and that the two election procedures yield similar amounts of strategic voting (Blais et al., 2010).

Further theoretical contributions show that Duvergerian equilibria (reducing the set of viable candidates to two) are more stable than non-Duvergerian equilibria (Fey, 1997), that the removal of the usual common-knowledge assumption produces a unique strategic-voting equilibrium in which the trailing candidate also receives votes (Myatt, 2007), and that, assuming arbitrary indifferences between candidates, pure strategy voting equilibria exist (Duggan and Sekiya, 2009).

A variant of the strategic voting theory models strategic voting under imperfect information as a choice between two lotteries, each of which is a gamble over the expected outcomes (Enelow, 1981). This *expected utility sophisticated* (EUS) voting rule follows the logic known from the beauty contest experiments in which perfectly rational behavior is not necessarily the best strategy if one cannot rely on the assumption that others' behavior is rational. This approach is tested experimentally in a voting environment against predictions assuming random, sincere, strategic and risk-averse behavior, showing that it explains voting patterns better than the other models (Smirnov, 2009). Actors may form expectations about the behavior of others which do not necessarily conform to the rationality assumption and still result in sophisticated, payoff-maximizing voting behavior.

This kind of strategic voting is relevant in plurality systems because under this rule elections always end with a majority for one of the candidates. Voting for a preferred, but chanceless, candidate reduces the winning potential of the next-best alternative and thus pushes the outcome even further away from the voter's policy preference. In proportional representation systems, however, elections often produce coalitions and thus induce a different kind of strategic voting. Votes for candidates unlikely to attract a sufficient number of other voters are only wasted if the candidate does not even pass a minimum threshold to gain seats in parliament. Otherwise, even a small party can tip the balance in favor of the voter's preferences if it becomes part of a coalition. Whereas voters can only vote on candidates, not on policies, which depend on the particular coalition formed, they still can condition their vote choices on their expectations about the likelihood of specific coalitions. Although the literature is not fully consistent in terminology,[2] it might make sense to reserve the term strategic voting to plurality rule, and to clarify the distinctive logic of proportional systems by naming this behavior tactical voting (McCuen and Morton, 2010). By a tactical vote, voters can make particular coalitions more or less likely and thereby indirectly decide on policy choices (Austen-Smith and Banks, 1988). Voters may thus vote tactically for their second-most preferred party in order to improve the chances of a coalition which is expected to implement a preferred policy. Although experimental evidence supports the proposition that voters are induced to tactical voting, and that this effect is mediated by their information level, the amount of tactical voting in the laboratory is considerably less than predicted by theory (McCuen and Morton, 2010).

In the run up to an election in multiparty proportional election systems, parties can signal with whom they would be willing to form a coalition. Experiments have shown that these pre-electoral coalitions have a clear impact on voting behavior. In a mock election among students, strong ideological congruence effects, promoting coalitions among ideologically proximate parties and dislike effects, penalizing announced coalitions with badly reputed parties, could be observed (Gschwend and Hooghe, 2008). In a survey experiment embedded in an electoral poll, voters responded strategically to coalition signals (Meffert and Gschwend, 2011). However, much insincere voting is not explicitly strategic. In particular, instead of swing voters, partisans seem to respond most strongly to coalition signals, punishing their party for unpopular coalition proposals.

### 2.2.5 Heuristics

The information requirements and cognitive demands on voters assumed by the models discussed in the previous paragraphs are considerable. As the level of political sophistication and knowledge in the population is generally low, these assumptions may not adequately capture actual processes. The citizens' lack of information and sophistication is considered both a problem to the rational theory of voting and the reason for 'the mismatch between what delegation demands and citizens' capabilities', or the 'democratic dilemma' (Lupia and McCubbins, 1998: 12). However, in an elaborate set of both laboratory and survey experiments that focus on the conditions of persuasion in different information settings and on the conditions of successful delegation, it is shown that subjects can make use of small cues that inform about the ability and willingness of agents and thus enable reasoned choice without full information (Lupia and McCubbins, 1998). This ability is strengthened by institutions such as a penalty for lying or a threat of verification of information provided (Boudreau, 2009).

An extensive literature has developed studying information shortcuts through which citizens form beliefs about the candidates' positions (Lau and Redlawsk, 2001). Lau and Redlawsk (2001) identify five types of heuristics used in elections: a candidate's party affiliation, ideology, appearance, endorsement by a group and poll results. Poll results appear to increase turnout in experimental elections when support for the candidates is about equal, while they decrease turnout when polls indicate large differences in support for the candidates (Großer and Schram, 2010). This indirectly supports the pivotal voter model because voter mobilization seems to be tied to the probability of being pivotal: Voters are more likely to abstain if they do not expect their vote to make a difference. Polls, as well as previous election results, also help voters to coordinate on a strategic vote, thus avoiding the election of the least-preferred candidate (Forsythe et al., 1993).

Generalizing on the idea of learning from available information that underlies the heuristic based on poll results, experimental evidence shows a very clear effect of the complexity of the choice situation on decision strategies (Van der Straeten et al., 2010). While strategic voting is prevalent in a one-round election, voting behavior in two-round elections is much better explained by a simple heuristic where voters in the second-round vote for the most-preferred candidate among the top two or three candidates from the first round.

By using heuristics, subjects can save substantially on information costs and significantly reduce the cognitive effort for generating expectations about outcomes. At the same time, such shortcuts may mislead voters. Survey and field experimental evidence on the impact of heuristics confirm this mixed picture. While – despite the fact that it is waning (Dalton and Wattenberg, 2000) – the salience of party identification is manifest in observational studies, it is unclear whether the mere assignment of party labels to subjects participating in experimental elections is sufficient to foster a level of identification that has implications for behavior (Schram and Sonnemans, 1996b). Nevertheless, a small identity effect, which increases when incentives to vote for a particular party or information are low, can still be observed (Bassi, Morton and Williams, 2011). Citizens' ideological and partisan preferences influence the perception of information. Voters appear to dismiss information that contradicts with their prior judgments or that is communicated by someone with divergent preferences (Ahn, Huckfeldt and Ryan, 2010; MacCoun and Paletz, 2009; Tilley and Hobolt, 2011). In a survey experiment conducted in Russia partisan cues are shown to not only influence the opinion of partisans, but also to affect nonpartisan votes

when a position represented by a party constitutes an unusually informative or credible signal (Brader and Tucker, 2009).

### 2.2.6 Framing and the volatility of political opinion

If subjects make use of simple heuristics instead of fully balancing out the
costs and benefits of different options, then they will also be disposed to
let themselves be guided by the conditions in which choices are presented.
The discovery of framing effects (Kahneman and Tversky, 1979) has had a
profound impact on many research areas in political science as it questioned
the premise of stable preference on which the theoretical edifice based on
rational choice was built. Gains and losses are differently valued and the
response to change thus depends on the context in which the change is
framed. With some delay, prospect theory has been introduced into the
realm of political science, although in the beginning it was almost exclusively in international relations (McDermott, 2004; Mercer, 2005). While
framing is clearly conceptualized in psychological experiments, the most
challenging problem for political scientists using prospect theory is to identify the relevant frame and to distinguish the frame from the actual choice
(Mercer, 2005: 4).

In political opinion formation, framing often takes the form of elite opinions disseminated through the media before subjects start making their
own opinion (Mendelsohn, 1996). Empirical research has documented that
in their opinions, citizens tend to follow other citizens whom they believe
to be better informed (Huckfeldt, 2001). Framing effects through influence
by others, however, are short-lived, reduced by individual expertise, and
eliminated by elite competition as well as deliberation in groups formed
by individuals holding conflicting opinions, in contrast to homogeneous
groups (Druckman, 2004; Druckman and Nelson, 2003). Moreover, because
the effect of information on opinion decays over time, the most recently
received message is weighted disproportionately and thus opinions change
adaptively over time (Chong and Druckman, 2010). In constellations in
which information is provided only by peers with conflicting interests, a
significant proportion of subjects is deceived by biased information to vote
against their own interests (Ryan, 2011).

### 2.2.7 Norms and social preferences

While framing effects focus on the way choice situations are presented to
subjects, norms and social preferences can be thought of as internalized
frames that add the consideration of other subjects' fates to the equation. Early on, and in line with analogous results in behavioral economics
(Camerer, 2003), results from experiments on voting behavior have been
difficult to reconcile with the assumption of purely selfish utility maximizing behavior (Eavey and Miller, 1984b). A different approach to solving
the voting paradox elaborates on the civic duty term in Riker and Ordeshook's

initial model (Feddersen, 2004; Feddersen and Sandroni, 2006). At the core of the "ethical voting" model is thus the idea that individuals receive a payoff from acting in accordance with ethical rules (Harsanyi, 1977; 1980), thereby developing a social preference theory of voting (Edlin, Gelman and Kaplan, 2007). Instead of relying on the infinitesimal probability of being pivotal in large elections, individuals are assumed to abide to some behavioral norm. Such "rule utilitarians" will vote for their favored candidate if their voting costs are below a certain threshold even if they are in a minority position, thereby generating turnout levels above zero. Results from observational research support predictions based on the ethical voting model in more detail than traditional pivotal voting models (Coate and Conlin, 2004; Coate, Conlin and Moro, 2008).

In order to improve the fit between the theoretical argument and the experimental results, the utility maximization and the ethical voting models have been integrated into a unified approach in which the dominating motivation depends on the pivotal probability. As the pivotal probability approaches zero, the relative importance of individual payoffs vanishes to the benefit of moral considerations (Feddersen, Gailmard and Sandroni, 2009). Therefore, the voting paradox is resolved in a more complex utility function. For an experimental test, the authors operationalize the abstract, and as such untestable, concept of rule utilitarianism in terms of the moral superiority of a distributional outcome. A vote for a more equal distribution of payoffs instead of an option that yields a better individual payoff is interpreted as indicating an expressive preference for a morally superior alternative. In this setup, the probability of expressive voting based on ethical considerations is shown to be indeed inversely related to the pivot probability (Feddersen, Gailmard and Sandroni, 2009).

A similar idea is at the heart of an approach that is explicitly based on social preference theory (Bolton and Ockenfels, 2000; Fehr and Schmidt, 1999). The basic departure of this perspective from traditional subjective utility theory is to extend the model by including a term that refers to the deviation of a player's payoff from the other players' payoffs. The two models differ in the formulation of this term: Whereas Fehr and Schmidt model the distance between each player and each other player individually, Bolton and Ockenfels use the distance of each player to the average of all players. Experimental evidence for committee decisions on distribution or redistribution shows that social preference models better predict voting behavior than models based on self-centered preference assumptions (Sauermann and Kaiser, 2010; Tyran and Sausgruber, 2006), thus confirming that the robust experimental results holding for the context of two- and more-player games (Bolton and Ockenfels, 2008; Frohlich, Oppenheimer and Kurki, 2004) extend to voting behavior. Expressive voting theory differs from social preference theory in suggesting a distinct logic of instrumental (selfish) and expressive voting (Feddersen, Gailmard and Sandroni, 2009), while the latter incorporates social preferences in an instrumental voting model.

The introduction of norm-guided behavior and social preferences into voting models actually touches on a broad theoretical and experimental discussion about redistributive justice (Konow, 2003) and seems to provide a natural microfoundation to this literature. As mentioned above, Feddersen, Gailmard and Sandroni (2009: 178) make this relation explicit and use voting in favor of an equal distribution as an indicator of expressive voting. However, the problem of analysis is thus implicitly shifted from turnout to the justice preferences of individuals (Frohlich and Oppenheimer, 1993; Michelbach et al., 2003; Scott et al., 2001; Traub, Seidl and Schmidt, 2009; Tyran and Sausgruber, 2006).

### 2.2.8    Learning to vote, or not

A final extension to models of turnout considers the time dimension more thoroughly by focusing on adaptive learning processes in voting behavior. Replacing the assumption of utility maximization by the idea of 'satisficing' (Simon, 1955) produces a model in which voters adapt their behavior to their assessment of the extent to which the outcome of the previous election was satisfactory (Bendor, Diermeier and Ting, 2003). The basic mechanism of the model is a feedback mechanism that increases the probability of voting when voters win and shirkers lose, or decreases when voters lose and shirkers win (Bendor et al., 2011; Collins, Kumar and Bendor, 2009). This model has been challenged for assuming casual voting, which seems at odds with survey-based knowledge of actual voting behavior, which suggests rather large extents of time-consistency in voting behavior, and a model of habitual voting has been suggested as an alternative (Fowler, 2006). To our knowledge, these models have not yet been subjected to experimental scrutiny.

The importance of developing and testing models of learning processes is underscored by the observation made in various experimental analyses of repeated elections that turnout and strategic voting undergo changes over time. As discussed above, and in line with the results of contribution games in general (Chan, Mestelman and Muller, 2008; Holt, 2007), turnout seems to be slightly and gradually decreasing over time (Schram and Sonnemans, 1996a). In contrast, the incidence of strategic voting is reported to grow in the course of an experimental session (Van der Straeten et al., 2010). These observations are compatible with the proposition that subjects learn to understand which behavioral strategies maximize their payoffs in the given situation and indeed call for an explicitly dynamic theory of voting.

### 2.2.9    Summary

Taken together, the experimental literature on voting behavior has substantially moved forward the research frontier. We consider three issues as the most challenging questions in this area. First, norms and social preferences must be considered an integral part of preference formation, but the extent to which subjects depart from rationality in the narrow sense depends on the institutional context and the cognitive frame relevant to the situation. Second, the rationality assumption is also challenged by information usage. In experiments, subjects make very reasonable decisions based on simple heuristic cues and incomplete information. And third, perhaps the most intricate challenge is the systematic assessment of effects related to time and sequencing, which involve issues such as adaptation, satisfaction and regret. All three challenges push assumptions about individual behavior clearly beyond the traditional rational choice core of game theoretic models without yet replacing this core with a new consensus about reasonable microfoundations.

## 2.3   Political institutions and voting rules

Although voting is and remains the single most individual and personal political activity in a democracy which gains its legitimacy by the fact of being unobservable by others, this act does not occur in a void. Instead, it is heavily conditioned by a variety of norms and rules that regulate the process of collective decision making. At several instances in the previous section, for example in the discussion of strategic and tactical voting, we have highlighted the differential impact that rules have on voting behavior in collective decisions. Actually, all experimental studies in political science define rules in some way or other that are meant to affect preferences and guide behavior. Comparative statics are analyzed by imposing certain conditions on subjects' behavior. Although a clear and unequivocal categorization is difficult to maintain, experimental research on institutions can be distinguished from the studies discussed above by an explicit focus on institutions that is the main interest of the theoretical argument to be tested.

Like in research on individual voting behavior, a paradoxical finding has initiated a burgeoning research field. The publication of the finding that under very general conditions in multidimensional space, majority rule can produce cycles through the entire set of outcomes (McKelvey, 1976), has had an impact that was at least comparable to the voting paradox. This analytically clear and theoretically compelling finding, later termed the "chaos theorem", was clearly at odds with practical experience. The key to resolving the paradox has been suspected to lie in the fact that the chaos theorem assumes an institution-free environment (Shepsle, 1979). Indeed, real-world decision processes are structured by institutional rules that, on the one hand, facilitate decision making but, on the other hand, risk being manipulated, thereby implicitly undermining the requirement of nondictatorship. The finding was disturbing, because it implies that the chances of individual preferences to be represented in the collective decision are unequally distributed. Institutions have a huge impact on the outcome of voting processes (Bottom et al., 2008). Thus, in the following we discuss vote aggregation mechanisms, voting rules and the quorum, and agenda setting (Wilson, 2007). Typically, the theoretical arguments are developed within a procedural setting in which a committee must decide on policies, and motions are voted sequentially in binary choices. In contrast to the literature on turnout and individual voting behavior, all members of the committee are usually assumed to vote. Nevertheless, many of the topics discussed above are also relevant for committee decisions.

### 2.3.1   The Problem of instability

At the core of the legitimation of democratic governance is the problem of aggregation: How should heterogeneous individual preferences, positioned in a one- or multidimensional space, be aggregated into a collective decision? Condorcet's cycling paradox (Mueller, 2003), Arrow's impossibility theorem (Arrow, 1963) and the chaos theorem (McKelvey, 1976) have unequivocally made it clear that aggregation rules are not innocuous and they can be manipulated. The interpretation of this result dominating formal political theory, which is the main source inspiring experimental work, has suggested in the 1970s and 1980s that the problems are paramount and that therefore democratic voting procedures must be considered meaningless (Riker, 1982). However, laboratory experiments inspired by various assumptions and results of the theorems, as well as detailed scrutiny of real-world examples, have generally disconfirmed the salience of the problem. Although the argument's assumptions are logically compelling, committees have typically neither produced cycles nor taken decisions that were far off the center of gravity of the involved preferences (Mackie, 2003).

A multitude of solution concepts predicting the outcome of spatial voting problems under pairwise sequential voting has been developed and examined experimentally (Fiorina and Plott, 1978; McKelvey, Ordeshook and Winer, 1978). Typically, these early experiments on spatial voting models employed simple majority voting under the plurality rule. They have shown that the core – the set of undominated outcomes – is resilient across different experimental designs (Eavey, 1996; Holt, 1999; McKelvey and Ordeshook, 1990). Given that many spatial voting games do not have a core, as shown by the chaos theorem, the search for solution concepts remained on the agenda. In the meantime, however, the exploration of institutional factors potentially affecting the outcome of majority voting has continued.

One avenue was to study the impact of bicameralism. According to the theory of the bicameral core (Hammond and Miller, 1987; Tsebelis and Money, 1997), subdividing the members of a committee into separate chambers that must both approve of a motion may generate a core if a unicameral committee does not have one, and therefore a bicameral system produces greater stability. Experimental studies testing this proposition found that the selected outcome corresponds to the core of the specific partition of the committee into two chambers and that the outcome responds to changes in the partition (Miller, Hammond and Kile, 1996). Moreover, bicameral committees appear to produce more stable outcomes than unicameral committees in experiments (Bottom et al., 2000).

The work on solutions for majority voting obtained new momentum with the development of a method for numerically approximating an alternative solution concept, the uncovered set, that is, the set of outcomes that are not covered by other outcomes (Bianco, Jeliazkov and Sened, 2004).[3] Both a reanalysis of previous experimental work on spatial voting (Bianco et al., 2006) and new experiments (Bianco et al., 2008) show that this solution concept can successfully improve the predictive capacity of spatial voting models. Although the uncovered set can be rather wide, it definitely reduces the number of expectable outcomes and thus gives evidence that the chaos theorem is an extreme case under specific and empirically rare conditions. Moreover, the implication of this development is that there exists a solution set of majority voting that is responsive to preference changes of pivotal voters and not necessarily conditioned by other institutional constraints (Bianco et al., 2008: 129). This does not, however, preclude the huge impact that institutions such as the percentage of yes-votes needed to pass a motion and the way votes are counted can have on the outcome. We now turn to these rules.

### 2.3.2   The quorum

One of the most fundamental problems of democratic rule is the proportion of a constituency that must approve of a motion to get it moved. The tension between distributional justice and the manageability of collective decisions has been captured early on by the distinction between external costs, which refer to the costs that those not taking part in the decision have to bear, and decision costs, which refer to the effort needed for reaching a decision (Buchanan and Tullock, 1962). Under the rule of one, dictatorship, decision costs are minimal because a single individual can decide the motion. However, at the same time, external costs are potentially unlimited. With an increasing proportion of approvals needed for a decision, decision costs grow, while external costs decline because more individuals can veto a motion. At the other extreme, unanimity, every single member of the constituency can veto a motion, which results in minimal external costs but potentially unlimited decision costs. In a direct experimental test of these arguments, the predictions are clearly supported (Miller and Vanberg, 2011).

Buchanan and Tullock's argument has been elaborated by subsequent theoretical work on the unanimity rule (Chen and Ordeshook, 1998; Mueller, 2003). Generally, the conclusion of this work is that unanimity rule produces Pareto-optimal outcomes. In comparison to intermediate situations, that is, qualified majority rules, the simple majority rule has been shown to optimize the representativeness of individual positions in a collective decision, and, given that conflict over interests easily translates into conflict over decision rules, to be least likely to be contested as a rule (Rae, 1969). In experimental work studying committees using the unanimity rule, the authors find that the core predicts the outcomes better than alternative solution concepts and thereby underscores the Pareto-optimality of decisions under unanimity rule (Laing and Slotznick, 1991).

Giving one player veto power reduces the core to a linear contract curve connecting the veto player's ideal point to the median line closest to the veto player's position, a prediction that is supported by experimental evidence (King, 1994). Similarly, the theoretical result that a two-thirds supermajority rule produces a core (Greenberg, 1977), has been confirmed experimentally (King, 1994). These results have also been supported by more recent experiments that revealed higher decision costs in the presence of veto players, an unequal distribution of power in favor of veto players and less willingness to compromise on the part of veto players (Kagel, Sung and Winter, 2010).

However, two different lines of reasoning have challenged this view. One argument posits that external costs can take two forms that cannot be treated as equivalent: inflicting harm on others, and rejecting favors for others (Guttman, 1998). If both types of external costs are considered, it can be shown that unanimity rule is almost never efficient and majority rule produces socially optimal outcomes. A second line of attack on received wisdom distinguishes between the retention of the status quo and the attraction to the status quo and posits that these two forces must be conceptualized differently (Dougherty and Edward, 2005). In a one-dimensional policy space, the authors show that unanimity is superior for maintaining the status quo if it is in the Pareto optimal set, but that majority is better in reaching the Pareto optimal set when the status quo is outside, because unanimity rule will maintain the status quo even if it is Pareto-suboptimal. This argument has also been extended to a multi-dimensional policy space (Dougherty and Edward, 2011). Experimental tests of implications of the model show that, first, majority rule is at least as likely as unanimity to attain the Pareto set, and that, second, it does so faster (Dougherty et al., forthcoming). Hence, the authors conclude that majority voting does not perform worse than unanimity rule for the external cost criterion, and it does better with regard to the decision cost criterion. By contrast, in a formal model endogenizing proposals, the unanimity rule makes voters better off than majority voting (Bond and Eraslan, 2010). We are not aware of an experiment explicitly testing the one perspective against the other.

Recently, other aspects relating to the impact of quorum rules have been modeled, in particular qualified voting rules and the effect of majority requirements. In an experimental comparison of the simple and the absolute majority rule, no clear advantage of the one or other rule in general could be found (Dougherty and Edward, 2010). Relative social welfare maximizing performance appears to depend very much on the criterion applied. Furthermore, the effect of the four options that voters have in dichotomous voting situations – voting "yes", voting "no", abstaining and staying at home – has been modeled in detail, without, to our knowledge, yet having been explicitly examined in an experiment (Laruelle and Valenciano, 2011).

### 2.3.3 Voting rules in multicandidate elections

The theory of voting equilibria has not only spurred a literature on individual voting behavior but also given new impetus to a literature exploring the effect of voting rules on election outcomes in multicandidate elections. Studies involve a subset of the following voting rules: one-round plurality, two-round majority, Borda counts, approval voting and the single transferable vote. Early experiments on voting rules tend to support Duverger's law that plurality rule leads to two-party systems (Rietz, 1993). These experiments furthermore show that Condorcet losers tend to win plurality-rule elections if these involve a split majority in a single-round election without information on voting preferences of others. This is not the case for approval voting and the Borda rule that tend to maintain votes for inferior candidates. For other voting rules, the support of a Duvergerian equilibrium requires either information derived from polls or from previous rounds in sequential voting games.

In follow-up studies, these initial findings are confirmed. Duverger's law holds under plurality rule and Condorcet losers occasionally win, but approval voting and the Borda rule often lead to close three-way races (Forsythe et al., 1996). In an experiment exploring the effect of the voting rule on the willingness to vote for motions that benefit others besides oneself, the plurality rule induced selfish voting behavior while approval voting included a motion benefitting both oneself and others as a second choice and this option was more likely to win (Baron, Altman and Kroll, 2005). Thus, approval voting seems to increase social welfare as compared to the plurality rule. Recently, the greater likelihood of approval voting, as compared to the one-round plurality and two-round majority rule, to select a centrist candidate has been confirmed again (Blais et al., 2010). Jointly, these experimental findings thus suggest that approval voting is better designed to select social welfare enhancing policies than alternative voting rules (Laslier, 2010). Field experiments in France (Baujard and Ingersheim, 2010) and Germany (Alós-Ferrer and Granić, 2010) support the practical feasibility of approval voting, underscore its acceptance by the voters and show that the tendency for moderate outcomes is increased.

### 2.3.4   Agenda control

Finally, if more than two proposals are on the floor, the voting sequence becomes another variable that is open to manipulation by strategically acting subjects. The effect of agenda control on the outcome is strong. A variety of theoretical and experimental work has shown that players who control the agenda can effectively pull the outcome towards their own ideal point (Romer and Rosenthal, 1977). Experimental tests of this prediction revealed, however, that observed outcomes fall anywhere on a line between the median voter's and the agenda setter's ideal points in both one-dimensional (Eavey and Miller, 1984a) and two-dimensional space (Kormendi and Plott, 1982), thereby confirming that even strong agenda setters cannot impose their position but need to bargain with the median voter. This also holds when the status quo is varied (Bottom, Eavey and Miller, 1996). In a variant of the model which experimentally examines the effect of dividing a committee into subcommittees, each controlling one of two dimensions, undominated outcomes are situated in the area between the two ideal points of the agenda setters and the status quo (Eavey and Miller, 1995). As it has been mentioned above, subjects in laboratory experiments tend to choose the agenda most favorable to their preferences (Smirnov, 2009).

### 2.3.5   Summary

In this section, we have identified three challenging questions relating to the macrostructure of politics. First, while we admit that the chaos theorem is a compelling theoretical problem, experimental evidence suggests that subjects are very well able to avoid the chaos. The main challenge is to identify a stable set of predictable outcomes. In this regard, the uncovered set is a promising candidate for unifying a hitherto diverse set of experimental results. Second, the relative performance of different quora is still disputed and results seem to depend to a large degree on the experimental design and the exact test conditions. Third, there is considerable evidence suggesting that the voting rules most widely applied in the real world, plurality and majority rules, may not be the socially best solution to the problem of aggregating preferences. Results from both laboratory and field experiments suggest that, at least under certain conditions, approval voting and Borda counts may generate more legitimacy and less discontent with policy.

## 2.4   Collective decision making

Equipped with knowledge about individual voting behavior and the effect of political institutions on outcomes, political scientists have started to explore the process of collective decision making in more detail. In this section, we report on the discussion of bargaining in legislatures and the implications of communication on collective decisions, a field in which formal social choice theory meets the theory of deliberative democracy. The question thus is: How do individuals interact under the condition of different rules?

### 2.4.1 Bargaining

Most of the models discussed above are basically static, one-shot voting games. A dynamic perspective on voting sequences is taken by multilateral bargaining theory (Baron and Ferejohn, 1989). Adjusting bilateral sequential bargaining theory (Muthoo, 1999; Nash, 1950; Rubinstein, 1982) to the multilateral setting, Baron and Ferejohn (1989) explore the problem of collective decision making in legislatures by bargaining under majority rule from a perspective that explicitly includes agenda setting and voting rules as constraints. They model a distributive decision as a sequence of (1) a stage in which one member is recognized for making a proposal, which is assumed to be a random draw from the legislators; (2) a stage for making amendments, which is either forbidden (closed rule) or allowed (open rule); and (3) a voting stage, in which the proposal is accepted or rejected by a simple majority vote. If the proposal is rejected, a new round of the sequence starts. The authors conclude from the formal analysis of their model that under the closed rule, a majority distributes the initial endowment among themselves, with the largest share being allocated to the proposer. The open rule, however, induces universalistic distributions in small legislatures and more equal distributions in large legislatures.

The model has been used extensively to study topics such as patronage (Baron, 1991), vote-splitting (Chari, Jones and Marimon, 1997), government turnover (Diermeier and Merlo, 2000) or the enforcement of collective goods programs (Baron, 1996). A variety of extensions and generalizations to the model have been explored. Proposal rights have been amended by veto rights, and the two have been shown to interact (McCarty, 2000): Being assigned the proposal right advantages a voter, but also increases her risk of being left out of a winning coalition. A veto right counteracts this vulnerability because it operates as an insurance against being left out. Replacing the initial constant endowment assumption by a stochastic process of surplus generation generates an incentive for voters to postpone their acceptance of a proposal to a later period (Eraslan and Merlo, 2002). These streams have been combined into a general bargaining model that also incorporates the possibility that the status quo is preferred to all other outcomes by some players, who thus have an incentive to delay agreement (Banks and Duggan, 2006). In particular, the authors show analytically that, in unidimensional policy spaces, the location of the status quo is a strong predictor of the outcome. If it is in the core, it will always be selected; if it is outside, it will never be selected. In an application of this general model to the trade-off between public and private goods, the individual valuation of the public and the private good determines the level of general welfare that can be attained (Volden and Wiseman, 2007). Particularistic spending can be discouraged when subjects either value the public or the private good much more than the other, but not when preferences are intermediate.

Experimental examinations of predictions derived from the Baron-Ferejohn bargaining model and some of its extensions, however, revealed that the model does not perform well in practice (Diermeier and Morton, 2005; Fréchette, Kagel and Morelli, 2005). A simple equal sharing rule outperforms both the Baron-Ferejohn model and a proportionality rule that predicts that the outcome will be proportional to the vote share of a party. The proportionality rule, in turn, performs better than the Baron-Ferejohn model. Diermeier and Morton discuss intrinsic fairness motivations, equal sharing as a focal point and the complexity of the experiment as potential causes for the deviation of the results from the theoretical expectations (Diermeier and Morton, 2005: 222–224). Political veto bargaining models have not been scrutinized experimentally (Cameron and McCarty, 2004), and to our knowledge this observation still holds today.

### 2.4.2   Communication

Perhaps equally consequential as the impact of experimental results of behavioral economics on the micro-fundament, and thus the modeling realism, of economics in general has been the systematic study of communication on the status of spatial models of collective decisions. In the context of clearly defined payoffs, monetary incentive structures induce utility maximizing behavior that makes behavior in narrowly circumscribed settings predictable. As long as the final behavioral decision is made in private, communication cannot have an effect on behavior because no binding commitments can be made. If the incentive structure is public knowledge, the subject cannot credibly announce a strategy that deviates from maximum individually available payoffs. From this perspective, all communication is mere cheap talk in strategic dilemmas (Farrell and Rabin, 1996).

While the narrow rationality assumption does seem to work rather well in the context of atomistic markets, these models are much less persuasive in nonmarket contexts, in particular in the case of group decision making. Similarly, with communication, the predictive capacity of spatial models turns out to be rather limited, because, 'Communication frees players to select alternatives unanimously preferred by a majority coalition to the dimension-to-dimension median, thus side-stepping the rules and the structure-induced equilibrium' (Eavey and Miller, 1995: 133). This does not imply that models based on subjective expected utility theory are moot. Early political science experiments that lacked computerized communication media routinely involved face-to-face interactions and thus did not ban or control for communication (Fiorina and Plott, 1978). With hindsight, the stunning aspect of the results of these experiments is not that they deviate from the expectations from formal theory, but the extent to which they support the expectations. The models do capture incentive structures in the context of strategic choice situations and basic logics of social interaction, and incentives can be successfully induced by monetary rewards even in the presence of communication.

Nevertheless, communication does make a difference. Communication prior to group decisions has a significant impact on the outcome (Croson, Boles and Murnighan, 2003; Sally, 1995). Also, the richness of communicative content (some form of limited content versus free-form chat interaction) appears to have a significant effect, suggesting that efficiency increases with communicative richness (Lev-On, Chavez and Bicchieri, 2010). Whether the media of communication affects the outcome is not definitively established. While early studies have found a very clear effect, suggesting that computer-mediated communication is less efficient than face-to-face interaction (Brosig, Weimann and Ockenfels, 2003), results from newer studies tend to nuance this proposition, suggesting that the medium affects the difficulty of developing mutual expectations (Bicchieri and Lev-On, 2007) but does not lead to qualitatively different behavior (Lev-On, Chavez and Bicchieri, 2010).[4]

### 2.4.3 Information sharing and deliberation

An important line of formal theoretical inquiry of communication in collective decision making has been the exploration of the extent of truthful information sharing under majority and unanimity rule in three-person committee decision making (Austen-Smith and Banks, 1996). Starting from the result that the unanimity rule increases the probability of taking erroneous decisions in juries as compared to other voting rules (Feddersen and Pesendorfer, 1998), a debate ensued whether a straw vote among jury members prior to the voting stage fosters nonstrategic voting and whether unanimity minimizes the probability of mistrial (Austen-Smith and Feddersen, 2005; 2006; Coughlan, 2000). In an experiment precisely capturing Austen-Smith and Feddersen's (2006) conceptualization of the model, results neither support the purported superiority of majority rule nor the proposition that communication induces honest sharing of information (Myers, 2010).

Whereas these studies limit the possibilities of communication to simple signals, free-form communication in multi-agent collective choice situations takes the form of deliberation. Deliberation is generally thought of as 'debate and discussion aimed at producing reasonable, well-informed opinions in which subjects are willing to revise preferences in light of discussion, new information, and claims made by other subjects' (Chambers, 2003: 309). Persuasion in the context of a free and equal exchange of thoughts, hence, is the core mechanism generating collective decisions. Couched within the ideals of deliberative democracy (Elster, 1998; Mutz, 2006), the possibilities for improving the quality of consideration, and – hopefully – decision, of policy problems in practice have been explored by 'deliberative polling' (Fishkin 2009), aiming to 'make the participants more like ideal citizens' (Luskin, Fishkin and Jowell, 2002: 460) by strengthening involvement, thought and information. Although not reaching the stringency of a true experiment, the deliberations among randomly selected citizens during deliberative polling events seem to have improved the overall level of reflection of decision making and generated more informed political positions (Fishkin, 2009). Apart from producing attitude changes, deliberation appears to bring preference distributions closer to single-peakedness, which avoids cyclical majorities for low-salience issues, albeit this result does not hold for high-salience issues (Farrar et al., 2010). Nevertheless, there is reason to ask to what extent such procedures might be practicable beyond singular events (McCubbins and Rodriguez, 2006).

The emphatic drive of deliberative democracy relies on the honesty of individual contributions to the deliberative process or at least on the capability of constituencies to identify and sanction dishonest contributions (Mutz, 2008; Ryfe, 2005; Thompson, 2008). The reliance on honest representation of preferences, however, is what the rational choice approach doubts: It views contributions as signals that may or may not be credible, depending on the institutionally mediated, strategic incentives to represent preferences truthfully (Austen-Smith, 1992). From this perspective, communicating the truth or not is a strategic decision. An expanding theoretical and experimental literature in political science has thus explored whether and how communication fosters collective decisions. Including deliberation into formal models is difficult because of the multifaceted and imprecise nature of free-form communication. As a result, theoretical elaborations and many experimental examinations have been restricted to rather shallow notions of deliberation.

In a first experimental test of computerized free-form deliberation that was performed as a set of dictator and ultimatum games with the opportunity to discuss proposals (Sulkin and Simon, 2001), allocations were significantly higher and decision processes have been considered as more fair if the discussion was scheduled prior to the proposal stage, but not after the proposal. Thus, the authors conclude, communication does not improve social preferences and fairness perceptions as such, but depends on the perception of participatory opportunities. The extension of the ultimatum game to N-person majority bargaining games with communication has revealed that the multidimensionality of the communication channel (face-to-face in contrast to computer-mediated chat) and the enforcement of public communication increase the ability of committees to agree on the most efficient outcomes socially, while keeping in force the strategic incentives to form exclusionary coalitions (Diermeier et al., 2008).

If free-form communication is introduced into the models of jury decisions discussed above, the incentives do not anymore depend on the voting rule, and the unanimity rule limits the set of possible outcomes as compared with other voting rules (Gerardi and Yariv, 2007). In contrast to models without communication, in which voting rules induce jury members to choose different outcomes and to communicate strategically, experimental examinations of jury decisions with free-form communication have shown that the variation in outcomes is significantly reduced and contributions are honest most of the time as soon as players can coordinate on a more efficient outcome through free-form communication (Goeree and Yariv, 2011). These findings are supported by the result that deliberation among equals in groups of four and larger does not improve social welfare if information sharing is costly, in contrast to expertise systems (McCubbins and Rodriguez, 2006).

The effect of deliberation on positions in political space, a core proposition of deliberative theory on the effectiveness of persuasion, is difficult to measure. One way to elicit deliberative contributions in a controlled environment is to build deliberation sequences into survey questionnaires (Kinder and Sanders, 1990). This has been implemented rudimentarily in a survey experiment in which respondents were confronted by the interviewer with systematically varied counterarguments to their response to an ideologically laden question (Jackman and Sniderman, 2006). The authors did not find an increase in ideological consistency attributable to this exchange. In a re-analysis of discussion transcripts from an early experiment testing Rawls' theory of justice (Frohlich and Oppenheimer, 1993), complex group-level factors, such as, for example, interactions between the gender composition and the decision rule, have been detected (Karpowitz and Mendelberg, 2007). While this research field is still in its infancy, it has a great potential for development (Karpowitz and Mendelberg, 2011).

The main source of disagreement between deliberative democratic theory and social choice theory seems to be different conceptions of contributions to political debate. Indeed, one can differentiate between different modes of communication (Dickson, Hafer and Landa, 2008). On the one hand, communication in a cognitive mode facilitates the clarification of matters of fact in the sense suggested by deliberative theory. On the other hand, in a strategic mode, communication helps to infer others' intentions from their statements and to manipulate others' decisions by particular messages of a cheap talk quality. In a laboratory experiment that studies contributions to deliberation conditional on the subject's level of comprehension, deliberative contributions turn out to be influenced by strategic incentives, in general, but many subjects fail to infer the individually most advantageous course of action from the available information and engage too much in deliberation, thereby not persuading, but alienating listeners (Dickson, Hafer and Landa, 2008). Thus, besides institutional incentive structures and group composition, the mode of communication is another factor that has to be put into the equation.

### 2.4.4   Summary

Digging into the details of the processes of collective decision making is perhaps the greatest challenge to experimental political science. Typically, experiments base the causal claim about the relationship between treatment and outcome on theoretical assumptions about unobserved mechanisms producing the outcome. Tracing the bargaining processes and using communication protocols for analyzing the deliberation processes opens up this 'black box' and allows us to actually identify social mechanisms at work in producing the outcome. However, the factors relevant in the effect of the group composition on the deliberative process and the outcome, such as personalities or the gender composition, are still insufficiently understood to systematically include in treatments and difficult, though not impossible, to control in laboratory settings. Deliberation seems to turn upside down many predictions derived from formal theoretical models assuming selfish utility-maximizing behavior on the part of voters. At least partly or under certain conditions it also seems to undermine structure-induced equilibria and to annihilate the effect of voting rules and procedures. On the one hand, this is disquieting, but on the other hand, this also provides a puzzle which generates new challenges. Given that in this field many different research traditions, most notably formal theory and deliberative democratic theory, meet, we expect it to become a major area of research in the near future.

## 2.5   Conclusion

We have presented a bird's eye view of a few important lines of research in political science involving the experimental examination of mainly, though not exclusively, formal theory-driven hypotheses. We have outlined the main ideas and the most challenging questions, at least in our opinion, and explored experimental evidence supporting or contradicting the propositions. The interim impression of roughly four decades of research is one of either a half-full or half-empty glass. We observe impressive advancement, but also diversity and conceptual confusion.

On the one hand, we can observe an emerging consensus about promising theoretical modules and established stylized facts. For example, the discipline has made quite some mileage since the voting paradox has been stated. Although the issue is perhaps not yet finally resolved, by the work of many heads the paradox has gradually evolved into models based on reasoned choice instead of rational choice and into the dynamic turnout models that seem to establish the current research frontier in this field. Much more than formal models and observational evidence, the clear and persuasive results of experimental work have facilitated this development. Likewise, the chaos theorem has been a catalyst for the understanding of institutional conditions of policy making. But again, the recent work on uncovered sets is the result of continuous reflection, revision and reconsideration of assumptions, conceptualizations and mechanisms that pushed the research frontier forward, leaving the original statement as an admired, though transcended, landmark behind. And again, it was experimental work that turned out to provide the decisive hints.

These developments underscore the relevance of the unifying impact that is attributed to the combination of game theory, evolutionary theory and experimental research for the behavioral science in general (Gintis, 2007).

On the other hand, despite all calls for cumulation (Granato and Scioli, 2004), at a closer look, results are still scattered, giving more the impression of a 'dappled world' loosely linked through a 'patchwork of laws' similar to the state of art attributed to physics (Cartwright, 1999). Although we have not delved deeply into the variety of theoretical assumptions and experimental designs that have been explored during the last four decades of research, the diversity of the work is both impressive and disconcerting. The more we investigate into the details of single studies, the more incommensurable the different contributions become. Every little research field has its own design specificities that undermine the comparability of results. Perhaps experimental results are not as 'dead on arrival' (Taagepera, 2007: 121; Taagepera, 2008) as many results from quantitative observational work. However, experimental work is still confronted with the fact that slight differences in reasonable assumptions can yield considerable differences in predictions, and slight variations in experimental designs can produce contradictory results. This is sufficient reason for more in-depth research that links the various findings and resolves the contradictions. Sometimes, such work may result in another big leap forward by unifying hitherto separate areas. But most of this work will not, and still must be done if we believe in the value of cumulation.

As a result, a commonly accepted set of experimentally corroborated propositions on which the various lines of research can build is still in its infancy. Not even the behavioral assumption of maximizing subjective expected utility that provided the bracket of formal theoretical models has survived experimental analysis without harm. Although this assumption made modeling easier, the utility maximizer turned out to be both too limited in scope as a model of behavior and too demanding as a description of human cognitive ability to remain the workhorse of experimental political science. Even more than the exchange decisions studied by behavioral economists, distributive decisions are guided by preferences that cannot be easily captured by the utility maximization assumption. Instead, communication turns upside down the structure-induced equilibria based on that assumption.

Although truthful representation of preferences appears to be one of the core disagreements between deliberative democracy and social choice theory, if one accepts the propositions that deliberation changes the incentives and induces greater co-operative dispositions, there seems to exist potential for reconciling the two perspectives (Dryzek and List, 2003; Landa and Meirowitz, 2009). Important failure predictions of social choice theory have been shown to be solved in practice, both in observational and experimental studies (Mackie, 2003). While deliberative democracy 'is concerned with identification of the functions that deliberation ought to, and indeed can, perform in democratic decision making', social choice theory 'is concerned with the clarification of the logical properties of available procedures for solving the aggregation aspects of democratic decision problems' (Dryzek and List, 2003: 28). The 'critical contrast', thus, 'is not between formalized theory and nonformalized theory, but between the game-theoretic focus on the deliberative environment and the normative behavioral focus on the behavior without inducing it from the environment' (Landa and Meirowitz, 2009: 430).

All considered, we can provisionally conclude that experimental research has brought about a watershed in political science. While old puzzles become obsolete and old truths are shattered, we hope to have shown that our discipline's understanding of some of the core problems of political science, voting behavior and policy making, has reached a new level by being based on experimentally tested propositions.

## Notes

1. We thank Rebecca Morton, Wolfgang Luhan and Markus Tepe for helpful suggestions and comments.
2. For example, Myatt and Fisher (2002) refer to 'tactical coordination' in the context of plurality systems.
3. The solution concept had been proposed in the early 1980s (Miller, 1980), but analytic solutions were 'impossible to calculate in all but the simplest cases' (Bianco et al., 2006: 840).
4. Notice that the studies cited in the text mark the beginning and current state of a decade in which text messages via cell phones (sms) and internet-based chat facilities have spread throughout the society and have now become normal means of communication. This might account for the differences in findings.

## References

Ahn, T.K., Robert Huckfeldt and John B. Ryan (2010) 'Communication, Influence, and Informational Asymmetries among Voters', *Political Psychology* 31, 763–787.

Alós–Ferrer, Carlos and Dura–Georg Granić (2010) 'Approval Voting in Germany: Description of a Field Experiment' in Jean–François Laslier and M. Remzi Sanver (eds.) *Handbook on Approval Voting* (Berlin: Springer).

Arceneaux, Kevin and David Nickerson (2009) 'Who Is Mobilized to Vote? A Re-Analysis of 11 Field Experiments', *American Journal of Political Science* 53, 1–16.

Aroopala, Christy (2011) 'Are Group Sources Always Credible? An Experimental Study of Sources, Stakes, and Participation', *Journal of Theoretical Politics*, 23, 87–110.

Arrow, Kenneth Joseph (1963) *Social Choice and Individual Values* New Haven: Yale University Press.

Austen-Smith, David (1992) 'Strategic Models of Talk in Political Decision Making', *International Political Science Review*, 13, 45–58.

Austen-Smith, David and Jeffrey Banks (1988) 'Elections, Coalitions, and Legislative Outcomes', *American Political Science Review*, 82, 405–422.

Austen-Smith, David and Jeffrey S. Banks (1996) 'Information Aggregation, Rationality, and the Condorcet Jury Theorem', *American Political Science Review*, 90, 34–45.

Austen-Smith, David and Timothy J. Feddersen (2005) 'Deliberation and Voting Rules' in David Austen–Smith and John Duggan (eds.) *Social Choice and Strategic Decisions. Essays in Honor of Jeffrey S. Banks* (Berlin: Springer).

Austen-Smith, David and Timothy J. Feddersen (2006) 'Deliberation, Preference Uncertainty, and Voting Rules', *American Political Science Review*, 100, 209–217.

Banks, Jeffrey S. and John Duggan (2006) 'A General Bargaining Model of Legislative Policy–Making', *Quarterly Journal of Political Science*, 1, 49–85.

Baron, David P. (1991) 'Majoritairian Incentives, Pork-Barrel Programs, and Procedural Control', *American Journal of Political Science*, 35, 57–90.

Baron, David P. (1996) 'A Dynamic Theory of Collective Goods Programs', *American Political Science Review*, 90, 316–330.

Baron, David P. and John A. Ferejohn (1989) 'Bargaining in Legislatures', *American Political Science Review*, 83, 1181–1206.

Baron, Jonathan, Nicole Y. Altman and Stephan Kroll (2005) 'Approval Voting and Parochialism', *Journal of Conflict Resolution*, 49, 895–907.

Bassi, Anna, Rebecca B. Morton and Kenneth Williams (2011) 'The Effect of Identities, Incentives, and Information on Voting', *Journal of Politics*, 73, 558–571.

Battaglini, Marco, Rebecca B. Morton and Thomas R. Palfrey (2010) 'The Swing Voter's Curse in the Laboratory', *The Review of Economic Studies*, 77, 61–89.

Baujard, Antoinette and Herrade Ingersheim (2010) 'Framed Field Experiments on Approval Voting: Lessons from the 2002 and 2007 French Presidential Elections' in Jean–François Laslier and M. Remzi Sanver (eds.) *Handbook on Approval Voting* (Berlin: Springer).

Bendor, Jonathan, Daniel Diermeier, David A. Siegel and Michael M. Ting (2011) *A Behavioral Theory of Elections* (Princeton: Princeton University Press).

Bendor, Jonathan, Daniel Diermeier and Michael Ting (2003) 'A Behavioral Model of Turnout', *American Political Science Review*, 97, 261–280.

Bianco, William T., Ivan Jeliazkov and Itai Sened (2004) 'The Limits of Legislative Actions: Determining the Set of Enactable Outcomes Given Legislators Preferences', *Political Analysis*, 12, 256–276.

Bianco, William T., Michael S. Lynch, Gary J. Miller and Itai Sened (2006) '"A Theory Waiting to Be Discovered and Used": A Reanalysis of Canonical Experiments on Majority–Rule Decision Making', *Journal of Politics*, 68, 838–851.

Bianco, William T., Michael S. Lynch, Gary J. Miller and Itai Sened (2008) 'The Constrained Instability of Majority Rule: Experiments on the Robustness of the Uncovered Set', *Political Analysis*, 16, 115–137.

Bicchieri, Christina and Azi Lev-On (2007) 'Computer–Mediated Communication and Cooperation in Social Dilemmas: An Experimental Analysis', *Politics Philosophy Economics*, 6, 139–168.

Blais, André, Simon Labbé-St-Vincent, Jean-François Laslier, Nicolas Sauger and Karine Van der Straeten (2010) 'Strategic Vote Choice in One-Round and Two-Round Elections: An Experimental Study', *Political Research Quarterly* online first.

Bolton, Gary E. and Axel Ockenfels (2000) 'ERC: A Theory of Equity, Reciprocity, and Competition', *American Economic Review*, 90, 166–193.

Bolton, Gary E. and Axel Ockenfels (2008) 'Self-Centered Fairness in Games with More Than Two Players' in Charles R. Plott and Vernon L. Smith (eds.) *Handbook of Experimental Economics Results* (Amsterdam: North Holland).

Bond, Philip and Hülya Eraslan (2010) 'Strategic Voting over Strategic Proposals', *Review of Economic Studies*, 77, 459–490.

Bornstein, Gary and Ilan Yaniv (1998) 'Individual and Group Behavior in the Ultimatum Game: Are GroupsMore 'Rational' Players?', *Experimental Economics*, 1, 101–108.

Bosman, Ronald, Heike Hennig-Schmidt and Frans van Winden (2006) 'Exploring Group Decision Making in a Power-To-Take Experiment', *Experimental Economics*, 9, 35–51.

Bottom, William P., Cheryl L. Eavey and Gary J. Miller (1996) 'Getting to the Core: Coalition Integrity as a Constraint on the Power of Agenda Setters', *Journal of Conflict Resolution*, 40, 298–319.

Bottom, William P., Cheryl L. Eavey, Gary J. Miller and Jennifer Nicoll Victor (2000) 'The Institutional Effect on Majority Rule Instability: Bicameralism in Spatial Policy Decisions', *American Journal of Political Science* 44, 523–540.

Bottom, William P., Ronald F. King, Larry Handlin and Gary J. Miller (2008) 'Institutional Modifications of Majority Rule' in Charles A. Plott and Vernon Smith (eds.) *Handbook of Eperimental Economics Results, Vol. 1* (Amsterdam: Elsevier).

Boudreau, Cheryl (2009) 'Making Citizens Smart: When do Institutions Improve Unsophisticated Citizens' Decisions?', *Political Behavior*, 31, 287–306.

Brader, Ted A. and Joshua A. Tucker (2009) 'What's Left Behind When the Party's Over: Survey Experiments on the Effects of Partisan Cues in Putin's Russia', *Politics & Policy* 37, 843–868.

Brosig, Jeannette, Joachim Weimann and Axel Ockenfels (2003) 'The Effect of Communication Media on Cooperation', *German Economic Review* 4, 217–241.

Buchanan, James M. and Gordon Tullock (1962) *The Calculus of Consent. Logical Foundations of Constitutional Democracy* (Ann Arbor: University of Michigan Press).

Camerer, Colin F. (2003) *Behavioral Game Theory. Experiments in Strategic Interaction* (Princeton: Princeton University Press).

Cameron, Charles and Nolan McCarty (2004) 'Models of Vetoes and Veto Bargaining', *Annual Review of Political Science*, 7, 409–435.

Cartwright, Nancy (1999) *The Dappled World. A Study of the Boundaries of Science* (Cambridge: Cambridge University Press).

Cason, Timothy N. and Vai-Lam Mui (1997) 'A Laboratory Study of Group Polarisation in the Team Dictator Game', *The Economic Journal*, 107, 1465–1483.

Chambers, Simone (2003) 'Deliberative Democratic Theory', *Annual Review of Political Science*, 6, 307–326.

Chan, Kenneth S., Stuart Mestelman and R. Andrew Muller (2008) 'Voluntary Provision of Public Goods', in Charles R. Plott and Vernon Smith (eds.) *Handbook of Experimental Economics Results, Volume 1* (Amsterdam: North–Holland).

Chari, Varadarajan, Larry E. Jones and Ramon Marimon (1997) 'The Economics of Split–Ticket Voting in Representative Democracies', *American Economic Review*, 87, 957–976.

Chen, Yan and Peter C. Ordeshook (1998) 'Veto Games: Spatial Committees under Unanimity Rule', *Public Choice*, 97, 617–643.

Chong, Dennis and James N. Druckman (2010) 'Dynamic Public Opinion: Communication Effects over Time', *American Political Science Review*, 104, 663–680.

Coate, Stehen and Michael Conlin (2004) 'A Group Rule–Utility Approach to Voter Turnout: Theory and Evidence', *American Economic Review*, 94, 1476–1504.

Coate, Stehen, Michael Conlin and Andrea Moro (2008) 'The Performance of Pivotal-Voter Models in Small-Scale Elections: Evidence from Texas Liquour Referenda', *Journal of Public Economics*, 92, 582–596.

Collier, Kenneth E., Peter C. Ordeshook and Kenneth C. Williams (1989) 'The Rationally Uninformed Electorate: Some Experimental Evidence', *Public Choice*, 60, 3–29.

Collins, Nathan A., Sunil Kumar and Jonathan Bendor (2009) 'The Adaptive Dynamics of Turnout', *Journal of Politics*, 71, 457–472.

Coughlan, Peter J. (2000) 'In Defense of Unanimous Jury Verdicts: Mistrial, Communication, and Strategic Voting', *American Political Science Review*, 94, 375–393.

Cox, Gary W. (1997) *Making Votes Count. Strategic Coordination in the World's Electoral Systems* (Cambridge: Cambridge University Press).

Croson, Rachel, Terry Boles and J. Keith Murnighan (2003) 'Cheap Talk in Bargaining Experiments: Lying and Threats in Ultimatum Games', *Journal of Economic Behavior and Organization*, 51, 143–59.

Dalton, Russell J. and Martin P. Wattenberg (eds.) (2000) *Parties Without Partisans. Political Change in Advanced Industrial Democracies* (Oxford: Oxford University Press).

De Rooij, Eline A., Donald P. Green and Alan S. Gerber (2009) 'Field Experiments on Political Behavior and Collective Action', *Annual Review of Political Science*, 12, 389–395.

Delli Carpini, Michael X. and Scott Keeter (1996) *What Americans Know About Politics and Why it Matters* (New Haven: Yale University Press).

Dickson, Eric S., Catherine Hafer and Dimitri Landa (2008) 'Cognition and Strategy: A Deliberation Experiment', *Journal of Politics*, 70, 974–89.

Diermeier, Daniel and Antonio Merlo (2000) 'Government Turnover in Parliamentary Democracies', *Journal of Economic Theory*, 94, 46–79.

Diermeier, Daniel and Rebecca B. Morton (2005) 'Experiments in Majoritarian Bargaining' in David Austen-Smith and John Duggan (eds.) *Social Choice and Strategic Decisions. Essays in Honor of Jeffrey S. Banks* (Berlin: Springer).

Diermeier, Daniel, Roderick I. Swaab, Victoria Husted Medvec and Mary C. Kern (2008) 'The Micro–Dynamics of Coalition Formation', *Political Research Quarterly*, 61, 484–501.

Dougherty, Keith and Julian Edward (2005) 'A Nonequilibrium Analysis of Unanimity Rule, Majority Rule, and Pareto', *Economic Inquiry*, 43, 855–864.

Dougherty, Keith and Julian Edward (2010) 'The Properties of Simple vs.Absolute Majority Rule: Cases Where Absences and Abstentions are Important', *Journal of Theoretical Politics*, 22, 85–122.

Dougherty, Keith and Julian Edward (2011) 'Voting for Pareto Optimality: A Multidimensional Analysis', *Public Choice* online first.

Dougherty, Keith, Brian Pitts, Justin Moeller and Robi Ragan (forthcoming) 'An Experimental Study of the Efficiency of Unanimity Rule and Majority Rule', *Public Choice*.

Druckman, James N. (2004) 'Political Preference Formation: Competition, Deliberation, and the (Ir)relevance of Framing Effects', *American Political Science Review*, 98, 671–686.

Druckman, James N. and Kjersten R. Nelson (2003) 'Framing and Deliberation: How Citizen's Conversations Limit Elite Influence', *American Journal of Political Science*, 47, 729–745.

Dryzek, John S. and Christian List (2003) 'Social Choice Theory and Deliberative Democracy: A Reconciliation', *British Journal of Political Science*, 33, 1–28.

Duch, Raymond M. and Randolph T. Stevenson (2008) *The Economic Vote. How Political and Economic Institutions Condition Election Results* (Cambridge: Cambridge University Press).

Duffy, John and Margit Tavits (2008) 'Beliefs and Voting Decisions: A Test of the Pivotal Voter Model', *American Journal of Political Science*, 52, 603–618.

Duggan, John and Yoji Sekiya (2009) 'Voting Equilibria in Multi–Candidate Elections', *Journal of Public Economic Theory*, 11, 875–889.

Eavey, Cheryl L. (1996) 'Preference–Based Stability: Experiments on Competitive Solutions to Majority Rule Games' in Norman Schofield (ed.) *Collective Decision Making: Social Choice and Political Economy* (New York: Kluwer).

Eavey, Cheryl L. and Gary J. Miller (1984a) 'Bureaucratic Agenda Control: Imposition or Bargaining?', *American Political Science Review*, 78, 719–733.

Eavey, Cheryl L. and Gary J. Miller (1984b) 'Fairness in Majority Rule Games with a Core', *American Journal of Political Science*, 28, 570–586.

Eavey, Cheryl L. and Gary J. Miller (1995) 'Subcommittee Agenda Control', *Journal of Theoretical Politics*, 7, 125–156.

Edlin, Aaron, Andrew Gelman and Noah Kaplan (2007) 'Voting as a Rational Choice. Why and How People Vote to Improve the Well–Being of Others', *Rationality and Society*, 19, 293–314.

Eldersveld, Samuel J. (1956) 'Experimental Propaganda Techniques and Voting Behavior', *American Political Science Review*, 50, 154–165.

Elster, Jon (ed.) (1998) *Deliberative Democracy* (Cambridge: Cambridge University Press).

Enelow, James M. (1981) 'Saving Amendments, Killer Amendments, and an Expected-Utility Theory of Sophisticated Voting', *Journal of Politics*, 43, 1062–1089.

Eraslan, Hülya and Antonio Merlo (2002) 'Majority Rule in a Stochastic Model of Bargaining', *Journal of Economic Theory*, 103, 31–48.

Farrar, Cynthia, James S. Fishkin, Donald P. Green, Christian List, Robert C. Luskin and Elizabeth Levy Paluck (2010) 'Disaggregating Deliberation's Effect: An Experiment within a Deliberative Poll', *British Journal of Political Science*, 40, 333–347.

Farrell, Joseph and Matthew Rabin (1996) 'Cheap Talk', *Journal of Economic Perspectives*, 110, 103–118.

Feddersen, Timothy J. (2004) 'Rational Choice Theory and the Paradox of Not Voting', *Journal of Economic Perspectives*, 18, 99–112.

Feddersen, Timothy J., Sean Gailmard and Alvaro Sandroni (2009) 'Moral Bias in Large Elections: Theory and Experimental Evidence', *American Political Science Review*, 103, 175–192.

Feddersen, Timothy J. and Wolfgang Pesendorfer (1996) 'The Swing Voter's Curse', *American Economic Review*, 86, 408–424.

Feddersen, Timothy J. and Wolfgang Pesendorfer (1998) 'Convicting the Innocent: The Inferiority of Unanimous Jury Verdicts', *American Political Science Review*, 92, 23–35.

Feddersen, Timothy J. and Wolfgang Pesendorfer (1999) 'Abstention in Elections with Asymmetric Information and Diverse Preferences', *American Political Science Review*, 93, 381–398.

Feddersen, Timothy J. and Alvaro Sandroni (2006) 'A Theory of Participation in Elections', *American Economic Review*, 96, 1271–1282.

Fehr, Ernst and Klaus M. Schmidt (1999) 'A Theory of Fairness, Competition, and Cooperation', *Quarterly Journal of Economics*, 114, 817–868.

Ferejohn, John A. and Morris P. Fiorina (1974) 'The Paradox of Not Voting. A Decision Theoretic Analysis', *American Political Science Review*, 68, 525–536.

Fey, Mark (1997) 'Stability and Coordination in Duverger's Law: A Formal Model of Preelection Polls and Strategic Voting', *American Political Science Review*, 91, 135–147.

Fiorina, Morris P. and Charles R. Plott (1978) 'Committee Decision under Majority Rule: An Experimental Study', *American Political Science Review*, 72, 575–598.

Fisher, Stephen D. and David P. Myatt (2002) 'Strategic Voting Experiments', *Nuffield College Politics Working Paper* 2002–W4.

Fishkin, James S. (2009) *When the People Speak: Deliberative Democracy and Public Consultation* (Oxford: Oxford University Press).

Forsythe, Robert, Roger B. Myerson, Thomas A. Rietz and Robert J. Weber (1993) 'An Experiment on Coordination in Multi–Candidate Elections: The Importance of Polls and Election Histories', *Social Choice and Welfare*, 10, 223–247.

Forsythe, Robert, Thomas A. Rietz, Roger B. Myerson and Robert J. Weber (1996) 'An Experimental Study of Voting Rules and Polls in Three–Candidate Elections', *International Journal of Game Theory*, 25, 355–383.

Fowler, James H. (2006) 'Habitual Voting and Behavioral Turnout', *Journal of Politics*, 68, 335–344.

Fréchette, Guillaume, John H. Kagel and Massimo Morelli (2005) 'Behavioral Identification in Coalition Bargaining: An Experimental Analysis of Demand Bargaining and Alternating Offers', *Econometrica*, 73, 1893–1937.

Frohlich, Norman and Joe Oppenheimer (1993) *Choosing Justice: An Experimental Approach to Ethical Theory* (Ewing: University of California Press).

Frohlich, Norman, Joe Oppenheimer and Anja Kurki (2004) 'Modeling Other-regarding Preferences and an Experimental Test', *Public Choice*, 119, 91–117.

Galeotti, Andrea, Sanjeev Goyal, Matthew O. Jackson, Fernando Vega–Redondo and Leeat Yariv (2010) 'Network Games', *Review of Economic Studies*, 77, 218–244.

Gerardi, Dino and Leeat Yariv (2007) 'Deliberative Voting', *Journal of Economic Theory*, 134, 317–338.

Gerber, Alan S. and Donald P. Green (2000) 'The Effects of Canvassing, Telephone Calls, and Direct Mail on Voter Turnout. A Field Experiment', *American Political Science Review*, 94, 653–663.

Gerber, Alan S., Donald P. Green and Christopher W. Larimer (2008) 'Social Pressure and Voter Turnout: Evidence from a Large–Scale Field Experiment', *American Political Science Review*, 102, 33–48.

Gintis, Herbert (2007) 'A Framework for the Unification of the Behavioral Sciences', *Behavioral and Brain Sciences*, 30, 1–61.

Goeree, Jacob K. and Leeat Yariv (2011) 'An Experimental Study of Collective Deliberation', *Econometrica* 79, 893–921.

Gordon, Stacy B. and Gary M. Segura (1997) 'Cross–National Variation in the Political Sophistication of Individuals: Capability or Choice?', *Journal of Politics*, 59, 126–147.

Gosnell, Harold F. (1927) *Getting out the Vote: An Experiment in the Stimulation of Voting* (Chicago: University of Chicago Press).

Goyal, Sanjeev (2007) *Connections. An Introduction to the Economics of Networks* (Princeton: Princeton University Press).

Granato, Jim and Frank Scioli (2004) 'Puzzles, Proverbs, and Omega Matrices: The Scientific and Social Significance of Empirical Implications of Theoretical Models (EITM)', *Perspectives on Politics*, 2, 313–323.

Green, Donald P. (2004) 'Mobilizing African-American voters using direct mail and commercial phone banks: A field experiment', *Political Research Quarterly*, 57, 245–255.

Green, Donald P. and Alan S. Gerber (2008) *Get Out the Vote: How to Increase Voter Turnout* (Washington D.C.: Brooking's Institution).

Greenberg, Joseph (1977) 'Consistent Majority Rules over Compact Sets of Alternatives', *Econometrica*, 41, 627–636.

Großer, Jens and Arthur Schram (2006) 'Neighborhood Information Exchange and Voter Participation: An Experimental Study', *American Political Science Review*, 100, 235–248.

Großer, Jens and Arthur Schram (2010) 'Public Opinion Polls, Voter Turnout, and Welfare: An Experimental Study', *American Journal of Political Science*, 54, 700–717.

Gschwend, Thomas and Marc Hooghe (2008) 'Should I Stay or Should I Go? An Experimental Study on Voter Responses to Pre–electoral Coalitions', *European Journal of Political Research*, 7, 556–577.

Guttman, Joel M. (1998) 'Unanimity and Majority Rule: The Calculus of Consent Reconsidered', *European Journal of Political Economy*, 14, 189–207.

Hammond, Thomas and Gary J. Miller (1987) 'The Core of the Constitution', *American Political Science Review*, 81, 1155–1174.

Harsanyi, John C. (1977) 'Morality and the Theory of Rational Behavior', *Social Research*, 44, 623–656.

Harsanyi, John C. (1980) 'Rule Utilitarianism, Rights, Obligations, and the Theory of Rational Behavior', *Theory and Decision*, 12, 115–133.

Holt, Charles A. (1999) Y2K Bibliography of Experimental Economics and Social Science Voting and Agenda Effects, http://people.virginia.edu/~cah2k/votey2k.htm, last access July 11, 2011

Holt, Charles A. (2007) *Markets, Games, & Strategic Behavior* (Boston: Pearson).

Huckfeldt, Robert (2001) 'The Social Communication of Political Expertise', *American Journal of Political Science*, 45, 425–438.

Jackman, Simon and Paul M. Sniderman (2006) 'The Limits of Deliberative Discussion: A Model of Everyday Political Arguments', *Journal of Politics*, 68, 272–283.

Kagel, John H., Hankyoung Sung and Eyal Winter (2010) 'Veto Power in Committees: An Experimental Study', *Experimental Economics*, 13, 167–188.

Kahneman, Daniel and Amos Tversky (1979) 'Prospect Theory: An Analysis of Decision Under Risk', *Econometrica*, 47, 263–292.

Karpowitz, Christopher F. and Tali Mendelberg (2007) 'Groups and Deliberation', *Swiss Political Science Review*, 13, 645–662.

Karpowitz, Christopher F. and Tali Mendelberg (2011) 'An Experimental Approach to Citizen Deliberation' in James N. Druckman, et al. (eds.) *Cambridge Handbook of Experimental Political Science* (Cambridge: Cambridge University Press).

Kerr, Norbert L. and R. Scott Tindale (2004) 'Group Performance and Decision Making', *Annual Review of Psychology*, 55, 623–655.

Keser, Claudia, Karl–Martin Ehrhart and Siegfried K. Berninghaus (1998) 'Coordination and Local Interaction: Experimental Evidence', *Economics Letters*, 58, 269–275.

Kinder, Donald R. and Thomas R. Palfrey (eds.) (1993) *Experimental Foundations of Political Science* (Ann Arbor: Michigan University Press).

Kinder, Donald R. and Lynn M. Sanders (1990) 'Mimicking Political Debate With Survey Questions', *Social Cognition*, 8, 73–103.

King, Ron (1994) 'An Experimental Investigation of Supermajority Voting Rules: Implications for the Financial Accounting Standards Board', *Journal of Economic Behavior and Organization*, 25, 197–217.

Kittel, Bernhard and Wolfgang J. Luhan (2011) 'Decision Making in Networks: An Experiment on Structure Effects in a Group Dictator Game', *Social Choice and Welfare*, Online First.

Konow, James (2003) 'Which is the Fairest One of All? A Positive Analysis of Justice Theories', *Journal of Economic Literature*, 41, 1188–1239.

Kormendi, Roger C. and Charles A. Plott (1982) 'Committee Decisions Under Alternative Procedural Rules. An Experimental Study Applying a New Non–Monetary Method of Preferences Inducement', *Journal of Economic Behavior and Organization*, 3, 175–195.

Kosfeld, Michael (2004) 'Economic Networks in the Laboratory: A Survey', *Review of Network Economics*, 3, 20–41.

Laing, James D. and Benjamin Slotznick (1991) 'When Anyone Can Veto: A Laboratory Study of Committees Governed by Unanimous Rule', *Behavioral Science*, 36, 179–195.

Landa, Dimitri and Adam Meirowitz (2009) 'Game Theory, Information, and Deliberative Democracy', *American Journal of Political Science*, 53, 427–444.

Laruelle, Annick and Federico Valenciano (2011) 'Majorities with a Quorum', *Journal of Theoretical Politics*, 23, 241–259.

Laslier, Jean-François (2010) 'Laboratory Experiments on Approval Voting', in Jean-François Laslier and M. Remzi Sanver (eds.) *Handbook on Approval Voting* (Berlin: Springer).

Lau, Richard R. and David P. Redlawsk (2001) 'Advantages and Disadvantages of Cognitive Heuristics in Political Decision Making', *American Journal of Political Science*, 45, 951–971.

Laury, Susan K. and Charles A. Holt (2008) 'Voluntary Provision of Public Goods: Experimental Results With Interior Nash Equilibria', in Charles R. Plott and Vernon Smith (eds.) *Handbook of Experimental Economics Results, Volume 1* (Amsterdam: North-Holland).

Lev-On, Azi, Alex Chavez and Christina Bicchieri (2010) 'Group and Dyadic Communication in Trust Games', *Rationality and Society*, 22, 37–54.

Levine, David K. and Thomas R. Palfrey (2007) 'The Paradox of Voter Participation? A Laboratory Study', *American Political Science Review*, 101, 143–158.

Luhan, Wolfgang J., Martin G. Kocher and Matthias Sutter (2009) 'Group Polarization in the Team Dictator Game Reconsidered', *Experimental Economics*, 12, 26–41.

Lupia, Arthur and Mathew D. McCubbins (1998) *The Democratic Dilemma. Can Citizens Learn What They Need to Know?* (Cambridge: Cambridge University Press).

Luskin, Robert (1990) 'Explaining Political Sophistication', *Political Behavior*, 12, 331–361.

Luskin, Robert C., James S. Fishkin and Roger Jowell (2002) 'Considered Opinions: Deliberative Polling in Britain', *British Journal of Political Science*, 32, 455–487.

MacCoun, Robert J. and Susannah Paletz (2009) 'Citizen's Perceptions of Ideological Bias in Research on Public Policy Controversy', *Political Psychology*, 30, 43–65.

Mackie, Gerry (2003) *Democracy Defended* (Cambridge: Cambridge University Press).

Mann, Christopher B. (2010) 'Is there a Backlash to Social Pressure? A Large-Scale Field Experiment on Voter Mobilization', *Political Behavior*, 32, 387–407.

Manza, Jeffrey, Clem Brooks and Michael Sauder (2005) 'Money, Participation, and Votes: Social Cleavages and Electoral Politics' in Thomas Janoski, et al. (eds.) *The Handbook of Political Sociology. States, Civil Society, and Globalization* (Cambridge: Cambridge University Press).

McCarty, Nolan (2000) 'Proposal Rights, Veto Rights, an Political Bargaining', *American Journal of Political Science*, 44, 506–522.

McCubbins, Mathew D. and Daniel B. Rodriguez (2006) 'When Does Deliberation Improve Decisionmaking?' *Journal of Contemporary Legal Issues*, 15, 9–50.

McCuen, Brian and Rebecca B. Morton (2010) 'Tactical Coalition Voting and Information in the Laboratory', *Electoral Studies*, 29, 316–328.

McDermott, Rose (2004) 'Prospect Theory in Political Science: Gains and Losses From the First Decade', *Political Psychology*, 25, 289–312.

McKelvey, Richard (1976) 'Intransitivities in Multidimensional Voting Models and Some Implications for Agenda Control', *Journal of Economic Theory*, 12, 472–482.

McKelvey, Richard D. and Peter C. Ordeshook (1986) 'Information, Electoral Equilibria, and the Democratic Ideal', *Journal of Politics*, 48, 909–937.

McKelvey, Richard D., Peter C. Ordeshook and Mark D. Winer (1978) 'The Competitive Solution for N–Person Games Without Transferable Utility, With an Application to Committee Games', *American Political Science Review*, 72, 599–615.

McKelvey, Richard and Peter Ordeshook (1985) 'Elections with Limited Information: A Fulfilled Expectations Model Using Contemporaneous Poll and Endorsement Data as Information Sources', *Journal of Economic Theory*, 36, 55–85.

McKelvey, Richard and Peter Ordeshook (1990) 'A Decade of Experimental Research on Spatial Models of Elections and Committees' in James M. Enelow and Melvin Hinich, J. (eds.) *Readings in the Spatial Theory of Voting* (Cambridge: Cambridge University Press).

Meffert, Michael and Thomas Gschwend (2011) 'Polls, Coalition Signals and Strategic Voting: An Experimental Investigation of Perceptions and Effects', *European Journal of Political Research*, 50, 636–667.

Mendelsohn, Matthew (1996) 'The Media and Interpersonal Communication: The Priming of Issues, Leaders, and Party Identification', *Journal of Politics*, 58, 112–125.

Mercer, Jonathan (2005) 'Prospect Theory and Political Science', *Annual Review of Political Science*, 8, 1–21.

Michelbach, Philip A., John T. Scott, Richard E. Matland and Brian H. Bornstein (2003) 'Doing Rawls Justice: An Experimental Study of Income Distribution Norms', *American Journal of Political Science*, 47, 523–539.

Michelson, Melissa R. (2003) 'Getting Out the Latino Vote: How Door-to-door Canvassing Influences Voter Turnout in Rural Central California', *Political Behavior*, 25, 247–263.

Miller, Gary J., Thomas Hammond and Charles Kile (1996) 'Bicameralism and the Core: An Experimental Test', *Legislative Studies Quarterly*, 21, 83–103.

Miller, Luis and Christoph Vanberg (2011) 'Decision Costs in Legislative Barhaining: An Experimental Analysis', *Public Choice*, online first.

Miller, Nicholas (1980) 'A New Solution Set for Tournament and Majority Voting', *American Journal of Political Science*, 24, 68–96.

Mueller, Dennis C. (2003) *Public Choice III* (Cambridge: Cambridge University Press).

Muthoo, Abhinay (1999) *Bargaining Theory with Applications* (Cambridge: Cambridge University Press).

Mutz, Diana C. (2006) *Hearing the Other Side. Deliberative versus Participatory Democracy* (Cambridge: Cambridge University Press).

Mutz, Diana C. (2008) 'Is Deliberative Theory a Falsifiable Theory?', *Annual Review of Political Science*, 11, 521–538.

Myatt, David P. (2007) 'On the Theory of Strategic Voting', *Review of Economic Studies*, 74, 255–281.

Myatt, David P. and Stephen D. Fisher (2002) 'Tactical Coordination in Plurality Electoral Systems', *Oxford Review of Economic Policy*, 18, 504–522.

Myers, Charles D. (2010) 'Decision Rules, Preferences, and Information Sharing', *Manuscript*, Princeton University.

Myerson, Roger B. and Robert J. Weber (1993) 'A Theory of Voting Equilibria', *American Political Science Review*, 87, 102–114.

Nash, John F. jr. (1950) 'The Bargaining Problem', *Econometrica*, 18, 155–162.

Nickerson, David (2008) 'Is Voting Contagious? Evidence from Two Field Experiments', *American Political Science Review*, 102, 49–57.

Ostrom, Elinor (2005) *Understanding Institutional Diversity* (Princeton: Princeton University Press).

Ostrom, Elinor and James Walker (2003) *Trust and Reciprocity. Interdisciplinary Lessons from Experimental Research* (New York: Russel Sage Foundation).

Palfrey, Thomas R. and Howard Rosenthal (1983) 'A Strategic Calculus of Voting', *Public Choice*, 41, 7–53.

Palfrey, Thomas R. and Howard Rosenthal (1985) 'Voter Participation and Strategic Uncertainty', *American Political Science Review*, 79, 62–78.

Panagopoulos, Costas (2010) 'Affect, Social Pressure, and Prosocial Motivation: Field Experimental Evidence of Mobilizing Effects of Pride, Shame, and Publicizing Voting Behavior', *Political Behavior*, 32, 369–386.

Rae, Douglas W. (1969) 'Decision–Rules and Individual Values in Constitutional Choice', *American Political Science Review*, 63, 40–56.

Rietz, Thomas A. (1993) Strategic Behavior in Multi–Alternative Elections: A Review of Some Experimental Evidence, *Discussion Paper 1026*, Evanston, IL: Center for Mathematical Studies in Economics and Management Science, Northwestern University.

Riker, William H. (1982) *Liberalism against Populism. A Confrontation Between the Theory of Democracy and the Theory of Social Choice* (Prospect Heights, IL: Waveland Press).

Riker, William and Peter Ordeshook (1968) 'A Theory of the Calculus of Voting', *American Political Science Review*, 62, 25–42.

Romer, Thomas and Howard Rosenthal (1977) 'Political Resource Allocation, Controlled Agendas, and the Status Quo', *Public Choice*, 33, 27–45.

Rubinstein, Ariel (1982) 'Perfect Equilibium in a Bargaining Model', *Econometrica*, 50, 97–109.

Ryan, John B. (2011) 'Social Networks as a Shortcut to Correct Voting', *American Journal of Political Science*, online first.

Ryfe, David M. (2005) 'Does Deliberative Democracy Work?', *Annual Review of Political Science*, 8, 49–71.

Sally, David (1995) 'Conversation and Cooperation in Social Dilemmas: A Meta–Analysis of Experiments from 1958 to 1992', *Rationality and Society*, 7, 58–92.

Sauermann, Jan and André Kaiser (2010) 'Taking Others into Account: Self–Interest and Fairness in Majority Decision Making', *American Journal of Political Science*, 54, 667–685.

Schram, Arthur and Joep Sonnemans (1996a) 'Voter Turnout as a Participation Game: An Experimental Investigation', *International Journal of Game Theory*, 25, 385–406.

Schram, Arthur and Joep Sonnemans (1996b) 'Why People Vote: Experimental Evidence', *Journal of Experimental Psychology*, 17, 417–442.

Scott, John T., Richard E. Matland, Philip A. Michelbach and Brian H. Bornstein (2001) 'Just Deserts: An Experimental Study of Distributive Justice Norms', *American Journal of Political Science*, 45, 749–767.

Sell, Jane (2007) 'Social Dilemma Experiments in Sociology, Psychology, Political Science, and Economics' in Murray Webster Jr. and Jane Sell (eds.) *Laboratory Experiments in the Social Sciences* (London: Academic Press).

Shepsle, Kenneth A. (1979) 'Institutional Arrangements and Equilibria in Multidimensional Voting Models', *American Journal of Political Science*, 23, 27–59.

Siegel, David A. (2009) 'Social Networks and Collective Action', *American Journal of Political Science*, 53, 122–138.

Simon, Herbert (1955) 'A Behavioral Model of Rational Choice', *Quarterly Journal of Economics*, 69, 99–118.

Smirnov, Oleg (2009) 'Endogenous Choice of Amendment Agendas: Types of Voters and Experimental Evidence', *Public Choice*, 141, 277–290.

Smith, Vernon (1976) 'Experimental Economics: Induced Value Theory', *American Economic Review*, 66, 274–279.

Sonnemans, Joep and Arthur Schram (2008) 'Participation Game Experiments: Explaining Voter Turnout' in Charles R. Plott and Vernon Smith (eds.) *Handbook of Experimental Economics Results, Volume 1* (Amsterdam: North–Holland).

Sulkin, Tracy and Adam F. Simon (2001) 'Habermas in the Lab: A Study of Deliberation in an Experimental Setting', *Political Psychology*, 22, 809–826.

Taagepera, Rein (2007) 'Predictive vs. Postdictive Models', *European Political Science*, 6, 114–123.

Taagepera, Rein (2008) *Making Social Sciences More Scientific: The Need for Predictive Models* (Oxford: Oxford University Press).

Thompson, Dennis F. (2008) 'Deliberative Democratic Theory and Empirical Political Science', *Annual Review of Political Science*, 11, 497–520.

Tilley, James and Sarah B. Hobolt (2011) 'Is the Government to Blame? An Experimental Test of How Partisanship Shapes Perceptions of Performance and Responsibility', *Journal of Politics*, 73, 316–330.

Traub, Stefan, Christian Seidl and Ulrich Schmidt (2009) 'An Experimental Study on Individual Choice, Social Welfare, and Social Preference', *European Economic Review*, 53, 385–400.

Trivedi, Neema (2005) 'The Effect of Identity–based GOTV Direct Mail Appeals on the Turnout of Indian Americans', *Annals of the American Academy of Political and Social Science*, 601, 115–122.

Tsebelis, George and Jeannette Money (1997) *Bicameralism* (Cambridge: Cambridge University Press).

Tyran, Jean-Robert and Rupert Sausgruber (2006) 'A Little Fairness May Induce a Lot of Redistribution in Democracy', *European Economic Review*, 50, 469–485.

van der Eijk, Cees and Mark Franklin (2009) *Elections and Voters* (London: Palgrave-Macmillan).

Van der Straeten, Karine, Jean-François Laslier, Nicolas Sauger and André Blais (2010) 'Strategic, Sincere, and Heuristic Voting under Four Election Rules: An Experimental Study', *Social Choice and Welfare*, 35, 435–472.

Volden, Craig and Alan E. Wiseman (2007) 'Bargaining in Legislatures over Particularistic and Collective Goods', *American Political Science Review*, 101, 79–92.

Wilson, Rick K. (2007) 'Voting and Agenda Setting in Political Science and Economics' in Murray Webster Jr. and Jane Sell (eds.) *Laboratory Experiments in the Social Sciences* (London: Academic Press).

Wong, Janelle S. (2005) 'Mobilizing Asian American Voters: A Field Experiment', *Annals of the American Academy of Political and Social Science*, 601, 102–114.

# 3
# Laboratory Tests of Formal Theory and Behavioral Inference

*Jonathan Woon*

One searches in vain for a detailed discussion of exactly how and when a model should be applied (...). If theorists blithely continue to prove more theorems, and applied scientists doggedly continue to gather more data, at some point data and theory might just miraculously conjoin. But we regard such a union as more likely to result from a determined effort than from a fortuitous accident (Fiorina and Plott, 1978, p. 576).

Political scientists seek to answer questions about political behavior, institutions and outcomes. Why do (or do not) people cooperate to achieve common goals? To what extent do elections induce politicians to follow the wishes of the public? Why is government unable to enact new laws demanded by popular majorities? At the most general level, the method of advancing scientific knowledge of politics involves developing theories and testing their predictions. Theories are often expressed in terms of models that are purposeful, abstract simplifications of the real world, and *formal theory* involves a set of concepts and methods for systematically constructing and analyzing *mathematical models*. Robert Powell (1999) provides a succinct definition of a model as a *'constrained, best effort to capture what the modeler believes to be the essence of a complex empirical phenomenon or at least an important aspect of it'* (24, emphasis original).

But in order to assess whether or not a model accurately captures the 'essence' of real-world politics, the empirical predictions from a model must be tested against systematic evidence. The results of empirical tests should then guide the theorist in refining or extending the model. Theory testing is therefore an essential component of what Roger Myerson (1992) calls a *'modeling dialog ...* a process in which theorists and empiricists work together interactively on the difficult task of finding tractable models that capture and clarify the important aspects of real situations' (64, emphasis original). Without this dialog, theoretical and empirical analyses might develop on separate, possibly divergent, paths and scientific progress would be significantly inhibited, as Morris Fiorina and Charles Plott so bitingly allude to in the epigraph.[1] The fact that Fiorina and Plott's call for a 'determined effort' to join theory and data is found in one of the earliest laboratory experiments testing the predictions of formal political theory indicates that laboratory experiments can contribute a great deal to the modeling dialog. Because the defining feature of laboratory experiments is the control that researchers have over the data-generating process, one obvious advantage of experimental control is that researchers can easily generate data to test a theory when naturally occurring data are otherwise unavailable.[2] In tests of applied game theory models, this involves implementing a game in the lab and observing whether subjects' choices accord with the theoretical predictions.

In this chapter, I argue that laboratory experiments play an important role in testing behavioral models because of the precise control that they afford.[3] To make this argument, I present a simple framework that can be used to understand the kinds of inferences that can be drawn from empirical tests of formal theory predictions and then compare the inferences that can be made from laboratory experiments and observational studies. I then discuss important design principles that follow from the framework and provide an illustration from an experiment that I conducted on democratic accountability. The example also illustrates other kinds of design decisions that a researcher faces when implementing a laboratory theory test.

## 3.1  A framework for inferences from theory tests

A formal model can be thought of as comprising three distinct models of an empirical phenomenon. First, there is a model of the social situation that describes who the players are, the possible choices they can make, the information that they observe and the outcomes that result from each possible combination of choices. In game theoretic terminology, this is called the game form. Second, there is a model of preferences that describes each player's goals, wants or needs in terms of a well-ordered ranking of the possible outcomes of the social situation. These preferences are typically represented by utility or payoff functions. Third, there is a model of behavior that completes the model by specifying the properties of how people choose their actions.[4] In noncooperative game theory, behavioral assumptions are captured by the notion of Nash equilibrium and related equilibrium concepts (for example, subgame perfect equilibrium or Perfect Bayesian equilibrium).[5]

Once each component is specified, the completed model is analyzed and solved, and the results of the analysis will include empirical implications – that is, testable predictions about outcomes and behavior. The following conditional statement summarizes how *empirical implications (EI)* follow logically from the joint assumptions of the model (the game form $G$, preferences $P$ and behavioral assumptions $B$).

$$G \wedge P \wedge B \rightarrow EI \tag{3.1}$$

If the data are consistent with the empirical implications, then it is reasonable to conclude that the model appropriately captures the essence of the phenomenon being modeled. But if the evidence instead disconfirms the empirical implication, then what inference can be made? As a matter of logic, statement (3.1) must be true if the theoretical analysis is done properly. Taking the contrapositive of (3.1) produces the equivalent statement:

$$\neg EI \rightarrow \neg G \vee \neg P \vee \neg B \tag{3.2}$$

Thus, falsifying the prediction implies that any one of the model's three components might be 'false'.[6] In other words, because the model is a set of joint assumptions, the theoretical implications of an empirical test must necessarily involve some degree of *indeterminacy*: we can infer that one or more of the components must be a *poor approximation* to the phenomenon being studied, but it might be difficult to know for sure which component the culprit is.

## 3.2.  Observational versus laboratory theory tests

Applying the framework helps to highlight a crucial difference between observational studies and laboratory experiments, and this suggests an important role for laboratory experiments in the modeling dialog. Two questions are of interest. First, given a falsified prediction, is it possible to resolve, or at least narrow down, the theoretical indeterminacy by establishing the empirical validity of some of the model's assumptions? For instance, establishing the validity of the game form would narrow down a model's failure to preferences or the behavioral model. Second, given that the theoretical indeterminacy is, or is not, resolved, what should the next step in the modeling dialog be?

Although it may sometimes be possible to gather sufficient evidence, the lack of control a researcher has over the data generation process in an observational study more often than not makes it difficult, if not impossible, to make a compelling case about the empirical validity of a model's assumptions. As a result, the theoretical indeterminacy will remain unresolved. Falsification might imply that the game form is improperly specified or that the assumptions about preferences are wrong, or that the behavioral assumption is inappropriate. It could also be due to the interaction of two components, or even the interaction of all three.

Typically, the theoretical response to observational falsification is to hold behavior *B*, and sometimes preferences *P*, constant while varying the model of the situation from *G* to *G'* in order to produce a new model that better predicts and explains the data. For many research topics, such as the study of institutions, this appears to be a sensible and practical methodological move insofar as the focus is on identifying key features of the institution. For instance, congressional scholars debating the role of parties in the lawmaking process hold preferences (for example, single-peaked preferences over a unidimenisonal policy space) and behavioral assumptions (for example, sequential rationality characterized by subgame perfect equilibrium) constant while varying the key players and order of moves in the game form. Pivotal politics models (Krehbiel, 1998) assume that the median legislator first proposes policies followed by the approval (or disapproval) from the veto and filibuster pivots (which represent supermajority voting rules). In contrast, party gatekeeping models (Cox and McCubbins, 2005) assume that a party leader first decides whether or not to allow an issue onto the agenda followed by a policy choice by the median legislator.

Daniel Diermeier and Keith Krehbiel (2003) tacitly acknowledge the theoretical indeterminacy and defend the practice of holding behavioral assumptions constant on the grounds that 'regular changes in behavioral postulates essentially guarantees that the field of study will fail to be cumulative' and if 'the behavioral postulate were abandoned, then all of the prior institutional theories that contributed to the base of knowledge would have to be re-analyzed to gain comparability' (p. 129). While frequent changes in behavioral postulates that prevent progress are certainly undesirable, holding behavioral assumptions constant in order to facilitate progress is defensible only up to a point.

It can be defended to the extent that existing knowledge supports the maintained behavioral assumptions as good approximations of reality or if it is impossible to evaluate the assumptions empirically. But because laboratory experiments provide important tools for evaluating behavioral models, clinging to behavioral assumptions is ill-advised for at least two reasons.[7] First, if more and more elaborate theories are built upon a foundation that ultimately collapses, a lot of 'progress' will be wasted when it comes time to rebuild them. Second, and more importantly, denying alternative behavioral assumptions severely limits the classes of theories and explanations that can be developed, and therefore inhibits scientific progress. The strict rational choice approach explains institutions as optimal collective choices (given preferences and constraints), while alternative behavioral theories might explain institutions as myopic choices or the results of adaptive processes.

In contrast to the persistent indeterminacy of observational studies, clearer inferences can be drawn from laboratory theory tests. The hallmark of laboratory experiments is the precise control that experimenters have over key features of the data-generating process. While experimental control has the obvious advantage that researchers can generate data that otherwise would not be available for theory testing, the more important consequence for the purposes of this discussion is that control ensures that the rules governing subjects' interaction in the laboratory exactly match the social situation described by the game form $G$. Doing so, therefore, immediately narrows (by disjunctive syllogism) the theoretical indeterminacy to preferences or behavior. Experimenters also can ensure that monetary payoffs from outcomes exactly match the preference structure of a model. By thus 'inducing value' (Smith, 1976), experimenters attempt to control preferences $P$, although this control is sometimes imperfect when subjects have intrinsic preferences (such as for fairness or other-regarding preferences). When control of preferences is successful, knowing that $G$ and $P$ correspond exactly to the formal model must then mean that a falsified prediction necessarily implies that the problem lies with the behavioral assumptions $B$.[8] To be clear, the proper inference is not that $B$ is 'universally false', but that the model of behavior $B$ does not accurately capture the essence of behavior in situations $G$ with preferences $P$.

Although the asymmetric nature of falsification implies that unambiguous conclusions can be drawn from disconfirming a prediction in the lab, I do not mean to suggest that confirming or verifying the predictions of a theory are any less important. To the contrary, it is easy for many applied and empirically oriented researchers in political science and other social sciences to dismiss the sparseness of a behavioral model such as Nash equilibrium or its rationality requirement out of hand. Experiments therefore provide evidence that a model 'works' and they should be taken seriously and therefore can be applied to explain behavior outside the lab. For example, experiments on jury voting and information aggregation support key predictions of Nash equilibrium theories, as Thomas Palfrey summarizes: 'many of the choice behaviors predicted by the equilibrium theories seem implausible, which makes their empirical validation in the laboratory quite surprising' (2009, p. 386).

Whereas the conventional response to observational falsification is to vary the game form or preferences, experimental falsification often leads to new models of behavior. Of course, these models need not involve wholesale rejection of the previous model. New models may retain key components of the old model that work well while altering the model where the assumptions are weakest. For instance, *quantal response equilibrium* (McKelvey and Palfrey, 1995, 1998) retains the core principle of Nash equilibrium that players' strategies are mutual best responses but differs in that players' actions are subject to stochastic error (as in probabilistic choice models). Alternatively, *level-K* or *cognitive hierarchy models* (for example, Nagel, 1995; Camerer, Ho and Chong, 2004) dispense with the equilibrium assumption of mutual consistency of beliefs and actions while retaining the assumption that players' strategies are best responses, but allow players to have mistaken beliefs about the behavior of others.

While control of the game form and preferences ensure that behavioral models can be tested, it is important to recognize that laboratory experiments have an important limitation: They cannot be used definitively to test a formal theory's assumptions about the game form and preferences. This issue is usually referred to by political scientists as 'external validity', which is the extent to which the inferences from a particular sample (laboratory or otherwise) generalize to other samples.[9] More precisely, a limitation of laboratory experiments for theory testing is that they cannot establish the correspondence between a formal theory and the real world. The reason is that the experimenter can implement $G$ and $P$ as stated in the model, but the empirical validity of $G$ and $P$ can only be established using nonexperimental data. In other words, experimental researchers must share the same concern as formal theorists about whether $G$ and $P$ accurately represent the real world.

Nevertheless, as I have argued, experiments play an important role in testing behavioral assumptions. Laboratory experiments therefore help to narrow down the set of behavioral models that might work outside the lab. That is, if a given behavioral model does not work in the lab when $G$ and $P$ are known, there is good reason to be skeptical that it will not work to explain behavior outside the lab either. If $B$ does not work in simple, controlled settings, why should it work in complicated, messy ones? Thus, laboratory experiments should be viewed as complements to, rather than substitutes for, observational studies; when experiments are used to pin down behavioral assumptions, observational studies can draw stronger inferences about whether the game form and preferences accurately capture the essence of the real-world situation.

## 3.3 Essential design principles

The framework suggests two simple, yet essential, design principles that should be followed in order to make meaningful, unambiguous inferences about the applicability of behavioral models:

(1) *The experiment should implement the game form $G$ and preferences $P$ as closely as possible.*
(2) *Subjects must understand the rules of the game but should not be told or given suggestions about how to behave.*

The first principle ensures that the results of the experiment can be interpreted clearly in terms of the behavior model, while the second principle ensures that behavior arises endogenously from subjects' reasoning and thinking (otherwise, the experiment would be a simulation). Subjects must understand the rules clearly, but this does not mean they are required to understand or perceive the game the same way that a game theorist does. After all, whether or not they do so is an empirical question.

Of course, in practice, adhering to these principles may not always be simple, especially for complicated games, or when the literal implementation of a game may conflict with other design considerations. For some purposes, there also may be good reasons for departing from these principles. Nevertheless, if the primary goal of the experiment is to make inferences with respect to behavioral models, then following these principles is crucial.

A simple experiment from the early history of game theory attests to the importance of the first basic principle. In 1950, Merrill Flood and Melvin Dresher devised a simple 2 × 2 (simultaneous move) matrix game (Flood, 1958) to test John Nash's recently developed noncooperative equilibrium theory (Nash, 1951). The game payoffs, given in pennies, are described in Table 3.1 (the first line in each cell). The game has a dominant strategy Nash equilibrium (Down, Left), but both players would be better off from the outcome (Up, Right) that results from playing dominated strategies (that is, the Pareto superior outcome is not a Nash equilibrium). The structure of this game would later become widely known as the Prisoner's Dilemma.

Flood and Dresher had the same two subjects (AA and JW) play the game 100 times, and they regarded each play as an independent observation. The observed frequencies of play in Table 3.1 (in parentheses) show that both subjects tended to play the dominated strategy and that the modal outcome is the Pareto superior (Up, Right) rather than the Nash equilibrium (Down, Left). Flood and Dresher regarded their finding as evidence against Nash equilibrium.

*Table 3.1*  Flood and Dresher's experimental test of Nash equilibrium

|  |  | Column (JW) | | |
|---|---|---|---|---|
|  |  | Left | Right | |
| Row (AA) | Up | −1, 2 (8%) | 0.5, 1 (60%) | (68%) |
|  | Down | 0, 0.5 (14%) | 1, −1 (18%) | (32%) |
|  |  | (22%) | (78%) | |

*Source*: Flood (1958), Notes: Payoffs (in pennies) are given by the pair of numbers in the top line of each cell. The observed frequencies (out of 100 plays) are shown in parentheses. The original action labels used in Flood (1958) are 'Row 1', 'Row 2', 'Column 1' and 'Column 2'.

Although Flood and Dresher's procedures would not survive the peer review process today (and they admitted that their experiment was only preliminary), two aspects of the design and interpretation of the experiment are noteworthy. First, it is interesting to note that Flood and Dresher's purpose was explicitly behavioral:

> To find whether or not subjects tended to behave as they should if the Nash theory were applicable, or if their behavior tended more toward the von Neumann-Morgenstern solution, the split-the-difference principle, or some other yet-to-be-discovered principle (Flood, 1958, p. 12).

Second, there is a poor correspondence between 100 plays of the experimental game between the same two subjects (who were also friends) and the single-shot nature of game they intended to implement. Today, their laboratory game would be quickly recognized as a (finitely) repeated game. Indeed, the lack of correspondence was noted by Nash himself (demonstrating a theoretical response in the modeling dialog):

> The flaw in this experiment as a test of equilibrium point theory is that the experiment really amounts to having the players play one large multi-move game. One cannot just as well think of the thing as a sequence of independent games as one can in zero-sum cases. There is much too much interaction, which is obvious in the results of the experiment... If this experiment were conducted with various different players rotating the competition and with no information given to a player of what choices the others have been making until the end of all the trials... this modification of procedure would remove the interaction between the trials (Nash's comments printed in Flood, 1958, p. 16).

While closely following the game form and preference assumptions is important for behavioral inference, the point here is not that the implementation must always be literal. Some features of the design will also depend on the theoretical interpretation of the behavioral model that goes beyond their formal mathematical definitions. For example, in the case of testing the Nash equilibrium predictions of static games, some form of repetition is often necessary. This is the case if Nash equilibrium is interpreted as a stable outcome of the game played by experienced subjects. Thus, subjects must play the game more than once to gain experience and so that the researcher can observe whether or not the outcome is stable. One solution, as Nash points out, would be to use random matching without feedback. Thus, the basic lesson from this example is that when it is not always possible or ideal to implement a game literally, experimenters must nevertheless have a clear understanding of how the behavioral assumptions apply to the game that is actually implemented. Usually, this is achieved by conducting additional theoretical analysis. When such analysis is not possible or if no proof of the empirical implication is otherwise possible, for example, the truth of (3.1) is not known, the experiment should be thought of as a 'stress test' rather than a direct test of the behavioral model.

## 3.4    Illustration: Democratic accountability

To illustrate the kinds of behavioral inferences that can be made from an experiment that follows these principles, I will discuss an example from my own work on electoral accountability (Woon, 2010). This illustration also demonstrates that when adhering to these two principles, a researcher still has wide latitude in designing the experiment and faces a number of important design choices. The additional aspects of the design that I will discuss are choices I made about the *complexity* of the game, the *parameters* to use and the amount of *meaningful context*.

An important question in democratic theory concerns the extent to which elections provide incentives for politicians to act in the interests of voters. V.O. Key's (1966) traditional theory of retrospective voting suggests that elections should provide powerful incentives even when voters do not fully understand the linkages between policies and outcomes. Voters only need to be able to judge the quality of outcomes, such as the health of the economy, and use a simple retrospective voting rule: Reward (re-elect) politicians for good outcomes and punish them (kick them out of office) for bad ones. Traditional retrospective voting can be thought of as a *sanctioning* device.

Subsequent rational choice theorizing, however, identifies an important limitation of the traditional theory (for example, Fiorina, 1981). If voters are forward-looking, then elections should instead be viewed as *selection* devices: Voters elect politicians based on expectations of future performance. Information about past outcomes is relevant only insofar as it helps to update beliefs about the incumbent. Several models formalizing the theory have identified conditions under which selection renders sanctioning an empty threat (for example, Canes-Wrone, Herron and Shotts, 2001; Fearon, 1999). Moreover, the selection view implies that politicians will have incentives to *pander*. That is, they will choose policies that convince voters – and even mislead them – into thinking that the politician possesses desirable characteristics (thus raising voter expectations about future performance) even when the politician knows that such policy choices are not in the best interests of voters.

Because real elections involve many factors beyond those that the formal theories focus on, laboratory experiments are well suited for creating a controlled environment for testing the behavioral predictions (and thus, the behavioral assumptions) of formal models of elections. In my experiment,

I used the model of Fox and Shotts (2009) to investigate whether elections are better viewed as sanctioning or selection devices. I chose their model because it identifies conditions under which selection and sanctioning are observationally distinct as well as conditions under which they are observationally equivalent.

The model involves policy-making before and after an election, and the sequence of actions in the model is as follows:

(1) Nature chooses a state of the world $\omega \in \{A,B\}$, the incumbent's type $t \in T$, the incumbent's signal $s \in \{A,B\}$ and the challenger's type $c \in T$.

(2) The incumbent chooses a policy $p \in \{A,B\}$.

(3) The voter observes both the policy $p$ and the state $\omega$, but not the type $t$, and chooses whether or not to re-elect the incumbent.

(4) Nature chooses a new state $\omega'$ and a new signal $s'$, and the elected politician (either the incumbent or challenger) chooses a new policy $p'$.

'Good' policies for voters are ones that match the state, while 'bad' ones are ones that do not match. There are eight possible politician types in the model, which are characterized by three attributes: (1) whether they are office or policy motivated, (2) their level of expertise and (3) whether they share the voter's policy preference or have an ideological bias for policy $B$.

The intuitive strategy for voters is to use a retrospective or *outcome-based rule*: vote for the incumbent if and only if the policy is 'good' ($p = \omega$), in order to induce office-motivated politicians to use their expertise (follow their signals). But there exists a perfect Bayesian equilibrium – describing optimal strategic behavior – in which voters instead use a *policy-based rule*: Re-elect politicians if, and only if, they choose $p = A$ (given that $\omega = A$ is more likely than $\omega = B$), which induces office-motivated politicians to ignore their signals and always choose $p = A$. This equilibrium can be thought of as a 'delegate' or 'pandering' equilibrium because voters only reward politicians for demonstrating that they do not have an ideological bias for policy $B$, and office-motivated politicians comply by always choosing $A$ even if they know it is worse for voters. Thus, the sequential rationality of perfect Bayesian equilibrium makes a distinctly different prediction about behavior than traditional retrospective voting.

### 3.4.1 Complexity

As someone who is knowledgeable about mathematical models, I recognize that I suffer from the 'curse of knowledge' (Camerer, Loewenstein and Weber, 1989). I might unconsciously perceive the game differently from subjects in the laboratory without the same knowledge. To mitigate the curse of knowledge, I try to imagine how I would think about the game if I were a subject in the lab. Although this is admittedly a subjective process, it led me to recognize that even though the game is an extreme simplification of real elections, it is nevertheless somewhat complicated – certainly more complicated than common experimental games such as a linear public goods game or the ultimatum game. I therefore simplified several aspects of the game that would make the rules easier to convey while still retaining the essence of the situation being modeled. One feature of the original model that was not absolutely necessary was that there is some probability that the policy issue in the second period is one of 'common value' – that all types shared the same preferences. Removing this feature simplifies the game form while preserving the delegate equilibrium.

The second feature that I simplified was the nature of post-election policymaking. Rather than implementing Step 4 in the game sequence described above – having Nature choosing $\omega'$, $s'$ and allowing the politician to choose $p'$ – the voter receives payoffs based directly on the type of politician elected to office in the second period. These payoffs are identical to the expected value of the voter's payoffs based on the elected politician's type, so again the modification simplifies the game while preserving the delegate equilibrium. This simplification also has other benefits. It reduces the amount of noise involved in subjects' payoffs and ensures that subjects clearly know the preference ordering over types. In other words, the modification involves greater control over subjects' preferences than if the realization of random variables and the politician's free choice in Step 4 were retained.

### 3.4.2  Parameters

Another important design consideration in testing formal theories is the selection of parameters. The model analyzed by Fox and Shotts has several exogenous parameters characterizing the distribution of states and politicians' types, and in a technical sense any feasible parameters can be used in the laboratory implementation of the game. However, some sets of parameters yield a greater number of useful observations for the purposes of discriminating between alternative theories (in this case, between selection/rationality and sanctioning/retrospection).

In the case of the accountability experiment, compare the outcome-based and the policy-based voting rules when they are described as strategies. In this case, a voter strategy specifies whether to elect the incumbent or challenger for each possible information set (each possible combination of policy and state). The two strategies are compared in Table 3.2. Notice that when the $\omega = A$, both strategies prescribe the same behavior. However, they make distinct predictions when $\omega = B$. Thus, in order to produce a sufficient number of observations where $\omega = B$, the probability of $\omega = B$ must be as high as possible subject to two constraints. The probability of state $A$ must be higher than the probability of state $B$ because this is a maintained assumption of the analysis. The distribution of states should also be easily

*Table 3.2* Comparison of alternative voting rules

| State (ω) | Policy choice (p) | Retrospective rule (Outcome-based) | Delegate equilibrium rule (Policy-based) |
|---|---|---|---|
| A | A | Incumbent | Incumbent |
| A | B | Challenger | Challenger |
| *B* | *A* | *Challenger* | *Incumbent* |
| *B* | *B* | *Incumbent* | *Challenger* |

represented as a simple fraction. While $Pr(\omega = B) = 0.499999$ would technically satisfy the first constraint, it is so close to 0.5 that subjects would not likely make the distinction, so I chose $Pr(\omega = B) = 0.4$. The probability can also be described as a 'four in ten chance'.

The second parameter of interest is the probability that politicians are office-motivated. This is because only office-motivated politicians respond to differences in voter strategies. I chose to let this probability be ¾, described as both a '75 per cent probability' and a 'three-in-four chance' which is large enough to ensure that many politicians would be office motivated while also ensuring that a sufficient number of politicians would be policy motivated and thus still contribute to voters' beliefs.

The third parameter of interest is the probability that politicians are ideological. The higher this probability is, the greater the incentive that voters have to select politicians in order to avoid ideological types. I therefore let this probability be ¾, as it is sufficiently high to ensure a unique equilibrium while being simple to describe.

The final parameter of interest is the probability that politicians have perfect signals. If this probability is sufficiently low, then the delegate equilibrium (and the policy-based voting rule) is the unique pure strategy perfect Bayesian equilibrium. I let this probability be ¾, which ensures that voters will not learn much about politicians' quality and will therefore focus on avoiding ideological types. I also conducted sessions in which this probability is ¼, which does not guarantee that the delegate equilibrium is unique, but enables me to test the comparative static prediction that delegate equilibrium voting behavior is less likely when the probability is higher.

### 3.4.3  Meaningful context

The final design consideration is whether the game should be described to subjects in 'context-free' abstract terms or with real-world context. An abstract representation of the game might describe the players' roles as 'Player 1' and 'Player 2' while calling them a 'Politician' and 'Voter' would involve some meaningful context. Many experiments testing game theoretic predictions, such as the Flood and Dresher experiment, use abstract context.

One reason for using an abstract context is to try to ensure that subjects' decisions depend only on strategic factors (the game form and their incentives) and to minimize the potential influences of nonstrategic or 'psychological' factors that might be triggered by the presence of real-world context. For example, when the Prisoner's Dilemma is framed as a 'Community Game' or 'Wall Street Game' the level of cooperative behavior changes in a systematic and predictable way (Liberman, Samuels and Ross, 2004). In this case, the experimenter has appeared to lose control over subjects' preferences, so using abstract context makes a lot of sense if the purpose of the experiment is to test abstract strategic thinking.

But removing real-world context also decreases the correspondence between the laboratory environment and the real-world situation that the experiment is intended to represent. The result may be a decision-making environment that is too artificial. Behavioral economist George Loewenstein argues that 'the context-free experiment is...an elusive goal' – that is, an abstract setting is simply an unfamiliar context – and that 'the goal of external validity is served by creating a context that is similar to the one in which...agents will actually operate' (Loewenstein, 1999, F30). Thus, in testing applied models intended to represent a specific class of real-world situations, a balance must be struck between ensuring control over the game form and preferences, and providing enough context so that the results may be interpretable in terms of real-world behavior.

An example from psychology in which some context increases the likelihood that subjects make objectively correct decisions is Wason's 'four-card problem' (Wason and Shapiro, 1971). In this task, subjects are given four cards, each with a letter on one side and a number on the other and are shown only one side of each card. Subjects are asked to turn over two cards in order to test the logical statement 'a vowel on one side implies an even number on the other'. When this task is presented in the abstract (with letters and numbers), only 10 per cent of subjects' choices are logically correct. However, when a logically equivalent problem is presented using a familiar context, such as checking IDs to ensure that alcoholic beverages are consumed by persons over the minimum drinking age, the proportion of correct choices improves dramatically to 89 per cent (Cosmides, 1989).

Because the Fox and Shotts model is motivated by and intended to represent a specific context (elections) rather than a more general model intended to apply to a variety of contexts (for example, collective action), some meaningful context is appropriate when implementing the game form in the laboratory. That is, the purpose of the experiment is to test voting behavior, but in a controlled setting in which the game form and preferences match the formal model, so meaningful context is appropriate. I therefore chose to tell the subjects that they would be playing two different roles, 'politicians' and 'voters', and that politicians' attributes were described as

*Table 3.3* Voter behavior

| State ($\omega$) | Policy choice (p) | Votes for incumbents | | N |
|---|---|---|---|---|
| | | Predicted | Observed | |
| A | A | 100% | 95% | 603 |
| A | B | 100% | 35% | 211 |
| B | A | 0% | 16% | 352 |
| B | B | 0% | 87% | 418 |

'office-seeking' or 'policy-seeking' 'motivations', 'pragmatic' or 'ideological' 'preferences' and 'perfect' or 'noisy' 'quality of information'.

In this case, the complexity of the game form is another reason for using meaningful context. Recall that there are eight politician types, characterized by three different kinds of attributes. Using some context also helps to orient subjects by helping them to understand and remember the game form, which enhances experimental control by minimizing confusion.

### 3.4.4 Results: unpacking rationality

Table 3.3 presents the predicted versus observed choices made by subjects in the role of voters from the experiment. Voting behavior for each possible information set (combination of $p$ and $\omega$) is compared to the delegate equilibrium prediction. The data clearly disconfirm the game theoretic prediction, as voters appear to consistently employ an outcome-based retrospective rule rather than a policy-based rule. Given the close implementation of the game form and preferences assumed by Fox and Shotts, the data (when viewed in light of the framework) strongly suggest that the behavioral assumptions captured by the perfect Bayesian equilibrium concept are poor approximations of behavior in this setting.

Can we say anything more about behavior other than the fact that perfect Bayesian equilibrium is not applicable in this context? It turns out that we can. First, note that the behavioral assumptions of perfect Bayesian equilibrium can be decomposed into three aspects of rationality: (1) choices that are consistent with preferences (basic rational choice), (2) choices that are best responses to other players' choices (strategic optimality) and (3) beliefs that are consistent with Bayes' Rule (Bayesian inference). Subjects' behavior is consistent with the first two notions, which narrows down the failure of rationality to the third.

To see why this is the case we need to consider the behavior of politicians in the experiment. Their behavior is shown in Table 3.4, which presents the predicted versus observed choice frequencies. Policy-motivated politicians have nonstrategic incentives; that is, their payoffs do not depend on what voters do and the data show that their actions are consistent with basic rational choice predictions. The data also show that office-motivated

*Table 3.4*  Politician behavior

| Type | Signal | Policy A chosen | | N |
|------|--------|-----------|----------|-----|
| | | Predicted | Observed | |
| Pragmatic | A | 100% | 95% | 17 |
| policy- | B | 0% | 17% | 36 |
| motivated | | | | |
| Ideological | A | 0% | 21% | 140 |
| policy- | B | 0% | 9% | 140 |
| motivated | | | | |
| Office- | A | 100% | 91% | 648 |
| motivated (all) | B | 100% | 20% | 564 |

politicians do not use equilibrium strategies, but their actions in the experiment are best responses to the voter's outcome-based strategy. Subjects' behavior is therefore also consistent with strategic optimality.

To understand further why there was such a strong behavioral tendency for voters to use a retrospective or outcome-based rule, I conducted a set of additional treatments. I hypothesized that the failure of voters to use a strategy consistent with correct Bayesian inferences might have been for two reasons. One possibility was the complexity of the inference problem (updating beliefs about eight possible types). In the face of such complexity, people tend to rely on some sort of decision heuristic rather than trying to solve for the fully optimal strategy. A competing (but not mutually exclusive) hypothesis was that subjects used an outcome-based strategy because they wanted to induce politicians to use their information to choose the best possible policy.

Although I do not have space to provide the full details of the additional treatments, the main principle underlying the design of the additional treatments was to modify the game in such a way as to remove the hypothesized source of nonequilibrium behavior while keeping the strategic incentives constant (that is, the delegate equilibrium was still the unique perfect Bayesian equilibrium). In this way, game theory provides a basis for the null hypothesis of no difference between the baseline experiment and the behavioral treatment (since the strategic incentives are identical), while the behavioral hypotheses imply that voters are more likely to use the equilibrium policy-based rule in the modified games (treatments). Although the data from the additional treatments remain inconsistent with the perfect Bayesian equilibrium point predictions, the treatment effects nevertheless provide support for both behavioral hypotheses.

## 3.5  Conclusion

In this chapter, I highlighted the advantages of laboratory experiments for testing formal theories. Precise control over the game form and preferences implies that laboratory methods are particularly well suited for testing and investigating the behavioral components of formal models. My experiment on democratic accountability provides an illustration that not only falsifies the package of assumptions captured by perfect Bayesian equilibrium, but also demonstrates that experimental methods can be used to pinpoint the source of an equilibrium concept's inapplicability. Experiments therefore play an especially important role in demarcating the bounds of rationality, identifying the circumstances when different rationality concepts do and do not apply.

While I have focused primarily on the benefits of laboratory experiments, it is also important to recognize their limitations. While controlled laboratory experiments permit strong inferences about *behavior given a social situation and preferences*, the strength of inferences about *real-world behavior* depends on how closely the laboratory environment corresponds to the relevant features of the real-world context the experiment is intended to investigate. The real-world validity of the artificial environment is therefore an important concern common to both laboratory experiments and formal theories. Laboratory experiments are best viewed as complements rather than substitutes for field and observational data.

## Notes

1. The concern about a gap between theoretical and empirical research has also motivated the Empirical Implications of Theoretical Models (EITM) movement in political science to deliberately encourage greater interaction between theorists and empiricists (Aldrich, Alt and Lupia, 2008). Note that I am neither arguing that all models must be tested – see Clarke and Primo (2007) on this point – nor that all theory must be formal, but rather that *when* models are intended to formalize an explanation for an empirical phenomenon, the modeling dialog is an important component of the research process.

2. The use of random assignment – which political scientists often associate with experiments – is not a necessary component of an experimental theory test, although it can often be useful to employ random assignment to identify a causal relationship in terms of a 'treatment effect'.

3. For extended discussion of epistemological issues related to experiments, see Morton and Williams (2010) and Bardsley et al. (2010). Morton and Williams also provide an extensive discussion of design issues, as do Kagel and Roth (1995) and Camerer (2003). For recent reviews of laboratory experiments in political economy see Palfrey (2006, 2009).

4. See Smith (1994) for a general three-part framework for understanding experiments consisting of the environment, institution and behavior.

5. In cooperative game theory and social choice theory, there is no explicit model of behavior. Instead, the solution concepts involve axiomatic properties of group choice, such as the core. Although the framework can be generalized by replacing the behavioral model with a solution concept (such as in Fiorina and Plott), I use the notion of a behavioral model because the discussion will revolve around noncooperative game theory.

6. Although I use the notation of propositional logic, I do not mean to imply that the goal of theory testing is to establish whether or not a model is 'true' or 'false'. Because models are simplifications of reality – and false by definition – I merely use truth values as a shorthand to mean whether or not the model sufficiently captures the essence of the situation.

7. A better defense of the rational choice paradigm is that analyses making strong assumptions such as Nash equilibrium or perfect Bayesian equilibrium provide us with knowledge of an ideal benchmark and that theoretical analysis should also investigate the consequences of behavioral departures from idealized models.

8. However, precise control over preferences is not always successful. Indeed, there is a vast literature on 'social preferences' (for example, Charness and Rabin, 2002) that suggests how laboratory payoffs do not always correspond to subjects' actual preferences. Although this presents a potentially serious confound to making inferences about behavior, it does not mean that it is impossible to induce preferences. For example, control is likely to be successful in settings with common values or binary outcomes. The structure of preferences in the model and how closely it can be implemented in the lab is a design issue that must be considered by the experimenter. For an expanded discussion of this issue, see Bardsley et al (2010, chapter 3).

9. See Levitt and List (2007) for a discussion of various concerns about the generalizability of laboratory experiments.

## References

Aldrich, John H., James Alt and Arthur Lupia (2008) 'The EITM Approach: Origins and Interpretations' in Janet Box-Steffensmeier, Henry Brady and David Collier (eds.) *The Oxford Handbook of Political Methodology* (Oxford University Press).

Bardsley, Nicholas, Robin Cubitt, Graham Loomes, Peter Moffatt, Chris Starmer and Robert Sugden (2010) *Experimental Economics: Rethinking the Rules* (Princeton University Press).

Camerer, Colin (2003) *Behavioral Game Theory: Experiments in Strategic Interaction* (Russell Sage Foundation and Princeton University Press).

Camerer, Colin F., Teck-Hua Ho and Juin-Kuan Chong (2004) 'A Cognitive Hierarchy Model of Games', *Quarterly Journal of Economics*, 119, 861–98.

Camerer, Colin, George Loewenstein and Martin Weber (1989) 'The Curse of Knowledge in Economic Settings: An Experimental Analysis', *Journal of Political Economy*, 97, 1232–54.

Canes-Wrone, Brandice, Michael C. Herron and Kenneth W. Shotts (2001) 'Leadership and Pandering: A Theory of Executive Policymaking', *American Journal of Political Science*, 45, 532–50.

Charness, Gary and Matthew Rabin (2002) 'Understanding Social Preferences with Simple Tests', *Quarterly Journal of Economics*, 117, 817–69.

Clarke, Kevin A. and David M. Primo (2007) 'Modernizing Political Science: A Model-Based Approach', *Perspectives on Politics*, 5, 741–53.

Cosmides, Leda (1989) 'The Logic of Social Exchange: Has Natural Selection Shaped How Humans Reason? Studies With the Wason Selection Task', *Cognition*, 31, 187–276.

Cox, Gary W. and Mathew D. McCubbins (2005) *Setting the Agenda: Responsible Party Government in the House of Representatives* (New York: Cambridge University Press).

Diermeier, Daniel and Keith Krehbiel (2003) 'Institutionalism as a Methodology', *Journal of Theoretical Politics*, 15, 123.

Fearon, James D (1999) 'Electoral Accountability and the Control of Politicians: Selecting Good Types versus Sanctioning Poor Performance' in Adam Przeworski, Susan C. Stokes and Bernard Manin (eds.) *Democracy, Accountability, and Representation* (Cambridge University Press).

Fiorina, Morris A. (1981) *Retrospective Voting in American National Elections* (New Haven, Conn.: Yale University Press).

Fiorina, Morris P. and Charles R. Plott (1978) 'Committee Decisions Under Majority Rule: An Experimental Study', *The American Political Science Review*, 72, 575–98.

Flood, Merrill M. (1958) 'Some Experimental Games', Management Science, 5, 5–26.

Fox, Justin and Kenneth W. Shotts. (2009) 'Delegates or Trustees? A Theory of Political Accountability', *Journal of Politics*, 71, 1225–37.

Kagel, John H. and Alvin E. Roth, eds. (1995) *The Handbook of Experimental Economics* (Princeton University Press).

Key, V.O., Jr. (1966) *The Responsible Electorate* (Belknap Press).

Krehbiel, Keith (1998) *Pivotal Politics: A Theory of US Lawmaking* (Chicago: University of Chicago Press).

Levitt, Steven D. and John A. List (2007) 'What Do Laboratory Experiments Measuring Social Preferences Reveal About the Real World?', *The Journal of Economic Perspectives*, 21, 153–74.

Liberman, Varda, Steven M. Samuels and Lee Ross (2004) 'The Name of the Game: Predictive Power of Reputations versus Situational Labels in Determining Prisoner's Dilemma Game Moves', *Personality and Social Psychology Bulletin*, 30, 1175–85.

Loewenstein, George (1999) 'Experimental Economics from the Vantage Point of Behavioral Economics', *The Economic Journal*, 109, F25–F34.

McKelvey, Richard D. and Thomas R. Palfrey (1995) 'Quantal Response Equilibria in Normal Form Games', *Games and Economic Behavior*, 10, 6–37.

McKelvey, Richard D. and Thomas R. Palfrey. (1998) 'Quantal Response Equilibria in Extensive Form Games', *Experimental Economics*, 1, 9–41.

Morton, Rebecca B. and Kenneth C. Williams. (2010) *Experimental Political Science and the Study of Causality* (Cambridge University Press).

Myerson, Roger B. (1992) 'On the Value of Game Theory in Social Science', *Rationality and Society*, 4, 62.

Nagel, Rosemarie (1995) 'Unraveling in Guessing Games: An Experimental Study', *The American Economic Review*, 85, 1313–26.

Nash, John F. (1951) 'Non-Cooperative Games', *Annals of Mathematics*, 54, 286–95.

Palfrey, Thomas R. (2006) 'Laboratory Experiments' in Barry R. Weingast and Donald A. Wittman (eds.) *The Oxford Handbook of Political Economy* (Oxford University Press).

Palfrey, Thomas R. (2009) 'Laboratory Experiments in Political Economy', *Annual Review of Political Science*, 12, 379–88.

Powell, Robert (1999) *In the Shadow of Power: States and Strategies in International Politics* (Princeton University Press).

Smith, Vernon L (1994) 'Economics in the Laboratory', *Journal of Economics Perspectives*, 8, 113–31.

Smith, V.L. (1976) 'Experimental Economics: Induced Value Theory', *The American Economic Review*, 66, 274–9.

Wason, P.C. and Diana Shapiro (1971) 'Natural and Contrived Experience in a Reasoning Problem', *Quarterly Journal of Experimental Psychology*, 23, 63–71.

Woon, Jonathan (2010) 'Democratic Accountability and Retrospective Voting: A Laboratory Experiment', Manuscript, University of Pittsburgh.

# 4
# Voting Mechanism Design: Modeling Institutions in Experiments

*Jens Großer*

## 4.1 Political engineering: mechanism design in political science[1]

In this chapter, I argue why laboratory experiments have the potential to become an indispensable tool of political engineering. Political engineers are concerned with the design of mechanisms, or political institutions and procedures (for example, electoral systems), that support desirable behavior and outcomes. Of course, what is desirable depends on the perspective of the decision maker (for example, a government, party or dictator). My focus is on the design of voting mechanisms for small groups which are concerned with the welfare and equality of income among their members. Other possible applications of mechanism design in political science include, but are not limited to, constitutions, fighting terrorism, conflict bargaining and environmental agreements. Although still relatively neglected in political engineering, laboratory experiments have become an established mechanism design tool in other areas, most notably auction and market design (for example, FCC combinatorial spectrum auctions, Brunner et al., 2010; Goeree and Holt, 2010; and $CO_2$ emissions markets, Burtraw et al., 2011). Experts in laboratory experimentation and game theory are often consulted to design these institutions, or to develop bidding strategies for firms that participate in trading. There is no reason why this could not happen in political engineering!

Beginning with Hurwicz (1960, 1972), theoretical mechanism design has developed as a branch of game theory, culminating in the Nobel Prize in Economics in 2007 for three of its pioneers: Leonid Hurwicz, Eric S. Maskin and Roger B. Myerson.[2] In traditional game theory, the analysis starts with specific institutions for which social, economic or political outcomes are predicted or explained. By contrast, in mechanism design, the direction of analysis is reversed. First, desirable outcomes are identified. Thereafter, it is investigated whether mechanisms exist that can generate these outcomes and, if so, what exactly the institutions and procedures must look like

(Maskin, 2008). In other words, mechanism design does not derive outcomes for specific games, but games are derived for specific outcomes. Typically, mechanism design assumes self-interested players with informational asymmetries among them and, given these assumptions, proper institutions and procedures need to be found that channel behavior towards pre-identified, desirable outcomes (see Maskin, 2008, for a simple, concrete example). The goals of experimental mechanism design are similar to those of its theoretical counterpart. An obvious key difference is that the laboratory is used for test-bedding specific mechanisms with respect to outcomes, and possibly underlying behavioral assumptions. In this chapter, my focus is on the experimental side of voting mechanism design.

To illustrate the possibilities of laboratory experiments for voting mechanism design, I will discuss four of my own studies with various co-authors. In two of these studies, we compare voluntary and compulsory voting. Political scientists and the media often consider high voting participation as desirable. Among other reasons, mobilization efforts likely encourage citizens to assume their democratic rights and yield more accurate representation of voter preferences in policymaking (Lijphart, 1997). Yet, many consequences of voter mobilization are still unexplored, and laboratory experiments and game theory can provide new perspectives on traditional views in political science. In Großer and Giertz (2006), we use a framework of pork barrel politics (for example Myerson, 1993) to compare voluntary and compulsory voting – that is maximal mobilization – with respect to income inequality. In Großer and Seebauer (2009) we are interested in information acquisition and aggregation, and the negative externality that uninformed voting can inflict upon aggregate welfare. This study also fits well into the growing literature on laboratory and game theoretical research on information aggregation and committee voting that started in the mid-1990s (for example Austen-Smith and Banks, 1996; Feddersen and Pesendorfer, 1998; Guarnaschelli, McKelvey and Palfrey, 2000).[3] In the same line of research, in Goeree, Großer and Rogers (2009), we study information aggregation and aggregate welfare for varying group sizes and elaborate on the optimal size of a committee. Finally, in Großer and Schram (2010), we investigate voting with and without information about others' preferences over policy alternatives and whether and how this information affects aggregate welfare. Note that it is quite common that others' preferences are revealed through deliberation, polls and so on, before voting takes place (for example Coughlan, 2000; Forsythe et al., 1993, 1996; Meirowitz, 2006).

Most studies discussed in this chapter use both laboratory experiments and game theory, which has proven to be a mutually beneficial relationship. Game theory provides an effective toolbox for describing specific institutions and procedures, and revealing the players' strategic incentives in these mechanisms. Its mathematical structure makes it relatively easy to test the games' assumptions and predictions in experiments. In turn, laboratory results often inspire game theoretical modeling when unexpected behavior is observed, yielding more realistic assumptions about the players' behavior (for example erroneous or bounded rational decision making in the quantal response equilibrium of McKelvey and Palfrey, 1995, 1998) or their motives (for example, concern for others in the social preference models of Bolton and Ockenfels, 2000; and Fehr and Schmidt, 1999). The combined use of laboratory experiments and game theory can prevent mechanism design from giving unrealistic or inapplicable advice (for example when procedures become too complex for people to make meaningful decisions) and inspire new institutional and procedural designs, often originating from conflicting results of both methods. Moreover, both laboratory experiments and game theory are particularly suited for picking up and analyzing institutional and procedural details that may crucially affect outcomes.[4] Finally, game theoretically designed mechanisms that are novel or rarely observed in the field can be test-bedded in the laboratory (for example storable voting, Casella 2005; Casella, Palfrey and Riezman, 2008). In this way, political engineers can produce observations relatively quickly and cheaply to gain an initial understanding of decision behavior and outcomes in unexplored institutions and procedures.

Political engineers may aim at advising designs of very specific institutions and procedures, potentially with immediate practical implications. Or they may be interested in more general, abstract phenomena and put minimal restrictions on the mechanisms they analyze. If application is the goal, institutional and procedural details are typically of importance. For example, a country's parliament may debate whether to continue using voluntary voting in general elections or to switch to compulsory voting while keeping all other electoral procedures unaltered. To avoid giving biased advice to parliament, a political engineer should ideally analyze the debated change within a context (that is a game or experimental design) that resembles as closely as possible the country specific, often historically developed, electoral system. By contrast, if the goal is to study more general, abstract phenomena of relevance for a larger class of mechanisms (for example for a variety of different voting rules), institutional and procedural details may be safely ignored. Most studies discussed in this chapter are of this more general kind of analysis.

Because theoretical mechanism design typically assumes self-interested rational players, outcomes are not only *predicted* but also *explained* by the underlying behavioral assumptions. By contrast, in experimental mechanism design, these assumptions are replaced by actual behavior. For some mechanisms and intentions of the designer, further modeling of actual behavior may not be necessary. However, in other cases it may be important to develop new behavioral assumptions. Consider, for example, the well-known double auction market of Vernon Smith (1962). The equilibrium outcomes, that is, market prices and quantities, are predicted by the intersection of supply and demand functions. Typically, players are given very little information about these functions and no further behavioral assumptions are made. Equilibrium outcomes are also efficient outcomes; that is, they yield maximal aggregate welfare. In the laboratory, supply and demand are induced by allocating trading values for hypothetical goods to sellers and buyers, and subjects from both sides of the market can post and accept prices with few restrictions. Typically, the experimental analysis focuses on market efficiency. The 'magic' of double auction markets is that observed outcomes quickly converge towards the efficient equilibrium predictions, as if driven merely by the institution and procedures and regardless of the subjects' motives and behavior. In fact, it has been shown that even simulated zero-intelligence traders who make random decisions achieve outcomes remarkably close to market efficiency, hence, behave *quasi rationally* (Gode and Sunder, 1993; Großer and Reuben, 2010). Although this is an impressive example of how mechanisms can virtually control outcomes, experimental mechanism design is also concerned with less powerful institutions and procedures in which the players' motives and behavior may have an important impact on outcomes (for example in bilateral bargaining). For such situations, it is useful for political engineers to have a more general model of behavior at their disposal (for example quantal response equilibrium or the social preference models mentioned earlier), which may help predict potential outcomes and guide the development of new mechanisms.

The remaining part of this section is organized as follows. First, I briefly describe three prominent experiments on voting mechanism design. Thereafter, I elaborate on how, so far, experiments have informed game theory that can be used for mechanism design. Finally, four of my own voting experiments with various co-authors are discussed and some conclusions are made.

## 4.2 Previous experiments on voting mechanism design

Game theoretical models of voting have improved substantially since the mid-1990s, and many predict and explain observed voting behavior and outcomes very well (see Goeree and Holt, 2005). Their predictions and assumptions are very specific and they can be tested in the laboratory at both the individual and aggregate level. Here, it is helpful to describe briefly three prominent examples of experiments in the realm of voting mechanism design.[5] To begin, McKelvey and Ordeshook (1984) show that even with substantial numbers of uninformed voters – about 55 per cent in their experiment – who do not directly observe the policy positions of two candidates, elections preceded by polls yield outcomes *as if* everybody is informed. In the experiment, two candidate-subjects chose policy positions in a two-dimensional spatial model of electoral competition (Downs,

1957; Hotelling, 1929) with electorates of 53 to 89 voter-subjects. The voters' induced policy preferences were distributed in a way that a unique informed Nash equilibrium exists. That is, if all voters could observe the candidates' policy positions, in equilibrium both candidates would choose the median preferences and voters would vote sincerely for the candidate who is 'closer' to their own preferences (or vote randomly if both candidates' positions are equally distant). Prior to Election Day, uninformed voters twice had the opportunity to infer some information about the candidates' policy positions from polls, though this was a rather complex task. All voters could either abstain or participate in the poll by indicating their support for a candidate, and candidates could change their positions after poll results were made public. McKelvey and Ordeshook found that candidate positions on Election Day were very close to those predicted by the informed Nash equilibrium, showing that elections with preceding polls can yield desirable outcomes, even when there are many initially uninformed voters.

Another interesting example is the agenda setting study of Levine and Plott (1977). They organized an intriguing field experiment on majority voting in the flying club they were members of. They manipulated the voting agenda over proposals about the size and composition of the aircraft fleet available to members, the organization of which was given into their hands. Prior to voting, they collected their co-members' preferences and set the agenda in a way in which they expected their own preferred outcome to emerge as the winner. They succeeded, to the anger of their co-members, who, afterwards were informed of the plot! Plott and Levine (1978) also developed the game theory of agenda setting and ran laboratory experiments to demonstrate that the single-observation field success was not a random outlier.

In a final example, Casella, Palfrey and Riezman (2008) study a *storable vote* mechanism that has not yet been applied in the field. In this mechanism (introduced in Casella, 2005), voters are granted a stock of votes that they can freely use across a series of simple majority elections over two alternatives. Because storable voting gives minorities the opportunity to save their votes for issues in which their preferences are strongest, minority interests can be better represented than in many other voting mechanisms. In the laboratory, Casella, Palfrey and Riezman (2008) indeed observe that minority preferences are better represented by storable voting than by standard simple majority voting, with only small differences in aggregate welfare between the two mechanisms.

### 4.3   How laboratory experiments have informed game theory

In recent decades, plenty of laboratory experiments have boosted the development of theoretical models that very successfully predict and explain decision behavior. Hence, these models may be important tools for political engineers. Among the most prominent examples are models of social preferences (for example Bolton and Ockenfels, 2000; Fehr and Schmidt, 1999) and quantal response equilibrium (McKelvey and Palfrey, 1995, 1998). In the following, I discuss these two theoretical developments in turn, beginning with social preference models.

Many experiments have shown that narrow self-interest alone cannot satisfactorily describe behavior in a variety of important decision-making situations. These include, but are not limited to, the prisoner's dilemma game (Dawes, 1980), public goods game (Isaac and Walker, 1988), ultimatum bargaining game (Güth, Schmittberger and Schwarze, 1992), dictator game (Hoffman et al., 1994) and trust game (Berg, Dickhaut and McCabe, 1995). All these simple games – which also serve as building blocks for more complex but equally well-known games[6] – are characterized by 'low competition' in the sense that only two players are involved (with the exception of $n$-player public goods games, which typically use $n \geq 3$). In the respective experimental games, observed behavior is not solely driven by self-interest but also by social preferences (for example, in some form of reciprocity or inequity aversion). For example, consider a standard ultimatum bargaining experiment in which a proposer-subject must divide $x$ dollars between herself and a receiver-subject. The receiver can either accept this division and both subjects are paid accordingly, or reject it and both receive nothing. Most proposed receiver-shares range between 40 per cent and 50 per cent of the amount at stake and are usually accepted, while smaller offers are prone to rejection (see Camerer, 2003). In stark contrast, a subgame perfect equilibrium for solely self-interested players predicts that receivers accept shares as low as 1 cent – because something is better than nothing – and, anticipating this, proposers offer only one cent. However, allowing for a realistic mix of self-interested and prosocial motives, social preference models can explain observed behavior very well (Bolton and Ockenfels, 2000; Fehr and Schmidt, 1999). To see the intuition, suppose a receiver in the ultimatum bargaining game is inequity averse – that is, the receiver dislikes differences between her share and the proposer's share. If the difference gets too large (because her own share gets too low), the receiver's inequity concerns may override her pecuniary concerns, triggering a rejection of the proposed division. Moreover, while a prosocial proposer may offer a fair share purely based on inequity concerns (for example, if $x = \$10$ she may propose the equal split of $5 for each subject), a self-interested proposer may offer substantially more than preferred because she fears rejection by a receiver who is potentially inequity averse. Similar arguments hold for the prisoner's dilemma, public goods, dictator and trust game experiments, in which social preference models can explain observed behavior very well, too. Hence, these models can prove to be very useful for political engineers who analyze low competition situations (for example, bilateral negotiations and conflicts). The distribution of self-interested and prosocial motives or types within a population of players is important information, because outcomes crucially depend on it. Mechanism design can help increase the probability of obtaining desirable outcomes by paying special attention to combinations of motives and types that tend to hinder this goal.

There are also many decision-making situations characterized by 'high competition' in the sense that more than two, possibly many, players are involved (for example, demonstrations, elections and other collective actions). For example, Fischbacher, Fong and Fehr (2009) show that adding just one proposer or receiver to a two-player ultimatum bargaining experiment already yields strong competition between the two subjects with the same role, to the advantage of the third subject. This suggests that high competition situations may decrease or eliminate the influence social preferences have on outcomes.[7] Another example is that of elections with compulsory voting over two alternatives, in which subjects typically vote according to their pecuniary self-interest (for example, Großer and Giertz, 2006).

The other successful theoretical development useful for political engineers is quantal response equilibrium (henceforth QRE; McKelvey and Palfrey, 1995, 1998). Many experiments have shown that decisions are often not *sharp* best responses to others' decisions, but *smooth* stochastic responses with more lucrative actions being chosen more frequently than less lucrative actions. The degree to which errors enter the decisions is represented by a nonnegative noise parameter, $\mu$. In a typical specification, if $\mu = 0$, decision makers make no errors and QRE reduces to the standard Nash equilibrium. At the other extreme, as $\mu \to \infty$ decision making becomes completely random. A common interpretation is that $\mu$ represents the degree of bounded rationality. For example, people may make mistakes while choosing an alternative or have erroneous perceptions about costs and benefits due to cognitive limitations.[8] QRE predicts behavior very well in many decision-making situations, for example, in voting and related binary decision experiments (for example, Goeree and Holt, 2005; Guarnaschelli, McKelvey and Palfrey, 2000; Levine and Palfrey, 2007).[9]

## 4.4 Voting mechanism design: some laboratory results

Here, four examples of my own research with various co-authors are discussed to demonstrate in more detail some of the possibilities of using laboratory experiments and game theory for voting mechanism design. Although these examples have no direct counterparts in the field, the questions we study are of more general interest to political engineers. All examples use simple majority voting over two alternatives, *A* and *B* (with random tie breaking), and decision-making costs of some kind. In two examples, we compare voluntary with compulsory voting to investigate information acquisition and welfare (Großer and Seebauer, 2009) and income inequality (Großer and Giertz, 2006). In the other two examples, we study optimal committee sizes (Goeree, Großer and Rogers, 2009) and how information about others' preferences affects voting and welfare (Großer and Schram, 2010).[10] In the following, I distinguish between studies with *common* and *private* preferences over the two alternatives, beginning with the former.

### 4.4.1 Voting with common preferences

Next, two voting experiments are discussed that use common preferences among voters in a single group. By common preferences I mean that everybody prefers the same alternative (henceforth, 'better alternative'). However, there is uncertainty about which alternative this may be. This can be either alternative with equal probability of 0.5 for each, which is common knowledge. Some voters have additional information. Specifically, they receive an $A$- or $B$-signal indicating that this alternative is better with probability $p > 0.5$, and that the alternative not shown by the signal is better with probability $1- p$. A signal is a Bernoulli trial that is drawn independently for each voter who receives a signal, where $p$ is used conditionally on the alternative which is indeed the better one.[11] Thus, voters may have different *opinions* about what is the better alternative, but everybody would support this alternative if it would only be known with certainty. Using this setup, Condorcet's jury theorem (1785) states that if there is no deliberation and if everybody receives a signal and casts a naïve vote for the alternative shown by her signal, the probability of choosing the better alternative by simple majority voting is increasing in the group size, $n$, and approaches 1 if $n$ goes to infinity. The following two examples modify this basic setup by introducing signal and voting costs, respectively.

### 4.4.2 Costly information acquisition

In Großer and Seebauer (2009), there are two decision-making stages. In the first stage, voters must decide on whether to acquire a signal at a cost, $c$, or to remain uninformed and bear no costs. In the second stage, either voluntary or compulsory voting takes place in which voting is costless. Each voter receives a benefit, $b > 0$, if the group decision is the better alternative and zero otherwise, irrespective of whether or not she acquired a signal. With voluntary voting, everybody decides on whether to vote for alternative $A$ or $B$, or to abstain. With compulsory voting, abstention is not an option and voters must vote for one of the two alternatives. Why is it interesting to study information acquisition under both voting mechanisms? In an important game theoretical study, Feddersen and Pesendorfer (*The swing voter's curse*, 1996) show that absent of voting costs and partisan voters, uninformed rational voters will abstain and 'delegate' voting to the informed voters. However, if the uninformed voters expect the outcome to be biased by partisans who always vote for their favorite alternative irrespective of the information in signals, they may vote to offset these partisan votes. The swing voter's curse has also found support in the laboratory (Battaglini, Morton and Palfrey, 2009). In contrast to these studies, we do not consider partisans, and signals are not provided exogenously, but must be acquired by the voters.

Importantly, voting uninformed inflicts an expected negative externality on the group.[12] To see the intuition, consider the decision problem of an uninformed voter when everybody else is informed and voting sincerely according to the information in signals. The only situation in which her uninformed vote is harmful is if it changes a one-vote lead by either alternative into a tie.[13] Without loss of generality, suppose $A$ is one informed vote ahead of $B$ and thus more likely to be the better alternative (because $p > 0.5$). Without the uninformed voter's vote, $A$ will surely win. By contrast, if she casts her vote randomly for one of the two alternatives,[14] the outcome will be a two-vote win for $A$ with probability 0.5 and a tie with probability 0.5. Since ties are broken randomly, $A$ will only win with probability 0.75 ($= 0.5 \times 1 + 0.5(0.5 \times 0 + 0.5 \times 1)$), as compared to 1 if the uninformed voter abstains. This decrease in $A$'s winning probability leads to an expected negative externality on the group, because given that $A$ is one informed vote ahead of $B$, alternative $A$ is more likely to be better. As a consequence of this externality, an uninformed rational voter abstains. Note now the key difference between voluntary and compulsory voting in our setup: In the former mechanism, an uninformed voter can avoid exerting an expected negative externality by abstaining, but in the latter, she cannot.[15]

In our experiment, we used $p = 0.75$, $c = 25$ points, $b = 200$ points, group sizes of three and seven and a within-subjects design in which in some sessions subjects made decisions in 30 rounds with voluntary voting and thereafter in 30 rounds with compulsory voting, and vice versa in other sessions (we varied the sequence across sessions to control for order effects). We used a random matching ('strangers') protocol, with groups of three or seven being randomly formed at the beginning of each round. For our setup and parameters, Bayesian Nash equilibrium predicts that players in groups of three buy a signal with a higher probability when voting is compulsory than when it is voluntary, but the reverse is predicted for groups of seven. By contrast, the QRE prediction for large enough $\mu$ is that players buy a signal with a higher probability when voting is compulsory for both group sizes. Our experimental results support the QRE predictions. Hence, subjects seem to account for the expected negative externality of uninformed voting by acquiring information more often. This results in higher aggregate welfare for compulsory than for voluntary voting, with the effect being more pronounced in smaller groups of three. However, whereas flipping a coin to decide between both alternatives adds on average 100 points ($= 0.5 \times 0 + 0.5 \times 200$) to each voter's payoff, our subjects earn on average only between 15 to 30 points more than in this random benchmark. Moreover, surprisingly, when voting is voluntary, a substantial number of subjects voted for one of the two alternatives even without buying a signal, contributing to the particularly low aggregate welfare in this mechanism.

This disillusioning result suggests there is room for improvement of voting mechanisms that involve information acquisition. Our experiment contributes novel arguments to the discussion of voting mobilization. There is a variety of good reasons why the media and many political scientists consider high voter participation as desirable (Lijphart, 1997). However, future research and discussions should more often take into account the level of information that the mobilized voters possess (see also Gerardi et al., 2009).

### 4.4.3 Costly voting and the optimal size of a committee

In Goeree, Großer and Rogers (2009), we study whether the result of Condorcet's jury theorem (1785), that larger groups choose the better alternative with a higher probability than smaller groups, also holds if voting is costly and voters have the option to save these costs by abstaining. As predicted by QRE for large enough $\mu$, but in contrast to Bayesian Nash equilibrium, we indeed observe that larger groups choose the better alternative more often. The reason is that even though voting rates decrease in group size, this effect is not strong enough to diminish, on average, the absolute number of voters who vote (which is what Bayesian Nash equilibrium predicts, but not QRE). Rather, larger groups do better because on average more subjects participate and voting is almost always sincere. This result is used to elaborate on the optimal size of a committee. We define a committee as a subgroup of voters who have the opportunity to participate in voting over the two alternatives, with consequences for the entire group.

There are two decision-making stages in our setup. In the first stage, each voter receives a *costless* signal (see endnote 11) and is informed about whether or not she is a committee member. Thereafter, committee members must decide on whether to participate in voting at a cost, $c$, or to abstain and bear no costs. In the second stage, simple majority voting over alternative $A$ and $B$ takes place, in which ties are broken randomly. In our experiment, we used $p = 0.75$, $c = 20$ points, $b = 120$ points and a fixed matching ('partners') protocol in which the same groups of eight subjects made decisions in 60 rounds. Each group faced three blocks of 20 rounds of committee sizes one, four and eight, respectively (we varied the sequence of blocks across sessions to control for order effects). Whether or not a subject was currently a committee member was randomly determined at the beginning of each round. Whereas Bayesian Nash equilibrium predicts an optimal committee size of one for our setup and parameters, QRE for large enough $\mu$ predicts this size to be eight (that is, all voters should be eligible). In the experiment, committee members who chose to participate voted almost always sincerely. Interestingly, the highest aggregate welfare observed was achieved neither by committees of size one nor eight (as predicted by Bayesian Nash equilibrium and QRE, respectively), but by committees of four. One possible explanation is that for this size committee, members vote more because they feel responsible for the four subjects who are not part of the committee but must rely on the committee's decision (interestingly, in a control treatment, voters in a group of four in which everybody could participate in voting did less so than our four committee subjects in a group of eight). However, there are other plausible explanations as to why an intermediate committee size performs best in our setup. It seems that more experiments are needed before political engineers can give confident advice about the optimal size of a committee.

### 4.4.4   Voting with private preferences

In this section, two experiments are discussed that use private preferences. By private preferences I mean that voters may prefer different alternatives, resulting in different benefits from voting outcomes. In one experiment, preferences are induced (Großer and Schram, 2010) and in the other experiment, they are endogenously determined through candidate competition (Großer and Giertz, 2006). The underlying framework in both studies is the participation game of Palfrey and Rosenthal (1983, 1985). In its basic version, $n$ players must decide over two alternatives, $i = A, B$, using simple majority voting (with random tie breaking). Each alternative is preferred by $n_i \in \{0,n\}$ players, with $n_A + n_B = n$, constituting two different voter groups.[16] Moreover, each voter decides on whether to vote for one of the two alternatives at a cost, $c > 0$, or to abstain (at no cost).[17] Each voter whose preferred alternative wins receives a benefit, $b > 0$, and nothing otherwise. Note that while voters in a model with common preferences may vote for different alternatives because they are uncertain about which one they all prefer, with private preferences they may do so because their tastes are different. In the following, two variations of the basic participation game setup are discussed.

### 4.4.5   Information about others' preferences

In Großer and Schram (2010), we study whether and how welfare is affected by information about the private preferences of others (for example, provided by polls). To do so, we compare participation games with *incomplete* information about others' preferences (that is, voters know their own taste but only a probability distribution of others' tastes; Palfrey and Rosenthal, 1985) to those with *complete* information (that is, the actual distribution of all voters' tastes is common knowledge; Palfrey and Rosenthal, 1983). In our experiment, we used $n = 12$, $c = 1$ point, $b = 3$ points, 100 decision rounds, and preference distributions $(n_A, n_B) \in \{(3,9), (4,8), (5,7), (6,6), (7,5), (8,4), (9,3)\}$, one of which was randomly determined at the beginning of each round. To avoid negative earnings, all voters received an additional point in each round and irrespective of the outcome, to cover potential voting costs. We varied information between subjects by showing the actual distributions at the beginning of each round in some sessions, while not showing them in other sessions.

In the experiment, we observed an overall increase in voting by 22 to 28 per cent when subjects knew the actual preference distribution, as compared to when this information was not provided. However, overall aggregate welfare was barely affected. Analyzing the effects of information on voting and aggregate welfare for each ($n_A$, $n_B$) separately, we find that welfare drops substantially when preferences are distributed equally (that is, when $n_A = n_B = 6$). The reason is that particularly many subjects voted in *ex ante* dead heats, which increases aggregate voting costs while aggregate benefits are independent of the outcome (aggregate benefits are the same, whichever candidate wins). By contrast, the effects of information on aggregate welfare are non-negative if preferences are distributed unequally (that is, when $n_A \neq n_B$). In these situations, majorities won more often than minorities when the actual preference distribution was shown to the subjects. As a consequence, we observe somewhat higher aggregate benefits with information than without information. For preference distributions (5,7) and (7,5), this increase is absorbed by an increase in voting costs due to informed subjects voting more, and aggregate welfare is barely affected. By contrast, for preference distributions (3,9), (4,8), (8,4) and (9,3), aggregate welfare generally increases in these situations.

Whereas our experimental results are poorly predicted by Bayesian Nash equilibrium, QRE captures many of the observed voting patterns and levels very well (as in other experimental participation games; Goeree and Holt, 2005). Preliminary computations suggest that our QRE predictions may be further improved if combined with models that derive predictions using group motives rather than individual motives (for example, Bacharach, 2006; Coate and Conlin, 2004; Feddersen and Sandroni, 2006). Naturally, our study is limited to some extent (for example, we focused on a symmetric probability distribution of preferences). However, a major advantage of our novel, simple setup is that it can accommodate a variety of more specific applications in which political engineers may be interested (for example, various electoral systems). We are optimistic that some of our results may turn out to be more general (for example, that information about others' preferences harms minorities), in the same way as our experiment complements the finding of many observational studies that people vote more in dead heats (for example, Blais, 2000).

### 4.4.6 Pork barrel politics and income inequality

In Großer and Giertz (2006), we compare voluntary and compulsory voting in a model of pork barrel politics (for example, Myerson, 1993).[18] There are two decision-making stages. In the fist stage, two candidates, $i = A, B$, compete by distributing a fixed budget, $w > 0$, across $n$ voters. Any selection of $x \geq 1$ specific voters is permitted. In case candidate $i$ wins the election, each of her $x$ selected voters receives benefits of $b = w/x$. Note that voter preferences are endogenously determined by the candidates' budget distributions, generating participation games (Palfrey and Rosenthal, 1983). Specifically, a voter prefers the candidate who promises her a larger share of the budget, and is indifferent between both candidates if both candidates offer her the same shares (including the case in which both do not consider her in budget spending). The candidates' budget distributions are made independently and are announced simultaneously. Thereafter, simple majority voting takes place (with random tie breaking) and there are voting costs, $c > 0$. When voting is voluntary, voters must decide on whether to vote for the budget distribution of candidate $A$ or $B$, or to abstain and save the voting costs. When voting is compulsory, they must decide on whether to vote for $A$ or $B$, or to vote blank (that is, vote for neither candidate) and bear the voting costs anyway. The vote outcome is made public, and the winning candidate receives $\sigma > 0$, while the loser receives nothing.

Why is a comparison between voluntary and compulsory voting interesting in this setup? Consider a political engineer who evaluates desirable outcomes with respect to income equality. Then, note that on average a candidate needs to offer larger budget shares to her selected voters when voting is voluntary than when it is compulsory. This is because her offer must not only exceed the opponent's offer, but with voluntary voting the benefit-differential between both budget shares must also suffice to make it profitable for her beneficiaries to bear the voting costs.[19] To achieve this, candidates must select fewer voters in their budget distributions. Consequently, we predict that budget spending will be more unequal with voluntary voting than with compulsory voting.

In the experiment, we used $w = 18$ points, thus $b = 18/x$ points, $c = 1$ point, $\sigma = 20$ points, and 51 decision rounds. To avoid negative earnings, all voters received an additional point in each round and irrespective of the outcome to cover potential voting costs.[20] A fixed matching ('partners') protocol was used, in which the two candidate- and 12 voter-subjects stayed together for all rounds and never changed their roles. We varied voluntary and compulsory voting between subjects. As predicted, we indeed observed that budget spending is more unequal when voting is voluntary. Candidates selected 33.13 per cent more beneficiaries in compulsory than in voluntary voting (the average numbers of selected voters are 6.71 and 5.04 out of 12 voters, respectively). It would also be interesting to investigate this inequality effect using observational data from the field, although it is more difficult to control for important details typical for electoral systems in practice. For example, one could study whether and how income equality was affected in countries like the Netherlands and Italy after they switched from compulsory to voluntary voting in 1967 and 1993, respectively.

## 4.5  Conclusions

In this chapter, I argued why laboratory experiments should become an indispensable tool for political engineers. While experiments and game theory are frequently used in other areas like spectrum auction design, they are still rarely utilized for the design of political institutions and procedures. I focused on political engineering at a more general, abstract level and demonstrated its possibilities based on results of small group experiments that I conducted with various co-authors. For example, we contributed novel arguments to the discussion on voter mobilization by comparing voluntary and compulsory voting. Specifically, we argued that getting people out to vote may not necessarily be desirable if many of the mobilized voters are uninformed about policy alternatives. We found that aggregate welfare is somewhat higher with compulsory voting (that is, with maximal mobilization) than with voluntary voting. However, the observed overall performance was rather low for both voting mechanisms. Moreover, within a model of pork barrel politics, we showed that compulsory voting yields more equal budget spending than voluntary voting. We also investigated the welfare effects of information about others' preferences (for example, provided by polls), and found that majorities typically gain from this information while minorities are unaffected or harmed. Finally, we elaborated on the optimal size of a committee and found that in our experiment, aggregate welfare is highest for a size in-between those predicted by Bayesian Nash equilibrium and quantal response equilibrium (that is, one and all voters, respectively). We conjectured that responsibility for other, noncommittee members in intermediate sized committees may increase voting towards the welfare optimal level.

At this point in the research program, our voting experiments and those of others cannot provide conclusive advice for applied mechanism design. However, they can be used as a starting point to investigate questions that are more specific. Moreover, in the general tradition of experimental methods, the robustness of existing results must be established through replication and stress testing in various decision making environments. Experimental mechanism design in political science has the potential to make progress in much the same way it did in other areas. We now have at our disposal important designer tools such as the successful quantal response equilibrium (McKelvey and Palfrey, 1995, 1998) and social preference models (Bolton and Ockenfels, 2000; Fehr and Schmidt, 1999), which can guide the development of new mechanisms in the laboratory and in game theory. There are plenty of opportunities for political engineering. For example, there is high demand for voting mechanism design in the United Nations, the European Union and other voting bodies (Bosman et al., 2005; Drouvelis, Montero and Sefton, 2010) and for peace design to keep conflicts (Dickson, 2009) and the nuclear race under control.

## Notes

1. I would like to thank Bernhard Kittel, Arthur Schram, Michael Seebauer and an anonymous commentator for helpful suggestions.

2. Hurwicz (2008), Maskin (2008) and Myerson (2008) are interesting reads of revised versions of their Nobel Prize lectures delivered in Stockholm, Sweden, on 8 December 2007.
3. See Gerling et al. (2005) for an interesting survey.
4. For example, the ending of Amazon auctions extends automatically when there is a bidding activity. In contrast, eBay auctions use fixed endings which allow buyers to 'snipe' (that is, to place relatively low bids in the very last moment to exclude further bidding competition), which may decrease a seller's revenue substantially (Ockenfels and Roth 2006).
5. Other prominent examples that are not further discussed here include, but are not limited to, Battaglini, Morton and Palfrey (2010); Fiorina and Plott (1978); Forsythe et al. (1995, 1996); Guarnaschelli, McKelvey and Palfrey (2000); Plott (1982). More examples of earlier experiments are given in the survey of McKelvey and Ordeshook (1990).
6. For example, the ultimatum bargaining game is the foundation of Baron and Ferejohn's (1989) legislative bargaining model. Or, two-candidate elections with costly voting are essentially threshold public goods games with binary contribution decisions in which the threshold number of votes needed by one voter group to beat the other group is endogenously determined by the votes cast in the opponent group (Palfrey and Rosenthal, 1983, 1985).
7. Bolton and Ockenfels (2000) and Fehr and Schmidt (1999) provide more examples. Interestingly, their social preferences models do predict competitive outcomes too, unless an unrealistic assumption is made in which nearly all players are solely inequity averse. In comparison, the social value orientation questionnaire of van Lange et al. (1997) typically indicates that between 35 and 45 per cent of the subjects are inequity averse.
8. The noise parameter, $\mu$, in QRE is also often used to measure learning behavior in experiments. For example, in a specification where $\mu = 0$ represents Nash equilibrium play and $\mu \to \infty$ fully random play, a decrease in the $\mu$-estimates across rounds indicates that decisions adjust in the direction of Nash equilibrium, that is, become less noisy.
9. There are relatively few attempts to combine (aspects of) the social preference models and QRE (for example, Anderson, Goeree and Holt, 1998; Fischbacher, Fong and Fehr, 2009).
10. The experimental software for Großer and Giertz (2006) and Großer and Schram (2010) was programmed using RatImage (Abbink and Sadrieh, 1995). For Großer and Seebauer (2009) we used z-Tree (Fischbacher, 2007) and the online recruitment system ORSEE (Greiner, 2004).
11. To illustrate this process, suppose $p = 0.7$ and that there are two urns, one containing seven blue and three yellow balls ('Blue' alternative) and the other containing seven yellow and three blue balls ('Yellow' alternative). Only one of the two urns is the better alternative, representing the 'true state of the world'. The group's task is to find out which urn this is, as it can be Blue or Yellow with equal probability of 0.5 for each. For voters who receive a signal, a ball is drawn from the urn representing the 'true state of the world'. A rational receiver uses Bayesian updating and knows now with probability $p = 0.7$ that the better alternative is Blue or Yellow, respectively, depending on the color of the ball drawn.
12. Similarly, partisan votes exert expected negative externalities on nonpartisans (and opponent partisans). In Feddersen and Pesendorfer (1996), the reason that uninformed rational nonpartisans may vote is to offset these negative externalities.

13. Another situation in which her vote affects the vote outcome is if it changes a tie into a win for either alternative. However, in this situation, there are equally many informed votes for both alternatives, which is not informative as compared to the initial knowledge that both alternatives are equally likely to be the better one. Hence, an uninformed vote does not do any harm in this situation.
14. We assume that there is no *a priori* reason (for example, incumbency of one alternative) why one alternative should be favored over the other if it is believed that both alternatives are equally likely to be the better one.
15. Note that I made the argument for a rational voter in the Bayesian Nash equilibrium. In QRE, an uninformed, boundedly rational voter may vote with some positive probability even when voting is voluntary, and thus, inflict expected negative externalities upon the group.
16. We define a group as the set of voters who prefer the same alternative.
17. A rational voter will never vote for the nonpreferred alternative because this alternative is strictly dominated by the decision to abstain.
18. We study pork barrel politics within the framework of a Colonel Blotto game that, originally, uses the following story: Two opposing generals must divide their armies across a number of battlefields. A general wins a battle if she sends more troops to this battlefield than her opponent, and wins the war if she wins the most battles.
19. A rational voter only votes with positive probability if the benefit-differential between both candidates' offers is at least twice as large as the voting costs (Palfrey and Rosenthal, 1983).
20. Whereas voter-subjects were paid for each decision round, candidate-subjects were paid between seven and nine rounds that were randomly drawn at the end of the experiment.

## References

Abbink, Klaus and Abdolkarim Sadrieh (1995) 'RatImage, Research Assistance Toolbox for Computer-aided Human Behavior Experiments', Discussion Paper No. B-325 (University of Bonn).

Anderson, Simon P., Jacob K. Goeree and Charles A. Holt (1998) 'A Theoretical Analysis of Altruism and Decision Error in Public Goods Games', *Journal of Public Economics*, 70, 297–323.

Austen-Smith, David and Jeffrey S. Banks (1996) 'Information Aggregation, Rationality, and the Condorcet Jury Theorem', *American Political Science Review*, 90, 34–45.

Bacharach, Michael (2006) *Beyond Individual Choice: Teams and Frames in Game Theory* (Princeton: Princeton University Press).

Baron, David P. and John A. Ferejohn (1989) 'Bargaining in Legislature', *American Political Science Review*, 83, 1181–206.

Battaglini, Marco, Rebecca Morton and Thomas Palfrey (2010) 'The Swing Voter's Curse in the Laboratory', *Review of Economic Studies*, 77, 61–89.

Berg, Joyce, John Dickhaut and Kevin McCabe (1995) 'Trust, Reciprocity, and Social History', *Games and Economic Behavior*, 10, 122–42.

Blais, André (2000) *To Vote or Not to Vote? The Merits and Limits of Rational Choice Theory* (Pittsburgh: University of Pittsburgh Press).

Bolton, Gary E. and Axel Ockenfels (2000) 'A Theory of Equity, Reciprocity, and Competition', *American Economic Review*, 90, 166–93.

Bosman, Ronald, Philip Maier, Vjollca Sadiraj and Frans van Winden (2005) 'Let Me Vote! An Experimental Study of the Effects of Vote Rotation in Committees', Manuscript, University of Amsterdam: CREED.

Brunner, Christoph, Jacob K. Goeree, Charles A. Holt and John O. Ledyard (2010) 'An Experimental Test of Flexible Combinatorial Spectrum Auction Formats', *American Economic Journal: Microeconomics*, 2, 39–57.

Burtraw, Dallas, Jacob K. Goeree, Charles A. Holt, Erica Myers, Karen Palmer and William M. Shobe (2011) 'Price Discovery in Emissions Permit Auctions' in R. Marc Isaac and Douglas A. Norton (eds.) *Experiments on Energy, the Environment, and Sustainability (Research in Experimental Economics, Vol. 14)* (Bingley: Emerald).

Camerer, Colin F (2003) *Behavioral Game Theory: Experiments in Strategic Interaction* (New York and Princeton: New Jersey: Russell Sage Foundation and Princeton University Press).

Casella, Alessandra (2005) 'Storable Votes', *Games and Economic Behavior*, 51, 391–419.

Casella, Alessandra, Thomas R. Palfrey and Raymond Riezman (2008) 'Minorities and Storable Votes', *Quarterly Journal of Political Science*, 3, 165–200.

Coate, Stephen and Michael Conlin (2004) 'A Group-rule Utilitarian Approach to Voter Turnout: Theory and Evidence' *American Economic Review*, 94, 1476–504.

Condorcet, Marquise de (Marie Jean Antoine Nicolas Caritat) (1785) Essai sur l'application de l'analyse à la probabilité des décisions rendues à la pluralité des voix (L'imprimerie Royale, Paris).

Coughlan, Peter (2000) 'In Defense of Unanimous Jury Verdicts: Mistrials, Communication, and Strategic Voting', *American Political Science Review*, 94, 375–93.

Davis, Douglas D. and Charles A. Holt (1992) *Experimental Economics* (Princeton, New Jersey: Princeton University Press).

Dawes, Robyn M. (1980) 'Social Dilemmas', *Annual Review of Psychology*, 31, 169–93.

Dickson, Eric (2009) 'Do Participants and Observers Assess Intentions Differently During Bargaining and Conflict?', *American Journal of Political Science*, 53, 910–30.

Downs, Anthony (1957) *An Economic Theory of Democracy* (New York: Harper and Row Publishers).

Drouvelis, Michalis, Maria Montero and Martin Sefton (2010) 'Gaining Power Through Enlargement: Strategic Foundations and Experimental Evidence', *Games and Economic Behavior*, 69, 274–92.

Feddersen, Timothy J. and Wolfgang Pesendorfer (1996) 'The Swing Voter's Curse', *American Economic Review*, 86, 408–24.

Feddersen, Timothy J. and Wolfgang Pesendorfer (1998) 'Convicting the Innocent: The Inferiority of Unanimous Jury Verdicts Under Strategic Voting', *American Political Science Review*, 92, 23–35.

Feddersen, Timothy J. and Alvaro Sandroni (2006) 'A Theory of Participation in Elections', *American Economic Review*, 96, 1271–82.

Fehr, Ernst and Klaus M. Schmidt (1999) 'A Theory of Fairness, Competition, and Cooperation', *Quarterly Journal of Economics*, 114, 817–68.

Fiorina, Morris P. and Charles R. Plott (1978) 'Committee Decisions under Majority Rule: An Experimental Study', *American Political Science Review*, 72, 575–98.

Fischbacher, Urs (2007) 'Z-Tree: A Toolbox for Readymade Economic Experiments', *Experimental Economics*, 10, 171–178.

Fischbacher, Urs, Christina M. Fong and Ernst Fehr (2009) 'Fairness, Errors, and the Power of Competition', *Journal of Economic Behavior & Organization*, 72, 527–45.

Forsythe, Robert, Roger B. Myerson, Thomas A. Rietz and Robert J. Weber (1993) 'An Experiment on coordination in Multi-candidate Elections: The Importance of Polls and Election Histories', *Social Choice and Welfare*, 10, 223–47.

Forsythe, Robert, Roger B. Myerson, Thomas A. Rietz and Robert J. Weber (1996) 'An Experiment of Voting Rules and Polls in Three-candidate Elections', *International Journal of Game Theory*, 25, 355–83.

Gerling, Kerstin, Hans Peter Grüner, Alexandra Kiel and Elisabeth Schulte (2005) 'Information Acquisition and Committee Decision Making: A Survey', *European Journal of Political Economy*, 21, 563–97.

Gerardi, Dino, Margaret A. McConnell, Julian Romero and Leeat Yariv (2009) 'Get Out the (Costly) Vote: Institutional Design for Greater Participation', Working Paper 121.

Gode, Dhananjay K and Shyam Sunder (1993) 'Allocative Efficiency of Markets with Zero-intelligence Traders: Markets as a Partial Substitute for Individual Rationality', *Journal of Political Economy*, 101, 119–37.

Goeree, Jacob K, Jens Großer and Brian W. Rogers (2009) 'Information Aggregation with Costly Voting: Theory and experiments', Working Paper.

Goeree, Jacob K and Charles A. Holt (2005) 'An Explanation of Anomalous Behavior in Models of Political Participation', *American Political Science Review*, 99, 201–13.

Goeree, Jacob K and Charles A. Holt (2010) 'Hierarchical Package Bidding: A Paper & Pencil Combinatorial Auction', *Games and Economic Behavior*, 70, 146–69.

Greiner, Ben (2004) 'The Online Recruitment System ORSEE 2.0 – A Guide for the Organization of Experiments in Economics', Working Paper Series in Economics 10 (University of Cologne).

Großer, Jens and Thorsten Giertz (2006) 'Candidates, Voters, and Endogenous Group Formation: An Experimental Study', Working paper.

Großer, Jens and Ernesto Reuben (2010) 'Redistributive Politics and Market Efficiency: An Experimental Study', Working paper.

Großer, Jens and Arthur Schram (2010) 'Public Opinion Polls, Voter Turnout, and Welfare: An Experimental Study', *American Journal of Political Science*, 54(3), 700–17.

Großer, Jens and Michael Seebauer (2009) 'Information Acquisition in Committees: An Experimental Study', Working paper.

Guarnaschelli, Serena, Richard D. McKelvey and Thomas R. Palfrey (2000) 'An Experimental Study of Jury Decision Rules', *American Political Science Review*, 94, 407–423.

Güth, Werner, Rolf Schmittberger and Bernd Schwarze (1982) 'An Experimental Analysis of Ultimatum Bargaining', *Journal of Economic Behavior and Organization*, 3, 367–88.

Hoffman, Elizabeth, Kevin McCabe, Keith Shachat and Vernon Smith (1994) 'Preferences, Property Rights, and Anonymity in Bargaining Games', *Games and Economic Behavior*, 7, 346–80.

Holt, Charles A. (2007) *Markets, Games, and Strategic Behavior* (Boston: Pearson, Addison Wesley).

Hotelling, Harold (1929) 'Stability in Competition', *Economic Journal*, 39, 41–57.

Hurwicz, Leonid (1960) 'Optimality and Informational Efficiency in Resource Allocation Processes' in Kenneth J. Arrow, Samuel Karlin and Patrick Suppes (eds.) *Mathematical Methods in Social Sciences* (Stanford: Stanford University Press).

Hurwicz, Leonid (1972) 'On Informationally Decentralized Systems' in C.B. McGuire, Roy Radner and Kenneth J. Arrow (eds.) *Decision and Organization: A Volume in Honor of Jacob Marschak* (Minneapolis: University of Minnesota Press).

Hurwicz, Leonid (2008) 'But Who Will Guard the Guardians?', *American Economic Review*, 98, 577–85.

Isaac, R. Mark and James M. Walker (1988) 'Group Size Effects in Public Goods Provision: The Voluntary Contribution Mechanism', *Quarterly Journal of Economics*, 103, 179–99.

Levine, David K. and Thomas R. Palfrey (2007) 'The Paradox of Voter Participation? A Laboratory Study', *American Political Science Review*, 101, 143–58.

Levine, Michael E. and Charles R. Plott (1977) 'Agenda Influence and its Implications' *Virginia Law Review*, 63, 561–604.

Lijphart, Arend (1997) 'Unequal Participation: Democracy's Unresolved Dilemma', *American Political Science Review*, 91, 1–14.

Maskin, Eric S. (2008) 'Mechanism Design: How to Implement Social Goals', *American Economic Review*, 98, 567–76.

McKelvey, Richard D. and Peter C. Ordeshook (1984) 'Rational Expectations in Elections: Some Experimental Results Based on a Multidimensional Model', *Public Choice*, 44, 61–102.

McKelvey, Richard D. and Peter C. Ordeshook (1990) 'A Decade of Experimental Research on Spatial Models of Elections and Committees' in Melvin J. Hinich and James M. Enelow (eds.) *Government, Democracy, and Social Choice* (Cambridge: Cambridge University Press).

McKelvey, Richard D. and Thomas R. Palfrey (1995) 'Quantal Response Equilibrium for Normal Form Games', *Games and Economic Behavior*, 10, 6–38.

McKelvey, Richard D. and Thomas R. Palfrey (1995) 'Quantal Response Equilibrium for Extensive Form Games', *Experimental Economics*, 1, 9–41.

Meirowitz, Adam (2006) 'Designing Institutions to Aggregate Preferences and Information', *Quarterly Journal of Political Science*, 1, 373–92.

Morton, Rebecca B. and Kenneth C. Williams (2010) *Experimental Political Science and the Study of Causality: From Nature to the Lab* (Cambridge, MA: Cambridge University Press).

Myerson, Roger B. (1993) 'Incentives to Cultivate Favored Minorities Under Alternative Electoral Systems', *American Political Science Review*, 87, 856–69.

Myerson, Roger B. (2008) 'Perspectives on Mechanism Design in Economic Theory', *American Economic Review*, 98, 586–603.

Ockenfels, Axel and Alvin E. Roth (2006) 'Late and Multiple Bidding in Second Price Internet Auctions: Theory and Evidence Concerning Different Rules for Ending an Auction', *Games and Economic Behavior*, 55, 297–320.

Palfrey, Thomas and Howard Rosenthal (1983) 'A Strategic Calculus of Voting', *Public Choice*, 41, 7–53.

Palfrey, Thomas and Howard Rosenthal (1985) 'Voter Participation and Strategic Uncertainty', *American Political Science Review*, 79, 62–78.

Plott, Charles R. and Michael E. Levine (1978) 'A Model of Agenda Influence on Committee Decision', *American Economic Review*, 68, 146–60.

Plott, Charles R. (1982). 'A Comparative Analysis of Direct Democracy, Two Candidate Elections, and Three Candidate Elections in an Experimental Environment', Social Science Working Paper 457 (California Institute of Technology).

Roth, Alvin E. (1995) 'Introduction to Experimental Economics' in John H. Kagel and Alvin E. Roth (eds.) *Handbook of Experimental Economics* (Princeton, New Jersey: Princeton University Press).

Smith, Vernon L. (1962) 'An Experimental Study of Competitive Market Behavior', *Journal of Political Economy*, 70, 111–37.

Van Lange, Paul A.M., Wilma Otten, Ellen M. N. de Bruin, and Jeffrey A. Joireman (1997) 'Development of Prosocial, Individualistic, and Competitive Orientations: Theory and Preliminary Evidence', *Journal of Personality and Social Psychology*, 73, 733–46.

# Part II
# Experimental Designs

# 5
# Strategic Voting in the Laboratory

*Nicolas Sauger, André Blais, Jean-François Laslier
and Karine van der Straeten*

The claim upon which most experiments in laboratories are conducted is that the random allocation of a treatment among various groups or individuals makes it possible to draw accurate inferences about causality. The laboratory is a context insulated from outside influences so that variations in behavior can be attributed to differences in treatment. Yet, the laboratory is not remote from all noises characterizing the 'real world'. The issue of internal validity is probably overlooked too often because threats to external validity appear to be the most important (McDermott, 2002; Green and Gerber, 2004). Most experiments in political science are faced with potential threats to internal validity which are often unavoidable. The good news is that most of these problems have no significant impact on the results; the outcomes of an experiment prove to be rather resilient to marginal changes of core characteristics (as remarked earlier by Fiorina and Plott, 1978). This is our general argument, supported by a series of experiments on electoral systems and strategic voting.

We report on a series of experiments held in 2006 and 2007 (Blais et al., 2007; Blais et al., 2011; Van der Straeten et al., 2010).[1] These experiments originate in the literature on electoral systems and their consequences on party competition and electoral outcomes. As Taagepera has put it, while their macro-level consequences are reasonably well understood along the lines of the 'duvergerian' agenda, the micro foundations of these regularities have still to be uncovered (Taagepera, 2007). To contribute to this, we have set up experiments aimed at understanding strategic voting. Strategic voting – as opposed to sincere voting, that is, voting for your first preference – has been considered to be a key explanation of the psychological effects of electoral systems, as voters anticipate the mechanical effects of electoral laws in transforming a distribution of votes into a distribution of seats (Duverger, 1951).

Two main debates have framed discussions on strategic voting: the extent to which voting decisions are based on strategic calculations on the one hand, and the type of cognitive process at play in these strategic calculations, on the other. These debates originate in the discrepancies between formal models predicting the number of 'viable' candidates (depending on the magnitude of constituencies), which are based on rational choice assumptions (Myerson and Weber, 1993; Cox, 1997) and mixed results provided by empirical studies of vote choice. Yet, most empirical studies cannot actually test the assumptions on which formal models are based because the required information is not available in individual surveys (Alvarez and Nagler, 2000). Hence the usage of laboratory experiments. They make it possible to control for preferences and then to understand the role of preferences and the mediation of the electoral system in vote choice. A number of laboratory experiments have indeed been run on this topic (for an overview, see Rietz, 2008 and Palfrey, 2009). The series of experiments we proposed differed from them by providing a more complex experimental setup, allowing multiple candidates, a large number of voters and variations in electoral systems.

The experimental design and its origins are described in details in the next section. The following section presents the main results. We end this chapter by an evaluation of the validity of these experiments, discussing the practical lessons in a concluding section.

## 5.1    Theory and experimental design

Our main focus in these series of experiments was to compare effects on voters' behavior of two specific electoral systems, plurality and majority run-off systems, in a context of presidential-like elections.

The two systems offer contrasted hypotheses in terms of strategic voting. On the one hand, plurality elections have been considered as a benchmark. Most theories of strategic voting have been developed on the basis of this electoral system and most empirical evaluations of the spread of strategic vote choice is based on countries with a plurality system (Alvarez and Nagler, 2000; Alvarez et al., 2006). The general assumption is that the plurality system fosters two-party competition because a significant number of voters do vote strategically. On the other hand, run-off elections have yielded divergent hypotheses. From a theoretical point of view, run-off elections offer large opportunities for a strategic vote. Cox (1997) claims that three effective candidates represent an equilibrium solution because the run-off makes it possible for two candidates to move to a second round. Competition takes place between the first losing candidate (the third candidate in the first round) and the second winning candidate (winner of a place in the run-off), assuming that voters are short-sighted and do not anticipate the effects of who makes it to the run-off on who actually wins the election. On the other hand, the empirical study of strategic voting produces mixed results, pointing either at the weak prevalence of such a logic in actual run-off systems or at the existence of 'perverted' forms of strategic votes such as 'inverse strategic voting' as in France in the 2002 presidential election (Blais, 2004). In this case, voters took for granted who was going to make it to the run-off and thus deserted their first preference to send messages to leading candidates. In few words, we can expect from the literature that both electoral systems are associated with a significant level of strategic voting, though the consequences of run-off systems are more uncertain. What is then the extent of the differences between these two systems? We devised an experiment to answer this question.

Protocol building is a lengthy process. Despite its obvious simplicity, the setup of our experiments has in fact been developed over a period of two years by a large team composed of theoretical economists and behavioral political scientists[2], none of whom specifically trained in experimental methods. Its basic features were quickly agreed upon. The experiments were designed to ascertain the impact of electoral systems on voters' behavior in a simple context; that is, attention was entirely focused on electoral rules.

From this general intention, two sharply contrasted options emerged. On the one hand was a protocol inspired by experiments in psychology to understand how people solve the trade-off between efficacy (through strategic adaptation to the viability of various options) and commitment to values. This is the approach followed by Lewis-Beck and Wittrock (2007). This protocol tries to be 'realistic' so that external validity should be enhanced. It is realistic in the sense that it tries to mimic more closely what actually happens in real-world elections. Subjects play their role in accordance with their own preferences and decide their vote after an electoral campaign (based on fake electoral statements, for instance). Efforts are made to act 'as if' these were actual elections. This makes it easier to interpret and generalize the results to actual elections since it is only the context of vote choice that is manipulated. The alternative option is closer to experimental economics. Its main characteristic is the inducement of preferences through monetary incentives.[3] This may be 'unrealistic' (people do not vote to earn money), but it greatly facilitates the interpretation since, assuming no systematic difference in the value of money across groups, there is no *a priori* difference across groups except for treatments. The emphasis is put, in this case, on the comparability and the possibility of replication of the experiments. The results are expected to be linked then, only to the experimental design and not, for instance, to the distribution of preferences in the target population. This substantially improves internal validity because there is no intervening and uncontrolled variable between the treatment and the behavior of interest.

Our team chose the option closer to behavioral economics. The experimental protocol remained to be set up. As we were interested in testing the effects of two-round majority run-off elections compared to plurality in the context of presidential-like elections, we chose a simple framework of unidimensional politics, single-peaked preferences and pay-offs distributed in accordance with the distance between voters' positions and the elected

Univ.-Bibl. Bamberg UB Bamberg ausgeschieden

candidate's position according to a purely linear transformation. Yet, as we show in the sequel, the trade-off between internal (quality of the inference within the target population studied, Morton and Williams, 2010: 255) and external validity (quality of the inference beyond the target population, Morton and Williams, 2010: 255) is not always clear cut.

The space we used in these experiments was represented by a horizontal axis, going from left to right[4], divided in 21 different positions. The experiments were conducted in groups of 21 subjects, more than what is generally observed in voting experiments. A unique position was randomly attributed to each subject[5], forming a flat distribution. The idea was to make the subjects' task as simple and as transparent as possible. Most of the fine-tuning of the protocol was about the exact positioning of candidates along this axis.

Determining the exact location of options (alternatively called candidates) was achieved after a few pre-tests. Contrary to many voting experiments, we preferred to have more than three candidates. The primary reason for this was to make it possible to differentiate different types of desertion of the first preference. With more than three candidates, it is possible to distinguish the optimal decisions from decisions which have a strategic underpinning, but which do not correspond to the prediction of a utility-maximization assumption. Another reason was external to the experiment and focused on contemporary developments in various political systems, having experienced the growth of fringe parties since the 1980s. We decided to have elections featuring five candidates. Figure 5.1 shows the exact positions of these candidates, which are perfectly symmetrical. This symmetry eases the analysis because it can be read as if positions (except for the median position) are replicated once.

Four more issues were discussed in the elaboration of the protocol: the number of subjects, their recruitment, the organization of the protocol in series of elections and the addition of a questionnaire.

The experiment was run in groups of 21 subjects. This number had been chosen as a kind of compromise between the usual small groups which one usually finds in lab experiments and larger groups, which would convey greater external validity. The assumption is that strategic behavior is driven by the potential impact of each individual vote choice (that is, the probability to be pivotal). Hence, smaller groups would tend to produce more strategic behavior. To test this hypothesis, a few larger groups of 63 subjects

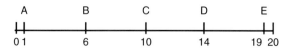

*Figure 5.1*   Positions of Candidates

were also included in our setup. Surprisingly perhaps, the extent of strategic voting did not seem to be affected significantly by the size of the group. The number of 21 was finally chosen in accordance with the facilities we had and the actual number of people we could host.

The recruitment of these subjects varied significantly because the protocol of our experiments included three different places of observation: Paris and Lille in France, and Montreal in Canada. Comparing plurality and run-off elections, we wanted to see if the patterns were different in Montreal, where people were less familiar with two rounds (we found little difference).[6] These locations had different modes of subject recruitment. In Paris and Montreal, subjects were invited from lists of experimental laboratories in which they voluntarily enrolled, while Lille subjects were undergraduate students in law following political science courses. Of course, this means the very context of experiments also varied, from in-class experiments in Lille, to laboratory experiments in Paris.

The participants were invited to vote in successive elections. These elections were divided in groups of four. During these four elections, the electoral system and voters' positions were held constant. This repetition aimed at enabling voters to gain a better understanding of the electoral system and to learn to coordinate. A secondary objective was to get more observations. Each group of subjects participated in two or three series of four elections, alternating randomly plurality and run-off in the first two series. When a third series was held, another electoral system was implemented, either the alternative vote or approval voting.

A related issue is which elections to consider for payments. We feared that if all elections were to 'count', learning and coordination would not be encouraged and the stakes might be considered to be too low since the general amount of money we could spend on the experiment was fixed. If the last election were the only one to be taken into account, a complex game might emerge over all the different ballots of the series, as we observed in pilot studies, which would lead some people to alter dramatically their behavior in the last election. This would have prevented us from using the whole series as actual observations. Hence the decision was made to select a 'decisive' election by a lottery. This made it possible to increase the apparent payoff of the experiment (a kind of payoff illusion). If there had been a payment for each election, gains would have been less than one-tenth in each election, and the difference between outcomes would have been likely perceived as minimal (with an expected gain of less than 1 euro by election).

The last main decision was the inclusion of questionnaires in the experiment. Two sorts of questions were asked. At the time of voting, subjects were asked to provide their expectations about each candidate's chances of winning on a scale ranging from zero to 10. This was done for about half the groups. The main advantage of doing so was direct access to the perceived viability of each candidate by voters, which is a key information in assessing strategic voting. We were concerned, however, that asking this question would alter the results because it was a clear and obvious hint about expected cognitive processes. Subjects may have been more strategic because they were almost invited to do so. Besides these questions about chances of winning, the protocol included a questionnaire at the end of the experiment to collect information about the subjects' socio-demographic profile and political preferences.

To sum up, the basics of our protocol was a laboratory voting experiment based on monetary induced preferences over a horizontal axis with a fixed set of options to be chosen among. The pay-offs were determined by a lottery among all election results and computed as the difference between 20 euros (or Canadian dollars) and the distance between the elected candidate's position and their own position. Two to three series of four elections were held in groups of 21 subjects, under different electoral rules (plurality, run-off, alternative vote, approval voting) which represented our main treatments. These experiments were held in 2006–2007, with 22 groups, 216 elections and 713 participants.

Several variants of this basic protocol were used in these different groups, including the number of participants (up to 63), the location and mode of the experiment and the use of questionnaires. These variations are documented in Table 5.1 Other variations have not been documented, such as who ran the experiment in the various locations, the political connotations instilled and all other unmeasured contextual characteristics. The year 2007 was an election year in France, the presidential (run-off) election being held in April. Politicization of subjects may have varied accordingly.

The rest of the chapter presents the main results and then turns to the discussion of their robustness and validity.

## 5.2   Results

Results from this protocol have been published in various papers (Blais et al., 2007; Blais et al., 2010; Van der Straeten et al., 2010) and are generally restricted to the comparison of one-round plurality elections to two-round run-off elections (except for Van der Straeten et al., 2010).

### 5.2.1   Aggregate results

Given the exact replication of the same protocol under plurality and run-off rules, any difference in electoral outcomes may be attributed to the effects of the electoral system, once controlled for explicit variations in the protocol. We also consider in this section two main characteristics of the elections observed to control for the difference between plurality and run-off systems, about which we have a direct interest. The first variation is group size, as it may have a direct impact on the opportunities for strategic behavior.

*Table 5.1*  Main Variants of the Protocol

| Place | Date | Number of Subjects | Electoral Systems | Number of Elections | Expectations about Outcomes |
|---|---|---|---|---|---|
| Paris | 2006–12–11 | 21 | 2/1/App | 12 | Yes |
| | | 21 | 1/2/App | 12 | Yes |
| | 2006–12–13 | 21 | 2/1/App | 12 | Yes |
| | | 21 | 1/2/App | 12 | Yes |
| | 2006–12–18 | 21 | 2/1/STV | 12 | No |
| | | 21 | 1/2/STV | 12 | No |
| | 2006–12–19 | 21 | 2/1/STV | 12 | No |
| | | 21 | 1/2/STV | 12 | No |
| | 2007–01–15 | 21 | 2/1/App | 12 | No |
| | | 21 | 1/2/App | 12 | No |
| Lille | 2006–12–18 | 21 | 2/1 | 8 | Yes |
| | 2006–12–18 | 21 | 1/2 | 8 | Yes |
| | 2006–12–18 | 61 | 1/2 | 8 | Yes |
| | 2006–12–18 | 64 | 2/1 | 8 | Yes |
| Montréal | 2007–02–19 | 21 | 1/2 | 8 | No |
| | | 21 | 2/1 | 8 | No |
| | 2007–02–20 | 21 | 1/2 | 8 | Yes |
| | | 21 | 2/1 | 8 | Yes |
| | 2007–02–21 | 63 | 1/2 | 8 | No |
| | | 63 | 2/1 | 8 | No |
| | 2007–02–22 | 63 | 1/2 | 8 | Yes |
| | | 63 | 2/1 | 8 | Yes |

1: Plurality elections; 2: Majority run-off; STV: Alternative vote; App: Approval voting

The second variation is the position of the election within the series of elections, since we can expect learning and communication effects to emerge.

At first glance, the results of our experiments are striking because of the similarity between plurality and run-off elections. In both cases, candidates *A* and *E*, holding extreme positions, never win, whereas candidate *C*, the Condorcet winner, is elected about half of the time. *C* is elected 42 times under plurality (48 per cent) and 48 times under run-off (55 per cent).[7]

The only difference in electoral outcomes is in fact to be found between small groups of 21 subjects and large groups of 63 subjects. Under the run-off system, candidate *C* is more likely to win in large groups (75 per cent) compared with smaller groups (47 per cent). This could be read as an indication of even higher strategic voting in larger groups. Yet, this result does not appear to be significant as we found no difference between larger and smaller groups under the plurality system. This difference can be thus regarded as a result of chance, due to the limited number of elections held in large groups (only six groups, amounting to 24 elections held under each rule).

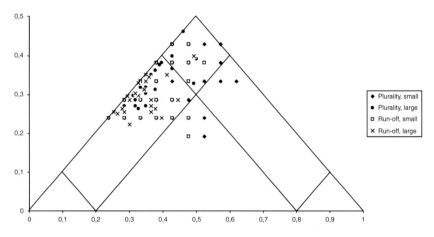

*Figure 5.2*   Scores of the Top-two Contenders (Nagayama triangles)

The comparative statics of our experiments should also be extended to the comparison of patterns of competition, beyond electoral results. Hypotheses about the effects of electoral systems have indeed focused on the number of viable parties rather than on which candidate is more likely to be elected. Even fragmentation, though higher in run-off elections as expected, does not show important differences. The number of effective parties (Laakso and Taagepera, 1979) grows from 3.2 under plurality to 3.6 under run-off.[8]

To explore in more depth the patterns of competition, we propose a visualization of them through the so-called Nagayama triangle technique (Grofman et al., 2004)[9] in Figures 5.2 and 5.3. These diagrams indicate the top two candidates on the one hand, and the second and third candidates on the other hand, depending on the electoral system and group size. Following Gary Cox (1997), we expect that plurality elections lead to close competition between first and second finishers, while run-offs lead to close competition between second and third finishers (closeness is here materialized as the fist diagonal on the graphs). This is not confirmed by these graphs. On the whole, dots do not cluster in accordance with these characteristics. Nevertheless, some interesting features emerge. First, there is apparently more variance for plurality elections compared to run-off. Second, fragmentation is confirmed to be less important in plurality elections (more dots close to the line $x + y = 1$). Third, some elections are dominated by one candidate in plurality (top finisher above the fifty per cent threshold); this is never the case under run-off.

If comparative statics at this general level do not reveal a sharp contrast between the effects of plurality and run-off methods, these results, in fact,

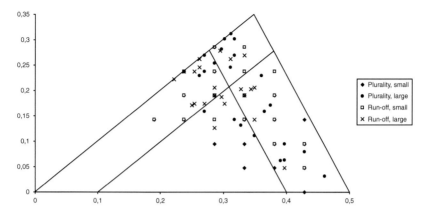

*Figure 5.3* Scores of the Second and Third Finishers (Nagayma triangles)

are overshadowed by similarities in the initial situation. Remember that the experiment is performed in series of four consecutive elections. Differences are indeed limited in the first election of the series but grow larger and larger during the series. Indeed, the dynamics of plurality and run-off elections are quite divergent. The third candidate sees its score decreasing steadily under plurality, while it is rather stable under run-off. Meanwhile, the first contender increases his score over all elections of series in plurality elections, whereas his score remains stable after the second election of the run-off series. This process can be viewed as the result of learning and reciprocal adaptation in the search of a situation of equilibrium. Neither situation, however, confirms Gary Cox's hypotheses on the effects of electoral systems. The gap between the first and second candidate increases under plurality, as does the difference between the second and third candidates under run-off. In other terms, voters apparently develop voting strategies which are different under these two electoral rules but neither case seems to correspond to expectations if voters were strictly instrumental.

### 5.2.2 Individual results

To uncover the individual logics resulting in these aggregate dynamics, we turn to the analysis of individual vote choice. This analysis is based on two components upon which these choices can be made: the voter's proximity to different candidates, and the voter's preference for a determined outcome. Proximity is taken for 'sincere' voting – that is, voters choose candidates closest to them. Preference over outcomes is different, since it entails expectations about the outcome of the election. In this context, the voter may try to influence the expected outcome. In order to do so, she can either not vote for weaker candidates (nonviable candidates with no chance of winning the

*Table 5.2*   A Conditional Logit Model of Vote Choice

| | Plurality elections | | | Run-off elections | | |
|---|---|---|---|---|---|---|
| | Model 1 | Model 2 | Model 3 | Model 1 | Model 2 | Model 3 |
| Distance | −0.48*** | −0.46*** | −0.48*** | −0.50*** | −0.48*** | −0.50*** |
| Viability (current election) | 0.13*** | | | 0.11*** | | |
| Viability (previous election) | | 0.16*** | | | 0.09*** | |
| Viability (perceived) | | | 6.90*** | | | 4.71*** |
| A | −1.58*** | −2.00*** | −1.12*** | −1.56*** | −1.93*** | −1.44*** |
| B | −0.20** | −0.19* | −0.18* | −0.18* | −0.09 | −0.05 |
| D | −0.37*** | −0.53*** | −0.38*** | −0.28*** | −0.20* | −0.13 |
| E | −1.78 | −2.09*** | −1.36*** | −1.71*** | −2.20*** | −1.56*** |
| Pseudo R² | 0.547 | 0.549 | 0.588 | 0.528 | 0.517 | 0.549 |
| N | 14200 | 10650 | 8200 | 14205 | 10670 | 8200 |

contest) or try to build from their pivotal position – if any – to influence the outcome.

To test for the importance of each of these components of vote choice, we follow Blais et al. (2010) to analyze individual vote choice through a conditional logit model. The general idea is to test the importance of both: the distance from a given candidate, and the candidate's viability to assess the probability a voter has to vote for this candidate. We use a simple measure of distance as the difference between the candidate's and the voter's positions. Three different measures of viability are considered: viability in the current election, measured as the difference between the score of the leading candidate and that of the candidate; viability in the previous election; and perceived viability, from questionnaire data.[10] The results of this analysis are shown in table 5.2.

The expectation is that the propensity to vote for a candidate decreases with distance from a candidate, and increases with her viability. We thus predict a negative coefficient for distance and a positive coefficient for viability. This pattern should hold for one-round and two-round elections alike. But strategic considerations should play less in run-off elections, and thus viability should have a weaker coefficient. As predicted, results presented in Table 5.2 return negative coefficients for distance and positive ones for viability. Yet, differences between plurality and run-off prove once again limited though rather consistent over all three measures of viability. Moreover, dummies controlling for effects linked to candidates are significant and always detrimental to fringe candidates. Desertion of the extremes is thus not only led by perceptions of viability but also by systematic effects due to candidates' positions. Notice that this effect is slightly stronger under plurality, reinforcing the conclusion of the stronger psychological effects of this electoral system.

The contrast between plurality and run-off systems is even sharper if attention is restricted to the last elections of each series. Including only the last two elections of each series, the coefficient associated with perceived viability decreases from 6.45 with a plurality system to 3.86 with run-off. The desertion of fringe candidates remains at a high level. We may also notice the specific negative coefficient attached to candidate D in plurality elections, whereas no significant effect is observed in run-off elections. This may be a further indication of the restrictive effect of the plurality system.

Van der Straeten et al. (2010) offer a detailed analysis of individual votes by determining for each of them whether it can be considered as 'instrumental' or not. They show that voters tend to vote instrumentally as long as the computations required to determine the optimal choice are not too complicated. Since the strategic recommendations are more complicated in two-round than in one-round elections, there is less instrumental voting with the two-round system, and voters' behavior is better explained by ad-hoc rules.

Our main conclusions are threefold. First, subjects adapt their behavior in accordance with the rules of the game, that is, the electoral system. Second, their behavior responds to the two main components assumed by strategic voting, that is, utility and viability. Third, plurality and run-off elections differ both in the extent of strategic voting and in how these strategic calculations are made, although these differences are limited in terms of actual results and become significant only after a period of learning.

## 5.3 Validity

As with any experimental setup, the question is whether these results have some validity. The issues of external validity and construct validity – do they reveal anything about behaviors in real elections? – are most difficult. One answer is that such an experimental design makes it possible to identify the upper bound for strategic voting possibilities. If voters in the laboratory do not strategically support candidates to change the balance in the second round in a run-off, it is difficult to believe that they would engage in such behavior in real elections. We prefer to focus on the issue of internal validity as the accuracy of the inferences made about causal effects of our main treatment variable.

As already shown, the interpretation of the results of these experiments heavily depends on which results are considered. If all elections are taken into account, the conclusion is an absence of difference linked to the electoral system. Differences become significant only in the last two elections of each series. In the same perspective, differences could also stem from the order in which a voting rule is utilized; that is, people may vote differently depending on whether they start with plurality or runoff. To control for that possibility, half of the groups were randomly assigned one round, and the other half two rounds for the first set of elections. The patterns reported here are very similar if we consider only the first set of four elections.

The issue of internal validity can also be addressed by estimating the consequences of 'uncontrolled' treatments. As documented in Table 5.1, both the inclusion of questionnaires about expectations concerning electoral outcomes and the location of the experiments were not randomized. For instance, questionnaires are systematically included in Lille, forty per cent of the time in Paris and in half of the sessions in Montreal. Location is not distributed randomly as well. This is all more problematic since the location is associated with diverse types of treatment variables. Group size distribution is not the same across places, with no large groups in Paris, but a majority of all small groups there. We were not able to take into account all these variations in our previous estimations because it would not only entail controlling for these variations, but also the interactions of these variations with our variables of interest. We propose here some simple tests to assess the extent that these uncontrolled variations may have biased our results.

### 5.3.1 Does measuring perceptions of viability affect behavior?

The first question to be addressed is whether tapping participants' perceptions of the candidates' chances of winning modifies their behavior. The concern here is a priming effect. It may be that when we ask people to indicate the various candidates' chances of winning, we lead them to pay more attention to viability considerations.

It is possible that some people do not 'naturally' think in terms of viability but were primed to consider it because we 'induced' them to think about the candidates' chances through our question which appeared on their ballot. If it were so, we would have unwillingly inflated the amount of strategic voting in our experiments.

We can check that possibility by comparing the vote obtained by candidates $A$ and $E$ in the series that included the question about expectations to the series without the question on the candidates' chances of winning. In about half of our groups (10/22), participants were not asked to rate the candidates' chances.

Table 5.3 presents the findings. There is no difference between the two sets of experiments and the small differences that emerge thereafter are in the direction opposite to the priming hypothesis (greater support for candidates $A$ and $E$ when people are asked about chances of winning). There is thus no evidence of a priming effect. The conclusion is that the great majority of participants 'naturally' think strategically; they do not have to be reminded that some candidates are not viable. Hence, our results are not biased by the inclusion in the analysis of data from both types of groups.

*Table 5.3*  Total Vote Share Obtained by Candidates A and E in Experiments With and Without Chances of Winning Question

|  | First Election (%) | | Second Election (%) | | Third Election (%) | | Fourth Election (%) | |
| --- | --- | --- | --- | --- | --- | --- | --- | --- |
| Can: | Without | With | Without | With | Without | With | Without | With |
| A & E | 20.0 | 20.3 | 8.8 | 11.3 | 4.1 | 8.1 | 2.7 | 6.2 |
| N | 295 | 418 | 295 | 418 | 295 | 418 | 295 | 418 |

### 5.3.2  Does location change behavior?

In terms of validity, one of the main advantages of our protocol has been replication across places. In this case, variations in the size of groups strengthen both internal and external validity. Internal validity, because it ascertains the role of our main treatment (controlled by group size), and external validity because elections are usually held in large groups. Yet, this has in fact weakened the internal validity of the experiment. There was no large group in one of the three locations (Paris) of our experiments because the facilities did not allow it. Location itself is a treatment, but not administered randomly over the set of subjects. It refers to the institutional context, the basic hypothesis being that familiarity with one electoral system (plurality in Canada, run-off in France) would make strategic use of the electoral system more likely.[11] Then, it would not have been the electoral system having an effect in itself, but socialization. Location is moreover not only about the national context. It also entails differences across the very academic context within which the experiments are conducted, for instance. We have already documented significant differences among Lille, Montreal and Paris series in terms of subject pools, recruitment and use of laboratory facilities. Nonrandom allocation of location is thus a significant breach on usual assumptions of experimental methods. Yet, the problem is not linked to a faulty construction of the protocol, since it is not possible to allocate subjects randomly to the different places.

Controlling for the effect of location directly is not easy because there is, for instance, no large group in Paris. At the aggregate level, there is no systematic difference among electoral outcomes. To go beyond this observation, we propose to proceed in two steps, building on the existence of a questionnaire on participants' characteristics in all three places. We first confirm the existence of systematic differences among subjects' characteristics, depending on location. We then observe to what extent these characteristics have systematic effects on behavior.

We use three different variables to define individual characteristics: gender, area of interest (humanities or sciences) and position on a left-right scale. Differences are indeed significant. Males represent 29 per cent of subjects in Lille, 48 per cent in Paris and 51 per cent in Montreal. In Lille,

*Table 5.4*  Probability of Voting Sincerely According to Voters' Positions and Subjects' Characteristics

|  | **Plurality elections** | **Run-off elections** |
|---|---|---|
| Constant | 4.33*** | 4.38*** |
| Distance to median | −0.29*** | −0.28*** |
| Difference between own and assigned position | −0.03* | −0.02 |
| Area of interest (humanities) | −0.16 | −0.03 |
| Gender (female) | −0.04 | −0.07 |
| Adjusted R² | 0.336 | 0.358 |
| N | 614 | 614 |

85 per cent of the subjects are mostly interested in humanities, 45 per cent of Paris' subjects have this interest and 41 per cent of subjects in Montreal have this interest. The distribution of left-right position of subjects is in fact what is most similar across the different locations. On a 0 to 20 scale, the average position is 9.32 in Lille, 9.27 in Paris 9.63 in Montreal.

Given these differences, the issue is whether they have an impact on vote choices. To get a simple indication of this impact, we run an OLS regression explaining the number of sincere votes cast by voters. According to previous results, this number of sincere votes should vary according to the position of the voter in the experiment (distance to the median position, more extreme positions being associated with more desertion). We expect individual characteristics not to have any significant effects. These characteristics are gender, area of interest and difference between the subject's left-right position and her personal self-placement on the same scale. The results of these regressions are presented both for the plurality and the majority rule in Table 5.4. As expected, none of the individual characteristics plays a significant role in the probability of casting a sincere vote. The only – substantially insignificant – exception is that increasing the distance between the subject personal self-placement on the left-right scale and her assigned position decreased its likelihood of casting a vote by three percentage points. The internal validity of the results of these experiments is then preserved because there is no systematic correlation between uncontrolled variations and variables of interest.

## 5.4   Conclusions

In this chapter, we have presented a series of experiments about the effects of electoral systems and the prevalence of strategic voting in the laboratory. We have shown that these systems are associated with different levels and different types of strategic reasoning, leading to different electoral outcomes once preliminary elections have conveyed enough hindsight and opportunities for coordination. In this respect, one of the first practical lessons drawn from these experiments concerns the definition of which observations (all of them or just the last ones) to be included in the final dataset if learning is allowed or suspected in a protocol.

Our protocol included several variants, including varying group size, order of the series of elections, inclusion of a questionnaire about expectations and so on. Besides the electoral system, the main variation has, however, been associated with the different locations where these experiments have been run (Lille, Montreal and Paris). Location was not randomized over the whole set of elections not only because the pool of subjects was not shared across these different locations, but also because supplementary treatments have not been distributed randomly across these locations. More generally, this chapter has shown that experiments are in fact often suffering from several uncontrolled and nonrandomized variations. This is due to the many parameters not included in protocols (from temperature in the lab to the mood of the instructor), and to more specific reasons. In our case, for instance, it was due to the large and international team of researchers having initiated these experiments. In other terms, these variations are unavoidable to some extent.

These uncontrolled or nonrandom variations should be avoided as far as possible. Also, more attention should be put on the careful organization of the different treatments included in the protocol, for instance through randomized-block designs. Yet, deviations from perfect randomization may bring significant added value to the experiment as did our international collaboration. In this case, we would argue that departure from pure randomization may be acceptable as long as there were strong assumptions that the nonrandom treatment has a priori no systematic effect and if enough supplementary controls are included in the protocol so as to be able to check for the absence of major bias and for the robustness of the results. Bias is, in this case, less likely because the experimental setting taps into some general – if not universal – type of behavioral response.

## Notes

1. We thank the various institutions and colleagues that made it possible to collect all data, especially the programme 'Deux tours' led by Annie Laurent and funded by the French Agence Nationale de la Recherche. We also thank Simon Labbé Saint-Vincent for assistance and fruitful discussions.
2. Besides the authors of this paper, these discussions included Bernard Dolez, Annie Laurent, Michael Lewis-Beck and Christian-Marie Wallon-Leducq, whom we thank here.
3. Another major difference between these two strands of research is the use of deception. Following the experimental economics tradition, we chose not use deception and we revealed all major components of the protocol to subjects.

4. Discussions were rather heated on whether or not this axis was represented as a left-right axis to the subjects because of the obvious political connotations.
5. Random draw within a fixed set of 21 positions, each position drawn being excluded for further draw. This was achieved either by distributing 21 different envelops, with a different position in each one, or by randomized allocation by the computer.
6. Of course, familiarity with the electoral system is not the only possible explanation of systematic difference. The point is, however, that the places of observation are not associated, fortunately, with systematic variations.
7. Differences are indeed sharper if electoral outcomes are compared to the results of other systems. With this same protocol, Van der Straeten et al. (2010) show that approval voting leads to the almost systematic election of the Condorcet winner, whereas it never wins under the alternative vote.
8. This number of effective parties is computed as $n=1/\Sigma(s_i)^2$ with $s_i$ being the vote share of each party.
9. 'Nagayama triangles' (and more especially the segmented version of Nagayama triangles) are used here as an exploratory method. Nagayama triangles are based on constituency-level data. This kind of diagram is used to show the vote share of the largest party on the x-axis, and the vote share of second largest party on the y-axis. Because the second largest party must receive fewer votes than the largest party, the feasible set of values in the diagram lies within a triangle bounded by the x-axis and segments of the line $x-y=0$ and $x+y=1$. These diagrams thus display information about the relative score of the two largest parties and information about the aggregated score of all the other parties (it is the distance between the plot and the nearest segment).
10. This perceived viability has been normalized by dividing the viability on a 10-points scale attributed to a candidate by the sum of the scores of all candidates.
11. Of course, the location of experiments is correlated with many dimensions of the electoral system, from national political culture to the academic system and laboratory facilities.

# References

Alvarez, R. Michael, Fred Boehmke and Jonathan Nagler (2006) 'Strategic Voting in British Elections', *Electoral Studies*, 25, 1–19.

Alvarez, R. Michael and Jonathan Nagler (2000) 'A New Approach for Modelling Strategic Voting in Multiparty Elections', *British Journal of Political Science*, 30, 57–75.

Blais, André (2004) 'Strategic Voting in the 2002 French Presidential Election' in *The French Voter: before and after the 2002 elections* (Basingstoke: Palgrave).

Blais, André, Simon Labbé-St-Vincent, Jean-François Laslier, Nicolas Sauger and Karine Van der Straeten (2011) 'Strategic vote choice in one round and two round elections: An experimental study', *Political Research Quarterly*, 64, 637–645.

Blais, André, Jean-François Laslier, Annie Laurent, Nicolas Sauger and Karine Van der Straeten (2007) 'One Round versus Two Round Elections: an Experimental Study', *French Politics*, 5, 278–286.

Cox, Gary W. (1997) *Making Votes Count: Strategic Coordination in the World's Electoral Systems* (Cambridge: Cambridge University Press).

Duverger, Maurice (1951) *Les partis politiques* (Paris: Armand Colin).

Fioriana, Morris and Charles Plott (1978) 'Committee Decisions Under Majority Rule: An Experimental Study', *American Political Science Review*, 72, 575–598.

Green, Donald P. and Gerber, Alan S. (2004) 'Experimental Methods in the Political Science', *American Behavioral Scientist*, 47, 485–487.

Grofman, Bernard, Alessandro Chiaramonte, Roberto D'Alimonte and Scott L. Feld (2004) 'Comparing and Contrasting the Uses of Two Graphical Tools for Displaying Patterns of Multiparty Competition', *Party Politics*, 10, 273–299.

Laakso, Markku and Rein Taagepera (1979) 'Effective number of parties: a measure with application to West Europe', *Comparative Political Studies*, 12, 3–27.

Lewis-Beck, Michael S. and Jill Wittrock (2007) 'Experimenting with French Election Rules: Initial Results', *French Politics*, 5, 106–117.

McDermott, Rose (2002) 'Experimental Methods in Political Science', *Annual Review of Political Science*, 5, 31–61.

Morton, Rebecca B. and Kenneth C. Williams (2010) *Experimental Political Science and the Study of Causality. From Nature to the Lab* (Cambridge: Cambridge University Press).

Myerson, Roger B. and Robert J. Weber (1993) 'A theory of voting equilibria', *American Political Science Review*, 87, 102–114.

Palfrey, Thomas (2009) 'Laboratory Experiments in Political Economy', *Annual Review of Political Science*, 12, 379–388.

Rietz, Thomas (2008) 'Three-way Experimental Election Results: Strategic Voting, Coordinated Outcomes and Duverger's Law' in Charles R. Plott and Vernon L. Smith, *The Handbook of Experimental Economic Results, Volume 1* (Amsterdam: Elsevier).

Taagepera, Rein (2007) 'Electoral systems' in Carles Boix and Susan C. Stokes, *The Oxford Handbook of Comparative Politics* (Oxford: Oxford University Press).

Van der Straeten, Karine, Jean-François Laslier, Nicolas Sauger and André Blais (2010) 'Strategic, Sincere, and Heuristic Voting under Four Election Rules: An Experimental Study', *Social Choice and Welfare* 35, 435–472.

# 6
# Survey Experiments: Partisan Cues in Multi-party Systems

*Ted A. Brader and Joshua A. Tucker*

## 6.1 Introduction[1]

While the vast majority of the chapters in this volume focus on experiments conducted in a laboratory setting, experiments have also long been prevalent in the discipline in the context of survey research. While many of these earlier experiments were designed with the idea of teasing out the nuances of survey research itself, the survey-based experiment remains an excellent option for researchers interested in exploring substantive questions of politics to this day (Gaines et al., 2006). With that in mind, the purpose of this chapter is two-fold. We begin by explaining the value of survey experiments as a research tool for political scientists generally. We then spend the bulk of the chapter illustrating the types of questions and challenges that can come up in survey experiments through the rubric of one particular experiment we designed to explore the effects of partisan cues in the multi-party systems of Poland, Hungary and Russia. We conclude the chapter with a brief discussion of the use of deception in survey experiments, including why it is often necessary and the extent to which it has different consequences from the use of deception in lab-based experiments.

## 6.2 Types of experiments

Let us begin with a modest attempt at defining the different types of experiments that are most commonly employed in political science. Experiments include at least two critical features. First, researchers manipulate the extent to which participants are exposed to some potential causal factor (a 'treatment') in a controlled manner, such that only one variable of interest is changed in any given treatment. In many experiments, some participants are not exposed to the variable of interest at all, or to a baseline level, in a condition commonly referred to as the 'control group'. Second, researchers randomly assign participants to the treatment and control conditions. They do so to ensure, to the greatest extent possible, that participants are identical across conditions on all observed *and unobserved* variables other than the treatment.[2] If these procedures are followed, then researchers can infer with considerable confidence that differences across conditions in any outcome measured (after exposure) have been caused by the change in the treatment. Thus, the primary value of experiments is that they allow researchers to draw conclusions about the causal effect of variables without worrying about endogeneity and selection bias concerns that often frustrate researchers using observational data.

One can group experiments in political science into three general types. In laboratory experiments, subjects interact with members of the research team and sometimes one another, typically in a pre-set location – quite often, but not always, an actual dedicated 'lab' space – and as a consequence, they often know that they are part of a study. Lab experiments afford researchers tight control over procedures and conditions, and also facilitate the use of special equipment for presenting materials and recording observations (for example, equipment for measuring physical reactions). Moreover, in most lab experiments, participants receive compensation, such as academic course credit or cash payment, for their participation. In contrast, the key feature of *field experiments* is that subjects have no idea that they are part of a study. These are experiments introduced into actual political or social processes: treatments are the real actions of citizens, groups or governments, and effects are assessed in terms of actual behaviors or other outcomes of interest. When ethical and logistical barriers can be overcome, field experiments offer an unparalleled window to the magnitude of the treatment effect in a rich, dynamic and natural environment. *Survey experiments*, in turn, lie somewhere between these two options. As the name implies, they are experiments embedded in surveys, and manipulations typically consist of slight alterations in the wording or order of questions or response options. Indeed, one extensive use of survey experiments has been to improve survey design itself, though political scientists can use the same sorts of manipulations in surveys to mimic public debate or other elements of the political process that shape opinions, learning and political behavior (Kinder and Sanders, 1990; Schuman and Presser, 1981). Table 6.1 provides a concise comparative summary of some of the more important characteristics of each type of experiment.

*Table 6.1* Comparing Experiments by Type

|  | Lab | Survey | Field |
|---|---|---|---|
| Participant awareness? | High | Moderate | Low |
| Control over procedures? | High | Moderate | Moderate |
| Sample resembles population? | Low | High | High |
| Artificiality of environment? | High | High | Low |
| Ability to monitor behavior? | High | Moderate | Low |

Survey experiments have a number of strengths that make them attractive research tools for political scientists.[3] First, they allow us to draw confident inferences about what shapes attitudes and behavior in the broader public. Scientific sampling procedures help generate a pool of subjects that is a representative sample of the general population or a particular subpopulation of interest. Second, most survey experiments are embedded in a larger survey that allows for the collection of rich observational data on covariates, which can be useful in testing or detecting factors that moderate the causal relationship under study. Third, they are increasingly easy to administer to representative samples worldwide thanks to the diffusion of infrastructure for commercial, governmental and academic survey research (Heath et al., 2005). Thus, the start-up costs of adding a survey experiment to an already-planned or regularly occurring survey are relatively low compared to many other forms of research. In addition, researchers can achieve economies of scale by placing multiple experiments on a single survey for their own studies or in collaboration with other scholars (Sniderman and Grob, 1996). In fact, recent years have seen the development of collective good resources, such as Timesharing Experiments in the Social Sciences (TESS), that allow scholars to conduct phone and Internet survey experiments for free using a peer-reviewed proposal process.[4] Finally, though survey respondents are aware that they are participating in a study, they typically do so in the comfort of their own homes and their participation consists usually of little more than answering a series of questions posed by an interviewer in person, over the phone or via computer. Moreover, unlike many lab experiments in which subjects' attention is drawn to a conspicuous treatment, subjects in survey experiments are more likely to believe that the interviewer is merely interested in their opinion and the treatment manipulations seem like just another inconspicuous part of the interview.[5]

## An Illustration: survey experiments on the effects of partisan cues

One important political question that is well suited for analysis using survey experiments is how partisan cues affect public opinion formation and individual decision making. By partisan cues, we mean labels or endorsements that *explicitly associate a policy, action or person with a political party*. By our count, other scholars have conducted almost two dozen experiments on the impact of party cues, most of them in the US.[6] Almost all of the early studies were lab experiments conducted on local convenience samples such as college students (Cohen, 2003; Druckman, 2001; Kam, 2005; Rahn, 1993; Rudolph, 2006; Stroud et al., 2005), but recent studies have increasingly used survey experiments to reach representative national samples (Arceneaux, 2008; Malhotra and Kuo, 2008; Sniderman and Hagendoorn, 2007). Research to date has focused on the impact that party cues have on candidate evaluation and voting, attribution of responsibility (blame) among public officials for bad outcomes, and the formation of policy preferences. Most of these studies have found that the presence of party cues substantially affects evaluations and preferences, typically by generating a favorable reaction to cues from a citizen's preferred party, and hostile reactions towards cues from an opposing party.[7]

Experiments to date have also tried to ascertain the limits of party cue effects and to identify the individual or situational factors that moderate their influence. For example, several studies have examined whether party cues affect educated or politically sophisticated citizens differently from their less savvy compatriots (Arceneaux, 2008; Cohen, 2003; Druckman, 2001; Kam, 2005; Maholtra and Kuo, 2008; Tomz and Sniderman, 2005; Van Houweling and Sniderman, 2005), while others have investigated the moderating role of personal importance attached to an issue (Malhotra and Kuo, 2008), trust in or familiarity with a party (Coan et al., 2008) or the value placed on social conformity (Sniderman and Hagendoorn, 2007). Scholars have also looked beyond individual differences to study whether the impact of party cues depends on the amount of detailed policy information available (Bullock, 2011), issue salience (Arceneaux, 2008), the clarity of party ideologies or performance (Merolla et al., 2007, 2008) and the difficulty or complexity of the issue (Coan et al., 2008; Merolla et al., 2007, 2008). Finally, some experiments have compared the impact of party cues relative to the impact of other factors, such as available details about the issues (Arceneaux, 2008; Bullock, 2011; Cohen, 2003; Rahn, 1993; Van Houweling and Sniderman, 2005), cues about the public office held by an official (Malhotra and Kuo, 2008), ideological cues (Tomz and Sniderman, 2005) and the emotional expressiveness of candidates (Stroud et al., 2005). Overall, studies have found that party cues tend to sway supporters even when the endorsed policy or candidate tends to deviate from the stereotypical positions of the party, often lessening in effectiveness only in extreme cases of complete stereotype violation.

In this chapter, we focus specifically on the question of how partisan cues affect public opinion formation on matters of policy. This is a fairly focused topic, but one with broad implications. An experiment designed to measure the effect of party cues can speak to the nature and strength of party identification in the public. For example, one can set up an experiment to test whether partisans respond more strongly and favorably to party endorsements than do other citizens. Such experiments are also useful for considering the extent to which party cues convey information to all citizens, irrespective of their preferred party. In other words, do party labels serve as useful heuristics that enable citizens to make good decisions in the absence of more complete information, or do they bias citizens to ignore available information and rely on their stereotyped impressions of, or gut feelings toward, parties (Brady and Sniderman, 1985; Lau and Redlawsk,

2001; Popkin, 1994)? Party cue experiments can tell us not only about citizens, but also about the parties themselves. Do parties differ in their ability to send credible signals, is their credulity restricted to particular domains and does all of this depend on their past performance in office and/or the ideological clarity of their platform (Brader et al., forthcoming; Lupia and McCubbins, 1998; Petrocik, 1996)? We can also use party cue experiments to assess the extent to which a particular public relies on parties as a guide to the political universe relative to other potential sources of guidance, such as ideology, social groups (for example, ethnicity, race, religion) or incumbency (Ansolabehere et al., 2006; Tomz and Sniderman, 2005; see also Kuklinski and Hurley, 1994 for a comparison of ideological and racial cues in the US). Finally, experimental studies of the effects of partisan cues can even help inform practical political decisions, such as the likely impact of printing party labels on election ballots, in public polls or in news reports on public figures (Malhotra and Kuo, 2008; Rudolph, 2006; Schaffner et al., 2001).

Designing an experiment to test the effects of partisan cues on public opinion in a two-party context is a fairly straightforward enterprise involving a single-factor, two-cell design. Using the United States as an example, interviewers could present all respondents with a policy question, for example, 'Do you support lifting the trade embargo on Cuba?' The control group could be told that 'experts' have proposed lifting the trade ban on Cuba. Then a treatment group could in turn be told that the Democratic Party had proposed lifting the trade ban on Cuba. The assumption would be that if parties provided cues, we should see more Democrats supporting lifting the ban in the treatment group than in the control group, and, similarly, more Republicans opposing lifting the ban in the treatment group than in the control group. If the researcher was at all concerned that somehow only using the Democratic Party in the cue was problematic, we could simply randomly alternate 'The Democratic Party has proposed lifting the trade ban on Cuba' with 'The Republican Party has opposed lifting the trade ban on Cuba', with the same set of predictions. Moreover, if we wanted to gauge the extent to which the magnitude of the effect varied based on pre-existing beliefs about the positions of parties on particular issues, we could switch to either a more politically charged issue – for example abortion – or a less politically relevant issue – for example some form of administrative reform.[8]

### 6.3   Party cue experiments in multi-party systems

The goal of our research, however, was to examine the effect of partisan cues in post-communist countries that feature multi-party systems; to date, we have conducted such research in five different post-communist countries: Russia (Brader and Tucker, 2009), Poland and Hungary (Brader and Tucker, forthcoming) and, more recently, Bulgaria and Moldova.[9] Replicating the two-party design in a multi-party context, however, introduces a number of important challenges. In a two-party system, it seems safe to say that providing a partisan cue that Party *A* supports a position on a particular issue ought to lead partisans of Party A to support that position and partisans of Party *B* to oppose that position. However, in a multi-party system, it requires a much more strenuous assumption to claim that just because Party *A* supports a proposal, supporters of Parties *B* and *C* will oppose that proposal. It is possible that we could find isolated examples of issues that work that way in a three-party system, but once we move to four parties and beyond this becomes increasingly difficult to sustain for most issues, and it is by definition impossible in the case of simple 'yes/no' approaches to policy issues (for example, whether one supports removing a trade embargo).

We therefore developed two new variants of the standard single-factor, two-cell experimental test of partisan cues on policy opinions that are suitable for testing in a multi-party setting. As would be expected, both introduce added layers of complexity, and thus place additional demands on the researcher in terms of experimental design, and in particular on the decision of what types of policy opinions can be included as part of the experiment. We refer to these two types of experiments as *single party cue* (SPC) experiments and *multiple party cue* (MPC) experiments.

### 6.3.1 Single party cue (SPC) experiments

Single party cue experiments are the simpler of the two. Here, respondents in the control group are told that experts have proposed a certain policy change. Respondents in the treatment group, in contrast, are told that *their preferred party* has proposed the same policy change. Our expectation in SPC experiments is that respondents who received the partisan cue (treatment group) would be more likely to support the proposal than those who did not (control group). Thus, we can check support for our hypothesis simply by comparing the average level of support for any given proposal across the control and treatment groups.

The SPC experiment presents the researcher with two distinct challenges. First, in order to provide members of the treatment group with a cue from their preferred party, we need to be able to ascertain which party is each respondent's 'preferred party'. In surveys conducted with computer assisted technology, this task can be automated through the use of algorithms that can draw on multiple questions in the survey. In surveys conducted without computer technology, however, this essentially entails picking a single question that interviewers can use to indentify the preferred party; requiring interviewers to use a more complicated algorithm during the interview that draws on multiple questions would invite serious measure error. Either way, though, there are likely to be some respondents who refuse to identify a preferred party, a point we return to below.

It is also worth noting at this point that the challenge of finding a 'preferred party' for the sake of the experimental design is *not* the same thing as dividing the sample of respondents into partisan identifiers and nonpartisan identifiers. While by definition partisan identifiers need to have a preferred party, it is of course possible that people who do not have a partisan identification can at the same time identify a preferred party. Otherwise, it would be impossible to use this experimental design to test the difference in the effects of partisan cues on partisan identifiers and non-identifiers. In practice, what this involves is having two separate thresholds: one for identifying a respondent's 'preferred party', and then a higher threshold for determining whether or not a respondent is a partisan identifier. In our case, we have used the following question to identify party preference:

*Which of the parties shown on this card do you like the best?*

Respondents who refused to answer this question were prompted twice more to do so, first by being asked which they liked best relative to the others, and then finally by being asked which they disliked the least. In contrast, we have used the following questions to measure whether or not respondents were partisan identifiers:

*Please tell me, is there any one among the present parties, movements and associations about which you would say, 'This is my party, my movement, my association?'*
  *Please tell me, does there exist a party, movement or association which more than the others reflects your interests, views and concerns?*
  *Do you usually think of yourself as close to any particular political party, movement or association?*
  *Is there a party to which you feel yourself a little closer to than the others?*

Of course, no matter what method one uses for indentifying a respondent's preferred party, there will always be some people who refuse to identify a preferred party. Since the experiment cannot be administered with some party being said to support the proposal in the treatment group, this leaves the researcher with two options. First, these individuals can simply be excluded from the experiment. The second option, however, is to choose a party to assign to individuals who refuse to provide their preferred party.[10] In doing so, it is important to remember that the researcher is now essentially setting up a new experiment: what is the effect of getting a cue from Party X, as opposed to what is the effect of getting a cue from your preferred party. Accordingly, the data from these two experiments should *not* be analyzed together in the same analysis, and this goes for respondents in the control group as well as the treatment group.[11] However, at this point in the game, the opportunity to run this new experiment – what is the effect of a cue from Party X – is essentially costless; these people are already here and participating in the survey. So there seems to be no good reason not to take advantage of this opportunity to collect more data. Then the question becomes *which* party to assign to these nonpreferred party types. Given the nature of the post-communist political context, we chose to assign the communist successor party in each country as the party making the proposal for these nonrespondents who were in the treatment group.[12] We did so because (1) we thought that this would be one of the best-known parties and (2) because we suspected that respondents who were not openly supportive of these communist successor parties might, on average, be more likely to *dislike* the communist successor party than any other party, which would open up the possibility of testing a 'negative partisan cue' hypothesis, which we discuss below. Other political contexts could lead to the choice of other interesting parties to be assigned as the supporter of the policy in question.

The second challenge of designing an SPC experiment is finding a policy that *any of the parties could conceivably support.* Thus, the universe of policy issues that could be featured in an SPC experiment is much smaller than in a partisan cue experiment in a two-party system, which, due to its dichotomous design, allows for the use of policy proposals that are supported by one party and opposed by the other. Moreover, since the design of the experiment requires that each respondent in the treatment group be told that her party supports the proposals, then almost by definition we are limited to policy proposals that are created by the researcher; while it is hypothetically possible for a proposed policy change to be supported by every major party, such occurrences are quite rare in the real world.

Due to the requirement that every party ostensibly is able to support the policy proposal in question, we were essentially forced to limit ourselves to nonpolitical policy proposals. In our experiments, we used topics such as administrative reforms, raising fees on public transportation to increase services, vaguely specified 'educational acts' and the like. Having gone through this process a number of times, we can confidently state that identifying country-appropriate topics for use in the SPC experiments is both challenging and time consuming. To do so, we took a three-step approach. First, we relied on our own knowledge of the country in question to try to come up with appropriate topics for the SPC experiments. We then circulated these topics to other scholars whom we considered experts on the politics of the country in question. Simultaneously, we included the questions in pre-tests of the survey instrument.[13] Finally, on the basis of the critiques we received from other scholars and the pre-test results, we modified the questions accordingly. Essentially what we were looking for were topics in which we had a relatively equal distribution of responses in terms of the likelihood that people would support the policy proposal, which, if anything, would lean a bit towards opposition so that our partisan cue could have more 'work' to do. To underscore the challenges of this process, even with our multiple-step process for choosing issues, we still ended up

*Table 6.2*    Policy topics by type of experiment and country

| | Single-Party Cues | | |
| --- | --- | --- | --- |
| | **Russia** | **Poland** | **Hungary** |
| **SPC1** | Transportation improvements (Metro) | Transportation improvements (Roads) | Transportation improvements (Metro) |
| **SPC2** | Weapon sales to China | Joint military exercise with Russia | Increase defense spending to NATO levels |
| **SPC3** | Import spent nuclear Fuel | Support Belorussian Opposition | Expand Internet access |
| **SPC4\*** | | 'Primary Education Restructuring Act' | 'Primary Education Restructuring Act' |
| | **Multi-party Cues** | | |
| **MPC1** | High School Exchange | High School Exchange | Healthcare Reform |
| **MPC2** | Administrative Reform (Subnational regions) | Administrative Reform (deputies in legislature) | Pipeline Projects |
| **MPC3** | Legal Guest Workers | Legal Guest Workers | Legal Guest Workers |

\*The 'Primary Education Restructuring Act' is a fictional act accompanied by no additional details.

with some questions that generated heavily skewed distributions, such as the question on whether or not Russia ought to import spent nuclear waste from other countries for reprocessing. This proposal was overwhelmingly disliked by respondents in the survey, and, consequently, made it very difficult indeed to find any effect for a party cue.

Table 6.2 Panel 1 summarizes the issues we used by country for the SPC experiments. In the Appendix, we provide examples of two SPC experiments.

### 6.3.2    Multiple party cue (MPC) experiments

Of course, politics often features debate over policy issues on which parties are likely to hold different positions. For this reason, we also created *multiple party cue* (MPC) experiments. In an MPC experiment, respondents in the treatment group are presented with a policy proposal, and then given a variety of different positions on that policy proposal, each of which is explicitly linked to a particular party. These usually ended up taking the form of 'Party *A* supports the proposal for Reason *X*; Party *B* supports for Reason *Y*; Party *C* opposes for Reason *Z*...etc.'[14] Respondents are then asked how they feel about the issue, and given the opportunity to choose from all of the different reasons. One complication here, of course, is that we might expect partisans of Party *C* to be partisans of that party precisely because they felt strongly about Reason *Z*. For this reason, the control group was presented with the exact same set of reasons for supporting or opposing the proposal, but without the party cue: they were simply told 'some people support the proposal for Reason $X$, some for Reason $Y$; some oppose for Reason $Z$, and so on'. In this manner, we were able to control for the extent to which supporters of a particular party might actually hold the same opinion as their preferred party – as in that case both the respondents in the control and treatment group ought to gravitate toward the preferred position equally – thus allowing us to interpret any findings purely as the result of the partisan cue. As with the SPC experiments, these 'proposals' were created by the researchers, and thus did not represent actual existing policy proposals.[15]

In the MPC experiment, therefore, our dependent variable is the extent to which people pick the *same* position as 'their' party.[16] If partisan cues matter, then, we should see more respondents in the treatment group, where the party cue is provided, picking the same position as their party than in the control group. The difficulty in constructing a good MPC experiment, however, lies in finding an appropriate issue for which there are actually enough different opinions on the issue that can be clearly differentiated into opinions that are associated with each party. In a two-party system, this is of course a trivial task; it is probably not likely to be that difficult in a three-party system either. But in countries with four to six major parties, this becomes very complicated very quickly. As a result, we tended to take a relatively nonsalient policy proposal and then read generic party positions back into positions on the proposal. So one example we used a number of times was a policy proposal concerning a high school student exchange program with another country. This is, of course, not likely to be a very salient political issue. But precisely because it is not a highly salient political issue, it gives us an opportunity to create positions for each party on the issue of the student exchange program that are closely related to the fundamental identity of the party. So in this case, a pro-business party could support the exchange program because it would expose the students to the workings of a successful market economy, while a far right religious party could oppose it because it would expose students to a godless culture. Table 6.2, Panel 2 (above) summarizes the topics we used by country; we also provide examples of two MPC experiments in the Appendix.

Similar to the SPC experiments, the biggest challenge in designing MPC experiments is coming up with viable topics. However, MPC experiments raise a number of issues above and beyond those we confronted in designing the SPC experiments. First, the researcher needs to be able to produce an issue for which there are *distinct and identifiable* positions for each of the different parties. By 'identifiable' we mean that it needs to be clear that the party in question really could hold this position on the issue under discussion.[17] By 'distinct' we mean that we need a different position for each of the parties. This in particular is where things can start to get tricky: just how many positions might we expect there to be on the subject of a student exchange program between Russia and Germany? In an ideal world, there would be already existing issues for which the parties all held distinct positions, and indeed this may often be the case in three- or even four-party systems. But it has been our experience that it is practically impossible to find any such existing issues in large party systems, which was one of the main factors pushing us towards creating our own hypothetical issues. Another related concern is that the analyst has to be careful *not* to inadvertently tap into a policy area in which there is already a major policy proposal on the table in the legislature. If this turns out to be the case, then the experiment risks contamination from the real world from a number of sources, but in particular we would be concerned that respondents in the control group would already associate the policy proposal in question with a political party.[18] We might also be concerned that respondents would be confused by differences between the researcher's description of the policy proposal and the respondent's *a priori* understanding of the existing policy proposal. To design our MPC experiments, we followed the same three-step procedure of relying on our own country knowledge, consulting with country experts and subjecting our initial topics to pre-tests.

Two other distinctions from the SPC experiments are worth noting, the first of which concerns identifying the respondent's preferred party. For the SPC experiments, the researchers need to be able to identify the respondent's preferred party *in order to administer the treatment*, precisely because the treatment is to link the policy proposal in question to the respondent's preferred party. That means that this information has to be both collected and applied during the survey itself. This is not, however, the case for the MPC experiments. In MPC experiments, the treatment is to provide information about the positions of *all* of the major parties, and therefore we do not need to know the respondent's preferred party. We do, however, need to know the respondent's preferred party in order to analyze the effects of the experiment, because the effect in question – whether the respondent picks the same position as her party more frequently following the treatment than the control – requires knowledge of a preferred party. However, to the extent that a preferred party does not need to be identified and then used during the survey itself, the MPC experiment is easier to implement. In the same vein, the MPC experiment also allows for a somewhat more sophisticated means of identifying the preferred party because algorithms can be applied after the data has been collected. Put another way, SPC experiments require a definitive decision about the identity of the preferred party during the experiment itself; MPC experiments allow this decision to be made later, and consequently we can actually analyze the effects of different decision rules in this regard and, therefore, the robustness of the measure.

One other significant difference between the SPC and MPC experiments concerns the length of the actual survey questions involved in the experimental treatments and control groups. As will be quickly apparent when looking at the sample questions in the Appendix to this chapter, MPC questions tend to be a lot longer than the SPC questions, especially as the number of parties involved increases. To the extent that researchers might be concerned about how much information respondents can process during the experiment, this could be a potential concern. We tried to alleviate this concern by making sure that when respondents were prompted to choose a position in the MPC experiment, they were given all of the information that was in the original presentation of the issue a second time. Computer-assisted interviewing could also make it easier for respondents to go back to the question and double check the information in it. Nevertheless, it is clear that the SPC experiments put fewer cognitive demands on the subject than the MPC experiments.

### 6.3.3 Additional features of partisan cue experiments

A number of additional points about both the SPC and MPC experiments are worth noting. First, in our studies, respondents took part in three or four SPC experiments and three MPC experiments.[19] We chose to include both SPC experiments and MPC experiments because these were pilot studies, and as both experimental designs were new, we really had no idea if one was superior to the other. Having gone through the process of running these experiments in multiple countries, we still do not have particularly strong feelings in this regard; neither of the experimental designs seems to outperform the other. Across all seven experiments, though, respondents were either assigned to the treatment or control group for all seven of the experiments, so they were *not* getting party cues for some policy issues and not for others.[20]

Second, we could not include partisan cues for every minor political party in the system. Choosing where to draw this line is always going to be a some-what subjective task. There is, of course, a trade-off between including every conceivable party a respondent could support and extending the number of parties for which we needed to generate policy positions in the MPC experiments.[21] Similarly, in the SPC experiments, allowing any possible party to be a respondent's 'preferred party' would eventually begin to place even further limits on the kinds of issues that any party could legitimately be said to support, especially as one begins to consider extreme fringe parties. In our work in Russia, Poland and Hungary, the decisions ultimately seemed fairly obvious – we included all of the parties with parliamentary represen-tation – and this left us with six parties each in Russia[22] and Poland[23] and four parties in Hungary.[24] While we would ideally have preferred to have had the same number of parties in all three countries, there just were no additional parties in Hungary that were supported by more than a handful of people.[25]

Table 6.3 provides a concise summary of the different features of SPC and MPC experiments.

*Table 6.3*    Single party cue vs. Multi-party cue experiments

|  | SPC | MPC |
|---|---|---|
| Complexity? | High | Low |
| Need to find policies that all parties can support? | Yes | No |
| Need to find policies that have distinct positions for all parties? | No | Yes |
| Need to limit number of possible parties ahead of time? | Not always | Yes |
| Preferred party needs to be identified prior to asking question? | Yes | No |

## 6.4    Analyzing empirical results from party cue experiments

In this section, we provide illustrations of four different types of analysis that one could perform using the experiments we designed: (1) testing the effect of learning that your preferred party supports a policy issue (from the SPC experiment) on your support for that issue; (2) testing the effect of learning that a communist successor party supports a policy proposal on your support for that issue (from the SPC experiment, using respondents who refused to provide a preferred party); (3) testing the effect of information on the party position of all major parties on whether it makes you more likely to pick the same position as your preferred party; and (4) testing whether partisan cues of either sort make one more likely to offer an opinion at all. For convenience sake, we present data from our Russian experiments in all of these cases.[26]

In Figure 6.1, we present the results of an SPC experiment in Russia, with people in the treatment group being told that their preferred party supports the policy in question. Accordingly, we expect the average level of support among members of the treatment group to be higher than the average level of support among members of the control group. This is precisely what we find for support of a proposal to increase metro fares while providing additional service ($p<.06$) and for selling technologically advanced weaponry to China ($p<.05$).[27] On the contrary, we find no evidence of the hypothesized effect in the case of the proposal to import spent nuclear fuel from other countries, which, as we previously noted, enjoyed very little support among the public overall. Note that these results *exclude* respondents who failed to provide a preferred party.

In Figure 6.2, we focus instead on the 27 per cent of respondents in the Russian experiment who refused to provide a preferred party. We suspected that being told that the communist successor party supported a proposal might actually have a negative effect on support for that issue among people who were not explicit supporters of the communist party. Interestingly, we find absolutely no evidence suggesting that this is the case. On both the

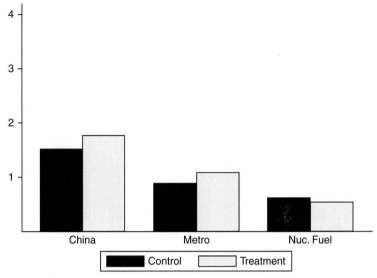

T-tests: China: p < .05 - Metro: p < .056 - Nuclear fuel: p < .78

*Figure 6.1* The Effect of Single Party Cues from One's Preferred Party in Russia

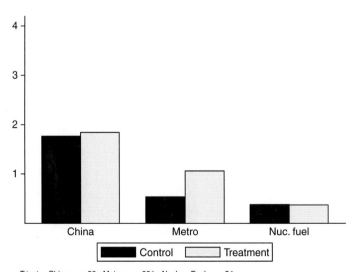

T-tests: China: p < .38 - Metro: p < .001 - Nuclear Fuel: p < .54

*Figure 6.2* The Effect of Single Party Cues from the Communist Party of the Russian Federation (KPRF)

China and Nuclear Fuel policy proposals, being told that the Communist Party of the Russian Federation (KPRF) supported the policy proposal had absolutely no effect on the opinions of Russians without a party preference. Intriguingly, however, on the one issue likely to have a disproportionate impact on poorer citizens – whether metro fares should be raised in the city of Moscow – the KPRF cue had a *positive* impact on respondents' attitudes towards the proposal. Thus far from exhibiting the negative effect on attitudes towards the policy proposal that we suspected might occur, it appears perhaps that the KPRF cue might have conveyed specific information linked to the connection between the KRPF and poorer citizens, namely that if the KPRF thought this was a good idea – even given the fact that it would raise metro fares, which would disproportionately hit their own constituents – then perhaps it really was a high 'quality' proposal. As the experiment was not explicitly designed to test for this kind of effect, this interpretation of the results of course remains speculative for now.

In Figure 6.3, we present results from a multiple party cue (MPC) experiment. Note as well that in this particular version of the results, we have limited the sample only to self-reported partisans in both the treatment and control groups. Here we find mostly what we expected: in all three cases, self-reported partisans are more likely to select their preferred party's policy position when they are given cues for the positions of all political parties than when they are not. In the case of administrative reform, the effect is dramatic, with approximately twice as many people

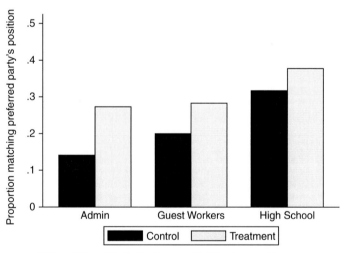

T-tests: Admin: p <.02 - Guest workers: p < .10 - High school: p < .20

*Figure 6.3*   The Effect of Multiple Party Cues on Matching the Position of One's Preferred Party for Self-Identified Partisans in Russia

selecting their party's position when presented with party cues than when not presented with the cues (*p<.02*). In the other cases, the effects are in the correctly predicted direction, although the magnitudes are not as large and we have less statistical confidence in the effects, especially in the case of the proposed high school exchange. It is also worth noting the limits of partisan cuing here: Despite seeing the predicted effects in all three cases, in no instance do any of the groups even approach 50 per cent congruence between respondents and their preferred parties. (Of course, given six parties, if respondents were just randomly picking a position, we would expect to see congruence in only about 16 per cent of the cases).

Finally, in Figure 6.4, we illustrate another hypothesis that can be tested with the experimental data we collected, whether partisan cues make respondents more likely at all to answer survey questions regarding their opinions on policy issues (Berinsky and Tucker, 2006; Berinsky, 2004). For this set of analyses, we can actually combine the SPC and MPC experiments – as both experiments feature a treatment group that received a partisan cue and a control group that did not – and we can even include the people from the SPC cue who received an assigned party, as they, too, received a partisan cue.[28] Figure 6.4 actually reveals an interesting pattern. Far from having a uniform effect, or even a consistent effect across SPC and

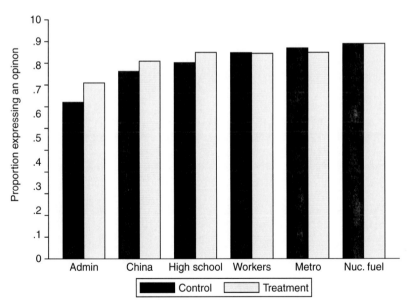

T-tests: Admin p < .03 - China p < .08 - School p < .05 - Workers p > .5 - Metro p > .5 - Nuclear fuel p > .5

*Figure 6.4*   The Effect of Partisan Cues on Opinion Giving in Russia

MPC experiments, partisan cues seem to encourage opinion giving only in areas in which some substantial portions of the population are tempted not to give an answer. Or to put this in more technical terms, there appears to be a ceiling effect at play here. Once more than 90 per cent of the population is willing to answer a question without a partisan cue, then adding a partisan cue seems to have little effect. However, as the proportion of the population in the control group offering an opinion declines below that level, then we begin to see statistically significant effects on opinion giving based on providing partisan cues.[29]

## 6.5   Deception in survey experiments

Having gone through our example of partisan cue experiments, it should be by now evident that it would have been impossible for us to have run these experiments without the use of deception. For both the SPC and MPC experiments, we, the researchers, crafted our own policy proposals, as well as – in the case of the MPC experiments – positions that we claimed the parties held on these policy proposals. Thus, the final question we wish to address in this chapter is whether this ought to be cause for concern. We, of course, debriefed our subjects after the surveys were completed, informing them that the policy proposals and party positions were in fact created by the authors of the study, while noting that we had attempted to formulate the party position using our best possible expectation of how the party would be likely to feel about the issue in question. So our concern is not whether people left our surveys with incorrect views about the positions of political parties due to our experimental manipulations, but rather the question of whether the deception in some sense creates flawed research in our specific case, or, perhaps even worse, damages the overall enterprise of experimental research.

In studies of behavioral economics that involve subjects receiving payoffs for their actions, such as the ones found in many other chapters of this volume, deception – especially in terms of how payoffs are calculated – is expressly forbidden. The concern here is two-fold. First, these types of experiments are designed to measure the effect of promised payoffs on subject behavior. If subjects do not believe they will actually receive the payoffs, then the results of the experiment are likely to be useless. Second, experimenters fear contamination of their subject pool. Laboratory experiments, by their very nature, are limited in the subjects they can attract. In many cases, they are drawing on a subsection of a student population that has opted to participate in experiments. These students may participate in multiple experiments (from different research projects) and they may also talk to one another. Thus, it is of paramount importance that any single experimenter does not contaminate the subject pool by conducting experiments involving deception.

On the contrary, deception is such a common practice in social-psychological experiments, that it would even be hard to imagine a chapter in a book like this devoting space to the topic.

So the question becomes: Are the survey experiments that we designed to study the effect of party cues likely to lead to the types of problems that give those who conduct lab experiments such concern over the use of deception? Consider first the nature of the deception in our experiment. It does not in any way involve compensation to the respondent for choices that she may make. Instead, it involves referencing a policy proposal that could exist, but does not actually exist at the moment. It also involves attributing positions to political parties on that policy proposal that we would expect the parties to hold, if they had to take such a position. The integrity of the experiment could, of course, be undermined if respondents did not believe that the parties would actually hold the positions we attributed to them, but fortunately the very design of the experiment completely aligns our incentives: We want to have policy positions for the party that seem credible. Thus, despite the fact that we need to invoke deception in our experiments in order to carry them out, the nature of the experiments insures that the deception is designed to be as realistic as possible. This is a very far cry from lying to someone about the amount of money you are going to give her at the end of a series of tasks.

Second, the nature of the subject pool is radically different in the case of survey experiments than it is when dealing with laboratory experiments. In our case, we were sampling from populations in the millions of people, as compared to a laboratory experiment which might be sampling from hundreds (or at best thousands) of students. While survey research has undoubtedly become more ubiquitous of late, the chance that a small number of survey-based experiments could somehow contaminate the larger enterprise of survey research seems infinitesimally small when working with large populations of potential respondents, such as national level surveys, or, as we used in Russia and Hungary, surveys of respondents in a capital city. It might, however, be a problem if researchers chose to focus their research on a very small population, such as students in a particular university, and this is worth bearing in mind in designing survey based-experiments. It is also worth noting, of course, that not all survey experiments need to involve deception; many will not. But it is our contention that while survey experiments should be sensitive to the potential dangers of applying deception in experiments, the use of the technique – as is the case in social-psychological research – should not be off the table.

From a pragmatic standpoint, however, this points out the need for survey researchers to be especially thorough in defending and justifying the use of deception in any application to internal review boards (IRBs) for permission to conduct experiments, which is usually research involving human subjects.[30] An IRB will typically focus on two key considerations. First, does the deception and experiment generally pose no more than a 'minimal risk' to a subject of physical, psychological, reputational or other harm? The standard for 'minimal' is usually gauged as a person facing no more risk of harm than he or she faces in everyday life. In the case of deception, for example, an IRB may ask whether the deception will cause the person to act in such a way that he is likely to experience serious regret later and that the 'action' cannot be easily undone. It is standard practice and typically required that deception, whether by commission or conspicuous omission, be revealed to subjects at the end of participation through a debriefing process. The second consideration for IRBs is to ask whether any risk, whether small or large, is necessary and warranted given the scientific and public value of the research. An IRB must be convinced that the deception is necessary to shed light on the object of study. Even when they are so convinced, they must also weigh the value of the science against the risk level. Few studies of public opinion or political decision making (in contrast, say, to studies seeking a cure for cancer) will likely outweigh any level of risk *higher than* 'minimal'.[31]

## 6.6  Concluding thoughts

As is argued throughout this volume, experiments represent an exciting avenue of research for political scientists, and survey experiments are no exception to this rule. Like other experiments, however, they require very careful attention to detail at the planning stage, and involve numerous decisions to be made by the researcher. In this chapter, we have illustrated both the challenges and potential payoffs involved in utilizing a particular type of survey experiment – designed to test the effect of partisan cues on public opinion formation – as part of a research agenda. Hopefully, this discussion can serve as a useful roadmap most specifically for those interested in studying the effects of partisan cues, but also more generally for those engaged in the larger enterprise of survey experiments.

## Appendix:   Examples of Single Party Cue (SPC) and Multiple Party Cue (MPC) Experiments

### SPC Example #1

*Treatment group*

<PARTY> has recently proposed raising fares on the Moscow Metro to pay for a number of improvements to the Metro.

*Control group*

A bill has been proposed that will raise fares on the Moscow Metro to pay for a number of improvements to the Metro.

Please tell us how strongly you personally support the proposal to make improvements to the Moscow Metro and pay for them by raising fares:

1. Strongly support making the improvements and raising fares.
2. Weakly support making the improvements and raising fares.
3. No opinion on whether the improvements should be made.
4. Weakly oppose making the improvements and raising fares.
5. Strongly oppose making the improvements and raising fares.

## SPC example #2

*Treatment group*

<PARTY> has recently proposed to remove most of the restrictions currently in place against selling modern and high tech Russian weapons systems to China. By selling China more advanced weapons that they currently do not have, Russia can continue to earn billions of rubles in sales and preserve jobs in the weapons industries. While there is of course always a chance that Russia and China could engage in a military conflict in the future, it is unlikely occurrence.

*Control group*

It has recently been proposed that Russia removes most of the restrictions currently in place against selling modern and high tech Russian weapons systems to China. By selling China more advanced weapons that they currently do not have, Russia can continue to earn billions of rubles in sales and preserve jobs in the weapons industries. While there is of course always a chance that Russia and China could engage in a military conflict in the future, it is unlikely occurrence.

Please tell us how strongly you personally support the proposal to remove existing restrictions on selling modern and high tech weapons systems to China:

1. Strongly support removing the restrictions and allowing China to purchase high tech weapon systems from Russia.
2. Weakly support removing the restrictions and allowing China to purchase high tech weapon systems from Russia.
3. No opinion on removing the restrictions and allowing China to purchase high tech weapon systems from Russia.
4. Weakly oppose removing the restrictions and allowing China to purchase high tech weapon systems from Russia.
5. Strongly oppose removing the restrictions and allowing China to purchase high tech weapon systems from Russia.

## MPC example #1

*Treatment group*

It has recently been proposed that Germany and Russia establish an exchange program for high school students. Under the terms of the proposal, 5,000 German high school students would study in Russia every year, and 5,000 Russian students would study in Germany. The costs of the program would be split between the German and Russian governments. Reaction to the proposal among Russia's political parties has been mixed. Unified Russia supports the proposal, because they think it will help deepen ties between Russia and Germany in the long run. The Union of Right Wing Forces also supports the proposal, because they believe that it will be a good opportunity for Russian students to learn Western business techniques. Yabloko supports the proposal, because they believe it would help more Russians learn about a country where citizens enjoy important social protections and civil rights. The Communist Party of the Russian Federation, however, opposes the measure, which they believe is just another state subsidy for the children of wealthy families, who will be the only ones that ever get to go to Germany. The Liberal Democratic Party of Russia opposes the measure because they think it is likely that some of the German students could end up spying on Russia. Motherland also opposes the proposal because there are already too many foreign students studying in Russia.

*Control group*

It has recently been proposed that Germany and Russia establish an exchange program for high school students. Under the terms of the proposal, 5,000 German high school students would study in Russia every year, and 5,000 Russian students would study in Germany. The costs of the program would be split between the German and Russian governments. Reaction to the proposal has been mixed. Supporters believe that it will help deepen ties between Russia and Germany in the long run, provide a good opportunity for Russian students to learn Western business techniques, and that it would help more Russians learn about a country where citizens enjoy important social protections and civil rights. Opponents of the proposal, however, argue that it is just another state subsidy for the children of wealthy families, who will be the only ones that ever get to go to Germany, that some of the German students could end up spying on Russia, and that there are already too many foreign students studying in Russia.

Which of these opinions best describes your views of the proposed exchange program between Russian and German students?

1. It should be supported because it will improve ties between Russia and Germany in the long run.

2. It should be supported because it will help Russian students learn Western business techniques.
3. It should be supported because Russian students will learn how a country can both provide social protection and respect civil rights.
4. It should be opposed because it will only help the children of wealthy families.
5. It should be opposed because the German students may spy on Russia.
6. It should be opposed because there are already too many foreigners studying in Russian schools.

## MPC example #2:

*Treatment group*

One question facing Russia today is whether or not the number of regions of Russia should be reduced by merging existing regions into new regions. One such merger is now occurring between Perm Oblast and the Komi-Permyatski autonomous okrug. Most political parties support reducing the number of regions, although they do so for a number of reasons. The Communist Party of the Russian Federation believes that reducing the number of regions will lead back to the Soviet system of linking administrative regions to economic production. United Russia believes that it will lead to more efficient administration of regions by eliminating poorly run regional administrations. The Union of Right Forces believes that regional consolidation would spur economic growth by reducing the number of trade barriers within Russia. The Liberal Democratic Party of Russia, however, supports reducing the number of regions as a step towards making Russia a unitary state where special status would no longer be granted to ethnic Republics. The Motherland party supports decreasing the number of Russian regions because it thinks it will increase the state's ability to constrain the power of oligarchs by strengthening the remaining regional governments. Yabloko, while not opposed to the mergers in principle, thinks that the discussion of merging regions distracts from the larger question of whether democracy and civil rights are respected in the regions.

*Control group*

One question facing Russia today is whether or not the number of regions of Russia should be reduced by merging existing regions into new regions. One such merger is now occurring between Perm Oblast and the Komi-Permyatski autonomous okrug. A number of different arguments have been made in favor of reducing the number of regions, although they do so for a number of very different reasons. Some like the proposal because they think reducing the number of regions will lead back to the Soviet system of linking administrative regions to economic production. Others believe it will lead to more efficient administration of regions by eliminating poorly run regional administrations. Another argument is that it will spur economic growth by reducing the number of trade barriers within Russia. Some people like the proposal because they think it is a first step to a unitary state where special status would no longer be granted to ethnic Republics, while others think it will increase the state's ability to constrain the power of oligarchs by strengthening the remaining regional governments. Finally, some people are concerned that the discussion of merging regions distracts from the larger question of whether democracy and civil rights are respected in the regions.

Which of the following best reflects your views regarding the effect of decreasing the number of regions in Russia?

1. Reducing the number of regions will help bring back a more Soviet style economy.
2. Reducing the number of regions will bring about more efficient government administration.
3. Reducing the number of regions will spur economic growth.
4. Reducing the number of regions will lead to the creation of a unitary state and weaken the power of ethnic republics.
5. Reducing the number of regions will weaken the oligarchs.
6. Reducing the number of regions is not nearly as important as ensuring that democracy and civil rights are respected in the regions.

## Notes

1. We thank the many, many individuals who have offered advice and assistance over the course of this project. Financial support for the data collection was generously provided by the Center for Political Studies at the University of Michigan and the Princeton Institute for International and Regional Studies.
2. Note that randomization does not *guarantee* an identical distribution of participants on all covariates. Indeed, given the large number of variables that may be relevant to any given outcome, we should expect that true random assignment would lead to at least one or two significant differences across conditions. Some researchers refer to this, somewhat misleadingly, as a 'failure of randomization'. It is not a failure of randomization per se, but rather a failure to achieve the ideal goal of randomization, which is perfectly matching treatment and control groups on *all* relevant variables. Many researchers check for such 'failures' on any measured covariates and, if differences are found, these variables are sometimes included as controls. Researchers can take extra steps in advance to reduce the likelihood of differences on some particularly potent and well-known covariates, by stratifying or 'blocking' subjects according to these covariates and randomizing within these strata (a process that can have additional benefits, such as allowing for more efficient estimates, if the covariates are to be treated as moderators).
3. For a detailed discussion of the advantages and disadvantages of survey experiments, see Gaines et al. (2006).
4. See http://tess.experimentcentral.org/, for more information.

5. While we cannot conclusively rule out the fact that some participants in a survey experiment might suspect that the survey contains some form of experimental treatments, it is our contention that the prevalence of survey research across a wide variety of fields (commercial, political and so on) has at the very least exposed large portions of the population to the fact that a survey is a 'normal' form of study that is involved in collecting the opinions of citizens, and not in subjecting them to experimental manipulations.

6. Very recently, other scholars have reported experiments on party cues in three countries outside the US. These include lab experiments on student samples in Canada and Mexico (Merolla et al., 2007, 2008) and a survey experiment on a national sample in The Netherlands (Sniderman and Hagendoorn, 2007). Although the latter study is principally framed as a test of whether conformist citizens can be 'led' on the issue of multiculturalism by their party leaders, the experiment features a key party endorsement manipulation.

7. Scholars may differ at times on what constitutes a small or large effect. For example, Bullock (2011) usefully directs our attention to the question of substantive significance, which is too often ignored in research. In doing so, he argues that party cue effects tend to be 'small', but his own evidence indicates average shifts in the range of 5 to 10 per cent of the scale on which the dependent variable is measured, and at times reaching 20 per cent. Another scholar may just as readily conclude that such an average shift, which is equivalent to completely reversing the opinion of 5 to 10 percent of the public from one position to the opposite with a simple label, is actually impressively 'large'.

8. We could even go so far as to flip flop the positions of the parties from where they normally stand and see if the partisan cue is strong enough to overcome the pre-existing association of certain parties with certain positions; see for example (Van Houweling and Sniderman, 2005).

9. We also conducted our experiments in three established democracies, the United States, Great Britain, and Sweden (Brader and Tucker, forthcoming).

10. On a computer-assisted survey, it might actually be possible to use earlier answers in the survey to impute the probability that each party would be that given respondent's preferred party. With such probabilities in hand, the researcher could then pick a rule (for example, assign the party with the highest probability; assign a party if any party has a greater than 75% likelihood of being a respondent's preferred party and so on) for using this information to guess at the respondent's preferred party. That being said, we have not yet personally attempted anything like this.

11. More specifically, people who refuse to provide a preferred party in the control group should be compared with the people who refused to provide a party in the treatment group for analyzing the experiment on 'What is the effect of a cue from Party $X$?', and people in the control group who did provide a party preference should be compared with people in the treatment group who did provide a party preference for analyzing the experiment on 'What is the effect of a cue from your preferred party?'.

12. In practice, this was the Communist Party of the Russian Federation in Russia, the Hungarian Socialist Party in Hungary and the Democratic Left Alliance in Poland.

13. In an ideal world, one would wait for the responses from the scholars before conducting the pre-tests, which we did when we could.

14. As discussed below, we tried some additional variants on this framework in our Hungarian survey.
15. Although, as opposed to the SPC experiments, there is no *a priori* reason why one couldn't employ a real policy proposal, provided it met the requirements of providing distinct positions for each of the parties. And we did actually attempt something similar to this in one of our Hungarian MPC experiments.
16. As the identification of whether people matched 'their' party is done after the survey during the analysis of the data, we can afford to be a little more sophisticated here in identifying a respondent's preferred party for the purpose of this analysis. We therefore use a simple algorithm that checks first whether respondents identify with a party using the standard question wording found on the Comparative Study of Electoral Systems surveys (Do you think of yourself as close to any particular political party, movement or association? Is there a party to which you feel yourself a little closer than to the others?). For respondents who fail to identify a party in response to this question, we then check whether they provide an answer to a party identification question used by Colton (2000), which is 'Please tell me, is there any one among the present parties, movements and associations about which you would say, "This is my party, my movement, my association?"' If they do provide a party in answer to this question, then that party is considered 'their party'. As would be expected, answers to the questions are very similar.
17. Of course, one could also design an experiment in which the idea was to see if the party cue was strong enough to overcome even a nonsensical position on the part of that party, but that is not the setup of the current experiment.
18. For more on other sources of potential contamination in survey experiments, see Transue et al. (2009).
19. In Russia, which is where the first set of experiments was carried out, there were only three SPC experiments; in Hungary and Poland, we added a fourth.
20. Whether varying the party cues by experiment would change the results could be a subject for further research, but in an effort to focus the power of the experiments on our primary research topic, we eschewed this and many other potentially interesting secondary experimental manipulations.
21. Again, varying the number of parties for different subjects within countries would make for an interesting follow-up experiment.
22. In Russia we included the four parties that achieved parliamentary representation from party lists – The Communist Party of the Russian Federation, United Russia, the Liberal Democratic Party of Russia and Motherland – as well as two prominent liberal parties that had not passed the minimum threshold to receive seats of the party lists, but still had representatives in the parliament from single member districts, Yabloko and the Union of Right Forces. (In the 2003 parliamentary election, Russia had still used a mixed electoral system; the 2007 Russian parliament was elected using only party lists). The Russian data were collected in the spring of 2006.
23. Citizen's Platform, Law and Justice, Samoobrona RP, the Democratic Left Alliance, the League of Polish Families and the Polish Peasant's Party. The Polish data were collected in the summer of 2006.
24. The Hungarian Socialist Party, FIDESZ-Hungarian Civic Party, the Alliance of Free Democrats and the Hungarian Democratic Forum. The Hungarian data were collected in the summer of 2007.
25. Given that the Hungarian experiment was already slightly different, we took the opportunity to try some slight variations in the MPC experiments, and therefore

one question (on gas pipelines) had only two potential answers, each of which was associated with two parties (in all the other MPC experiments each answer was associated with one party) and in one question (on increasing legal guest workers) we had all of the parties supporting the proposal, but for different reasons.

26. For those interested in these findings, we discuss them in much greater detail in Brader and Tucker (2009).

27. P-values are from one-tailed t-tests comparing the difference of means across the control and treatment groups. We employ one-tailed t-tests because we have a clear hypothesis about the direction of the predicted effect.

28. Of course, researchers could also assess the effect on opinion giving across those who got a cue from their preferred party and those who got the assigned cue in the SPC experiments. We are obviously leaving a lot on the table here in our effort just to provide some cursory illustrations of empirical results from our experiments. We also want to be clear that in our surveys, the SPC and MPC experiments were presented in the same section of the survey, and indeed were intermingled with one another. So in both cases, the questions asked prior to experiments – for example, those soliciting party preference – were asked prior to both the SPC and MPC experiments.

29. It is important to note that our claims about the distinction in the effects when more or less than 90% of the survey population answered the question is of course simply an observation based on the figure, and not a statistical test. A statistical test of this nature would require many more experiments than the six reported on here. We thank an anonymous reviewer for highlighting this point.

30. More information about IRBs can be found here (http://en.wikipedia.org/wiki/Institutional_review_board) and here (http://www.hhs.gov/ohrp/). While IRBs are very common at American universities, an anonymous reviewer of this chapter pointed out that such boards are less common elsewhere. Researchers in these cases face essentially two choices. Ideally, they would work with their home institutions to establish IRBs, which may ultimately make it easier for the institutions to receive external research funding from organizations that require IRB approval for research projects. Alternatively, researchers should be that much more diligent on their own without an oversight board in assuring that any deception used in their experiments violates neither ethical norms nor the concerns of behavioral economists noted previously.

31. It is also worth noting that there are certain subjects that could not even be studied without the use of at least mild deception, such as tolerance. Telling a subject that you were involving him or her in a study of tolerance would contaminate the results to such an extent that our ability to learn anything from the results would be severely hampered. We thank an anonymous reviewer for raising this point.

## References

Ansolabehere, Stephen, Shigeo Hirano, James M. Snyder and Michiko Ueda (2006) 'Party and Incumbency Cues in Voting: Are They Substitutes?' *Quarterly Journal of Political* Science, 1, 119–137.

Arceneaux, Kevin (2008) 'Can Partisan Cues Diminish Democratic Accountability?' *Political Psychology*, 30, 139–161.

Berinsky, Adam J. (2004) *Silent Voices: Public Opinion and Political Participation in America* (Princeton, N.J.: Princeton University Press).

Berinsky, Adam and Joshua A. Tucker (2006) '"Don't Knows" And Public Opinion Towards Economic Reform: Evidence from Russia', *Communist and Post-Communist Studies*, 39, 1–27.

Brader, Ted and Joshua A. Tucker (2009) 'What's Left Behind When the Party's Over: Survey Experiments on the Effects of Partisan Cues in Putin's Russia', *Politics and Policy*, 37, 843–868.

Brader, Ted and Joshua A. Tucker (forthcoming) 'Following the Party's Lead: Party Cues, Policy Opinion, and the Power of Partisanship in Three Multiparty Systems', *Comparative Politics*.

Brader, Ted, Joshua A. Tucker, and Dominik Duell (forthcoming) 'Which Parties Can Lead Opinion? Experimental Evidence on Partisan Cue-Taking in Multiparty Democracies', *Comparative Political Studies*.

Brady, Henry E. and Paul M. Sniderman (1985) 'Attitude Attribution: A Group Basis for Political Reasoning', *American Political Science Review*, 79, 1061–78.

Bullock, John G. (2011) 'Elite Influence on Public Opinion in an Informed Electorate', *American Political Science Review*, 105, 496–515.

Coan, Travis G., Jennifer L. Merolla, Laura B. Stephenson and Elizabeth J. Zechmeister (2008) 'It's Not Easy Being Green: Minor Party Labels as Heuristic Aids', *Political Psychology*, 29, 389–405.

Cohen, Geoffrey L. (2003) 'Party Over Policy: The Dominating Impact of Group Influence on Political Beliefs', *Journal of Personality and Social Psychology*, 85, 808–822.

Colton, Timothy J. (2000) *Transitional Citizens: Voters and What Influences Them in the New Russia* (Cambridge, Massachusetts: Harvard University Press).

Druckman, James N. (2001) 'Using Credible Advice to Overcome Framing Effects', *Journal of Law, Economics, and Organization*, 17, 62–82.

Gaines, Brian, James H. Kuklinski and Paul J. Quirk (2006) 'The Logic of the Survey Experiment Reexamined', *Political Analysis*, 15, 1–20.

Heath, Anthony, Stephen Fisher and Shawna Smith (2005) 'The Globalization of Public Opinion Research', *Annual Review of Political Science*, 8, 297–333.

Kam, Cindy (2005) 'Who Toes the Party Line? Cues, Values, and Individual Differences', *Political Behavior*, 27, 163–82.

Kinder, Donald R. and Lynn M. Sanders (1990) 'Mimicking Political Debate with Survey Questions: The Case of White Opinion on Affirmative Action for Blacks', *Social Cognition*, 8, 73–103.

Kuklinski, James H. and Norman L. Hurley (1994) 'On Hearing and Interpreting Political Messages: A Cautionary Tale of Citizen Cue-Taking', *Journal of Politics*, 56, 729–51.

Lau, Richard R. and David P. Redlawsk (2001) 'Advantages and Disadvantages of Cognitive Heuristics in Political Decision Making', *American Journal of Political Science*, 45, 951–71.

Lupia, Arthur and Mathew D. McCubbins (1998) *The Democratic Dilemma: Can Citizens Learn What They Need to Know?* (New York: Cambridge University Press).

Malhotra, Neil and Alexander G. Kuo (2008) 'Attributing Blame: The Public's Response to Hurricane Katrina', *Journal of Politics* 70, 120–35.

Merolla, Jennifer, Laura Stephenson and Elizabeth J. Zechmeister (2007) 'La Aplicación de los Métodos Experimentales en el Estudio de los Atajos Informativos en México', *Política y Gobierno*, 14, 117–42.

Merolla, Jennifer L., Laura B. Stephenson and Elizabeth J. Zechmeister (2008) 'Can Canadians Take a Hint? The (In)Effectiveness of Party Labels as Information Shortcuts in Canada', *Canadian Journal of Political Science*, 41, 673–96.

Petrocik, John R. (1996) 'Issue Ownership in Presidential Elections, with a 1980 Case Study', *American Journal of Political Science*, 40, 825–50.

Popkin, Samuel L. (1991) *The Reasoning Voter: Communication and Persuasion in Presidential Campaigns*. Chicago: University of Chicago Press.

Popkin, Samuel L. (1994) *The Reasoning Voter: Communication and Persuasion in Presidential Campaigns*, 2nd edition (Chicago: University of Chicago Press).

Rahn, Wendy (1993) 'The Role of Partisan Stereotypes in Information Processing about Political Candidates', *American Journal of Political Science*, 37, 472–96.

Rudolph, Thomas J. (2006) 'Triangulating Political Responsibility: The Motivated Formation of Responsibility Judgments', *Political* Psychology, 27, 99–122.

Schaffner, Brian F., Matthew Streb and Gerald Wright (2001) 'Teams without Uniforms: The Nonpartisan Ballot in State and Local Elections', *Political Research Quarterly*, 54, 7–30.

Schuman, Howard and Stanley Presser (1981) *Questions and Answers in Attitude Surveys: Experiments on Question Form, Wording, and Context* (New York: Academic Press).

Sniderman, Paul M. and Douglas B. Grob (1996) 'Innovations in Experimental Design in Attitude Surveys', *Annual Review of Sociology*, 22, 377–99.

Sniderman, Paul M. and A. Hagendoorn (2007) *When Ways of Life Collide: Multiculturalism and Its Discontents in the Netherlands* (Princeton, N.J.: Princeton University Press).

Stroud, Laura R., Jack Glaser and Peter Salovey (2005) 'The Effects of Partisanship and Candidate Emotionality on Voter Preference', *Imagination, Cognition, and Personality*, 25, 25–44.

Transue, John E., Daniel J. Lee and John H. Aldrich (2009) 'Treatment Spillover Effects across Survey Experiments', *Political Analysis*, 17, 143–61.

Tomz, Michael and Paul M. Sniderman (2005) 'Brand Name and the Organization of Mass Belief Systems', Unpublished manuscript (Stanford University).

Van Houweling, Robert P. and Paul M. Sniderman (2005) 'The Political Logic of a Downsian Space', Working Paper Series 44, *Institute of Government Studies, UC Berkeley*.

# 7
# Experimental Triangulation of Coalition Signals: Varying Designs, Converging Results

*Michael F. Meffert and Thomas Gschwend*

## 7.1 Experiments as flexible tools for theory testing

It is probably fair to say that political science has not been a welcoming discipline for experimental research (McDermott, 2002). Our discipline has always expressed skepticism about the usefulness and the prospects of experimental designs to address the key research questions we care about. But the more political scientists have started to think carefully about causal relationships and what is required to test them, the more they came (or should come) to realize that our traditional methodologies and research designs are also not sufficient. The latter have serious limitations as well, and some of these limitations can be addressed by experimental methods. Because experimental designs have unique strengths compared to other research designs, it is not surprising that the use of experiments has evolved and increased over time (Morton and Williams, 2010). Put simply, experiments are flexible tools for theory testing that allow us to establish causality by clearly separating causes and effects.

In this chapter, we will focus on one particular but striking advantage of experiments. When the key explanatory factor lacks variance, that is, when no observable data to test a theory is available, experiments can provide an elegant solution for this problem. Even if they come with their own difficulties and drawbacks, political science can only gain by embracing experimental designs. They not only provide an answer when traditional methods fail, but also open up new opportunities and possibilities for political science research.

As an illustrative example throughout this chapter, we use the effect of pre-election coalition signals by parties on strategic vote decisions and discuss three different experimental approaches designed to test this effect. Coalition governments are a common outcome in many multi-party systems, and voters might take possible coalitions into account at the ballot box after the next election. During campaigns, parties sometimes signal to voters the desirable and undesirable coalition partners. For instance, German parties often resort to explicit appeals for strategic voting in the form of a 'rental vote' (*Leihstimme*). Supporters of one of the two major parties, Christian Democrats (CDU/CSU) or Social Democrats (SPD), are asked to 'rent out' their vote in favor of the preferred small coalition partner when the latter is in danger of falling short of a minimum vote threshold (for example, the Free Democrats). In case of such a failure, the major party will likely have no prospects to lead the next government, even when running strong. A more detailed motivation of our substantive research question is provided below. First, however, we elaborate our argument that experiments are a flexible tool for theory testing, discuss some advantages and disadvantages of experimental designs and introduce the concept of experimental triangulation.

We start with the assumption that researchers want to test a theory. As textbooks instruct us, this requires a careful definition of the theoretical concepts, the derivation and specification of observable implications and the selection of appropriate cases that allow the measurement of causes and effects (King et al., 1994; Gschwend and Schimmelfennig, 2007). When selecting cases, researchers will often face the challenge that appropriate observable data is simply not available to test a theory adequately. Suppose we are interested in the effect of a particular contextual factor on individual behavior such as a coalition signal or other specific campaign messages. If such a message is sufficiently loud and clear, all informed voters will receive it. But how would we be able to determine if it had any effect? If the message was constant throughout the campaign, our key explanatory variable would lack variance. We have only data from this one election, a single case. Thus, all respondents in an election survey will have been exposed to the same message, and no respondent would have received an alternative, counterfactual message. It would not be possible to determine the impact of a constant message with any level of confidence. In fact, any political scientist interested in the effects of institutions and institutional rules on political behavior will almost certainly face a similar challenge.

What can be done in such a situation? If increasing the number of cases is not an option, crafting a clever experimental design can provide a methodological solution. Experiments are ideal for exactly this kind of situation because they enable the researcher to create the necessary variance. Guided by theory, the researcher can operationalize and manipulate the explanatory factor(s) in such a way that meaningful causal tests become possible. Experiments essentially create scenarios that represent different states of the world. By randomly assigning the manipulated explanatory factors to participants, we can make comparisons and estimate the causal effects. The differences (or lack thereof) between treatment and control groups will tell us whether participants react and behave as hypothesized.

Reducing the complexity of the real world to theoretically meaningful but often very narrow differences naturally raises the question of external validity. A simple manipulation does not represent reality as we experience it in everyday life, nor should it do that. The advantage of experiments is to submit hypotheses to causal tests, if necessary by breaking up complex causal chains into smaller steps that can be tested individually. Thus, experiments can systematically address what happens under theoretically relevant circumstances, even if they may not occur this way in the real world (for example, Mook, 1983). After successfully demonstrating the predictive value of a theory, researchers are well advised to address the external validity of their findings. This might require additional experiments or observational data from surveys and similar designs. In fact, the combination of complementary research designs might often be the best strategy.

Experiments are by no means a free lunch. They frequently require tough decisions. There are no cookbook recipes that tell us what to do and how to test a particular theory. Different experimental designs come with different advantages and disadvantages, and a researcher will have to decide which design is most appropriate in a given situation. For example, a researcher who wants to rule out all confounding influences on her measures of causes and effects needs to fully control all aspects of the study by creating or inducing all key variables, including the preferences of participants. Any measure that relies on pre-existing preferences is not fully controlled by the researcher and might introduce some confounding factor. At other times, however, it might make perfect sense to leverage participants' pre-existing preferences, especially in realistic decision contexts. It would be futile to try to directly manipulate a powerful predisposition such as party identification. A simple party label will automatically elicit strong reactions and beliefs. A smart experimental design will at minimum simply measure and control such powerful reactions but ideally take advantage of them and utilize them within the experimental design.

What is the best experimental design? The short answer is that it does not exist. Every researcher will have to decide on the most appropriate design to test a certain theory in a given context. If a single experiment cannot give a complete and satisfying answer, as it is frequently the case, more than one experiment might be the solution. We call such a research strategy *experimental triangulation*. Researchers vary the operationalization of key measures or the setup of the experiment in order to test different aspects and mechanisms of the hypothesized cause-and-effect relationship. Taken together, this set of experiments offers a more complete and valid explanation of the social phenomenon of interest.

The term triangulation is borrowed from celestial navigation where it indicates a technique to infer one's geodetic position from the measurement of different sights such as the sun and the horizon (a role taken over by satellites for modern GPS-based navigation). In the social sciences, the concept can be traced back to the idea of improving measurement by using different measures. More specifically, Campbell and Fiske (1959) proposed the multi-trait–multi-method matrix to obtain more valid measures of traits. The first explicit reference to triangulation we are aware of was made by Webb et al. (1966):

'Once a proposition has been confirmed by two or more independent measurement processes, the uncertainty of its interpretation is greatly reduced. The most persuasive evidence comes through a triangulation of measurement processes. If a proposition can survive the onslaught of a series of imperfect measures, with all their irrelevant error, confidence should be placed in it. Of course, this confidence is increased by minimizing errors in each instrument and by a reasonable belief in the different and divergent effects of the source of error' (p. 3).

The concept of triangulation has been extended beyond measurement in several ways. Denzin (1970) outlined various types of triangulation, among them the use of independent data sources (data triangulation), different researchers (investigator triangulation) and different research methodologies (method triangulation). While not without criticism (for example, Blaikie, 1991), triangulation can be defined as a process in which different measurement strategies or sources of information validate each other and overcome their potential individual weaknesses to enhance the confidence in our conclusions.

Like multiple measures of a single concept, we can talk about triangulation with a multi-method approach when we devise independent tests of the same theory with different methods. If multiple but complementary theory tests come to similar conclusions, we have more confidence in the research findings. But as Mathison (1988) points out, different measures, methods and sources might not always converge but rather offer inconsistent or even contradictory outcomes. A triangulation strategy consequently can lead to a much more complex and thorough understanding of a social phenomenon.

In this chapter, we elaborate how scholars can, within the same methodological paradigm, creatively leverage different experimental designs to triangulate their findings within the same research program. With multiple experiments, we can use the specific strengths of one particular experimental paradigm to address and compensate for the limitations of another experimental paradigm. The obvious advantage in contrast to, say, a regular multi-method approach, is that through experimental triangulation scholars do not have to compromise the strengths of experimental designs *per se* with the use of other methodologies to triangulate theory tests. While multi-method designs are of course still possible and even desirable, we argue that the particular strength of experimental triangulation is that it facilitates the use of experiments as a flexible tool to devise several independent tests of the same theory. Of course, different designs might sometimes lead to different answers, raising the question about how to evaluate and interpret such divergent results. We will return to this question in our conclusion.

## 7.2    Illustrative example: Coalition signals and strategic voting in multi-party systems

In first-past-the-post systems, a strategic voter is typically defined as someone who cast his or her vote for a party other than the most preferred party because the former has a better chance of winning (Cox, 1997; Fischer, 2004). According to the theory of strategic voting, a strategic vote requires an instrumental motivation and rational expectations about the outcome of the next election. According to this definition, it is necessarily insincere. At first glance, studying strategic voting in multi-party systems might seem to be a hopeless endeavor (but see Cox, 1997). But more recently, several studies have offered evidence that strategic voting not only makes sense in multi-party systems using proportional representation (PR) but have offered supporting evidence as well (for example, Abramson et al., 2010; Blais et al., 2006; Bargsted and Kedar, 2009; Meffert and Gschwend, 2010). These studies suggest that voters not only defect from marginal parties but have a variety of reasons to cast a strategic vote.

The theory of strategic voting assumes that voters cast their ballot in order to maximize their expected utility based on their party preferences and their expectations about the outcome of the next election (Cox, 1997). With coalition governments, strategic voters must not only form expectations about the likelihood of which parties will win representation in parliament but also consider which coalitions are viable and likely. Based on these expectations, they can decide how to vote in order to best influence government formation, if only to influence the weight of each party in an almost certain coalition (Meffert and Gschwend, 2007). Given the complexity of the decision task, it is likely that voters use simple heuristics such as coalition signals by parties to simplify the decision task. Especially coalition signals should help voters to narrow down the large number of theoretically possible coalitions to the relevant few.

At the individual level, strategic voting is typically studied with survey data from particular elections. The challenge to determine the effect of coalition signals on voting behavior is by now a familiar one: A single election usually does not provide much variation in the key independent variables, polls and coalition signals. Both tend to be fairly stable and consistent before elections, and every voter will receive more or less the same information. Consequently, it is not possible to determine with confidence that a strategic voter would have decided differently if the polls had suggested a different election outcome or if parties had offered different coalition signals.

In order to overcome this lack of variance, we turn to experimental designs. This strategy allows us to create theoretically relevant decision scenarios in and outside the laboratory that should either facilitate or inhibit strategic voting. We use experimental manipulations to create variance in the key explanatory factors, and the comparison of treatment and control groups allows us to directly test our hypotheses about coalition signals.

## 7.3  Coalition signals in three experimental designs

Testing the causal effects of coalition signals requires that coalition signals vary, either in terms of their presence or absence or in terms of their nature (valence), advocating (positive) or ruling out (negative) a specific coalition. The basic design and operationalization can follow a simple logic. By randomly assigning different versions of the coalition signal to participants, it is possible to determine whether signals have the hypothesized impact by comparing the key outcome variable for the different experimental groups. Experiments allow the systematic variation of coalition signals and measure their effect on randomly assigned groups.

Experiments can take many different shapes and forms. The settings can range from a tightly controlled lab environment over a real-world field setting to (often representative) surveys, and methodological rules and standards differ by tradition (Morton and Williams, 2010). Experiments in the economic tradition tend to confront participants with abstract, context-free and transparent decision scenarios. The information available to participants might be incomplete, creating uncertainty, but it should never be deceptive or false. In order to rule out external and potentially confounding influences, preferences are induced and assigned by the experimenter and not based on existing preferences of participants. This gives the experimenter in economic experiments a very high degree of control. The abstract nature of these experiments and the induced preferences make it possible to assess the quality of decision making in a straightforward manner. Because the correct decision is known to the experimenter, it is very easy to determine good and bad or optimal and wrong decisions. Participants experience success and failure as monetary gains and losses.

Following these basic principles, we designed an economic experiment that presented participants with an abstract game with fictitious parties and induced party preferences in a laboratory setting (Meffert and Gschwend, 2007). The coalition signals were operationalized as salient information but associated with high ambiguity and uncertainty. The quality of the decision was determined as a monetary payoff. Table 7.1 presents an overview of the key characteristics of our studies.

Psychological experiments, on the other hand, try to create realistic decision scenarios, not in terms of mundane realism, but in the sense that they rely on pre-existing individual preferences and differences and try to pose

*Table 7.1*   Key Characteristics of Studies

| Key Aspect | Economic Lab Experiment | Psychological Lab Experiment | Survey Experiment |
|---|---|---|---|
| Context | Abstract Game | Real Campaign | Real Campaign |
| Party Preferences | Induced (no ties) | Measured (ties possible) | Measured (ties possible) |
| Coalition Signals | Salient and Transparent (uncertain) | Subtle and Unobtrusive (realistic) | Salient and Transparent (hypothetical) |
| Vote Decisions | Monetary Payoff (optimal) | Hypothetical Vote Decision | Hypothetical Vote Decision |
| Sample | Convenience Sample (Students) | Convenience Sample (Students) | Representative Sample |

decision scenarios that capture the attention and involvement of the participants (McDermott, 2002). A key difference to economic experiments is the frequent use of concealment and deception for experimental manipulations. The information given to participants is optimized to create a convincing manipulation, not to provide objective and verifiable facts. From an ethical perspective, the use of concealment and deception makes it mandatory that participants are debriefed at the end of the study. Any misrepresentation of the facts needs to be corrected.

Psychological experiments of electoral decision making rely frequently on fictitious scenarios in order to control the amount and content of information available to participants. However, it is very common to use existing parties and existing party preferences, relinquishing much more control than economic experiments. The psychological experiment described below went one step further by embedding it in two ongoing state election campaigns in Germany (Meffert and Gschwend, 2011). The decision scenario presented to participants was thus highly realistic, and most information provided to participants was taken from the actual party platforms. However, the experiment still took place in a laboratory setting with a convenience sample of student participants. The experiment used deception to operationalize and manipulate coalition signals and poll results. The manipulated information was embedded in a subtle and unobtrusive way in other campaign information. The goal was to create theoretically relevant decision scenarios that should (not) induce strategic voting. The key dependent variable was a hypothetical vote decision in the state election, but not tied to any monetary payoff or incentive (though participants received a fixed participation fee).

Laboratory experiments usually use convenience samples that pose a challenge to external validity and the generalization of the study results to the world outside. In this respect, cross-sectional surveys with a general population sample have a clear advantage over laboratory experiments, even if they fall short when assessing causal relationships. That said, it is sometimes possible to combine the advantages of randomized manipulations and control of laboratory experiments with the representative nature of general population surveys. If a manipulation can be included in a survey questionnaire, the combination of a randomized experimental manipulation with a representative population sample is a near perfect solution.

In the survey experiment described below, respondents were interviewed in a pre-election survey and confronted with four scenarios in the form of short vignettes, in a randomized order. The vignettes presented respondents with different coalition signals and asked for any (hypothetical) changes in vote intentions. Needless to say, these respondents did not receive a financial incentive for participation or 'optimal' answers.

### 7.3.1 Economic experiment

The main purpose of the economic experiment was a causal test of strategic voting in multi-party systems with proportional representation, minimum vote thresholds and coalition governments under ideal conditions; all participants had an induced monetary incentive for strategic voting and no incentive for expressive or habitual voting (for details, see Meffert and Gschwend, 2007). An important initial design decision was to use a decision scenario with four parties because three parties allow only for a trivial number of coalitions while five parties already lead to an (exponentially increasing) explosive number of coalitions and highly complex decision scenarios. The election scenario consisted of four parties (A to D) competing for the votes of 15 voters, distributed randomly in a two-dimensional space. Voters could maximize their expected utility by moving the location of the next government as close as possible to their own location, compared with or relative to the government location after a sincere vote for the preferred (closest) party. The reduced distance constituted the monetary payoff, while wrong decisions that moved the government further away from the voter location constituted a monetary loss. A voter decision (or government) is called optimal if no other party choice (government) leads to a higher payoff. The participant was the only swing voter while the other 14 simulated voters always supported their preferred party (see Figure 7.1).

The critical component of the decision scenarios was how coalition governments would be formed after an election. The procedure followed four sequential rules. The first and very obvious criterion was an *absolute majority* of seats in parliament for a single party. If no party had the support of a majority, a coalition government became necessary. The key rule was the *minimum distance* of two (or three) parties in the political space that reached an absolute majority. The following two rules were used to break any ties that might exist after the second rule. First, a two-party coalition would beat a three-party coalition (*minimum number of parties*), and if this still could not resolve the tie, the coalition with the lower vote share would

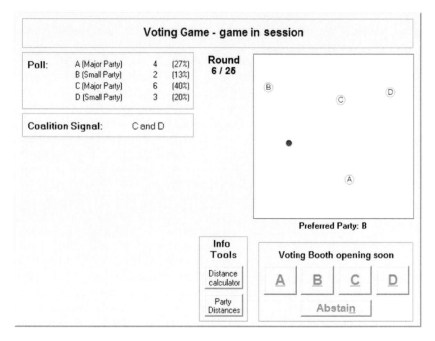

*Figure 7.1*   Game Screen of Economic Experiment

be formed (*minimum vote share*). If all four rules failed to produce a government, the election ended in a stalemate without any payoff. It is important to note that government formation was explicitly and entirely based on the electoral strength and proximity of the parties. Pre-electoral coalition signals played no part in government formation and thus should *not* have played any role for voters. Participants were fully informed and familiar with the rules of government formation.

The experiment tested the influence of two critical information sources, polls and coalition signals, by manipulating their availability to voters. Polls were based on the actual distribution of the party preferences in a given election scenario and available with an 80 per cent probability. But even if not available, voters would still receive information about the relative size of the parties, whether it was a major (>25 per cent) or a minor (<25 per cent) party. The operationalization of the coalition signal was more difficult to implement. Ideally, an experimental manipulation is fully randomized and independent from other manipulated factors such as, in this case, the strength and location (or proximity) of the parties. If implemented this way, the signal would show two (or three) randomly chosen parties. However, a signal generated this way would frequently be meaningless, for example by displaying two small parties or two parties at the opposite ends of the political space. It would have no meaning and participants would not take it seriously. The signal had to be both plausible but uncertain – that is, sometimes providing 'good' information and sometimes 'bad' information – good in the sense that the coalition in the signal would indeed lead to a successful, optimal outcome, while a bad signal would indicate a coalition that represents an unsuccessful election outcome. Consequently, the coalition signal was based on a simple decision rule: It showed the two parties closest to each other but required that at least one of the two parties was a major party. This rule essentially represents a simple heuristic for government formation that might or might not be successful. It is also based on information that was always available to participants, the distance of the parties in the political space and the approximate size of the parties (that is, at least one major party).

In about half of the randomly generated decision scenarios selected for the experiment, the signal showed the coalition that represented the optimal government for the voter. In the other half, it displayed a suboptimal government. Note that even if the signal shows the optimal government, these parties do not necessarily include the party that the participant should vote for in order to produce this government. While the parties in the signal were thus determined by a simple rule, the visibility of the signal to participants was randomized with equal probability. Participants were only told that the signal shows parties that wish to form a coalition, not how the signal was generated. Because the coalition signal played no role in actual government formation, it should be irrelevant information for participants.

The results of the experiment, however, show that the signal did influence the decisions of the participants. Table 7.2 distinguishes between easy elections with an optimal coalition signal and difficult elections with a suboptimal signal, as well as the availability of poll and signal information. If we take the decision scenarios without polls and signals as the baseline, participants were able to make optimal decisions in 51 per cent of the easy elections and 31 per cent of the difficult elections. The availability of polls increases the proportion of optimal decisions to 64 and 41 per cent, respectively. The impact of the signal, when no poll was available, is equally strong, but conditional on the quality. Good signals in easy elections increase the share of optimal decisions to 65 per cent, while bad signals in difficult elections lower the share of optimal decisions to 22 per cent. If both the poll and signal are available, the share of optimal decisions in easy elections increased further, but only slightly, to 68 per cent. In difficult elections, the availability of a poll appears to have helped voters to counteract the bad signal. They made optimal decisions in 38 per cent of the elections. The results of the economic experiment suggest that even voters with a strategic (monetary) incentive tend to rely on coalition signals as a heuristic. If the

*Table 7.2* Share of Optimal Decisions by Election Difficulty and Available Information

|  | No Info | Poll Only | Signal Only | Poll and Signal |
|---|---|---|---|---|
| Scenarios | % (BSE) | % (BSE) | % (BSE) | % (BSE) |
|  | N | N | N | N |
| Easy Elections | 51.7 (3.1) | 64.2 (1.5) | 64.8 (2.8) | 67.7 (1.4) |
|  | 269 | 1097 | 301 | 1123 |
| Difficult Elections | 30.9 (2.3) | 40.8 (1.2) | 21.8 (2.1) | 37.6 (1.2) |
|  | 408 | 1651 | 427 | 1699 |

*Note*: Entries are proportions, with bootstrapped standard errors in parentheses and the number of decisions in each cell. The number of decisions varies due to the random assignment of poll and signal manipulation, the former with unequal probability.

signal is accurate, it can very well substitute for a poll, but if it is bad, voters who follow it tend to make the wrong decisions.

### 7.3.2   Psychological experiment

The psychological experiment operationalized coalition signals in a highly realistic way. As before, the experiment focused on strategic voting and it was conducted in a laboratory setting. However, it was embedded in two real, contemporaneous German state election campaigns in January 2006. The general design and procedure of the study involved exposure to campaign information about the five major parties, with information taken from actual election platforms of the parties. Participants played the role of a voter and were instructed to inform themselves before the upcoming election. The information was presented on a computer-based information board that always showed six newspaper-style headlines with information. Clicking on a headline opened another window with the associated short article (see Meffert and Gschwend, 2011, for details).

The main purpose of the experiment was to test a specific version of strategic voting in PR systems with minimum vote thresholds, threshold insurance. Supporters of a major party might vote for the preferred junior coalition partner if the latter is in danger of falling short of the threshold. Previous research has shown mixed support in favor of such rental votes or *Leihstimmen* (for example, Gschwend, 2007; Pappi and Thurner, 2002). At the same time, supporters of small parties that are fairly certain to fall short of the threshold should defect from their party and rather vote for another party that will affect government formation in a beneficial way. In order to test these assumptions and the role of polls and explicit coalition signals by parties, the study used the actual party preferences of the participants.

The manipulation of polls and coalition signals specifically targeted the preferred parties of each participant. At the beginning of an experimental session, participants indicated their party preferences by ranking the five most relevant parties, the two major parties Christian Democrats (CDU) and Social Democrats (SPD) and the three minor parties Free Democrats (FDP), the Greens (Die Grünen) and the Left Party (Die Linke/WASG). This ranking determined which parties were used for the subsequent manipulations. First, the highest ranked major party determined the assignment of a participant to one of two states, CDU supporters to Baden-Württemberg and SPD supporters to Rhineland-Palatinate. These parties were the respective incumbent parties in each state and both were expected to be re-elected by large margins. In other words, the expected winner in each election was held constant for all study participants. It should be noted that the study was conducted in the city of Mannheim, located right on the border between these two states, allowing for a fairly seamless assignment of participants to these different states.

Next, the most preferred small party was used for the poll and coalition signal manipulation. The poll manipulation varied the expected performance of the small party above and below the minimum vote threshold. The signal manipulation used the preferred major and minor parties to either explicitly mention this coalition or to avoid any reference to it. In short, the two most preferred parties of each participant were used for manipulations in order to create standardized election scenarios, but the manipulations themselves, the closeness to the threshold and an explicit coalition signal, were randomized.

Participants were exposed to manipulated polls and signals in two ways during the 'campaign'. Participants were exposed to six headlines on the information board that changed in a fixed interval of 45 seconds, whether or not participants clicked on and read any of the articles. Five headlines on each screen always represented the issue positions or candidates of the five parties (one headline for each party). The sixth headline covered either polls or other, fairly generic state information. In total, the 90 headlines and articles available to respondents covered 13 issues and two candidates for each party as well as five manipulated polls, five generic polls and five state-specific but generic topics. The order was randomized.

After two screens with headlines, the campaign was interrupted for a pre-election poll that first asked participants to indicate their vote intention at that point, followed by a screen ostensibly showing the results of an actual state election poll (Figure 7.2). Participants saw a table with the manipulated numerical poll results on the left and a verbal summary (for numerically challenged participants) on the right. At the bottom were two statements attributed to the two preferred parties of each participant. Phrased in the style of newspaper headlines, they either mentioned a coalition or just stated typical campaign statements in response to the poll. Using the parties CDU and FDP as examples, the statements without signal read:

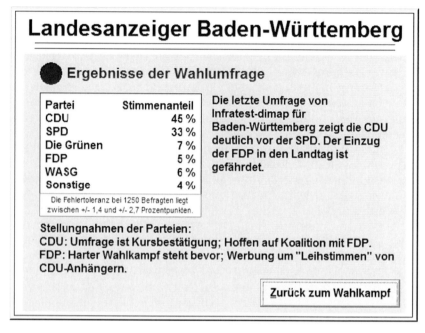

## Landesanzeiger Baden-Württemberg

● **Ergebnisse der Wahlumfrage**

| Partei | Stimmenanteil |
|---|---|
| CDU | 45 % |
| SPD | 33 % |
| Die Grünen | 7 % |
| FDP | 5 % |
| WASG | 6 % |
| Sonstige | 4 % |

Die Fehlertoleranz bei 1250 Befragten liegt zwischen +/- 1,4 und +/- 2,7 Prozentpunkten.

Die letzte Umfrage von Infratest-dimap für Baden-Württemberg zeigt die CDU deutlich vor der SPD. Der Einzug der FDP in den Landtag ist gefährdet.

**Stellungnahmen der Parteien:**
**CDU: Umfrage ist Kursbestätigung; Hoffen auf Koalition mit FDP.**
**FDP: Harter Wahlkampf steht bevor; Werbung um "Leihstimmen" von CDU-Anhängern.**

Zurück zum Wahlkampf

*Figure 7.2*   Poll Results Screen of Psychological Experiment

CDU:  Poll confirms we are on the right track; Will fight for every vote
FDP:  Campaign will be tough; Need to better motivate supporters

In the version with a coalition signal (as shown in Figure 7.2), the statement read instead:

CDU:  Poll confirms we are on the right track; Hope for coalition with FDP
FDP:  Campaign will be tough; Appeal for 'rental votes' by CDU supporters

Note that the first part of these statements was always identical and only the second part changed. All participants saw this screen and thus were guaranteed to be exposed to the signal manipulation.

The second opportunity to encounter the manipulated information was as part of the headlines and articles on the information board. However, participants had to actively choose and read these five articles with manipulated poll and signal information. It does provide a hard behavioral measure of interest in and exposure to poll information. The five articles repeated the same poll and signal information from the pre-election poll discussed above. Each article focused on a different aspect, but basically restated the same information. As a rule of thumb, one or two paragraphs restated the poll results and one paragraph discussed coalitions, either mentioning the explicit coalition signal or at a fairly unspecific level. In each experimental condition, every participant was exposed to the same information or content. Only the names of the parties changed according to the individual party preferences of each participant. In terms of programming, the party names were 'variables' in a text mask (which also included all the verbs associated with the parties because, grammatically, the Greens are a plural noun and require a different verb form than the singular nouns FDP and WASG).

The operationalization of polls and coalition signals in this experiment has the clear advantage of tapping the actual party preferences of the participants and using a real election campaign as decision scenario and backdrop. This clearly improves the external validity of the study but it also imposes certain limitations. First, reality constrains the manipulation of polls and signals to a plausible range. For the polls, the winning major party in each state could not be changed, only the forecasts for the small parties could plausibly range from four per cent to ten per cent (with a minimum vote threshold of five per cent). The WASG was running for the first time in both states, creating some uncertainty about its strength. The only baseline salient to participants could have been the results of the previous general election several months earlier in which the three minor parties reached fairly similar and strong results (FDP: 9.8 per cent, Green Party: 8.1 per cent, Left Party/PDS/WASG: 8.7 per cent).

The coalition signal posed a bigger challenge. In both states, the FDP was the junior partner in the incumbent coalition and thus the designated coalition partner after the next election. In both states, however, the situation was more fluid and alternative coalitions could not be ruled out. In both states, the Greens were a plausible alternative coalition partner while the WASG was more or less ruled out by both major parties. Because the signal manipulation automatically used the preferred parties of each participant, the signal could have shown fairly absurd combinations, in particular a coalition of the conservative CDU with the far-left WASG. This was judged to be an acceptable risk, correctly as it turned out, because such a party preference ranking was highly unlikely. Less serious, but more difficult to solve, was the fact that some signals would show the incumbent coalition, while others would propose a new coalition. Thus, the coalition signals had to be phrased very carefully. They were attributed, for example, to 'different politicians in both parties' to make them plausible for any coalition, incumbent or not. The phrases used typical, sometimes off-the-record statements by politicians during real campaigns. Given this complexity, the complete experimental design was tested first in a large pilot study. This test was successful, but as a result, it became necessary to include another poll condition in the main experiment. The manipulation checks of poll and signal manipulations were successful as well, and post-study comments and feedback by participants indicated hardly any suspicion of the manipulated polls and coalition signals.

The results, however, brought some surprises. Only ten participants (or 7.5 per cent of participants in the close-poll conditions that were expected to induce strategic voting) could be classified as strategic voters, pre-empting a meaningful analysis of the effect of coalition signals on strategic voting. However, about a quarter of the participants did defect from their top-ranked party and voted 'insincerely' for some other party, independent of the poll manipulation. In a multivariate model predicting insincere voting, coalition signals have a modest positive impact, again suggesting that coalition signals do play a role in vote decisions. But compared to the strong signal effect in the economic experiment, the realistic but fairly subtle signal in the psychological experiment appears to have only a minor impact.

The small number of strategic voters can in part be explained by one of the key and necessary design features. Because the preferred large party was always the certain winner and never faced real competition or even trailed the opponent, this party was essentially removed from strategic considerations that might exist otherwise. Only a replication in other contexts would allow a test of strategic voting under such circumstances. Last but not least, the manipulation of coalition signals during a real election campaign carries a significant risk because real parties might make an announcement during data collection that might undermine the study purpose. In our case, this did not happen.

### 7.3.3 Survey experiment

Experimental manipulations can also be included in representative population surveys, though with less control and with the need for fairly obvious manipulations. Coalition signals are very well suited for this purpose because they merely require that survey respondents are exposed to them before the relevant questions. Thus, our third implementation of coalition signals is fairly straightforward. As part of a representative pre-election survey before the 2006 Austrian General Election, participants were exposed to four different vignettes of hypothetical coalition announcements by Austrian parties. As in the psychological experiment, a real election campaign as decision context and background always poses the acute risk that real events might interfere with the manipulations, such as a party making an unexpected coalition announcement. Unlike laboratory experiments with fictitious decision tasks, a survey that is several weeks in the field offers hardly any control over contextual factors and the study setting that might undermine the manipulated messages. Consequently, the coalition signals had to be phrased explicitly and transparently as hypothetical statements in order to work even in a changed setting.

In order to both avoid such surprises and to create sharply contrasting vignettes, the hypothetical coalitions always mixed and matched one of the two major Austrian parties, the conservative People's Party (ÖVP) or the Social Democrats (SPÖ), with one of the two smaller parties that were expected to perform very well in the election, the moderate but left-of-center Greens (Die Grünen) and the far-right and populist FPÖ (which incidentally was fairly explicit in ruling out any participation in government).

These vignettes were presented shortly after asking the standard question about vote intentions. They were introduced by the statement that '[m]ost parties have not made a clear announcement about possible coalitions after the election' and followed by four vignettes, in randomized order:

- For which party would you vote if the Greens would clearly reject a coalition with the SPÖ and announce the intention to form a coalition with the ÖVP?
- For which party would you vote if the Greens would clearly reject a coalition with the ÖVP and announce the intention to form a coalition with the SPÖ?
- For which party would you vote if the FPÖ would drop its intention to not participate in any coalition and rather announce the intention to form a coalition with the ÖVP?
- For which party would you vote if the FPÖ would drop its intention to not participate in any coalition and rather announce the intention to form a coalition with the SPÖ?

The response to each vignette was recorded with the same party list that was used for the standard vote intention question. This allows within-respondent comparisons of changes in (hypothetical) vote intentions.

Because the vignettes focus on specific parties but were given to all respondents, it is reasonable to expect effects primarily on those respondents who are directly affected by these coalition signals, in particular supporters of the Greens and the FPÖ. Table 7.3 gives a short illustration of how respondents reacted to the vignettes. Among supporters of the Green Party, a signal in favor of the ÖVP and against the SPÖ led to a considerable drop of support, while a signal in favor of the SPÖ did not change the support at all. The latter was the preferred coalition of a large majority of Green Party supporters. Among FPÖ supporters, however, any departure from the declared governmental abstinence, whether in favor of the ÖVP or the SPÖ, led to a drop of support for the FPÖ. In both cases, coalition signals affect the vote intentions of supporters. For the Greens, the coalition partner matters and the SPÖ is the clear favorite. For FPÖ supporters,

*Table 7.3*   Vote Intention for Preferred Party of Green Party and FPÖ Supporters

| | Vote Intention for Preferred Party (PP) | | |
|---|---|---|---|
| | **Initial** | **Vignette with ÖVP-PP Signal** | **Vignette with SPÖ-PP Signal** |
| Preferred Party | % (SE) | % (SE) | % (SE) |
| Greens (*n* = 308) | 65.9 (2.7) | 53.6 (2.8) | 65.6 (2.7) |
| FPÖ (*n* = 86) | 62.7 (5.2) | 51.2 (5.4) | 51.2 (5.4) |

*Note*: Entries represent the proportions of Green Party or FPÖ supporters who intend to vote for their preferred party in each condition, with standard errors in parentheses. The preferred party is defined as the party rated highest among all parties.

government participation in itself leads to a drop of support, suggesting that at least some supporters see their vote as a protest vote against the mainstream parties. Even if the effects are again more limited, the third study once more supports the notion that coalition signals matter, in a real election and with a representative sample of voters.

## 7.4   Conclusion: Comparing and evaluating the results of different experiments

How do we know that coalition signals actually have an effect on voters' decision making? If we had merely used observational data, we would almost certainly have faced the problem that our key independent variable, coalition signals, would not have varied much in each of the election campaigns. We simply would not have the necessary variance for a meaningful test of our hypothesis. Instead, we used different experimental designs that allowed us to 'inject' variance by manipulating coalition signals in theoretically meaningful ways. This approach makes a test of the causal hypothesis possible and suggests that coalition signals matter, and not only for strategic voting.

The different operationalizations of coalition signals demonstrate that experiments are flexible tools to test causal relationships even if there is not enough variance in the key explanatory variable. Given that the lack of variance is a frequent problem for research questions in political science, researchers would be well advised to consider and adopt experimental strategies as well. It can not only overcome the limits of other designs but provide the opportunity to address new and seemingly intractable questions. And using an experimental triangulation strategy by employing different types of experiments can further enhance and strengthen our confidence in the findings. In our case, three experimental designs from different experimental traditions – economic, psychological and survey research – have given us a

*Table 7.4* Key Results of Studies

| Key Aspects | Economic Lab Experiment | Psychological Lab Experiment | Survey Experiment |
|---|---|---|---|
| Coalition Signals | Highly Effective | Marginal Effect | Conditional Effect |
| Interpretation | Useful but Risky Heuristic | Nonstrategic Heuristic | Deliberate Decision |

mostly converging, sometimes inconsistent, but never contradictory pattern of results. Table 7.4 provides a brief summary.

The unambiguously good news is that no matter the type of experiment, coalition signals matter! We saw in the economic experiment (that deliberately induced in all participants a strategic mindset) that the manipulation of coalition signals was highly effective. Coalition signals facilitated strategic voting and emerged as a useful heuristic that simplified participants' decision task. But it is a risky heuristic because a given coalition signal might involve parties that are not the optimal vote choice for a participant. Thus, coalition signals can help but also lead voters astray if they trust them blindly.

In the psychological experiment (in which voters could follow either strategic or expressive motivations in a real election context), we found merely a marginal impact of coalition signals on participants' vote choice. Voters were more likely to defect from their top-ranked party and vote for some other party when coalition signals were present. The fact that participants deserted their preferred party even if the polls did not indicate any instrumental benefit suggests that coalition signals affect not just strategic voting but that they have a more complex impact. It suggests that coalition signals are a simple heuristic for both strategic and merely insincere voters but that they might even elicit the expression of a genuine coalition preference. The experiment suggests that the investigation of coalition signals requires a closer look at coalition preferences as well.

The results of the survey experiment replicate and complement the results of the two previous studies. Coalition signals changed respondents' vote intention systematically in our representative sample of Austrian voters. We find evidence for those effects not for all signals and on all respondents, but primarily on those who are directly affected by the signals. In contrast to the two other studies, in which coalition signals were an unobtrusive facet of the information environment, the vignettes in the survey experiment explicitly linked the coalition signals with the vote intention. Thus, respondents could not even process this information heuristically. Rather, they were forced explicitly and deliberately to think about the consequences of different signals on their vote decision, leading to clear and observable shifts in vote intentions.

Our triangulation strategy with different types of experiments leverages the strength of each design to address the limitations of the others. For example, the economic experiment gave us full control over participants' preferences, the signal manipulation and any contextual influences. In the survey experiment, our control was very weak because we had no influence over what happened in the actual campaign. On the other hand, the survey experiment used a real election and it was based on a representative sample, giving it much higher generalizability than the convenience sample in our laboratory experiments.

In terms of internal validity, the psychological experiment falls somewhere in the middle. The standardized decision scenarios and randomized manipulations certainly provide a high degree of internal validity, but it is rather difficult to find the hypothesized effects. Subtle manipulations met real and strong political preferences, severely limiting our ability to 'push' participants around.

For a pure theory test, our concern is more with internal than external validity. The fact that we can replicate the strong effects of coalition signals in the abstract economic experiment in weaker form with both a laboratory experiment and a survey experiment during real election campaigns gives us the confidence to conclude that coalition signals are an important factor that requires more attention in future research.

How can we best assess and compare the different impact of coalition signals across very different experiments? We have two answers. First, it remains puzzling for us how to *directly* compare the size of the effects, and in fact it might even be a futile endeavor. These differences might merely be random, but it is a priori more likely that different types of experiments exert their own 'design effects' similar to so-called 'house effects' of different survey institutes that often produce different numbers even when surveying the same population at the same time. A third possibility is that the differences vary systematically with the different contexts in which they were conducted. Only replications with similar experiments in different contexts will allow us to answer this question. On a more positive note, the second answer is that the findings of all three experiments support and complement each other while indicating stronger and weaker effects under different conditions. This, after all, is the ultimate purpose of experimental triangulation.

To sum up, we argued that experiments are flexible tools for theory testing. Our results indicate that experiments are particularly useful in situations in which key explanatory factors lack variation. This is a challenge we often face when designing a study. We have shown some of the strengths and weaknesses of different experimental designs, and the benefits of using an experimental triangulation strategy to both conduct conclusive causal tests of our theories and to generate a complementary and more generalizable pattern of findings. Our hope is that we have convinced our readers that despite all the difficulties and drawbacks, well-designed experiments offer new possibilities for interesting research in political science.

## References

Abramson, Paul R., John H. Aldrich, André Blais, Matthew Diamond, Abraham Diskin, Indridi H. Indridason, Daniel J. Lee and Renan Levine (2010) 'Comparing Strategic Voting Under FPTP and PR', *Comparative Political Studies*, 43, 61–90.

Bargsted, Matias A. and Orit Kedar (2009) 'Coalition-Targeted Duvergerian Voting: How Expectations Affect Voter Choice under Proportional Representation', *American Journal of Political Science*, 53, 307–23.

Blaikie, Norman W.H. (1991) 'A Critique of the Use of Triangulation in Social Research', *Quality & Quantity*, 25, 115–36.

Blais, André, John H. Aldrich, Indridi H. Indridason and Renan Levine (2006) 'Do Voters Vote for Government Coalitions? Testing Downs' Pessimistic Conclusion', *Party Politics*, 12, 691–705.

Cox, Gary W. (1997) *Making Votes Count. Strategic Coordination in the World's Electoral Systems* (Cambridge: Cambridge University Press).

Campbell, Donald T. and Donald W. Fiske (1959) 'Convergent and Discriminant Validation by the Multitrait-Multimethod Matrix', *Psychological Bulletin*, 56, 81–105.

Denzin, Norman K. (1970) *The Research Act in Sociology: A Theoretical Introduction to Sociological Methods* (Chicago: Aldine).

Downs, Anthony (1957) *An Economic Theory of Democracy* (New York: Harper Collins).

Fisher, Stephen D. (2004) 'Definition and measurement of tactical voting: the role of rational choice', *British Journal of Political Science*, 34, 152–66.

Gschwend, Thomas (2007) 'Ticket-Splitting and Strategic Voting under Mixed Electoral Rules: Evidence from Germany', *European Journal of Political Research*, 46, 1–23.

Gschwend, Thomas and Frank Schimmelfennig (2007) *Research Design in Political Science. How to Practice What They Preach?* (Houndmills, Basingstoke: Palgrave).

King, Gary, Robert O. Keohane and Sidney Verba (1994) *Designing Social Inquiry: Scientific Inference in Qualitative Research* (Princeton, NJ: Princeton University Press).

Mathison, Sandra (1988) 'Why Triangulate?' *Educational Researcher*, 17, 13–7.

McDermott, Rose (2002) 'Experimental Methodology in Political Science', *Political Analysis*, 10, 325–42.

Meffert, Michael F. and Thomas Gschwend (2007) *Strategic Voting under Proportional Representation and Coalition Governments: A Simulation and Laboratory Experiment* (SFB 504 Working Paper No. 07–55, University of Mannheim).

Meffert, Michael F. and Thomas Gschwend (2010) 'Strategic Coalition Voting: Evidence from Austria', *Electoral Studies*, 29, 339–49.

Meffert, Michael F. and Thomas Gschwend (2011) 'Polls, Coalition Signals, and Strategic Voting: An Experimental Investigation of Perceptions and Effects', *European Journal of Political Research*, 50, 636–667.

Mook, Douglas G. (1983) 'In Defense of External Invalidity', *American Psychologist*, 38, 379–87.

Morton, Rebecca B. and Kenneth C. Williams (2010) *Experimental Political Science and the Study of Causality: From Nature to the Lab* (Cambridge, Cambridge University Press).

Pappi, Franz U. and Paul W. Thurner (2002) 'Electoral Behaviour in a Two-Vote System: Incentives for Ticket Splitting in German Bundestag Elections', *European Journal of Political Research*, 41, 207–32.

Webb, Eugene J., Donald T. Campbell, Richard D. Schwartz and Lee Sechrest (1966) *Unobtrusive Measures: Nonreactive Research in the Social Sciences* (Chicago, Rand McNally).

# Part III

# Exploring and Analyzing Experimental Data

# 8
# Statistical Analysis of Experimental Data

*Susumu Shikano, Thomas Bräuninger and Michael Stoffel*

## Introduction

While an increasing number of observational studies in modern political science use quite sophisticated statistical methods, experimental studies often continue to apply rather simple statistical instruments like t-tests or analysis of variance (ANOVA). At first sight this is surprising if one considers that many modern statistical methods had been developed and invented for the analysis of data generated in random experiments (see, for example, Fisher, 1935). It is, however, less surprising if one considers that more sophisticated statistical methods were developed much later in order to cope with specific data problems in observational studies. Looking from the perspective of the random experimentalist, the most serious statistical challenges in observational data arise from treatment imbalance and from the violation of the assumption that the independent variables are distributed independently and identically at random.

Experimental studies, on the other hand, do not have to worry about biased estimation due to treatment imbalance as long as the random assignment in data collection is successful. Does randomizing make such kinds of ex-post statistical analysis redundant? The answer is no, of course. Even though random assignment enables us to estimate a less biased treatment effect, a couple of statistical techniques can help us to increase statistical power and the quality of the inferences we make. One of the most widely known techniques is the analysis of covariance (ANCOVA), which integrates further covariates into ANOVA. ANCOVA can be interpreted as a combination of ANOVA and linear regression and as a special case of multi-level modeling. The latter fact points to applying multi-level modeling to experimental data as this opens a variety of possible model specifications.

The aim of this chapter is to elaborate the basic idea above and to present an application to a concrete experimental study. In the remainder of this chapter, we proceed as follows. The next section discusses problems of the ex-post-facto design, whereas the third section elaborates the basic ideas of

ANCOVA and its relationship to multi-level modeling. Subsequently, we present an application of the proposed method to data generating in an experiment on committee voting. We conclude with a short summary.

## 8.1   Development of statistical techniques in the ex-post-facto design

Most of the sophisticated statistical techniques used in observational studies are motivated by some deficits of the ex-post-facto design in comparison with the experimental design. The experimental design enables causal inferences by random assignment to experimental and control groups and explicit manipulation of treatments. More specifically, the experimental design prevents third variables from biasing the estimation of average causal effects of the interested treatment. By contrast, the ex-post-facto design in observational studies cannot guarantee balanced covariates between the treatment and control groups. The treatment imbalance can cause biased estimation of the treatment effect. In terms of regression models, this is expressed in violating the assumption that the stochastic component (residuals) and the deterministic component (forecasted values) are independent from each other. To avoid this, we conventionally use multiple regression models in which relevant control variables are added to the treatment variables. The logic extends to other types of generalized linear models with different types of dependent variables such as binary or multinomial logit, Dirichlet or poisson regression.

Another challenge for observational studies is the assumption underlying random experiments that random variables are independent and identically distributed. This assumption often is violated in observational data because of serial correlation, grouped structure of data or heteroscedasticity. This violation leads to inefficient estimates so that correction of underestimated standard errors is another important topic motivating advanced statistical techniques. To analyze data with serial correlation, different kinds of time-series analytical models have been developed. Datasets with grouped structure can be analyzed more appropriately with multi-level models which include panel data or time series cross-sectional data models as special cases. Furthermore, for different kinds of statistical models, a heteroscedastic extension has been developed.

The common goal of this variety of extended statistical models is to compensate for the deficiencies inherent to observational data as compared to experimental data. This, however, does not necessarily mean that the use of advanced statistical models is redundant for experimental data. While a successful random assignment (e.g., no lack of compliance with the treatment assignment) guarantees unbiased estimation of average treatment effects, certain statistical models can provide more efficient estimates. As an example, we introduce ANCOVA and multi-level modeling in the next section.

## 8.2 ANCOVA and multi-level modeling

In analyzing experimental data, one often begins by comparing averages of observed outcomes among different treatment groups. The basic model may be written down as follows:[1]

$$y_{ij} = \mu + \alpha_j + e_{ij} \tag{8.1}$$

where $y_{ij}$ is subject $i$'s outcome of interest in the $j$th experimental treatment, $\mu$ is the overall mean of $y_{ij}$, $\alpha_j$ is the effect of treatment $j$ and $e_{ij}$ is a random variable representing the uncontrolled variation. If we denote the mean outcome or dependent variable score of the $j$th treatment by $\mu_j$ then:

$$\alpha_j = \mu_j - \mu \tag{8.2}$$

$$e_{ij} = y_{ij} - \mu_j \tag{8.3}$$

Substituting (8.2) and (8.3) into equation (8.1), we can rearrange it as follows:

$$y_{ij} = \mu + (\mu_j - \mu) + (y_{ij} - \mu_j) \tag{8.4}$$

As randomized assignment guarantees independence between treatment and uncontrolled variance, we can decompose the total variation in the data into a treatment and an error component:

$$\sum_{i=1}^{N}\sum_{j=1}^{J}(y_{ij}-\mu)^2 = \sum_{j=1}^{J}N_j(\mu_j-\mu)^2 + \sum_{i=1}^{N}\sum_{j=1}^{J}(y_{ij}-\mu_j)^2 \tag{8.5}$$

where $N_j$ is the number of test persons in treatment $j$. Based on this decomposition, ANOVA tests for the statistical significance of differences in averages by comparing the following statistic:

$$F = \frac{\dfrac{\sum_{j=1}^{J}N_j(\mu_j-\mu)^2}{J-1}}{\dfrac{\sum_{i=1}^{N}\sum_{j=1}^{J}(y_{ij}-\mu)^2}{N-J}} = \frac{\dfrac{\sum_{j=1}^{J}N_j\alpha_j^2}{J-1}}{\dfrac{\sum_{i=1}^{N}\sum_{j=1}^{J}e_{ij}^2}{N-J}} \tag{8.6}$$

to the F-distribution with $J-1$, $N-J$ degrees of freedom. The formula represents the ratio of the mean square of the treatment or model component over the mean square of the error component. Obviously, the researcher desires to achieve a value as large as possible for this statistic. One way to approach this ideal is having either a larger 'variation between treatments' (enumerator of Equation 8.6) or very different average values for each treatment. The other way to receive a large value for F is to lower the denominator, that is, the 'variation within treatments'. This can be done by integrating further covariates that explain the uncontrolled variation within treatments. This is the basic idea underlying the analysis of covariance (ANCOVA). The basic model of ANCOVA is as follows:

$$y_{ij} = \mu + \alpha_j + \beta Z_{ij} + e_{ij} \qquad (8.7)$$

Here, $Z$ represents covariates that can explain part of the variation of the dependent variables within treatments, and $\beta$ is a vector of regression coefficients. By integrating additional covariates, we can reduce the uncontrolled variation and, thereby, improve statistical power.

This relationship is visualized in Figure 8.1, which is based on simulated data. The distribution of points in the two panels is identical, with the dots representing the scores of the treatment group and the circles depicting the scores of the control group. The lines in the left panel give the average scores for the treatment and the control group without considering a third variable z. The dependent variable scores for the treatment group (solid line) have a higher average than those for the control group (dashed line). Note that

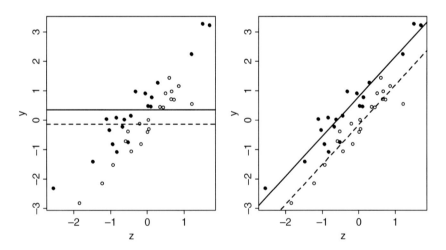

*Figure 8.1*   ANOVA and ANCOVA

within treatment variation is large, that is, the variation of individual points around the line. Once we include the additional variable $z$ into the model, we can redraw both lines in the right panel and, apparently, the variation of points around the lines, that is uncontrolled variation, which is much smaller. Recurring to the difference between ANOVA and ANCOVA, it is obvious that the left panel corresponds to the former and the right one to the latter.

ANCOVA can be considered as a special case of multi-level modeling. For those who are familiar with multi-level modeling, the parallel between both methods should be apparent in the right panel. This is equivalent to one specification of a multi-level model, the varying fixed intercept model without group-level predictors. Here, the group-structure in the dataset is represented by the treatment. While this flexibility makes the usage of multi-level modeling in the analysis of experimental data reasonable per se, multi-level models have a bunch of additional advantages compared to ANCOVA for experimental studies in political science. These refer to (1) the scale of dependent variable, (2) repeated measurements, (3) inclusion of random effects and (4) the integration of treatment (group)-level predictors.

To begin with, outcome or dependent variables in experimental studies often have quite different and naturally defined scales. In political science, dependent variables of interest are often binary or multinomial. To give an example, in the application presented below, the dependent variable is the vote for or against a stop motion in the collective choice process of a five-person committee. The dependent variable clearly has to be coded binary. ANCOVA, however, requires a metric scale for the dependent variable. This restriction does not apply to multi-level models which can easily be extended to other scales using logit, probit or other link functions. For example, we can model a binary dependent variable using a logit link.

$$Pr(y_{ij} = 1) = logit^{-1} (\mu_j + \beta Z_{ij}) \tag{8.8}$$

Second, many experimental studies are designed to use repeated measurement. That is, test persons are measured several times in the same or in different treatments. For example, in the experiment presented below, each test person belongs to either a cost- or noncost treatment (independent factor) and takes a series of votes in four different configurations (related factor). The design is presented in Table 8.1.

In this context, the assumption of independence of samples is not fulfilled. Since conventional ANCOVA ignores the intra-treatment (group) correlation, the problem should be solved by extending conventional ANCOVA by the inclusion of a subject effect:[2]

$$y_{ijk} = \mu + \pi_{i(j)} + \alpha_j + \gamma_k + \beta Z_{i(j)k} + e_{ijk} \tag{8.9}$$

*Table 8.1* Experimental design of example in Section 8.3

| Treatment j | Subject i | Configuration k | | | |
| | | 1 $\gamma_1$ | 2 $\gamma_2$ | 3 $\gamma_3$ | 4 $\gamma_4$ |
| --- | --- | --- | --- | --- | --- |
| Cost $\alpha_1$ | 1 | | | | |
| | 2 | | | | |
| | 3 | | | | |
| | 4 | | | | |
| Non-Cost $\alpha_2$ | 5 | | | | |
| | 6 | | | | |
| | 7 | | | | |
| | 8 | | | | |

Here, $\pi_{i(j)}$ represents the subject-level effect of the *i*th test person. Again, the representation is equivalent to a whole class of multi-level models. Extending ANCOVA in the way above by adding subject-level fixed effects raises another problem, however. Since the model has to consider as many subject effects as there are test persons, we lose a large amount of degrees of freedom and, consequently, statistical power of analysis. At this stage, the third advantage of multi-level modeling becomes relevant, namely the possibility to include random effects.

If we model the subject-level effect in Equation (8.9) as a random effect, we assume the $\pi_{i(j)}$ to be independent draws from a normally distributed random variable, or:

$$\pi_{i(j)} \sim N(0, \zeta^2) \tag{8.10}$$

In this setup, $\pi_{i(j)}$ is not a series of fixed unknown quantities but a single random variable instead. Therefore, a dramatic loss of degrees of freedom is prevented. We should note that moving from fixed effects to random effects is also associated with a conceptual change in the interpretation of the subject effects. If we consider subject effects as random effects, we assume that our test persons are randomly sampled from a larger population. This is a quite reasonable assumption. Yet, it would be incorrect if one models treatment effects ($\alpha_j$ or $\gamma_k$ in Equation 8.9) as random effects. In general, we do not think of treatments as being sampled from a population of all possible treatments, but rather, treatments as finite possibilities so that it seems more appropriate to model them as fixed effect.

The fourth advantage of using multi-level modeling is that one can also consider group-level predictors. This is particularly useful in modeling subject effects. From estimating the model in Equation 8.9, one can conclude subject-level variation is so and so large or relevant but the source of this variation remains unknown. If one, however, has information about predictors for this variation, we can actually model the subject level effect:

$$\pi_{i(j)} = \delta_0 + \delta Z'_{i(j)} + e'_{i(j)}$$

$$e'_{i(j)} \sim N(0, \zeta^2) \tag{8.11}$$

Note that specifying a model according to Equation 8.10 already exhausts the variation for the subject level and including Equation 8.11 does not introduce additional variation to this level.

To sum up, there are good arguments for using multi-level modeling for the analysis of experimental data. Treatment effects would typically be modeled as a regular fixed effect. If the experimental design includes repeated measures of single subjects or different settings or configurations within a treatment, we would possibly model these effects at the subject- or other level as random effects.

## 8.3 Example application: an experimental study of decision costs

In the beginning of this section, we briefly present the goal and design of our experiment. Subsequently, we apply the method discussed above to the data. More detailed information about the experimental setup can be found in Bräuninger, Shikano and Stoffel (2008).

### 8.3.1 Goal and design of the experiment

While standard collective choice theory takes the generic instability of majority rule voting as a fact (McKelvey, 1976), empirical observations suggest that real-world and laboratory committees come to a conclusion more often and easier than expected. We explore the rationale of one plausible explanation, that is, the effect of decision or opportunity costs of participating in collective decision-making on the individual voting behavior and the collective choice outcomes at the aggregate level.

We start with the standard assumption of a policy space given by a nonempty, compact and strictly convex subset of the multi-dimensional Euclidean space, $X \subseteq R^k$. The set of agents within the committee is given by $N = \{1, \ldots, n\}$, $n$ odd. Agents have Euclidean preferences, where $x_i$ denotes the ideal point of actor $i$. Decisions are taken by simple majority. In the conventional model, agents would vote for policy change if, and only if, the new policy is closer to their ideal point than the status quo. The act of voting itself is assumed to be costless. Introducing decision costs means that the utility of a policy change must outweigh the costs that are incurred in the process of decision-making itself. Let these costs be denoted by $\varepsilon_i$. Of course, these costs may be specific to individuals; for instance, they may reflect current opportunity costs of committee voting instead of following some leisure activity. Then, when alternative $x$ is paired against alternative $y$, agent $i$ votes for $x$ if and only if:

$$\| x_i - x \| < \| x_i - y \| - \varepsilon_i \tag{8.12}$$

We focus on opportunity costs as a constraint for strategic choice. We think of committee agents (or the participants in our experiments) as individuals for whom time is a scarce resource. Regardless of whether they have committed for committee membership (for example, legislators) or are paid for participating (for example, the participants in our experiments), any individual has an opportunity set of (valued) activities he can spend time on if the committee (or laboratory) session ends sooner rather than later. Clearly, these opportunity costs are privately borne, and they depend on both individual opportunity sets and how these are valued as compared with possible outcomes of the collective choice process.

To test the above idea, we set up two series of experiments in which participants were paid for selecting an alternative in a two-dimensional policy space by majority vote in a five-member committee. At the beginning of the session, participants were grouped randomly into five-member committees and seated at individual desktop computers. In the laboratory, there were 20 PCs in total making up four five-member committees, but participants were not told who their fellow committee members were. All interactions, that is the making of and voting on proposals, were made on the computer; participants were not allowed to communicate directly and could not look at the terminal of any other participant.[3] Subjects participated in four committee sessions in which they could earn money. Each of these sessions started with a random assignment of preference sets to subjects, followed by a number of proposal and voting stages that continued until a majority of committee members agreed to close the session and move to the next one. The total payment of subjects was the sum of the payments of the four sessions. At the end of the experiment, payments were made in private.

All in all, a total of 135 individual participants were recruited making up 27 experimental committees and 108 committee sessions for collective choice processes and outcomes. Subjects were recruited from the pool of registered lab participants at the University of Mannheim.[4] From the 27 committees, 16 were subjected to a 'no-cost' treatment and eleven committees to a 'decision cost' treatment (see below). Participants were told that the experiment would not last longer than one hour; median actual duration of the experiment was about 50 minutes (including time for payment).

In a single session, the committee can change the status quo under majority rule employing a forward moving agenda. Preferences of committee members are Euclidean over the two-dimensional policy space $X = [0,10] \times [0,10]$. The

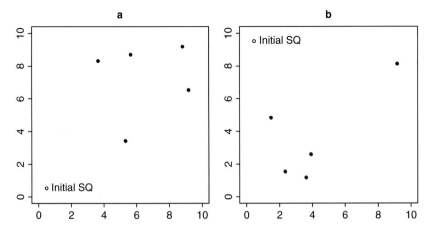

*Figure 8.2* BSS and FP Configuration of Ideal Points

committee session starts with a random assignment of participants to ideal points, which are then shown to all subjects together with the initial status quo policy (SQ). For the four sessions, we used two configurations of ideal points. In session 1, the setting shown in Figure 8.2a was used (henceforth BBS configuration); in session 2, a configuration used by Fiorina/Plott (1978) (Figure 8.2b; henceforth FP configuration). In neither of these settings does a Condorcet winner exist. Configurations used in sessions 3 and 4 were point reflections of BSS and FP configurations with center (5, 5).

What follows the assignment of ideal points is a number of proposal periods. In each proposal period, one committee member is randomly chosen to make a proposal for changing the current status quo. The proposal is presented to all participants, who then vote between the proposal and the status quo. The simple majority winner then becomes (or remains) the (new) status quo. At the end of any proposal period, committee members take a vote on whether to continue with another proposal or to stop and make the current status quo the final outcome. If the stop motion fails a simple majority, a new proposal period begins with the random selection of a proposer. If the stop motion is supported by a simple majority, the session ends and members receive their payoff.[5]

The main treatment variable in the experiment is whether or not committee members bear costs from the collective choice process. As we think of these costs as opportunity costs of committee decision-making instead of pursuing some other activity, participants in the decision-cost treatment are assessed a fee for any voting on a proposal, whether it is accepted or not. Notably, this is different from the *cost of change* setting used by Herzberg and Wilson

(1991: 180), in which subjects in the majority coalition bear costs for successfully changing the status quo. In the no-cost treatment, the payoff is a linear function of the Euclidean distance of ideal point $x_i$ of actor $i$ and outcome $x$, or, in terms of the experimental currency ('Taler'):

$$p_{ij} = 17 - 3.75 \times \| x_i - x \|. \tag{8.13}$$

In the decision-cost treatment, the payoff is lowered by .25 currency units for each proposal period, that is:

$$p_{ij} = 17 - 3.75 \times \| x_i - x \| - .25 \times \textit{\#proposals}. \tag{8.14}$$

The earnings of a participant at the end of the experiment were his total payoff in the four sessions (converted from 'Taler' into Euros) plus a fixed amount of four Euros. Mean pay-off in the no-cost treatment was 9.69 Euros and 9.12 Euros in the decision-cost treatment (with SD of 2.57 and 2.39).

### 8.3.2 Data analysis

In this experiment, we were interested in whether the cost treatment increases a test person's willingness to support the stop motion. To model the binary dependent variable (1: support for the stop motion; 0: rejection), we utilize a logit model. We proceed stepwise as follows: The first model is estimated without a multi-level structure and includes only one treatment variable (cost treatment). This is a logit-type pendant to conventional ANOVA with a metric dependent variable. In the second model, we include further theoretically relevant covariates to increase the statistical power of the analysis, like conventional ANCOVA. In the third model, we consider a further treatment variable (configuration). Finally, we introduce subject effects as random effects in a fourth model.

We need some notes concerning the theoretically relevant covariate, which is included in all but the first model. Although diverse covariates can be integrated, we proceed here based on a minimalist model. That is, the committee members decide to vote for or against a stop motion solely based on its cost and utility. In addition, the utility of using the stop motion can be operationalized differently; we assume that committee members are forward-looking and that they will cast their vote in a prospectively strategic way. With perfect foresight, the strategy of a rational decision-maker should correspond to the equilibrium strategy in an extensive form game with a random fall-back stop rule (which, however, we do not know). In the following, we are less demanding when assuming that committee members are able to look one step ahead. That is, expecting a favorable outcome in the next period based on the same status quo, a member would vote *against* a proposal in the current period even when it goes along with a higher payoff than the status quo. Therefore, the difference in the payoff between the (new or old) status quo

*Table 8.2* Estimation results (posterior distribution)

| | Model 1 | | Model 2 | | Model 3 | | Model 4 | |
|---|---|---|---|---|---|---|---|---|
| | Mean | sd | Mean | sd | Mean | sd | Mean | Sd |
| Cost treatment | 1.290 | 0.515 | 2.135 | 0.637 | 2.123 | 0.645 | 1.904 | 0.753 |
| Configuration 1 (BSS) | | | | | 0.150 | 0.208 | 0.165 | 0.224 |
| Configuration 2 (FP) | | | | | –0.027 | 0.232 | –0.084 | 0.242 |
| Configuration 3 (BSS) | | | | | 0.097 | 0.210 | 0.058 | 0.198 |
| Utility Diff. | | | –0.189 | 0.015 | –0.192 | 0.015 | –0.208 | 0.011 |
| Constant | –0.301 | 0.076 | 1.270 | 0.128 | 1.211 | 0.184 | 1.201 | 0.172 |
| Sigma (subject) | | | | | | | 0.660 | 0.156 |

* In Models 3 and 4, Configuration 4 (FP) is a reference category.

and the best outcome in the next period is considered as relevant covariate. We call this covariate the (one period) 'prospective utility differential'.

Table 8.2 shows estimation results of four different model specifications. Model 1 is the logit pendant to a one-way ANOVA. More specifically, the probability of voting for the stop motions are compared between the cost and noncost group. In the noncost treatment, 43 per cent of all votes are casted for the stop motion and under the cost treatment, 51 per cent are casted for the stop motion. This difference shows up in Model 1, in which the cost treatment has a positive effect (1.290) on the probability of voting for a stop motion.

In model 2, we consider one theoretically relevant covariate, the prospective utility differential. This covariate has, as expected, a negative effect (-0.189). That is, the larger the possible utility gain expected for the next round, the less likely the committee member is to vote for the stop motion. Another important result is the change in the positive effect of the cost treatment (2.135). By including the prospective utility differential, the average effect of the cost treatment increases substantially while the error of the estimate remains at the same level. Obviously, the statistical power of the analysis is improved by including the utility differential. This improvement can also be visualized. If we compare the average probabilities of voting for stop motions, the difference between the cost and no-cost condition is 8 percentage points (51 per cent vs. 43 per cent). Once we also consider and control for the prospective utility differential, this difference becomes larger. This can be seen in the left panel of Figure 8.3 that shows the effect of the prospective utility differential on the vote probability in both treatments (solid line for noncost and dashed line for cost treatment). At a value of 10 on the utility differential, for instance, committee members under the noncost condition would vote for the stop motion with less than 40 per cent probability, while the probability for an agent under cost treatment is about 80 per cent. This makes up a difference of about 40 percentage points. Note that the difference between both treatments is not constant due to the non-linear model. In any case, the contrast between treatments became clearer by introducing a further covariate.

Model 3 then introduces the other treatment variable, the spatial configuration of ideal points of committee members used in the experiment. The estimation result in Table 8.2 suggests that there is no substantive impact of the preference configurations and their variance is large.

The right panel of Figure 8.3 further confirms this result. Comparing the difference between solid (noncost treatment) and dashed lines (cost treatment), there are only small deviations among both classes of lines. Moreover, including these treatments hardly affects the effect of the cost/non-cost treatment. Therefore, we can conclude that the difference between preference configurations can be ignored.

In Model 4, we finally consider the multi-level structure by including the subject-level effects as random effect. Which kind of change can we find at the effect of cost/noncost treatment? According to Table 8.2, inclusion of the subject-level effects reduces the average effect (1.904) and increases its variance (0.753). The statistical power is therefore slightly, but not dramatically, reduced. This might be interpreted such that random assignment to both treatments does not work perfectly. The reduction of the effect was

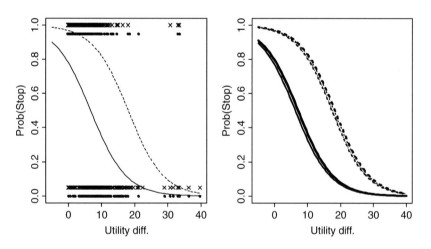

*Figure 8.3*   Model 2 and Model 3

* The solid lines are the effect of utility differential under the noncost treatment. The dashed lines are under the cost treatment. In the right panel, the effects under different preference configurations are drawn using different linewidths.

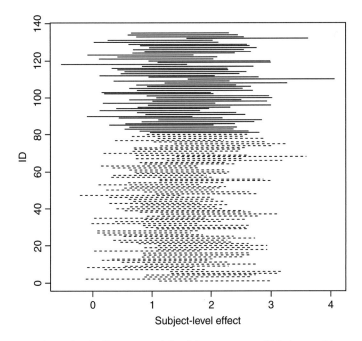

*Figure 8.4* Subject-level Effects in Model 4 (90 per cent -credible intervals)

* Solid lines are noncost treatment. Dashed lines are cost treatment.

absorbed by the subject-level effects, which are visualized in Figure 8.4. The figure presents the subject-level effects for all 135 test subjects in the 90 per cent-credible interval. The more positive the effect is, the more likely it is that the test subject tends to vote for stop motions. The figure shows certain individual differences whose magnitude is, however, rather limited. For this observation, we can conclude that the cost/noncost treatment has a substantial effect that goes beyond the individual differences among test subjects.

## 8.4 Conclusions

In this chapter, we advocated to apply multi-level modeling to experimental data. Multi-level modeling is a generalized form of ANOVA and ANCOVA, which have traditionally been used in the analysis of experimental data. Due to its generality, multi-level models are able to capture a wider range of real-world specifications and complexities in settings without loss of the basic idea underlying analyses with ANOVA and/or ANCOVA.

What kind of improvement can we expect by applying multi-level modeling? First, we have shown that by including subject-level (random) effects we can consider differences between individuals, which we otherwise could not fully control for (even not in an experimental setting). Second, the random effect model allows us to consider subject-level effects without losing many degrees of freedom. Theoretically, this modeling strategy thus increases the efficiency of estimation. In fact, if this is not the case, it is a warning signal that randomization might not work perfectly. Third, another possible application, which we did not mention above, is the estimation of a distinct effect of the additional relevant covariates for each treatment group. Utilizing such a procedure, we can relax another assumption of ANCOVA, namely that the two lines in the right panel in Figure 8.1 must have identical slopes. This constraint is an unrealistic assumption in many experimental designs. In a nutshell, the flexibility offered by multi-level modeling can help to further exploit the rich information hidden in experimental

## Notes

1. ANOVA and ANCOVA can be formulated in different ways. To make their relationship to multi-level modelling clear, we take a generalized linear model approach (see, for example, Rutherford. 2001).
2. This does not necessarily work. In a simple single-factor design with repeated measures as follows:

$$y_{ij} = \mu + \pi_{ij} + \alpha_j + \beta Z_{ij} + e_{ij},$$

   the subject effect and the additional covariates are redundant.
3. The experimental software used is z-Tree (Fischbacher, 2007). Code is available on the authors' webpage.
4. For the recruitment of participants, the software package ORSEE was used (Greiner, 2003).
5. While the stop motion provides committee members with the possibility to bring the session to an end on their own, a fall-back stop rule had to be considered in case no stop motion receives majority support. Previous experimental studies have dealt in different ways with the problem. Salant/Goodstein (1990) restrict the number of proposal periods to five, Fiorina/Plott (1978) are silent about the unbounded horizon of the game. While the setup of the Fiorina/Plott experiment is misspecified (possible states are undefined for the participants), limiting proposal time or proposal periods to a fixed number induces a finite game which participants can solve by backward induction. We therefore decided to specify a finite game in which the length of the game, however, is not known to participants by certainty. More specifically, participants were told that any committee session can end (making the current status quo the final outcome) at any time between zero and ten minutes but the randomly chosen maximum duration is unknown to them. Eventually, we chose stop times between nine minutes and ten minutes, but this fall-back stop rule had to be invoked only once.

## References

Bräuninger, Thomas, Susumu Shikano and Michael Stoffel (2008) 'An Experimental Study of Decision Costs in Majority Rule Voting', prepared for the Workshop 'Experimental Political Science' at Hanse-Wissenschaftskolleg, Delmenhorst.

Fisher, Ronald A. (1935) *The Design of Experiments* (Edinburgh: Oliver & Boyd).

Fiorina, Morris and Charles R. Plott (1978) 'Committee Decisions under Majority Rule', *American Political Science Review*, 72, 575–598.

Fischbacher, Urs (2007) 'z-Tree: Zurich Toolbox for Ready-made Economic Experiments', *Experimental Economics*, 10, 171–178.

Greiner, Ben (2003) 'An Online Recruitment System for Economic Experiments' in Kurt Kremer, Volker Macho (eds.) *Forschung und wissenschaftliches Rechnen*, GWDG Bericht 63, Göttingen: Ges. für Wiss. Datenverarbeitung, 79–93.

Herzberg, Roberta and Rick Wilson (1991) 'Costly Agendas and Spatial Voting Games: Theory and Experiments on Agenda Access Costs', in Thomas Palfrey (ed.) *Experimentation in Political Science* (Ann Arbor: University of Michigan Press).

McKelvey, Richard D. (1976) 'Intransitivities in Multidimensional Voting Models and Some Implications for Agenda Control', *Journal of Economic Theory*, 12, 472–482.

Rutherford, Andrew (2001) *Introducing ANOVA and ANCOVA: A GLM Approach* (London: Sage).

Salant, Stephen W. and Eban Goodstein (1990) 'Predicting Committee Behavior in Majority Rule Voting Experiments', *RAND Journal of Economics*, 21, 293–313.

# 9
# Experimental Chats: Opening the Black Box of Group Experiments

*Thomas Kalwitzki, Wolfgang J. Luhan and Bernhard Kittel*

## 9.1 Introduction

The problems of collective decision making and voting – as one of the models of aggregating individual to collective preferences – belong to the defining research questions of political science. In their early overview of experimental political science, Kinder and Palfrey highlight the flexibility of the experimental method to study different levels of aggregation and to explicitly address the problem of aggregation (Kinder and Palfrey, 1993). Indeed, voting and collective decision making has become a major field of experimental research, not only in political science (Palfrey, 2008; Wilson, 2007; McDermott, 2007) but also in the adjoining disciplines of behavioral economics (Schram, 2003) and social psychology (Moscovici and Zavalloni, 1969; Kerr et al., 1996). In his highly influential summary of the state-of-the-art in behavioral economics, Camerer (2003) listed group decision making as one of his top 10 open research questions in experimental research. His argument was that the vast majority of experimental studies resorted to the game theoretic standard hypothesis of the irrelevance of the decision maker, and therefore conducted experiments mainly with individuals as decision makers. Given the sufficient flexibility of the experimental approach, Camerer suggests a promotion of collective decision experiments – also to produce facts in order to stimulate theoretical advancement. Since Camerer's invitation, the already substantial stream of research appears to have sped up in progression (Cooper and Kagel, 2005).

Contrary to the claim that the decision maker is irrelevant, we follow the social psychological perspective that groups add another – social – layer of complexity to decision making that can neither be reduced to individual decision making nor be studied on the basis of individual behavior alone (Levine and Moreland, 1990; Kerr and Tindale, 2004). While modern game theoretic approaches include social preference models (Bolton and Ockenfels, 2000; Fehr and Schmidt, 1999) and thus have advanced our possibilities to explore other-regarding behavior and mutual consideration, there is still a difference between interaction among individuals and group processes. Strategic interaction among rational actors is one part, inter-personal processes like persuasion, intimidation, deception or leadership cannot be easily integrated into such models but seem to play an important role in real-world deliberation processes preceding group decisions. In this chapter, we explore the possibilities of studying group processes in experimental settings.

In many recent experimental collective action studies, the process of group decision making has been recorded; on the one hand, as a mere byproduct of the communication device (for example, logfiles of online chats), on the other hand, as a topic of separate evaluation. We claim that an extended analysis of these protocols of group decision processes is suitable to address many items on Camerer's top 10 list. In this chapter, we propose an approach that combines quantitative and qualitative methods for studying experimental data in order to facilitate deeper insights not only into the processes leading to group decisions, but also to individual decision making in the group context.

The methodological contribution of this chapter will be to show that the – hitherto idle – recorded group communication processes are nothing less than complete recordings of the actual process of collective decision making. The detailed analysis of these data can illuminate the process of decision making that has so far been unobservable to social sciences. This analysis, however, requires a combination of qualitative and quantitative research methods, which might be the reason why it has not been done before.

## 9.2 Collective Decision Makers

Though the focus of this chapter lies on methodological issues rather than on group decision making, a short introduction to previous group decision making experiments might be useful. The scope of experimental studies on group decision making ranges from social psychology, to economic and political decision making.

Although the standard models of economic and political game theory largely neglect the type of the decision maker by simply assuming individual decision making, many economic decisions are taken by groups such as families, company boards, management teams, committees or central bank boards. This shortcoming has, of course, led to a large and still growing body of literature. In their survey, Cooper and Kagel (2005) find team decisions to be closer to standard game theoretic predictions in the majority of studies. This means that teams usually display a higher level of rationality and/or more egoistic behavior than individual players. For example, teams are observed to act more selfishly in the dictator game (Luhan et al., 2009),[1] propose as well as accept smaller transfers in the ultimatum game (Bornstein and Yaniv, 1998) and display less trust and trustworthiness (Cox,

2002). Teams behave more in line with game theoretic predictions in the centipede game by exiting at earlier stages (Bornstein et al., 2004), and in beauty-contest games by converging more quickly to the equilibrium than individuals (Kocher and Sutter, 2005).

But the (experimental) comparison of individual and group behavior is not an innovation to social sciences. Social psychologists have worked on this very issue virtually for decades (Levine and Moreland, 1998). While social science has largely dealt with the question of whether groups behave differently than individuals and the *influence of* as well as the *effects on* certain environments, social psychology has investigated the question of why these differences arise in the first place. One very prominent, yet controversial, example is the explanation for the observed increased competitiveness of groups, termed 'discontinuity effect' (Wildschut et al., 2003). The rationale for this effect is twofold. First, group membership increases the anonymity of the individual and thereby reduces the individual responsibility for collective action. Competitive action can be justified more easily – to others and to oneself. Second, when groups interact with groups, a more competitive opponent is expected and competitive actions are taken in anticipation of the other group's behavior.

### 9.2.1   Observing the Process vs. Assessing Final Outcomes

In the vast majority of experimental studies on group as well as on individual decision making, the analysis of subject behavior is limited to the evaluation of observed actions taken by the subjects as the final outcomes of the experimental design. The communication process is implemented only in order to enable cooperation and it is therefore excluded from the analysis as such. The whole process of decision making is concurrently also excluded from consideration, leading to an analysis of outcomes without attention to the process that produced these outcomes.

This is definitely not due to analytical slackness. Rather, it is based on two methodological reasons: On the one hand, the analysis follows the specific theoretical methodology of testing hypotheses focusing on final outcomes (Samuelson, 2005). On the other hand, individual decisions are – because of their intraindividual nature – not observable by means of social science methods. Individual decision making is a cognitive process that will often, but does not necessarily, involve social determinants. Obviously, the realm of mental activity belongs to psychology, while social sciences study the emerging actions that affect or are driven by the social environment of the acting person. Consequently, emerging differences between individual and group decisions that can be interpreted as a field of intersection between psychology and social sciences are mostly justified by (socio-) psychological group theories. The 'group polarization' theory introduced above might serve as an example. Although the theory describes certain individual strategies and procedural elements within the process of group decision making,[2] Cason and

Mui (1997) test theoretical predictions using only the observed outcomes. This is just one example for a prevalent method used, for example, in economics and political science (Blinder and Morgan, 2005; Bosman and van Winden, 2002; Cox, 2002), but also in social psychology (Insko et al., 1987). Of course, a clear-cut test of ex ante formulated hypotheses is only possible using observational data on decisions and actions. But a more extended view on research methods and the combination of approaches developed in different scientific areas might permit analyzing the process of decision making itself and the reasons and motivations that drive the final outcome. In this way, hypotheses are not only tested by the comparison of outcomes in treatment and control groups whereby the statistical irrelevance of other factors is ascertained by random assignment of subjects to groups, but we are also able to make empirically more informed statements about the process leading from the treatment to the outcome. This is in line with the idea of causation as a mechanism.

One increasingly popular attempt to expand social science research is the field of 'neuroeconomics' (Glimcher and Rustichini, 2004; Glimcher, 2004; Camerer et al., 2005; Glimcher et al., 2009). This combination of economics, psychology and neuroscience studies the functions of the brain in evaluating risks, assessing pros and cons and ultimately making decisions. Hence, neuroeconomics attempts to open the 'black box' of decision making at the level of individuals. Given that so far we have no means of studying intra-brain processes that lead to decisions other than visualizing brain activity, this avenue currently seems the most promising way to shed light on the mechanisms of individual decision making.

We contend, however, that in contrast to the study of individual decisions, we do not yet need to resort to such techniques for the study of collective decision processes, because all the information relevant for the social scientific study of collective decisions is available in an experimental study of group decision making. While neuroeconomics aims to open the 'black box' of the intraindividual process of decision making by the means of neuroscientific methods, we propose a method to take a look into the 'black box' of interindividual decisions by making use of qualitative research methods and experimental data already at hand. Our approach is exploratory in the same sense as neuroimaging has been during its first steps. We attempt to interpret the signals that individuals involved in collective decision making send – without being able to manipulate individual states. Within the otherwise controlled experimental setting, hence, we consider these signals as field data that can be explored by traditional techniques of interpretative research. Unlike individual decisions, the process of decision making in groups is not unobservable to social sciences. Hence, the methodological requirement for visualization is replaced by the requirement for a clear definition of observability and method.

## 9.2.2    Interaction and Communication

In laboratory research, interaction among group members can be facilitated in various ways. The simplest form of communication is the publication of information about prices and quantities on the screen in market experiments with single players who make individual decisions isolated from other participants – without any communication.

This is the typical basic setup in classical economic experiments (Smith, 1994, 2005). The most complex form is the formation of groups that can interact freely, an approach common in social psychology but which also has a long tradition in political science (Fiorina and Plott, 1978), and has been taken up in economics more recently (Bosman et al., 2006). This continuum of complexity is duplicated by a reverse continuum of experimental control. In anonymous market situations, the experiment is as fully isolated from social interaction as possible by excluding all outside interference except for the personality, character and previous experiences of the participants. In open group discussions, in contrast, control is minimal and social processes are unleashed in groups without clearly circumscribed limits.

Unsurprisingly, it has been established that the channel of communication, which defines the extent to which interaction among participants is possible, affects the outcome of experiments. For example, successful cooperation in a public goods setting has been shown to depend on the opportunity of coordination before individual decisions are taken (Brosig et al., 2003). This poses a challenge to the validity of comparisons of results along the continuum from the isolated individual to the group. For example, in the team dictator game reported by Cason and Mui (1997), in which teams interacted face-to-face, team choices turned out to be dominated by the other-regarding team member. In contrast, Luhan et al. (2009) found that groups tended to be more selfish than individuals in a replication of this study using a computerized chat facility that restricts communication to written chat contributions. Although uncontrolled group discussions are not inaccessible for analysis because they can be observed and videotaped, the availability of the full repertoire of communication and the lack of anonymity causes too many factors to be left uncontrolled to unambiguously trace differences in outcomes to the manipulated factor. In other words, in such situations, the treatment signal is difficult to detect in the noise of multi-channel communication within the group. In fact, this data differs from field data only by the fact that the interaction situation is artificial.

Hence, if control over factors related to social interaction and communication is relevant, it may make sense to restrict communication channels to the minimum necessary to facilitate interaction within a group. The requirements for limiting social interaction to those communications necessary for group formation and decision making in the experimental setting are (1) anonymity, (2) free choice of communication contents and (3) deliberation. While any setting that involves face-to-face deliberation fails to meet criterion (1), any setting that restricts communication to information about choices by others fails to meet criteria (2) and (3). In our view, the setup chosen by Luhan et al. (2009) is the only one currently known in which all three requirements are fulfilled.

## 9.3  The Observation of Group Decision Processes

Compared to other methods of data collection, the main advantage of experiments is the highly structured procedure allowing for a maximum of control and, as a result, maximal internal validity (Friedman and Sunder, 1994; Thye, 2007). This advantage comes at the cost of high levels of abstraction. The ecological validity – the degree to which these results can be generalized to situations outside of the laboratory – is therefore in question (Zelditch, 2007). Nevertheless, understanding social mechanisms in group decisions may eventually provide stylized facts that can be used as building blocks for the interpretation of empirical findings and as starting points for more elaborate models of group decision making.

In group decision experiments, a fundamental part of control is effectuated through the provision of a clearly defined decision rule and the restriction of communication channels. The resulting observations are contentually linked to the specific controlled process of group decision making. Hitherto, however, information on the specific process of intra-group decision making and inter-individual negotiation that is contained in the dataset generated during an experiment remained beyond the scope of observation and assessment. Instead, the standard procedure for collecting information on this process is a debriefing questionnaire at the end of the experimental session which is either conducted computerized or as a face-to-face interview. This kind of data collection is typically done individually with subjects producing a specific dataset. It is to be emphasized that the compatibility of this type of data is a fundamental advantage. The data can be related to the experimental data in statistical analysis as controls or explicative variables.

At first view, a questionnaire at the end of a session might be considered to be as close to the actual decision process as possible. Although it is certainly closer than any survey can attain for field data, this does not necessarily mean that it is close enough to yield unbiased – valid – data. Between the decision making process itself and the questionnaire, a variety of acts have been made and, most probably, a participant in the experiment has had many different thoughts. Thus the distance may be considerable and it might appear as a problem. Ex-post interviews are no more than subjective reconstructions of the decision making process by the participants. This definitely sets limits to the comprehension of the actual interactions within the group by the researcher. Furthermore, in addition to the retrospective design of the data collection technique the subjective reconstruction has to be expressed in words. This has to be seen as a further construction process which is influenced by the form and the specific topics of the interview or questionnaire (Smith, 2008).

In laboratory experiments, ex-post interviews are not the only means of obtaining data on the decision process. 'Modern' experiments are being conducted via computer and the administration of the communication between the workstations (and therefore between the participating subjects) is implemented via specialized software with the possibility to coordinate the communicative interaction as a treatment condition.

The basic idea for our approach, from a pragmatic as well as from a methodological point of view, is to utilize the information automatically stored by the experimental software. This allows us to reconstruct a full real-time protocol of the group decision process. Considered pragmatically, the allocation of a communication channel, usually a chat function, produces an additional dataset. To run the chats error-free, the server has to build a real-time protocol file. This file saves the communication data so that the process of group decision making is described by the developing chat. The database produced is a real-time group communication collected in a highly controlled experimental setting which also ensures full integrity of the data.

From a methodological perspective, the reglementation of communication depending on the experiment is an advantage not to be underestimated. In face-to-face communication which uses all communication channels, language, mimic and gesture affect decision making considerably. Hence, every dataset constructed from such data has to be considered as a selection only. Due to the enormous amount of potential data, every observational dataset will always just preserve the few data which have been chosen by the specific focus of the collection. Although one way of collecting data from face-to-face communication is to video-tape the complete process and, in principle, a researcher could go back to the original material in order to validate interpretations, the extreme amount of time and effort involved in preparing such data for interpretation puts limits to feasibility. Considering this, there are two aspects of such approaches to be acknowledged. First, most of the data available in principle will not be studied at all. Second, the samples of information studied are subject to a not definitely specifiable arbitrariness.

We contend that our approach deals with the trade-off between completeness of data and the time and effort needed in a more efficient way. Because of the restriction of communication to chats, we can safely presume that the record of communication in the group decision process is complete and the remaining source of error variation can be ascribed to intra-individual specifics like personality and previous experiences. The following procedure for an integration of 'real-world data' into an otherwise experimental design thus offers a more efficient way of analysis than a study of face-to-face communication and a more valid way than would be possible through an ex-post questionnaire.

### 9.3.1 Nesting a Qualitative Study in an Experimental Framework

Typical economic or political science experiments are designed for the analysis of individual decisions. Groups merely enter as contextual factors and communication between individuals is considered a means for individuals to collect the information necessary to reach a decision. Communicative acts are not an object of analysis, but part of the experimental framework.

We suggest to extend the analysis of the participants' actions from a completely different perspective. Although the experiment is an externally controlled situation, by the subjects it is also experienced as a real existing social situation in which communication channels are limited to chats.[3] This change of perspective allows us to reorganize the interindividual communication data as a process and to subject it to a qualitative data analysis. The change of perspective also implies a change in research question. Instead of asking 'Which effect has the manipulation of one factor on the outcome', we ask '*In which way* does this manipulation lead to the change in outcome'. We thus trace the process from the manipulated factor to the realization of a particular outcome in order to understand the mechanisms effectuating the outcome. Hence, we take a look into the black box of group experiments.

In a sense, this endeavor is a variant of the attempt to combine different methodological perspectives in order to answer research questions. We assume that methodological plurality helps to produce better, or at least broader, insights. To some extent, the approach can be considered a variant of the application of mixed methods (Bergman, 2009). However, in the case of our proposal of an ex-post extension of the methodological frame of analysis, we do not attempt to locate the approach within the family of mixed methods in a strict sense because – in our view – this could only be sensibly formulated in an ex-ante research program. This would imply that at an early stage of the research process, several perspectives of data collection and analysis have to be planned and attuned under the guidance of one particular methodological paradigm (Morse, 2002). In the study presented here, this has not been the case, but the idea to look at the data from the perspective described in this chapter arose only during the work on the data. Needless to say that there is no reason not to plan a joint procedure in advance for future projects.

We are thus in a situation in which two different, though related, questions are studied with two different, though related, data sets: While the experimental study focuses on the outcomes of the manipulation of certain factors that are the result of particular individuals actions, the qualitative study focuses on the group processes that preceded the actions and that are documented in the protocols of communication. They are related by being generated in one experimental session, and therefore the data can be linked. This approach can be located under the wide roof of triangulation. In the current case we add a qualitative analysis of the communication process of decision making committees to the quantitative analysis of decision making outcomes. We thus do not aim at extending the validity of results, as is usually intended in triangulative strategies, but to gain complementary results which furnish a broader, more encompassing and more complete picture of the object of analysis (Flick, 2008). By studying the contents of the 'black box', we hope to improve our understanding of the processes going on among the participants during the experiment. The mode of integration is thus not determined by methodological rules but by the object of analysis (Kelle and Erzberger, 1999).

### 9.3.2   Qualitative chat analysis

Since the type and quality of data is the core precondition of a valid analysis and interpretation, data collection is among the aspects of a research project to be most carefully planned and prepared. This part of a research project, however, is hardly an issue for the analysis of experimental chat protocols. In computer-based experiments that entail communication between particy-ipants, the protocols are a byproduct of the experimental procedure. Within this context we thus record and observe real-life data. As a consequence, we do not need any specific techniques to elicit 'truthful'[4] responses from the participants that yield valid and reliable material for analysis. The protocol is all there and participants produce it while going through the experimental procedure. The challenge for analysis hence is the next step, finding adequate techniques for exploring the protocols.

In structural terms, the chat protocols are similar to the transcripts of face-to-face discussions that are often used in the qualitative research tradition in psychology, sociology and political science (Peräkylä, 2005). They involve several speakers who interact and respond to each other. Apart from these general characteristics, the protocols have specific traits that separate them from the material typical for qualitative research. On the one hand, due to the strict isolation of the experimental conditions, the data on interactions are complete with regard to the contributions to communication. There are neither elements missing due to unrecorded communications nor due to connections between participants external to the specific interaction situation. Thus, in contrast to transcripts of non-experimental group processes – that only present a tentative and selective picture of the real situation (Weihe et al., 2008; Nullmeier et al., 2008) – the limitation to electronic chats generates an unfiltered representation of communication. On the other hand, the anonymity of the situation, the (desired) maximum of social distance (Hoffman et al., 1996; Bohnet and Frey, 1999) and the artificial limits on communication result in a separation of the situation from the social world of the participants. In this sense, the approach trades ecological for internal validity.

From these characteristics of the data we derive three postulates determining the choice of instruments for analyzing the material. First, the controlled and anonymous situation of communication precludes the need to include other social influences into the analysis. Any analysis only reflects the recorded discussions and the final decisions taken by the participants. Second, the ad-hoc constellation of the groups, the general limits on discussion time, but also the interaction sequences – that are typically rather short – imply that we can consider the chats as a separate, complete and closed sequence. Statements that involve generalizations across several chats can only refer to individuals who participate in several consecutive sequences during an experimental session. In this vein, for example, we have to take into account that past experiences of a participant may affect behavior in later sequences. This may be made apparent by an analysis of subjects. Nevertheless, communication patterns may exhibit some specific traits that can be observed repeatedly across different sequences. Third, the real-life data stemming from an artificial situation only allow for (maximally) verified statements about behavior in the specific experimental situation. For interpretations and generalizations beyond this situation more research has to be conducted.

In principle, techniques such as conversation analysis, document analysis, discourse analysis or process analysis could be very useful tools for the study of this data. As of now, however, we explore the possibilities entailed in a simpler and more straightforward approach, qualitative content analysis in the tradition of Mayring (2004, 2007). Qualitative content analysis combines a set of techniques for the analysis of communication material. They share two core aspects: Firstly, they are characterized by the usage of defined procedural schemata that assure intersubjective traceability of the course of analysis and thus permit the implementation of quality criteria. Secondly, definite category systems are employed that are either based on ex-ante theoretical considerations or that emerge from the analysis as an empirical result (Titschner et al., 2000). This method is widespread in various fields in sociology, psychology and education science (Mayring and Gläser-Zikuda, 2005).

The methodology of qualitative content analysis is structured along three procedures, or steps that can, but need not, be aligned sequentially: summary, explication and structuring (Titschner et al., 2000; Mayring, 2007). The relative emphasis which is laid on either of these three procedures depends on the properties of the material studied. The summary procedure aims at the reduction of the textual material and the condensation to its core messages. It results in a comprehensible text covering the contents of the original text. Mayring (2007) augments this procedure by a stepwise, inductive categorization of the material which combines statements of the same kind in some analytically relevant sense.

The procedure of explication, in contrast, does not condense the contents but aims at clarification of unclear passages, thereby making use of additional material. This additional material can either stem from within the text (narrow content analysis) or be information external to the text such as timing, sequence, assigned role or incentive structure (broad content analysis).

The procedure of structuring can be applied in four different modes: a formal, a contentual, a typifying and a scaling mode (Mayring, 2007: 82ff). In all modes, the researcher attempts to extract a particular structure from the material. The specific mode is selected depending on whether this structure is expected to be either based on formal properties of the text, the contents of the text, a classification or typology according to a predefined set of types, or on an allocation of values on scales. For this task, concrete dimensions of structuring are identified on the foundation of theoretical propositions, which are then used as an elaborate system of categories for the reconstruction of the structures inherent in the discussion. Which mode is used depends on the research question and we will elaborate on this procedure in more detail below (9.4.3).

After having summarized, explicated, and/or structured the texts, processes of chat communication can be traced systematically in order to identify the different steps that constitute the collective decision process. The material can then be used for answering questions related to the macro level of collective decision making as well as the micro level of individual behavior in the context of a collective decision problem.

At the micro level, the study of participants behavior can address their stated intentions (for example related to an upcoming vote), enunciated reflections and considerations, and finally the participants' actual decision. Conceptualized as a process in time, this analysis can uncover not only the influences of the group on the subject, but also, in reverse direction, the share of the individual in the group deliberation. Thereby we obtain insights into different modes of individual action.

At the macro level, the modality by which the final group outcome, for example the election result, has been generated interactively can be revealed. Thereby, light can be shed on the process of negotiation and on promises by group members, the observance of which finally leads to a specific result of the deliberation.

The results of this analysis can be considered valuable in their own right because they add analytical depth to the analysis of the effect of manipulating certain factors typical of experimental research. They uncover the variety of processes underlying the relationship between manipulation and outcome and thus add nuance to the findings. In addition, it is quite likely that they will reveal unexpected linkages and processes which point towards new questions that can be studied experimentally. But apart from these classical strengths of qualitative research, one can also ask questions about the frequency and spread of different types of processes. Given that the experimental situation isolates the chat sequences from factors external to the design and that the remaining linkages between the sequences through the repeated involvement of the same individuals within one experimental session can be controlled, statistical analyses yield valid results. Hence, to the extent that the processes of summary, explication and structuring have led to the identification of a limited set of categories, chat sequences can be classified and statistical techniques can be used to study relationships between characteristics of sequences at the macro level, but also between characteristics of individuals in the context of chat sequences.[5]

## 9.4   Example: Strategic voting and voter turnout

In this section we present an exemplary application of qualitative content analysis as described above. We use a dataset from Kittel et al. (2009), who investigate costly voting in multiparty elections. The authors find significant evidence that communication increases both strategic voting[6] and participation. In order to present the qualitative research design, the procedure and the results of this approach, the experimental setup as well as the relevant results will be described briefly; a more detailed discussion on equilibria, parametrization, results and so on, can be found in Kittel et al. (2009).

### 9.4.1   Experimental design and results

Building on Palfrey and Rosenthal (1985), an election is modeled with $N$ voters divided into four possible preference types $E, F, G, H$. The election involved three party candidates $A$, $B$, and $C$. Two voter types are considered to be partisans, with type $E$ strictly preferring party $A$ and type $H$ strictly preferring party $B$ and being indifferent over the other options. Voters of type $F$ (and $G$, respectively) have a first preference for party $A$ ($B$), a second preference for $B$ ($A$), and a third preference for $C$. According to the strategic voting theory (Cox, 1997; Myatt, 2007), these latter voters may wish to vote strategically for their second preference if their first preference is less likely to win in order to prevent a win by their least preferred party $C$.

In the experiments these preferences are induced through voters' payoffs according to table 9.1.[7] In the experiment there are $M$ votes cast automatically for party $C$ in every period. Voting is costly with voting costs $c$ independently randomly drawn from the interval [0, 55]. The experiment consisted of 19 periods with participants being randomly rematched into groups of various size and varying distributions of voter types. In every period, the subjects were informed about the size of the electorate (group),

*Table 9.1*   Payoffs (Kittel et al., 2009)

| Voter Type | Party Wins | | |
|---|---|---|---|
| | A | B | C |
| E | 155 | 75 | 75 |
| F | 155 | 105 | 55 |
| G | 105 | 155 | 55 |
| H | 75 | 155 | 75 |

the distribution of voter types, the size of *M* and their individual voting costs.

Three treatment conditions were introduced in order to test three predictions:

| | |
|---|---|
| *Party Labels* | From the sixth period on, subjects were labeled as 'members' of either party *A* or party *B*. |
| *Communication* | *Party Chat*: In periods 13 to 19 subjects could chat with their party members. |
| | *All Chat*: In periods 13 to 19 subjects could chat with the whole electorate. |

Participants were either scheduled to the *Party Chat* or the *All Chat* treatment. The difference between the two chat treatments was solely the division of the electorate into communication groups. The distribution of voter types, the payoff structure, and so on, remained exactly the same.

The chat in both treatments was free-form. It was, however, not allowed to make any statements that might lead to an identification of the sender (for example name, gender, field of study, position in the lab, and so on). Each chat was implemented in the experiment to last at most ten minutes and then terminate automatically. Only three groups exhausted this time, all other groups had left the chat well in advance of automatic termination.

Summing up briefly, the predictions to be tested were: (1) Party labels as well as communication will increase strategic voting. (2) Participation will increase with party labels as well as with communication. (3) Party *C* will win fewer elections in party label and/or communication treatments than without these conditions.

Kittel et al. (2009) report evidence of increased voter coordination in the communication treatments while strategic voting increased significantly as compared to the other conditions. In the baseline condition without labels and communication only 9.8 per cent[8] of type *F* and *G* voters voted strategically whereas this number increases to 20.2 per cent in the all chat and 24.9 per cent in the party chat treatments. Communication is also found to increase voter turnout in general, resulting in a decreased probability of the least favored party winning the election (78.1 per cent in the baseline versus 19.4 per cent in the all chat treatment).

## 9.4.2 Dataset

The experimental data consist of six sessions in total, four of which featured chat communication. For the exposition of the analytical possibilities of the approach we chose only one of these four sessions featuring party chat communication.[9] As mentioned above, in the party chat treatment the electorate was divided in two groups that had to vote jointly in order to prevent party *C* from winning the election – but without the possibility of intergroup communication. Because of this communication structure the coordination in order to beat party *C* was inordinately more difficult. This higher complexity in coordination between unconnected voter groups, on the one hand, complicates the analysis, but, on the other hand, facilitates the analysis of more elaborate coordination concepts (see section 9.5).

## 9.4.3 Applied methods

At a general level, we are interested in tracing the formation process of the quantitative results. We thus explore the mechanisms underlying the outcome and leave other possible research aims discussed above aside. Our main focus of interest is in the behavior of voters: In which way did the participation in the group decision process affect their voting behavior? More specifically: Were voters persuaded to change their intentions during the chat? At an early stage of data examination we realized that we could capture the deliberation processes preceding the decisions only slowly and step by step along single dimensions. In a first step, which will be the topic of this example, we asked three questions. First: What were the intentions of the swing voters (*F* and *G*) when entering deliberations? This question relates to the issue of strategic voting. Second: What were the intentions of the voters, in particular the partisans (*E* and *H*), when entering deliberation? This question focuses on whether and how deliberations affect turnout. And third: Which deliberations resulted in optimal voting behavior?

Although the questions pick up the central hypotheses of the study described above, they are not meant as additional tests but to provide a specific, complementary contribution to the understanding of the outcome. The first two questions (sections 9.5.1 and 9.5.2) involve an inductive categorization which we develop according to figure 9.1, which is based on Mayring (2007). For answering the third question (section 9.5.3) we employ a typifying structuring (Mayring, 2007: 90ff). Both techniques make use of MAXQDA, a software for Computer-Aided Qualitative Data Analysis (CAQDAS).

In order to answer the first two questions that ask about the voting intentions of swing voters in particular (strategic voting) and voters in general (turnout), we have to identify an ex-ante selection criterion that specifies the units of analysis. The focus of the question on initial intentions suggests taking first chat-statements of each participant because they are the contributions to the deliberation that is closest to the initial point.[10]

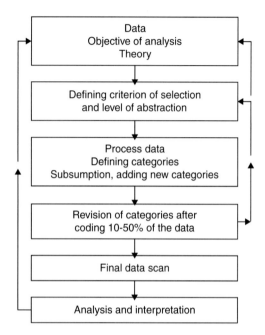

*Figure 9.1*   Process of inductive categorization based on Mayring (2007: 75)

With regard to the level of abstraction of the categorization, we decided to take every single difference in the first statements as its own category. This is motivated by the extremely short text segments and the narrowly circumscribed research question, which cannot be answered by relying on broader categories. An inductive analysis of individual statements yielded seven, respectively five categories for the first and second question. In sections 9.5.1 and 9.5.2, we will describe them in detail, report frequencies of the different categories, and interpret the findings with respect to the results of the quantitative analysis reported in Kittel et al. (2009).

The third question relates to the optimal group vote outcomes in the sense of maximizing the total payoffs of the group. In theory, given the $M$ automatic votes for candidate $C$, an optimal group vote is a combination of strategies in which the minimum number of 'yes'-votes ($M + 1$) is cast that makes the most-preferred party (given the situation, hence it might be a strategic vote for the second choice at the individual level) win the election and in which those voters participate who have the minimum voting costs and in which all others abstain. In order to explore the deliberation processes that resulted in optimal voting behavior we selected only positive outcomes, hence those chat sequences that actually resulted in an optimal vote.

As the dimensions of typification we differentiated between modes of negotiation. Although concrete deliberation processes cannot be predicted, we can identify three theoretical variants of the process at an abstract level. These turned out to fit the data well and could be maintained after scrutinizing their adequacy ex post. After analyzing the relevant chats we summarized their empirical frequencies and compared these findings with the quantitative results in Kittel et al. (2009). In the current case, this analysis added challenging nuances to the previous results.

## 9.5 Substantiating hypotheses on strategic voting and voter turnout

### 9.5.1 Inducement for swing voting

Kittel et al. (2009) found that the potential 'swing voters' $F$ and $G$ displayed higher rates of strategic voting in the communication treatments than in the baseline treatments. The question is now whether these subjects had to be convinced to do so or not, and which mechanisms during the communication process led to this increased observation of strategic voting.

In the 18 elections with prior communication (within parties) 112 potential swing voters had the option to cast their vote, 54 voters of type $F$ and 58 of type $G$. 54 (48.2 per cent) of these voters chose to abstain, 32 (28.6 per cent) voted for their first preference, 25 (22.3 per cent) voted for their second preference and one subject voted for party $C$.[11] While in the periods without communication we can only hypothesize about the motivation of swing voters and assume rational behavior, the chat protocols enable us to take a closer look at the origin of the swing votes. More precisely, we examine whether the swing voters are convinced to vote strategically during the group discussion, or whether they already intended to do so when entering the chat.

We focus on the 25 swing voters who actually cast a strategic vote, observing that only in five cases the swing voters had to be convinced to vote strategically while the remaining 20 subjects displayed the disposition to vote for their second preference already in their first statements. Within these two groups we differentiate seven different initial positions of swing voters.

*Proactive decisions to vote strategically* were identified twice. These subjects actively approached the other group members with the idea to vote for a specific party, which, according to their payment structure, should be their second preference. We thus not only found the willingness to vote for the second preferences, but in addition, an active promotion of this strategy. This is a clear indication that subjects comprehended the situation and the benefits of a strategic vote for the whole group.[12]

*Active decisions to vote strategically* were taken five times. Again, the subjects stated that they planned to vote for their second preference, but these subjects declared this for themselves only, without the attempt to convince their group mates. The subjects also appear to conceive the merits of the strategic vote but focus on their decision as a part of the group decision only.[13]

*Willingness to vote strategically* was indicated by seven subjects. Their first statements in the group discussion signaled a principal disposition to vote for their second preference. This is not due to a misunderstanding of their roles, because most of these subjects refer to their contrary first preference and their possible losses.[14]

*Conditional willingness to vote strategically* was indicated by four subjects. They submitted a first statement that conditioned their vote on the votes of the other group members. They stated a basic willingness to vote with the basic requirement that the other group members will vote for the same party. Most of these conditional statements indicated the willingness to vote for either party, as long as a majority would vote for that party. Only one subject indicated the willingness to vote for her second preference, as long as the other group members would also do so.[15]

*Approvals of agreement* were observed only towards the end of the discussion. As these two subjects remained silent until their confirmatory messages when the decision was already taken, these were their first statements. In these they merely approved the group's decision. Though we cannot judge whether these subjects had to be convinced to vote for their second preference, the chat protocols allow us to draw some inference about the subjects initial disposition. Both of the chats were extremely short and the proposal to vote for a specific party took place without any prior discussion. All approving statements directly followed this proposal. We therefore conclude that the swing voters did not have to be convinced but rather agreed on the party they intended to vote for anyway.[16]

*Intention to abstain* was stated in their first message by three subjects. These statements very clearly revealed the initial disposition not to vote at all. These subjects were subsequently convinced to vote for their second preference by the other group members.[17]

*Intention to vote for the first preference* was expressed incipiently by two subjects. Both of these statements were forwarded relatively early during the discussion and repeated at a later point. Both subjects were observably convinced to vote for their second preference by the obvious majority for that party.[18]

We find that the majority of actual swing voters (80 per cent) entered the chat with the intention to vote strategically. The five subjects that had to be persuaded to vote for their second preference reacted mainly to the argument that the majority of voters (members of their as well as of the other party) would vote for this specific party. This is, on the one hand, in line with the theoretical prediction of rational behavior based on the expected utility of the vote.[19] On the other hand, according to this observation the chat should not be superior to other communication media that would merely transfer information on the planned actions of the group members. A simple statement about which party each player intended to vote for would then have the same effect on the swing voters. This information was, however, already available in the no communication treatments. The distribution of voter types should – in principle – serve exactly this purpose. Nevertheless, we find significantly lower numbers of strategic votes in these treatments (Kittel et al., 2009). This information appears not to have convinced the swing voters.[20] Only personal chat statements such as 'I am going to vote for A', appear to be considered credible evidence on which the subjects subsequently build their strategies.

### 9.5.2 Inducement to vote

Similar to section 9.5.1, we explore the question whether the voters had to be convinced to vote during the group discussion, or whether they had been craving for a chance to coordinate their votes. This can again be found in the course of the chat with special emphasis on the first statements. We again analyze the 18 elections with prior communication (periods 13–19). In total, 154 voters of all types participated. 75 subjects abstained from voting, 79 cast a vote: 58 voters of type *G* and *H* (potential swing voters), 21 voters of type *E* and *H* (partisans).

Using five categories of initial positions similar to those described in section 9.5.1, we find that the majority of subjects (87.3 per cent) did not have to be convinced to vote, but rather stated the intention to vote already when entering the chat. We identified the following five types.

Subjects were classified as belonging to the type *proactive decision to vote* if they actively approached the other group members with the idea to vote either for a specific party or generally to vote jointly. We find 20 subjects falling into this category.

Statements were classified as *active decisions to vote* if subjects stated their intention to vote but did not try to convince the other players. Though some active subjects acted proactively later during the course of the experiment, their first statement did not involve any reference to a common action. 40 subjects submitted an active first statement.

*Conditional willingness to vote* has been expressed by four subjects, who are identical to those four that has been classified in this category in the last section. The stated intention to vote was conditioned on an unanimous or majority action of the group. The subjects stated clearly that they were willing to act only as part of a large fraction of the group.

*Approval of agreements* is a type in which the first statement did not include an independent action. The subjects confirmed a previously forwarded proposal by other group members. This proposal was either the result of a group discussion (that did not include the approving subjects) or was an individual opinion. We identified five subjects in this category.

The subjects who expressed their *intention to abstain* in their first statement were the only ones that had to be actively convinced to vote by the other group members. They did proclaim their plan to abstain but changed their minds during the communication process. We found ten subjects who were convinced to vote by the others.

Though most theoretical predictions of higher turnout rates after group communication refer to some process of persuasion, we find that only a minor part of the voters have actually been convinced by others. Our results show that the communication process is rather used as a mere source of information on the preference distributions in the electorate. Subjects update their beliefs on the possible outcomes and appear to act very rationally in accordance with the prospective electoral results. This is best demonstrated by the subjects who condition their vote on the actions of the other group members. They are willing to vote but only if a majority of voters will do so as well, thereby maximizing the probability of voting for the right candidate.[21] Although this is merely a small minority of voters, we find the mirror image confirming this thesis in the group of subjects that did abstain. Here, 47 per cent (35 subjects) initially claimed not to vote and acted accordingly after the chat.

The second to largest group are the non-voters whose first messages were actively (19 per cent) or proactively (20 per cent) indicating the willingness to vote. So besides the subjects who planned to abstain and then did so, there is a large fraction of players who searched to convince as many people as possible to vote, only to abstain themselves and absorb the profits from free riding.

### 9.5.3   Optimal election outcomes

We define an optimal election outcome as a situation in which exactly $M + 1$ votes are cast for either party $A$ or party $B$. This is a wider definition than the social optimum where exactly those voters with the highest voting costs and, consequentially, lowest gains from voting are appointed to abstain. We do not expect this high level of coordination to occur often. In principle, three scenarios provide plausible explanations for the emergence of an optimal vote:

   i. A collective decision, in which some subjects are determined to bear the voting costs while others are determined to abstain.
  ii. A collective decision in which the voters coordinate on a voting strategy different from the optimal vote. In this scenario a number of individuals break the engagement, thereby incidentally creating the optimal outcome.
 iii. No coordination takes place at all and the optimal number of votes emerges only by chance. Though theoretically possible, this event appears to be rather unlikely and did in fact never happen in the 12 periods without communication.

Our example dataset contains 41 elections (or sequences/periods), 18 of them including a communication phase prior to the actual election. Out of those 41 elections only five resulted in an optimal vote, all of them occurring in chat treatments. A special feature of our dataset is that the chats were restricted to the members of each party $A$ and $B$, respectively. This exacerbated the coordination process, as none of the parties included a sufficient number of voters to decide the election in their favor. The five optimal votes were the result of coordination in ten subgroups (parties $A$ and $B$ in each election) each unaware of the decision taken in the other subgroup. The three possible scenarios described above apply to each of the subgroups, resulting in six possible paired scenarios. Obviously the first scenario described above is not possible without inter-party coordination or at least beliefs about the decisions of the other party. Without the elicitation of the beliefs from the chat protocols we can only state that in three of five votes both subgroups resorted to the strategy of unanimous votes for one party and individual defections (abstentions) led to an optimal vote (group 1 in period 17, group 1 and 2 in period 19). In group 4 of period 18 party $A$ decided not to coordinate their votes while party $B$ coordinated on an unanimous vote. Party $A$ of group 1 in period 16 also coordinated on an unanimous vote while party $B$ decided to provide only two votes, thereby constituting the only case of a coordination on an optimal vote to be found in our dataset.

Beyond this brief characterization we found clear evidence for a fixed underlying scheme for the interplay of the subgroups in all examined cases. This scheme comprises a set of recursive typifications which structure the decision situation. We identify three elements of typification that allow for an advanced coordination also between the subgroups.

a. The first step is the independent decision of both subgroups which party may serve as a focal point for the election. Apparently the number of partisans in both subgroups is the predominant decision criterion, followed by the number of swing voters sharing the same first preference. More specifically, a specific party ($A$ or $B$) will be the focal point for the coordination if a) this party features the majority of partisans and b) the subgroup to which these voters belong is larger than the second subgroup.

b. This former group receives the status of a 'leader group'. The members of the leader group appear to coordinate largely without referring to the behavior of the other subgroup. This way the group 'leads' the coordination process by creating a foreseeable coordination result. The second subgroup is allotted the complementary position of the 'follower group', which strongly relies on (and refers to) the predicted choice of the leader group.

c. It is obvious that the leader group has – strictly speaking – no possibility for tactical voting, for example by anticipating the number of votes for one specific party and coordination on the minimal required number of complementary votes. Given their status of a leader group, the expected coordination result is an unanimous vote for the party whose partisans are members of the group, or at least an unanimous vote. The possibilities for strategic behavior of the follower group emanate exactly from this expected behavior of the leader group. Only this anticipation of a foreseeable vote by the leader group facilitates the strategic, complementary behavior of the follower group, thereby fostering optimal election outcomes.

All of these elements stem from and have been found in the chat protocols of the experimental elections. The fact that only in one election the planned strategic behavior of the follower group led to the optimal outcome (group 1 in period 16), rather than defection, can obviously be attributed to risk aversion: Though all follower groups refer to the most certain vote of the leader group, most groups resort to an unanimous vote as 'the only possibility to *assure* that Party X wins the election'. By deliberately casting too many votes for a specific candidate the follower group seeks to minimize the risk of loosing the vote because of wrong assumptions about the leader party. Evidently, coordination for an unanimous vote is also much easier to propagate as it avoids the discussion of who shall bear the costs of voting and who may take a free ride, only enjoying the benefits. Still, it should be noted that in group 1 in period 17, two subjects very actively convinced the rest of the group to vote unanimously while themselves defecting by abstention in the actual voting phase. This group reached an optimal election outcome only *prima facie* via scenario ii but actually via a planned strategy (scenario i) that was not revealed to all group members. Hence we can add two interesting nuances to previous findings. First, only one of the five optimal votes was the result of intended strategic coordination on the outcome that was realized. Second, some 'sneaky' voters have been able to manipulate the deliberation process in such a way as to generate the possibility to free ride on the willingness of others to contribute to the public good of a defeat of party $C$.

### 9.5.4 Discussion

In analyzing the process of group decision making we expand the originally purely quantitative analysis in Kittel et al. (2009). We find that the coordination process is used rather to update the subjects' beliefs about the preference distributions in the group than to convince rank-breaking group members. Apparently, the potential swing voters are well aware of benefits from strategic voting. Only the smallest part of type $F$ and $G$ voters have to be convinced to vote for their second preference. In most cases, subjects confronted with the challenge of strategic voting seek to confirm the higher probability of their second preferred party winning the election during the deliberation. The same appears to hold true for voter turnout rates. In our view, this does in no way question the results of Kittel et al. (2009), but rather confirms the rational and strategic voter theories in displaying the high level of rationality – in the sense of cutoff-cost equilibria – observed. A further proof for the high levels of comprehension found in this experiment is the leader-follower pattern of parties. Even without the possibility to communicate, some chat parties manage to coordinate on an optimal vote. Admittedly, this is true only for 1.3 per cent of the considered elections, but one has to keep in mind that in the majority of elections the groups were at least successful in coordinating on one candidate – without communication.

## 9.6  Conclusion

We have started from the consideration that the typical social science experiment remains silent about the causal path via which the treatment is linked to the outcome, although there may certainly exist theoretical propositions about these paths. In the case of experimentation with individuals, discontent with this situation has encouraged the foundation of the interdisciplinary field of neuroeconomics. This field attempts to trace the decision process in the subjects' minds by studying brain activity. In the emerging field of experiments on group decision making, researchers do not need to explore brain activity to understand the processes leading to the decision – these processes are observable with tools available to social scientists. Hence, in addition to research on behavioral differences between individuals and groups, the exploration of individual behavior within groups provides an opportunity to study group decision processes. Using chat facilities as a communication medium of group experiments produces unique material about intra-group interactions and the collective decision making process. In fact, it provides researchers with a complete protocol of all relevant communication and events contained in the 'black box' of group experiments, and thus allows them to look inside this box.

We have shown that scrutinizing this source of information both strengthens and adds nuance to the results from more conventional experimental research. In particular, one striking result was that the process of deliberation itself had less impact on individual voting decisions than the comprehension of the strategic trade-offs which the subjects faced. Although such a finding is too isolated and too much circumscribed by the experimental design to warrant drawing big conclusions, it might hint at a possible need to nuance the effect of deliberation on decisions (Steiner et al., 2004; Hajer and Wagenaar, 2003; Thomson, 2008; Austen-Smith and Feddersen, 2006; Landa and Meirowitz, 2009). Another unexpected result we found is that four of the five outcomes that turned out to be 'optimal' appeared to be less the result of successful strategic coordination than of chance. This means that assumptions about rationality in behavior under-lying the formal models of strategic voting that are currently employed may be too optimistic to capture real-world processes (Myatt, 2007).

In this chapter, we have only scratched the surface of the possibilities of qualitative analysis of chat protocols. We see much potential in the following areas: First, given that the software does not only automatically record the workstation from which a contribution to the chat was made but also registers the exact moment at which the contribution was sent, the process of decision making can be represented as a score. This implies that we can make use of the more extensive tools that have been developed for the holistic study of decision making in real committees developed in the score approach (Nullmeier et al., 2008). We can explore different phases and sequences in the decision making process, trace the effects of infor-mation asymmetries between subgroups of electorates and obtain more fine-grained information about the way in which proposals emerge from deliberation. Communication in the experimental setting is much simpler, though more artificial than in real-world settings. Therefore, it is possible in qualitative experimental work to abstract from many factors interfering with the model that undermine the strength of theory tests in observational studies. Thus, our approach may provide a bridge between the crisp tests of formal theories by experiments (producing high internal validity), and the proximity to the complexities of real-world group decisions encountered in observational studies (strong on ecological validity).

Second, an interesting route of exploration may be to study the behavior of individuals in more depth. Some participants explicitly express their motiv-ations, while others hide their real intentions or lie about their preferences in order to mislead the other group members and to free ride on the group's choice. All the information necessary for identifying such behavior is avail-able as the chat protocols contain statements about intended behavior, and the induced preferences in the context of the experimental procedure elicit real behavior.

Third, the study of chat protocols allows us to explore basic assumptions underlying social science experiments about the extent to which induced preferences do indeed cause behavior. Because of the possibility to follow the reflections of individuals about their aims and preferences in group discussions, we can make more informed judgments about the validity of these assumptions.

Finally, in the context of groups, individuals quickly take on particular roles. While being anonymous situations by design, we have been surprised by the speed at which roles within the group have been distributed. Role taking in the experimental groups, however, seems to be intensely related to individual character traits, because we also found hints at the persistence of roles of individuals across different chat sequences in one and the same experimental session. But on the other hand, experiences in early sequences of an experimental session may cause individual learning processes. Such processes can thus be studied under highly isolated conditions.

Although experimental and interpretative work may seem to be methods that are as far apart in ontological, epistemological and methodological terms as one can imagine, we hope that our study helps to reveal the potential of a more pragmatic distribution of different but complementary roles for different approaches.

## Notes

1. The findings in the seminal paper by Cason and Mui (1997) have been repeatedly interpreted and cited as teams being more generous than individuals in the dictator game. Cason and Mui (1997) do in fact only report that teams whose members feature heterogeneous preferences take more other-regarding decisions than individuals.

2. The two most prominent theories explaining this fact that the very same subjects take different decisions individually and in a group (choice shifts) are the Social Comparison Theory (SCT) (Festinger, 1954) and the Persuasive Argument Theory (PAT) (Vinokur and Burnstein, 1974). SCT claims that subjects consider the other group members to find out the 'socially correct' decision and seek to position themselves on the extremes of the socially correct position. PAT assumes that individuals make decisions based on pro and con arguments, with the option featuring the most pro arguments being selected. During discussion the group members forward these arguments, which leads to an updating of individual information and finally to a collective choice of the option with the most shared pro arguments.

3. Note, however, that the artificiality is only a matter of degree. For the current cohorts of students, communication with strangers via online chats belongs to their everyday experiences.

4. 'Truthful responses' typically refer to actions that represent the subjects' real preferences. In our analysis, 'true' or 'unbiased' observations are based only on the experimental situation, which is completely observed.

5. Note that this constellation implies a complex multi-level structure. We are confronted with individuals (level 1) within chat sequences (level 2), who are, however, reallocated to new sequences within one experimental session. We thus have two levels and potential autocorrelation between level-2 units caused by behavior at level-1. See Shikano et al., in this volume.

6. In a strategic voting situation the agents have a clear preference structure over multiple candidates ($n > 2$). If an agent observes that his favourite candidate cannot win the election, she can either vote sincerely for this candidate or vote strategically for a second-preferred candidate in order to prevent an even less preferred candidate from winning the election.

7. The payoffs are displayed in experimental points. The conversion rate was 2.5 points per euro or each token was worth 40 euro cents.

8. Own calculation from raw data.

9. Session dated October, 22, 2008.

10. This decision leaves some uncertainty, because participants who kept silent during early phases of a deliberation may already have been influenced by statements of others before their view is recorded. In principle, it might be possible to

question and perhaps adjust the first statements of late contributors to the discussion in a procedure of explication. This, however, depends on the availability of cues that challenge the interpretation of first statements. In the material studied for this chapter, we have not found indications of such endogeneity.

11. As the group (group 2 in period 17) coordinated on a vote for party B, this vote may have been cast accidentially, because the buttons for party B and C were aligned next to each other.

12. Original message: 'wir müssten uns alle mit auf B stürzen, weil die andere partei das wählt', translation: 'we all have to jump at B with them because that is what the other party is voting' (14_2_1: 541).

13. Original message: 'Wählertyp A und wähl B', translation: 'votertype A voting B' (17_2_2: 548).

14. Original message: 'mh, also für mich eigentl B gut, und für die A, aber A wär für mich auch ok'; translation: 'Well, in principle B would be good for me, and A would be good for them, but A would also be o.k. for me' (18_4_1: 451).

15. Original message: 'habe zwar hohe kosten (49) aber wenn alle mitmachen, dann wähle ich b', translation: 'my voting costs are high (49) but if everybody participates I will vote for B' (19_2_2: 554).

16. In this case, the chat analysis cannot illustrate the decision process, but this remains an intrapersonal process social sciences cannot observe.

17. Original message: 'nicht bei mir. zu hohe wahlkosten', translation: 'not with me, too high voting costs' (16_1_1: 550).

18. Original message: 'bin für b', translation: 'I'm in favor of B' (19_1_2: 561).

19. The exact theoretical predictions can be found in Kittel et al. (2009).

20. Polls are another means of gathering and disseminating such information among actors in a voting context (Forsythe et al., 1993). We consider this as an intermediate situation between the two treatments discussed in the text. If, as our results suggest, authentic statements by actors involved in the communication process are important, we would expect the results of this condition to be closer to our no-communication treatment.

21. Models based on such conditional strategies have been explored by Coate and Conlin (2004) and Feddersen and Sandroni (2006).

## References

Austen-Smith, David and Timothy Feddersen (2006) 'Deliberation, Preference Uncertainty, and Voting Rules', *American Political Science Review*, 100, 209–17.

Bergman, Manfred Max (2009) *Mixed Methods Research* (London: Sage).

Blinder, Alan S. and John Morgan (2005) 'Are Two Heads Better than One? Monetary Policy by Committee', *Journal of Money, Credit and Banking*, 37, 789–811.

Bohnet, Iris and Bruno S. Frey (1999) 'Social Distance and other-regarding Behavior in Dictator Games: Comment', *The American Economic Review*, 89, 335–9.

Bolton, Gary E. and Axel Ockenfels (2000) 'ERC: A Theory of Equity, Reciprocity, and Competition', *American Economic Review*, 90, 166–93.

Bornstein, Gary, Tamar Kugler and Anthony Ziegelmeyer (2004) 'Individual and group decisions in the centipede game: Are groups more "rational" players?', *Journal of Experimental Social Psychology*, 40, 599–605.

Bornstein, Gary and Ilan Yaniv (1998) 'Individual and group behavior in the ultimatum game: Are groups more "rational" players?', *Experimental Economics*, 1, 101–8.

Bosman, Ronald, Heike Hennig-Schmidt and Frans Van Winden (2006) 'Exploring Group Decision Making in a Power-to-take Experiment', *Experimental Economics*, 9, 35–51.

Bosman, Ronald and Frans van Winden (2002) 'Emotional Hazard in a Power-to-Take Experiment', *The Economic Journal*, 112, 147–69.

Brosig, Jeannette, Joachim Weimann and Axel Ockenfels (2003) 'The Effect of Communication Media on Cooperation', *German Economic Review*, 4, 217–41.

Camerer, Colin (2003) *Behavioral game theory: Experiments in strategic interaction* (Princeton University Press: Princeton, NJ).

Camerer, Colin, George Loewenstein and Drazen Prelec (2005) 'Neuroeconomics: How Neuroscience Can Inform Economics', *Journal of Economic Literature*, 43, 9–64.

Cason, Timothy N. and Vai-Lam Mui (1997) 'A Laboratory Study in Group Polarisation in the Team Dictator Game', *The Economic Journal*, 107, 1465–83.

Coate, Stephen and Michael Conlin (2004) 'A Group Rule–Utilitarian Approach to Voter Turnout: Theory and Evidence', *American Economic Review*, 94, 1476–504.

Cooper, David J. and John H. Kagel (2005) 'Are Two Heads Better than One? Team versus Individual Play in Signaling Games', *The American Economic Review*, 95, 477–509.

Cox, Gary W. (1997) *Making Votes Count: Strategic Coordination in the World's Electoral Systems* (Cambridge University Press).

Cox, James C. (2002) 'Trust, Reciprocity, and Other-regarding Preferences: Groups vs. Individuals and Males vs. Females', in Rami Zwick and Amnon Rapoport, (eds.), *Experimental Business Research* (Dordrecht: Kluwer).

Feddersen, Timothy and Alvaro Sandroni (2006) 'A Theory of Participation in Elections', *American Economic Review*, 96, 1271–82.

Fehr, Ernst and Klaus M. Schmidt (1999) 'A Theory Of Fairness, Competition, and Cooperation', *Quarterly Journal of Economics*, 114, 817–68.

Festinger, Leon (1954) 'A Theory of Social Comparison Processes', *Human Relations*, 7, 117–140.

Fiorina, Morris P. and Charles R. Plott (1978) 'Committee Decisions under Majority Rule: An Experimental Study', *American Political Science Review*, 72, 575–98.

Flick, Uwe (2008) *Triangulation*, 2nd edition (Wiesbaden: VS Verlag für Sozialwissenschaften).

Forsythe, Robert, Roger B. Myerson, Thomas A. Rietz and Robert J. Weber (1993) 'An Experiment on Coordination in Multi-candidate Elections: The Importance of Polls and Election Histories', *Social Choice and Welfare*, 10, 223–47.

Friedman, Daniel and Shyam Sunder (1994) *Experimental Methods: A Primer for Economists* (Cambridge: Cambridge University Press).

Glimcher, Paul W. (2004) *Decisions, Uncertainty, and the Brain: The Science of Neuroeconomics* (Cambridge: The MIT Press).

Glimcher, Paul W. and Aldo Rustichini (2004) 'Neuroeconomics: The Consilience of Brain and Decision', *Science* 306, 447–452.

Glimcher, Paul W., Colin Camerer, Russell A. Poldrack and Ernst Fehr (eds.) (2009) *Neuroeconomics. Decision Making and the Brain* (Harvard: Academic Press).

Hajer, Maarten A. and Hendrik Wagenaar (eds.) (2003) *Deliberative Policy Analysis. Understanding Governance in the Network Society* (Cambridge: Cambridge University Press).

Hoffman, Elizabeth, Kevin McCabe and Vernon L. Smith (1996) 'Social Distance and Other-regarding Behavior in Dictator Games', *The American Economic Review*, 86, 653–60.

Insko, Chester A., Robin L. Pinkley, Rick H. Hoyle, Bret Dalton, Guiyoung Hong, Randa M. Slim, Pat Landry, Brynda Holton, Paulette F. Ruffin and John Thibaut (1987) 'Individual versus Group Discontinuity: The Role of Intergroup Contact', *Journal of experimental social psychology*, 23, 250–67.

Kelle, Udo and Christian Erzberger (1999) 'The integration of qualitative and quantitative methods. Methodological models and their significance for practising social research', *Kölner Zeitschrift für Soziologie und Sozialpsychologie*, 3, 509–31.

Kerr, Norbert, Robert MacCoun and Geoffrey Kramer (1996) 'Bias in Judgement: Comparing Individuals and Groups', *Psychological Review*, 103, 687–719.

Kerr, Norbert and R. Scott Tindale (2004) 'Group Performance and Decision Making', *Annual Review of Psychology*, 55, 623–55.

Kinder, Donald R. and Thomas R. Palfrey (1993) 'On Behalf of an Experimental Political Science', in Donald R. Kinder and Thomas R. Palfrey (eds.) *Experimental Foundations of Political Science* (Ann Arbor: The University of Michigan Press).

Kittel, Bernhard, Wolfgang J. Luhan and Rebecca Morton (2009) 'Communication and Voting', Manuscript, University of Oldenburg.

Kocher, Martin G. and Matthias Sutter (2005) 'The Decision Maker Matters: Individual versus Group Behaviour in Experimental Beauty-contest Games', *Economic Journal*, 115, 200–23.

Landa, Dimitri and John Meirowitz (2009) 'Game Theory, Information, and Deliberative Democracy', *American Journal of Political Science*, 53, 427–44.

Levine, John M. and Richard L. Moreland (1990) 'Progress in Small Group Research', *Annual Review of Psychology*, 41, 585–634.

Levine, John M. and Richard L. Moreland (1998) 'Small Groups' in Daniel T. Gilbert, Susan T. Fiske and Gardner Lindzey (eds.), *The Handbook of Social Psychology* (Boston: McGraw-Hill).

Luhan, Wolfgang J., Martin G. Kocher and Matthias Sutter (2009) 'Group Polarization in the Team Dictator Game Reconsidered' *Experimental Economics*, 12, 26–41.

Mayring, Philipp and Michaela Gläser-Zikuda, (eds.) (2005) *Die Praxis der Qualitativen Inhaltsanalyse* (Weinheim: Beltz).

Mayring, Philipp (2004) 'Qualitative Content Analysis' in Uwe Flick, Ernst von Kardorff and Ines Steinke (eds.) *A Companion to Qualitative Research* (London: Sage).

Mayring, Philipp (2007) *Qualitative Inhaltsanalyse* (Weinheim: Beltz).

McDermott, Rose (2007) 'Experimental Political Science' in Murray Webster, Jr. and Jane Sell (eds.) *Laboratory Experiments in the Social Sciences* (Burlington: Academic Press).

Morse, Janice M. (2002) 'Principles of Mixed Methods and Multimethod Research Design', in Abbas Tashakkori and Charles Teddlie (eds.) *Handbook of Mixed Methods in Social & Behavioral Research* (London: Sage).

Moscovici, Serge and Marisa Zavalloni (1969) 'The Group as a Polarizer of Attitudes', *Journal of Personality and Social Psychology*, 12, 125–35.

Myatt, David P. (2007) 'On the Theory of Strategic Voting', *Review of Economic Studies*, 74, 255–81.

Nullmeier, Frank, Tanja Pritzlaff, Anne C. Weihe and Achim Wiesner (2008) *Entscheiden in Gremien. Von der Videoaufzeichnung zur Prozessanalyse* (Wiesbaden: VS Verlag für Sozialwissenschaften).

Palfrey, Thomas R. and Howard Rosenthal (1985) 'Voter Participation and Strategic Uncertainty', *The American Political Science Review*, 79, 62–78.

Palfrey, Thomas R. (2008) 'Laboratory Experiments' in Barry R. Weingast and Donald Wittman (eds.) *The Oxford Handbook of Political Economy* (Oxford: Oxford University Press).

Peräkylä, Anssi (2005) 'Analyzing Talk and Text' in Norman K. Denzin and Yvonna S. Lincoln (eds.) *The Sage Handbook of Qualitative Research* (London: Sage).

Samuelson, Larry (2005) 'Economic Theory and Experimental Economics', *Journal of Economic Literature*, 43, 65–107.

Schram, Arthur (2003) 'Experimental Public Choice' in Charles K. Rowley and Friedrich Schneider (eds.) *Encyclopedia of Public Choice* (Deventer: Kluwer).

Smith, Vernon L. (1994) 'Economic in the Laboratory', *Journal of Economic Perspectives*, 8, 113–31.

Smith, Vernon L. (2005) 'Behavioral Economics Research and the Foundations of Economics', *The Journal of Socio-Economics*, 34, 135–50.

Smith, Vernon L. (2008) *Rationality in Economics: Constructivist and Ecological Forms* (Cambridge, Cambridge University Press).

Steiner, Jürg, André Bächtiger, Markus Spörndli and Marco R. Steenbergen (2004) *Deliberative Politics in Action. Analysing Parliamentary Discourse* (Cambridge, Cambridge University Press).

Thomson, Dennis F. (2008) 'Deliberative Democratic Theory and Empirical Political Science', *Annual Review of Political Science*, 11, 497–520.

Thye, Shane R. (2007) 'Logical and Philosophical Foundations of Experimental Research in the Social Sciences' in Murray Webster Jr. and Jane Sell. (eds.) *Laboratory Experiments in the Social Sciences* (Burlington, Academic Press).

Titschner, Stefan, Michael Meyer, Ruth Wodak and Eva Vetter (2000) *Methods of Text and Discourse Analysis* (London: Sage Publications).

Vinokur, Amiram and Eugene Burnstein (1974) 'Effects of Partially Shared Persuasive Arguments on Group-induced Shifts: A Group-problem-solving Approach', *Journal of Personality and Social Psychology*, 29, 305–15.

Weihe, Anne C., Tanja Pritzlaff, Frank Nullmeier, Tilo Felgenhauer and Britta Baumgarten (2008) 'Wie wird in politischen Gremien entschieden? Konzeptionelle und methodische Grundlagen der Gremienanalyse', *Politische Vierteljahresschrift*, 49, 339–59.

Wildschut, Tim, Brad Pinter, Jack L. Vevea, Chester A. Insko and John Schopler (2003) 'Beyond the Group Mind: A Quantitative Review of the Interindividual-Intergroup Discontinuity Effect', *Psychological Bulletin*, 129, 698–722.

Wilson, Rick K. (2007) 'Voting and Agenda Setting in Political Science and Economics' in Murray Webster Jr. and Jane Sell (eds.) *Laboratory Experiments in the Social Sciences* (Burlington, Academic Press).

Zelditch Jr., Morris (2007) 'The External Validity of Experiments That Test Theories' in Murray Webster Jr. and Jane Sell (eds.) *Laboratory Experiments in the Social Sciences* (Burlington, Academic Press).

# Part IV

# Challenges to Inferences from Experiments

# 10
# On the Validity of Laboratory Research in the Political and Social Sciences: The Example of Crime and Punishment

*Heiko Rauhut and Fabian Winter*

## 10.1 The controversy of crime and punishment

Policies against crime often focus on more extensive crime control schemes and more severe punishments (Foucault, 1977; Garland, 2001). Examples are the 'zero tolerance' policy or the program 'three strikes and you're out' (Cohen, 1985; Dreher and Feltes, 1997; Austin et al., 1999; Zimring, 2001; Hudson, 2002).

However, the empirical support for the deterrent effect of punishment severity on crime is limited. Gibbs (1968) and Tittle (1969) compared official crime rates in areas with different levels of punishment severity. Sellin (1961) compared murder rates in US states which allow for capital punishment with those which do not. None of the three studies could demonstrate that crime rates were lower in areas with more severe punishments. Ross (1973, 1975) studied whether an increase in the level of punishment in one region caused lower crime rates. The results showed that the deterrent effects were limited in time. After an initial decrease, crime rates bounced back (see also Sherman, 1990). Therefore, many current reviews raise serious doubts that severity of punishment has a strong impact on crime (Cook, 1980; Von Hirsch et al., 1999; Doob and Webster, 2003), whereas more 'optimistic' views on the effects of punishment severity on crime have been raised elsewhere (Cameron, 1988; Nagin, 1998; Levitt, 2002).

Laboratory experiments may provide additional insights and uncover the causal mechanisms with greater clarity than traditional methods. The disadvantage of traditional methods, like observational and field data, is that they often do not allow for causal inferences due to unmeasured or unknown third variables. This results in doubts as to whether correlations are causal or spurious. In contrast, laboratory experiments allow us to vary the variables of interest deliberately and hold everything else constant.

There is increasing popularity of performing laboratory research on the violation of informal norms (see for selected influential experiments Yamagishi, 1986; Ostrom et al., 1992; Horne and Cutlip, 2002, and for reviews Diekmann, 2003 and Fehr and Gintis, 2007). However, there are still only few experiments on the violation of formal norms, that is, criminal behavior. One counter-example is the experiment by Falk and Fischbacher (2002), who studied reciprocity of criminal decision-making. Here, subjects could earn individual property in a knowledge quiz. Then, subjects were randomly matched in groups of four and they could decide to steal money from their fellows. Using the strategy method,[1] subjects could condition their stealing decision on the theft rate in their group. The authors concluded that crime is reciprocal, because individuals stole more in groups with higher theft rates. Bosman and van Winden (2002) conducted an experiment on punishment of 'criminal' decision-making. In the so-called 'power-to-take' game, two players earned their own property. Then, one player could take any fraction of the other player's earnings. However, the victim could punish the perpetrator so that she could destroy any fraction of her own property before it was taken.[2]

Despite substantial contributions of laboratory researching identifying causal mechanisms in the political and social sciences, many questions remain disputed. Scepticism may be fueled by concerns about the validity of generalized causal inferences of laboratory experiments. In this chapter, we discuss the validity of laboratory research and exemplify selected issues using one laboratory study on crime, control and punishment whose theoretical and empirical aspects have been discussed elsewhere (Rauhut, 2009). We discuss its validity with reference to the typology introduced by Shadish et al. (2002). This typology may be used as a checklist for the construction of experimental designs and the assessment of respective results.

## 10.2   A validity typology for the development and assessment of experimental designs

Validity can be understood as a measure of the approximate truth of an inference.[3] Campbell (1957) suggested the first systematic classification of validity. He defined *internal validity* as the question 'Did in fact the experimental stimulus make some significant difference in this specific instance?' (p. 297). Thus, internal validity is concerned with the question of whether the correlation between treatment and outcome reflects a *causal* relationship.[4] Causality can be defined with the *counterfactual model*.[5] A causal effect is the difference between what did happen (factual) and what would have happened if the state of the world was different (counterfactual). Shadish et al. (2002, p. 38) defined *internal validity* more precisely as the 'validity of inferences about whether observed covariation between *A* (the presumed treatment) and *B* (the presumed outcome) reflects a causal relationship from *A* to *B* as those variables were manipulated or measured.'[6]

Spurious correlations can be ruled out in two ways. Either the same subjects are assigned to different treatments at a different time (*within-subjects design*), or different subjects are assigned to different treatments at the same time (*between-subjects design*). The disadvantage of a within-subjects design is that subjects may learn or may be exposed to different kinds of history effects between the first and the second treatment so that their behavior may be incomparable. Another disadvantage is the exposure to the full set of treatment conditions, which may put subjects into the position to get to know the research question, triggering a social desirability bias (Friedman and Sunder, 1994, p. 39). For a between-subjects design, the comparison groups have to be similar. This is usually ensured by randomly assigning subjects to different treatments. Between-subjects designs only allow the investigation of population effects, while the assessment of the same subject's reaction to different stimuli is excluded by construction of the design.

*External validity* is concerned with the question as to whether the findings are generalizable. More precisely, external validity can be defined as the 'validity of inferences about whether the cause-effect relationship holds over the variation in persons, settings, treatment variables, and measurement variables' (see Shadish et al., 2002, p. 38). A threat to external validity may be that experiments are often highly local. They are conducted at one particular university and the population often consists of convenience samples like students.

In addition to internal and external validity, Shadish et al. (2002) extended the typology by introducing statistical conclusion and construct validity. *Statistical conclusion validity* is concerned with the accurateness of the statistical estimates. More specifically, statistical conclusion validity can be defined as the 'validity of inferences about the correlation (covariation) between treatment and outcome' (Shadish et al., 2002, p. 38).[7] Typical concerns are violated assumptions of statistical tests and the so-called 'fishing problem', which means that repeated tests are conducted to find significant relationships which are uncorrected for the number of tests. Statistical conclusion validity is deeply entrenched with the choice of the design. Therefore, it is crucial to construct experiments such that there is a fair chance that the hypothesized correlations can be measured with sufficient statistical certainty. For example, if different types of players are compared, it is statistically more efficient to use groups of similar size.

Moreover, *construct validity* refers to the similarity between real-world phenomena and their measurements in the laboratory. Construct validity can therefore be defined as the 'validity of inferences about the higher order constructs that represent sampling particulars' (Shadish et al., 2002, p. 38). It is necessary to operationalize abstract concepts with decision-making tasks such that they are easily comprehensible by subjects and adequately represent higher order constructs. It is not possible to formulate strict guidelines. This requires the profound knowledge, intuition and creativity of the experimenter.

Shadish et al. (2002: 37, Fn. 4) mention another important dimension of validity, *ecological validity*, only in passing. According to Morton and Williams (2010: 265), this validity type refers to '[w]hether the methods, materials, and settings of the research are similar to a given target population'. In other words, this type of validity is concerned about the extent to which the environment in which the experiment takes place reflects situations experienced in natural environments. Put colloquially, ecological validity reflects the connection between laboratory and 'real-world' situations. Hence, construct validity and ecological validity are two distinct challenges to inferences made from experiments. The first is foremost an issue of adequate operationalization of the relevant theoretical variables and their correct measurement in the experiment. This may involve a more or less naturalistic setting, hence they have more or less ecological validity.

## 10.3   Technical implementation

The remainder of this chapter will discuss the four different types of validity with reference to an experiment originally reported in Rauhut (2009). In total, 196 subjects were sampled. These subjects were randomly chosen from an address pool of 692 students and randomly allocated to one experimental session. Each subject participated only once in the experiment. The address pool consisted of students from many different fields from the University of Leipzig. Each subject was offered a show-up fee of 5 euros for participation in the experiment, which was paid at the end of the experiment. The experiment was conducted using the software z-tree (Fischbacher, 2007). On average, participants earned 4.35 euros, in addition to the show-up fee (9.35 euros in total). The experiment lasted for about one hour, so that the average earnings are comparable to student wages paid in the area of Leipzig.

## 10.4   Designing experiments on crime and punishment

The idea of a 'rational' treatment of crime and punishment was introduced by Cesare Beccaria (1819, first published 1764) in his essay 'On Crimes and Punishment'. He argued that humans have a free will or choice and are rational in terms of maximizing their own profit under given restrictions. Gary Becker (1968) formalized these ideas and applied a market equilibrium analysis to crime and punishment.[8] In this view, a thief is a thief and a professor is a professor because this profession makes both better off given their preferences and restrictions: 'Someone willing to pay that price

*Table 10.1* The Inspection Game

|  |  | Inspector m | | |
|---|---|---|---|---|
|  |  | Inspect |  | Not Inspect |
| Citizen $i$ | Crime | $g - p, r - k$ | $\Leftarrow$ | $g, 0$ |
|  |  | $\Downarrow$ |  | $\Uparrow$ |
|  | No crime | $0, -k$ | $\Rightarrow$ | $0, 0$ |

The payoffs denote $g$ gains from crime, $p$ punishment, $k$ inspection cost, $r$ rewards for successful inspection with $p > g > 0$ and $r > k > 0$.

will commit the crime – and, from the standpoint of economic efficiency, should' (Friedman, 1995, 45).

However, the model of Becker (1968) ignores strategic decision-making, because the detection probability is exogenous. More precisely, this ignores that the detection probability is generated by the incentive structure, beliefs and decisions of inspectors. The models on tax evasion consider this aspect. Here, an endogenous audit probability is introduced in the standard model (Allingham and Sandmo, 1972). It is assumed that the tax authority can either impose costly audits which guarantee detection of tax fraud, or it can leave tax evasion undetected. Later models allow for continuous choices such that the audit probability depends on the amount of declared income by the taxpayer. Taxpayers can choose different extents of tax fraud by reporting a certain amount of income to the tax authority. The difference between real and reported income is the so-called *tax gap*, which measures the extent of fraud.[9]

A strategic model of crime and punishment was introduced by Tsebelis (1989, 1990) with the so-called 'inspection game'. The model considers citizens, who can decide to commit a crime to receive criminal earnings $g > 0$. Further, there are inspectors who can decide to spend some effort $k > 0$ to detect criminals. If they detect them, the inspectors receive rewards $r > k$ and criminals receive punishments $p > g$. The incentive structure is given in Table 10.1.

The model implies that citizens prefer to commit a crime if not inspected, but to abide by the law if inspected. In contrast, inspectors prefer to perform inspections if citizens are criminal and not to inspect if citizens are law-abiding. Because there is no dominant strategy, actors have to 'mix' their strategy. This means that players choose a certain probability to perform one of the alternatives. The idea is that rational actors try to outsmart their opponents. Outsmarting only works if citizens choose the probability of committing a crime at the indifference point of inspectors, and inspectors choose the probability of inspection at the indifference point of criminals.

The intuition of this logic may be illustrated by the following consideration: A criminal who commits a crime no matter what will be, sooner or later, sent to prison. On the other hand, a 'big-brother-state' which invests in an omnipresent control regime will be highly inefficient because the crime rate will drop and control activities will no longer amortize. Therefore, both parties will choose a mixed strategy instead of a pure one.

This structure has the counterintuitive implication that more severe punishment does not result in lower crime rates, but in lower control rates. This effect can be derived with equilibria in 'mixed' strategies. We denote $s_i$ as the probability that citizen $i$ chooses to commit the crime and $c_m$ as the probability that inspector $m$ will inspect citizen $i$. We can write the payoff function $\pi$ for citizen $i$ who plays against inspector $m$ as

$$\pi_i(s_i, c_m) = s_i(g - c_m p)$$

The payoff function $\varphi$ for inspector $m$ who plays against citizen $i$ is

$$\phi_m(s_i, c_m) = c_m(s_i r - k).$$

Note that in contrast to the model proposed by Becker (1968), the game theoretical model introduces the detection probability as an endogenous variable, generated by the strategic decision making of inspectors. The best response for citizen $i$ can be determined by calculating the first partial derivative $\dfrac{\partial \pi_i}{\partial s_i}$ as

$$s_i^*(c_m) = \begin{cases} 1 & \text{if } g - c_m p > 0 \\ [0, 1] & \text{if } g - c_m p = 0 \\ 0 & \text{if } g - c_m p < 0. \end{cases}$$

The first partial derivative $\dfrac{\partial \phi_m}{\partial c_m}$ returns the best response for inspector $m$ as

$$c_m^*(s_i) = \begin{cases} 1 & \text{if } s_i r - k > 0 \\ [0, 1] & \text{if } s_i r - k = 0 \\ 0 & \text{if } s_i r - k < 0. \end{cases}$$

It can be seen that there are no Nash equilibria in pure strategies due to $p > g > 0$ and $r > k > 0$ so that citizens and inspectors have to mix their strategies. A mix of strategies is only in equilibrium if both actors make their opponent indifferent between both alternatives. If one actor is not indifferent, she will take advantage and exploit the other, giving an incentive for the other to change her strategy. Given the indifference conditions above, we can calculate the equilibrium in mixed strategies for the decision to commit a crime for citizen $i$ as

$$s_i^* = \frac{k}{r} \qquad (10.1)$$

The equilibrium in mixed strategies for inspectors to invest in control is

$$c_m^* = \frac{g}{p}. \tag{10.2}$$

Due to the fact that $p$ and $r$ can be found in the denominator, $s^*$ and $c^*$ are decreasing functions of reward and punishment respectively. This proves the counterintuitive implication that more severe punishment does not result in lower crime rates, but in lower control rates.

## 10.5  Construct validity

### 10.5.1  From simple games to laboratory tests of theories

Simple game theoretical models highlight a particular strategic structure of a social situation, be it voting, environmental protection or crime. In fact, this boils down to a small set of simple games. While these models may be a parsimonious yet intriguing representation of the problem, they may neglect some crucial differences between, say, crime and environmental protection. In order to design a laboratory test of a simple game model, it is often necessary to incorporate more elements into the incentive structure. Sometimes, only this extension allows valid inferences to the constructs of the theory.

A laboratory test of a theory about crime, control and punishment should appropriately operationalize the theoretical constructs. The inspection game is a theory about crime. More specifically, it is a parsimonious model of how norm violators and enforcement personnel react to severity of punishment and success fees or other nonmaterial inspection rewards. The inspection game highlights the strategic interaction between criminals and inspectors in these situations. The original structure of the inspection game described above only models a pure 'discoordination' situation. One party is interested in a mismatch (that is, committing a crime if there is no control) while the other party is interested in a match (that is, performing control if there is crime).

The logic of discoordination games also applies to other settings. At penalty kicks in football, the shooter tries to shoot in a different corner than the one in which he expects the goal-keeper to jump, whereas the goal-keeper tries to jump in the same corner (Chiappori et al., 2002; Palacios-Huerta, 2003; Moschini, 2004; Berger and Hammer, 2007).

However, it could be the case that people behave differently in discoordination games with respect to shooting penalty kicks in football or inspecting crimes. Thus, equilibrium predictions in mixed strategies could apply to, say, football kicks, but not to inspections. That is, theoretical predictions for discoordination behavior may work for one set of discoordination games, but not for another. There may be an interaction between the specific kinds of discoordination behaviors, i.e., football or crime, and treatment variables, i.e., the general payoffs of a discoordination game. These interactions should be specified by the theory. It is a theoretical question of whether the theory applies to a larger or smaller set of phenomena. However, it is also a measurement problem: If the theory applies to one kind of discoordination game but not to another, the specific constructs to which it applies should be appropriately operationalized in the laboratory. In fact, this is a challenge for construct validity.

We argue that inspection of crimes may be different from penalty kicks in football because crime causes negative externalities to third parties, i.e., to the victims. Optimizing criminal activities and inspection expenditures may not only be motivated by optimal responses between criminals and inspectors, but also by moral concerns, reciprocity or social norms with respect to the harm done to the victims. Such considerations are unlikely to play a role in football, where externalities are excluded by the commonly accepted rules of the game.

In order to represent the constructs *crime* and *inspection of criminals* accurately, we include externalities to third parties in the game theoretical model as well as in the experiment. This modification of the game yields higher construct validity by creating a specific discoordination situation which resembles the one between criminals and inspectors. This is a theoretical refinement with the aim of yielding a more accurate theoretical representation of the constructs crime and inspection.

It seems only natural to model social interactions in which inspectors control perpetrators who steal money from victims. This can be realized by combining Tsebelis' inspection game with the prisoner's dilemma. Here, two citizens can decide to steal money from each other. Theft, however, is inefficient so that mutual theft causes mutual welfare losses, which creates a prisoner's dilemma. The strategic interaction structure between criminals is given in Table 10.2.

The complete structure of strategic interactions of criminals and inspectors is modeled as follows: There are two inspectors who can decide to inspect citizens. More formally, the decision to commit a crime is denoted by $s_i$ for citizen $i$ and $s_j$ for citizen $j$ with 1 indicating crime, and 0 no crime. At the same time, inspector $m$ plays against citizens $i$ and inspector $n$ against citizen $j$. The

*Table 10.2*   Crime as a Prisoner's Dilemma

|  |  | Citizen j | | |
| --- | --- | --- | --- | --- |
|  |  | Crime | | No Crime |
| Citizen *i* | Crime | $g-l, g-l$ | $\Leftarrow$ | $g, -l$ |
|  |  | $\Uparrow$ | | $\Uparrow$ |
|  | No Crime | $-l, g$ | $\Leftarrow$ | $0, 0$ |

The payoffs denote $g$ criminal gains and $l$ victim's losses with $l > g > 0$.

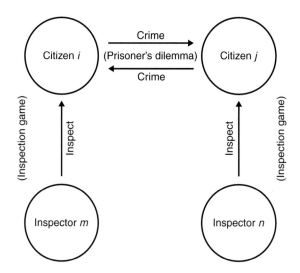

*Figure 10.1*   The Extended Inspection Game

Inspection and crime are dichotomous decisions (yes/no) with fixed payoffs. Criminal citizens are always detected if they are inspected.

inspection decisions are denoted with $c_m$ and $c_n$ with 1 indicating inspection and 0 no inspection. This creates a four-player system: Citizen $i$ can decide to steal money from citizen $j$ and citizen $j$ to steal money from citizen $i$. If both commit a theft, both receive the payoff $g$ and have losses of $l$ with $l > g$. The inspectors can invest in inspection with cost $k$. They receive reward $r$ with $r > k$ if their citizen actually committed a theft. The caught citizen receives punishment $p$ with $p > g$. This design is illustrated in Figure 10.1.

We can write the payoff function $\pi$ for both citizens $i$ and $j$ as

$$\pi_i = s_i g - s_j l - c_m s_i p \tag{10.3}$$

$$\pi_j = s_j g - s_i l - c_n s_j p \tag{10.4}$$

The respective payoff functions $\varphi$ of the inspectors $n$ and $m$ are given by

$$\varphi_m = c_m (s_i r - k) \tag{10.5}$$

$$\varphi_n = c_n (s_j r - k). \tag{10.6}$$

The derived Nash predictions in the extended inspection game are equivalent to the ones in the simple inspection game.[10] The mixed Nash equilibrium strategy for citizens to commit a crime ($s^*$) is such that the inspector is indifferent between performing control or not.

The incorporation of victims into the inspection game significantly enriches our theoretical model of crime and control: It captures the interaction between inspector and inspectee and it includes the notion of welfare losses which usually go along with criminal behavior. The game theoretical predictions are equivalent in the simple and in the extended inspection game. In addition, the new dilemma structure of the game narrows the domain of the model: While Tsebelis' inspection game could, in principle, also be applied to football, our extension limits the application to discoordination games which *include* externalities.

### 10.5.2   Monetary earnings and 'real' theft decisions

Until now, we have discussed how Tsebelis' (1990) *theory* of crime and punishment could be extended to incorporate such important features as victims of crime and social welfare losses. Now, however, we will stress the importance of an appropriate translation of the theoretical terms into variables that are measurable in an *experiment*.

Crime requires property. Property in the theoretical model is assumed to be zero, but the game should be robust to affine transformation. Since our model enables losses through crime and punishment, an experimentalist who wants his subjects to be sufficiently motivated to take their decisions seriously and to be motivated to participate in future experiments should take care that they earn money for participating in the study and they do not leave the lab bankrupt. This can be created in the lab by giving subjects an initial endowment. We decided, however, to let subjects earn their money in an initial knowledge quiz in which subjects generate their individual earnings. This has been done in previous experiments (Falk and Fischbacher, 2002; Gächter and Riedl, 2005) and typically creates stronger feelings of individual property than the provision of 'windfall gains' (Shefrin and Thaler, 1992). Just providing subjects with money is like bargaining over a cake which nobody had to bake (see Güth and Kliemt, 2003 and for further discussion and related experimental evidence, Berger et al., forthcoming). In the experiment reported below, subjects earned their own individual money by giving correct answers to 30 multiple choice questions concerning politics, art, geography, science and mathematics. Inducing a feeling of earned property has the additional advantage of enhancing ecological validity of the experiment, which we will discuss later.

### 10.5.3   Repeated interactions as a measure of mixed strategies

The measurement of mixed strategies requires us to measure 'probabilistic' decision-making. *Repeated measurements* were used for this purpose. Subjects were assigned to the role of either citizen or inspector and kept this role until the end of the experiment. Subjects played the inspection game in 30 consecutive periods, using a stranger-matching design. This protocol randomly matches two citizens with each other and each citizen with one inspector in each period. The average of subjects' repeated decisions were used as a measure of mixed strategies. This means that a test compares the ratio of criminal decisions and inspection decisions with the equilibria in mixed strategies.[11]

An alternative way of matching subjects is often termed *absolute stranger matching:* Subjects who interacted once, never meet again. This method has the advantage that direct reciprocity can be excluded as an explanatory factor for cooperative behavior. To conduct an experiment with 30 periods and two types of subjects with an absolute stranger matching protocol would, however, require 64 subjects per session.[12] This exceeds the maximum number of participants in typical computer labs.

### 10.5.4 Empirical assessment of construct validity

Three methods for assessing construct validity were used. First, subjects were asked to complete control questions at the beginning of the experiment. After filling in an answer, subjects were given the right answers on the screen. The questions had an increasing degree of complexity. They asked about the structure of the game, the payoffs and the matching protocol. Second, subjects were asked to write qualitative comments after completion of the experiment. Finally, we conducted several qualitative group interviews after the payments and recorded them on tape and video. This provided us with some certainty that our experimental subjects understood the game theoretical incentive structure in the experiment. Therefore, all three methods could substantiate construct validity of the experimental design.

In addition to the questions of understanding the incentive structure, we were interested in whether subjects interpreted the incentive structure as a typical situation between criminals and inspectors. We asked subjects about their associations with similar real-life situations. The subjects in the role of citizens thought of fare-dodging, shoplifting, theft, speeding, smuggling or cheating with scholarships. Inspectors were thought of as police, private control agents, governmental controls or, more playfully, of playing cops and robbers. Since the statements in the qualitative interviews reflect situations of crime and punishment, they provide evidence that the construct's crime and inspection were appropriately operationalized by the extended inspection game.

## 10.6 The logic of ecological validity

The 'realism' of lab experiments in the social sciences is limited. Hence, many scholars dismiss its results because they question its generalizability. This scepticism may be fueled by the abstractness of experimental designs (Levitt and List, 2007), a criticism which may be subsumed under *ecological validity*. Ecological validity is concerned with the question of 'whether the methods, materials and settings of the research are similar to the target environment' (Morton and Williams, 2010, p. 195).

Ecological validity, however, mainly demands careful model building. Think of a *parsimonious* theory $T^p$, which assumes a causal relationship from *A and B* to $C$ ($A \wedge B \rightarrow C$), in which this relationship could be confirmed in a lab experiment. If this relationship could not be confirmed in the 'real world', this does not necessarily mean that the theory is wrong or the experimental design is flawed. It could simply be a sign that $T^p$ neglected to specify its domain and to admit that it is restricted to, say, the lab. Of course, this theory would not be of much value to the social scientist usually interested in generalizing beyond the lab. However, the solution is not redesigning the experiment, but changing the theory. If some feature $D$ existent in the field is important there but not in the lab, and $B$ is existent and important in the lab but not in the field, then the *rich* theory $T^r$ should explicitly state

$$(A \wedge B \wedge \neg D) \vee (A \wedge D \wedge \neg B) \rightarrow C),$$

instead of only ($A \wedge B \rightarrow C$). To put it differently, ecological validity is of high importance if there is an interaction between the experimental treatments and the location of the study. But again, this is mainly a task for the theory, not for the experiment.

This argumentation implies that there is no end in itself to creating 'realistic' settings in the lab. For example, one could create a more realistic laboratory setting of the inspection game by putting those taking the role of inspectors in police uniforms and those of citizens in prison clothing. Subjects could be invited to a computer laboratory inside a prison and they could play the game in an animated video game of cops and robbers instead of a puristic computer interface showing merely all payoffs and choices of others. However, if there is no theoretical reason why differences in settings matter, too much realism can blur the effects. The more complex the experimental stimulus, the more difficult the isolation of the exact cause of the effect. Is it the particular clothing the subjects are asked to wear, the specifics of the building they sit in, the animated features in the video game, or is it actually the monetary incentives of the game?

Any experimental treatment consists of many parts, some of which are the variables of the theory and others are characteristics of the settings and procedures. Shadish et al. (2002, 10) call this set *molar treatment, 'molar here referring to a package that consists of many different parts'*. Experiments are good at identifying a causal relation between molar treatments and molar outcomes by randomizing subjects to different treatments. Shadish et al. (2002, 2009) call a relationship between molar treatment and molar outcome a *causal description.* However, it is difficult to say which of the elements of the molar package actually cause the effects. 'Clarifying the mechanisms through which and the conditions under which that causal relationship holds ... [is] what we call causal explanation' (Shadish et al., 2002, 2009). This is why it is no end in itself to create 'realistic' settings, which include in addition to the variables of interest a rich set of characteristics and specifics of the setting. In contrast, in laboratory experiments it is more advisable to create a parsimonious, abstract setting which focuses on the variables of interest, i.e., the incentive structure of the game, in order to have less confounding effects of the setting.

The systematic and experimental assessment of ecological validity has not yet found its deserved attention in many social sciences.[13] Too few studies have investigated the effects of gradual, one-step-at-a-time increases in ecological validity. This research would be necessary to isolate causal factors and move forward from causal descriptions to causal explanations. In a notable exception, List (2006) compared the results of gift exchange in a lab experiment over monetary stakes to those obtained from the same game over sports trading cards. In addition to changing the object of trade, he systematically varied experimental subjects; one condition consisted of students and the other of professional card traders. In the lab, the results of the professional traders paralleled those of the students: Higher prices were reciprocated with higher quality. However, this correlation diminished when List and his assistants moved from the lab to the field: Professional traders at a sports-card show did not honor higher offers when the products were of higher quality.

However, even this study was not systematic enough to reveal the exact causal factors. List's study compared apples with oranges when observing differences in the lab and in the marketplace. Many important variables are different in the lab and the field, hindering the isolation of the causal effects. A more fine-grained design would help us understand which parts of ecological validity are in fact causal.

Note that our discussion above about the introduction of 'victims' and 'property' into the experimental setting of crime and punishment was mainly intended to show that this increased construct validity. The aspect that crime harms third parties is a theoretical refinement of the game and an improvement of the measurement of crime in the laboratory. This refinement is less relevant for ecological validity, because a change of the payoff structure of the game does not make the setting of the experiment more similar to, say, a field setting where real ticket collectors try to chase real fare dodgers.

## 10.7 Internal validity

In experimental political science, random assignment of subjects to treatments is the 'gold standard' to generate high internal validity. The random assignment of subjects to different treatments guarantees that subjects in different treatments are similar with respect to any known or unknown confounding variables. Random assignment, however, necessitates a large number of subjects because of random noise. Typically, about 20 subjects are assigned to one experimental session and about six to 10 sessions are conducted.

*Within-subjects* designs are often applied because of their higher statistical power compared with *between-subjects* designs. However, order effects may bias treatment effects and threaten internal validity of within-subjects designs: Differences between treatment one and two could be due to treatment effects, but as well as to fatigue, learning or timing effects between treatments. It is thus crucial to conduct two experimental series which interchange the order of treatments. This allows disentangling order and learning effects from treatment effects.

The crime and punishment experiment consisted of two different treatments in which punishment severity and its order was varied. In each of the ten experimental sessions, $N=20$ subjects took part.[14] Experiment 1 consisted of five sessions, in which subjects were allocated to mild punishment for periods 1–15 and severe punishment in periods 16–30. In experiment two, treatments were reversed. and subjects were first assigned to 15 periods of severe punishment and then to another 15 periods of mild punishment. Note that the subjects kept their role as citizens and inspectors after the change of punishment severity.

## 10.8   Statistical conclusion validity

Statistical conclusion validity is concerned with two different types of statistical inferences. Do outcome variables statistically differ between treatment and control, and how strong are these differences? In the case of the crime and punishment experiment, three design elements were considered to yield sufficient statistical power. These are discussed below.

### 10.8.1   Detection of statistical differences by means of appropriate payoff parameters

The choice of payoff parameters should represent realistic scenarios and foster fair tests of treatment conditions. Therefore, the mild punishment treatment is specified such that it is just unprofitable to commit a crime if caught. In the severe punishment treatment, caught criminals face substantial monetary losses.

More specifically, citizens simultaneously had to decide whether or not to steal $l = 1$ euro from each other. Stealing one euro from the victim yielded a gain of $g = 0.5$ euro to the perpetrator. This made the criminal monetary exchange socially inefficient, so that the game can be represented as prisoner's dilemma between citizens. Inspectors could pay $k = 0.1$ euro inspection costs to reveal the decision of the respective citizen. In the case that the citizen committed a theft, the inspector received the reward of 0.2 euro and the citizen received a punishment. In the low punishment condition, the citizen received the punishment of 0.6 euro, and in the severe punishment condition, 2.50 euros. The money was introduced in terms of experimental tokens and at the end of the experiment transferred into money. The choice of these parameters yields a predicted crime rate of 50 per cent for both treatments and an inspection rate of 83 per cent for mild and 20 per cent for severe punishment, which can be deduced from the model in section 10.5.1.

The reason monetary incentives for inspectors are lower compared with citizens is as follows. In the course of the game, citizens lose money and inspectors stay at about their original income level. This creates the problem that large payment differences will occur which are not due to individual decision-making but random assignment to the respective roles. In order to avoid this, one can either let inspectors earn less money in the knowledge quiz, or treat inspectors and citizens with a different exchange rate between experimental tokens and money. A different exchange rate has the advantage of comparable incentives in the knowledge quiz and may trigger similar attachments to the individual earnings among citizens and inspectors. We therefore implemented different exchange rates, namely citizens received ten cents and inspectors two cents for each experimental token.[15]

### 10.8.2 Detection of statistical differences by means of appropriate group sizes

In society, there are many citizens and few police officers. In order to increase construct and ecological validity of crime and control in the laboratory, one could think of an implementation that considers an experimental session with 20 subjects, consisting of 19 citizens and 1 inspector. While this may be a scenario somewhat closer to reality, such an experiment would yield considerably less statistical power for inspectors than for citizens. In the first experiments on crime and punishment, we tested such designs (Rauhut, 2008); however, the greater ecological validity is dearly bought at the expense of low statistical power for the behavior of inspectors.

Statistical considerations brought us to the conclusion to implement the same number of citizens and inspectors. As discussed in section 10.5.1, we introduced a four-player system. At the beginning of the experiment, subjects were not yet told their role in order to motivate them to learn the rules for both roles. After completion of the control questions, we randomly split the subjects, half into citizens and half into inspectors. Each experimental session consisted of five of these four-player systems, adding to a total of 20 subjects per session.

### 10.8.3   Testing the robustness of statistical differences by means of repeated measurements

The robustness of a statistical conclusion can, in general, be tested in two different ways, either using the same statistical test for different samples, or using the same sample for different statistical tests.

To address the first issue, two experiments were conducted, consisting of five experimental sessions each. In each session, 20 subjects could make 15 crime or inspection decisions in mild punishment, and 15 decisions in severe punishment scenarios. The statistical robustness of treatment effects can be demonstrated by reporting the effects for each session separately, because the same statistical method is applied to different samples from the population.

Figure 10.2 demonstrates that the severity of punishment affects both crime and inspection behavior in each session in a similar way. More severe punishments reduce crime *and* inspection rates.[16] This pattern is robust for all sessions except for the inspection rate in session two. This pattern can be confirmed by experiment 2, yielding another robustness test (see Figure 10.3).[17]

With reference to the game theoretical hypotheses 1 and 2 and the respective predictions stated above, there are too many inspections in the

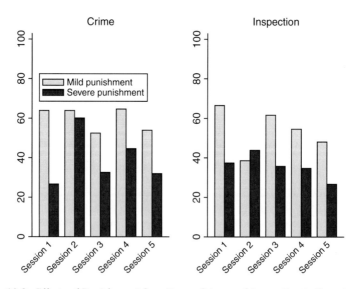

*Figure 10.2*   Effects of Punishment Severity on Crime and Inspection in Experiment 1.
The y-axis denotes crime (left) and inspection rates (right) averaged over all periods. The x-axis denotes experimental sessions. Experiment 1 implemented 15 periods mild punishment (grey bars) followed by 15 periods severe punishment (black bars). Each bar represents 150 decisions (except session 3, with 135 decisions). *Data source:* Rauhut (2009).

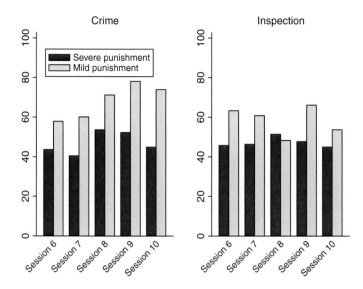

*Figure 10.3* Effects of Punishment Severity on Crime and Inspection in Experiment 2

Data display and axes similar to Figure 10.2. Experiment 2 implemented 15 periods severe punishment (black bars) followed by 15 periods of mild punishment (grey bars). Each bar represents 150 decisions. *Data source:* Rauhut (2009).

severe punishment condition and too few inspections in the mild punishment condition. This may be understood as an indication of bounded rationality.[18]

### 10.8.4 Testing the robustness of statistical differences by means of different statistical approaches

Another way to assess statistical conclusion validity is to address the same question with different statistics. Remember that subjects play multiple periods of the same game resulting in 5880 observations in total. The decisions are, however, not independent of each other, but correlated within subjects and her history of play. Consequently, errors in decisions are not independent and identically distributed as assumed by standard models. Uncorrected OLS-models would therefore give overly optimistic, that is, too narrow confidence intervals, leading to a premature rejection of the null-hypothesis. Multi-level models take correlated errors intro account.

In what follows, the session data is pooled to demonstrate the statistical power of punishment effects on crime and inspection behavior. Logistic random intercept models are estimated. The data consists of 2940 crime decisions clustered in 98 citizens and 2940 inspection decisions clustered in 98 inspectors. A random intercepts model with random subjects intercepts

*Table 10.3*   Effects of Punishment Severity on Crime and Inspection Behavior

| Fixed Effects | Experiment 1 | | Experiment 2 | |
|---|---|---|---|---|
| | (1) Crime | (2) Inspection | (3) Crime | (4) Inspection |
| **Fixed Effects, Subjects' Level** | | | | |
| Intercept | 0.45 ** | 0.13 | 0.96 *** | 0.41 * |
| | (0.14) | (0.18) | (0.22) | (0.18) |
| Severe Punishment | –0.94 *** | –0.90 *** | –1.19 *** | –0.56 *** |
| | (0.12) | (0.12) | (0.13) | (0.12) |
| **Random Effects, Subjects' Level** | | | | |
| Std. Dev. of Intercepts | 0.59 | 1.28 | 1.88* | 1.19 |
| | (0.17) | (0.34) | (0.48) | (0.31) |
| –2 LogLikelihood | –923.7 | –871.1 | –845.8 | –929.8 |
| BIC | 1869.2 | 1764.0 | 1713.5 | 1881.6 |
| n(decisions) | 1440 | 1440 | 1500 | 1500 |
| N(subjects) | 48 | 48 | 50 | 50 |

Logistic random intercepts models. Experiment 1 (2) consists of 1440 (1500) decisions clustered in 48 (50) citizens and 48 (50) inspectors. Standard errors are given in parentheses. Statistical inference is denoted with * $p < 0.05$, ** $p < 0.01$, *** $p < 0.001$. Severe punishment is a dummy variable (0 denotes mild and 1 severe punishment).

adjusts standard errors for cluster effects within subjects. The propensity to commit a crime in the mild punishment conditions is compared with the severe punishment condition. This is done by creating a dummy variable for the experimental treatment. The same procedure is used for inspections. Separate models for experiments 1 and 2 are estimated to analyze robustness and to examine order effects. This yields the estimation of four different logistic regression models (Table 10.3). Models are estimated with Stata 9.2, using the XTLOGIT procedure (see Rabe-Hesketh and Skrondal, 2005).

Table 10.3 reports significant punishment effects for crime and inspection. The implementation of similar numbers of citizens and inspectors proved to be useful, as all punishment effects are significant at the 0.1-per cent level.

Robustness of results was confirmed with linear growth curve models and logit random intercept models, yielding qualitatively similar results (see Rauhut, 2009).

## 10.9   External validity

Typically, experiments use convenience samples of students. Experimenters often do not use a systematic sampling frame nor do they collect data from the general population instead of student populations. Having no proper sampling frame is a threat to external validity, because conclusions from the student sample may not be generalizable to other populations. And in fact, the anthropologists Henrich et al. (2010) question the value of information obtained by WEIRD subjects,[19] and present evidence that students differ in many dimensions compared to people from other social classes, educational backgrounds or countries.

Convenience samples, moreover, make it problematic to generalize from student samples to the general student population, as subjects typically self-select into experiments. Those interested in earning money or those interested in science may have a higher selection likelihood. Therefore, laboratory experiments are often criticized for their limited external validity.

However, it is questionable whether one should rely primarily on external validity and neglect internal, construct and ecological validity. Morton and Williams (2010: 275) argue that scientific work without internal consistency is virtually worthless. How is generalization from one population to another possible if the causes of the effects are blurred by a poor design? In this sense, internal validity is a precondition of external validity.

There is a well known tradeoff between experiments, which are strong in internal validity, and field studies, which are strong in external validity. Triangulation of methods may foster theoretical and empirical progress in the political and social sciences. Nevertheless, we believe that laboratory experimentation is particularly useful for testing theoretical propositions and causal mechanisms, because they yield data with high internal validity, ruling out alternative explanations for the findings.

## 10.10   Conclusions

Laboratory experimentation is a promising method for the advancement of the political and social sciences. This was illustrated with the example of crime and punishment. Laboratory experiments facilitate the test of theoretical mechanisms in a direct way and with high internal validity.

The construction of laboratory experiments should follow certain quality criteria, which can be differentiated in internal, construct, external and statistical conclusion validity. This chapter discussed different concepts of validity exemplified by laboratory experiments on criminal and control behavior. In this way, laboratory experimentation can fruitfully complement field research. The reported experiment demonstrated why field studies often find only weak effects of punishment severity on crime. The argument is that the strategic interplay between criminals and inspectors creates lower effects of punishment severity on crime than one may intuitively expect because more severe punishments do not only lower crime, but they also lower inspection activities in society and crime rates can remain at surprisingly high levels. This mechanism can only be closely investigated in the laboratory because of the high control of treatment variables and the observability of all criminal decisions (and not just only those which are detected by the police).

## Acknowledgements

We thank Bernhard Kittel, Wolfgang Luhan, Karsten Donnay, Sergi Lozano, Christoph March and one anonymous reviewer for insightful and constructive comments on our manuscript.

## Notes

1. See for the original contribution Selten (1967) and for a recent discussion Rauhut and Winter (2010).
2. Later experiments showed that this result is sensitive to the way earnings are generated (Bosman et al., 2005), which was also confirmed in an ultimatum game experiment (Winter et al., forthcoming).
3. There are many typologies distinguishing different aspects of validity. For a review on the history of validity concepts, a classification of validity and its importance for political science, see Morton and Williams (2010). For further discussion of validity in experimental economics see Friedman and Sunder (1994); Kagel and Roth (1995); Friedman and Cassar (2004); Guala (2005); Plott and Smith (2008) and Bardsley et al. (2010). An introduction to experimental sociology is given by Webster and Sell (2007) and Willer and Walker (2007). Horne and Lovaglia (2008) introduce experimental criminology. Statistical treatments of experimental data is given by Morgan and Winship (2007).
4. Note that internal validity is sometimes subdivided into statistical, causal and construct validity (see Morton and Williams 2010 for a discussion). We will, however, refer to the classification of Shadish et al. (2002) in this article.
5. For a discussion of causality see Lewis (1973, 2000) and Shadish et al. (2002, p. 3–12).
6. For a mathematical treatment of internal validity, causality, the counterfactual model and why random assignment works to guarantee similarity among treatment groups see Winship and Morgan (1999).
7. Note that statistical conclusion validity refers to the statistical accurateness of the estimators, for example, as to whether certain distributional assumptions are fulfilled to return unbiased estimates. Therefore, statistical conclusion validity does not refer to the question of whether causal inferences can be drawn from the statistical model. This question of causality is addressed by internal validity.
8. For reviews of the economic approach of crime and punishment, see Friedman (1995) and Ehrlich (1996).
9. For a review on models of tax fraud see Andreoni et al. (1998) and for the respective original publications Yitzhaki (1974); Beck and Jung (1989) and Cronshaw and Alm (1995).
10. This is the case because criminal behavior is a dominant choice if no inspection is performed. The hypotheses can be derived by using the same logic of best responses described in section 3. For a more detailed discussion, see Rauhut (2009).
11. An alternative measurement of mixed strategies may be the strategy method (Selten, 1967). Alternatively, subjects could be asked to enter probabilistic decisions using a wheel of fortune.

12. The number of possible new pairings for $n$ citizens is given by $(n(n-1))/2$. In each of the 30 periods, all citizens are matched simultaneously in pairs of two citizens, so that there are $n/2$ pairs of citizens in each period. Thus, the minimum number of $n$ citizens can be calculated by solving $30 \times \dfrac{n}{2} = \dfrac{n(n-1)}{2}$ for $n$; hence $n = 31$. Because even numbers are needed for pairings, and $n$ has to be doubled because the same number of inspectors are needed for inspecting the citizens, the minimum number of subjects is given as 32 x 2 =64.

13. One exception is psychology, where effects of experimenters, experimental settings, and social desirability have been stressed since more than 100 years (see for instance Pierce (1908).

14. Except session 3, in which only 16 subjects showed up.

15. Note that different exchange rates do not affect the game theoretical predictions. Citizens and inspectors learned their exchange rate only after they were informed about their role. Citizens and inspectors only knew their own exchange rate, but they were told that there is a different exchange rate due to unequal earnings over the course of the game.

16. For a more detailed discussion of the hypothesized effects and its empirical confirmation, see Rauhut (2009).

17. For statistical significance tests of the effects of punishment severity on crime and inspection, see the logit models in table 10.3 in section 10.8.2.

18. For a comprehensive discussion and respective simulations of bounded rationality in the inspection game, see Rauhut and Junker (2009); Rauhut (2009).

19. The acronym WEIRD stands for White Educated Industrialized Rich and Democratic countries, where the lion share of experiments has been carried out.

## References

Allingham, Michael G. and Agnar Sandmo (1972) 'Income Tax Evasion: A Theoretical Analysis', *Journal of Public Economics*, 1, 323–38.

Andreoni, James, Brian Erard and Jonathan Feinstein (1998) 'Tax Compliance', *Journal of Economic Literature*, 36, 818–60.

Austin, James, John Clark, Patricia Hardyman and D. Alan Henry (1999) 'The Impact of 'Three Strikes and You're Out'", *Punishment Society*, 1, 131–162.

Beccaria, Cesar Bonesana Marquis (1819, first published 1764) *An Essay on Crimes and Punishment* (Philip H. Nicklin).

Beck, Paul and Woon-Oh Jung (1989) 'Taxpayers' Reporting Decisions and Auditing Under Information Asymmetry', *The Accounting Review*, 64, 468–487.

Becker, Gary S. (1968) 'Crime and Punishment: An Economic Approach', *Journal of Political Economy*, 76, 169–217.

Berger, Roger and Rupert Hammer (2007) 'Die doppelte Kontingenz von Elfmeterschuessen', *Soziale Welt*, 4, 397–418.

Berger, Roger, Heiko Rauhut, Simone Prade and Dirk Helbing (forthcoming) 'Bargaining over Waiting Time in Ultimatum Game Experiments', *Social Science Research*.

Bosman, Ronald, Matthias Sutter and Frans van Winden (2005) 'The Impact of Real Effort and Emotions in the Power-to-take Game', *Journal of Economic Psychology*, 26, 407–429.

Bosman, Ronald and Frans van Winden (2002) 'Emotional Hazard in a Power-to-take Experiment', *Economic Journal*, 112, 147–69.

Cameron, Samuel (1988) 'The Economics of Deterrence: A Survey of Theory and Evidence', *Kyklos*, 41, 301–23.

Campbell, Donald T. (1957) 'Factors Relevant to the Validity of Experiments in Social Settings', *Psychological Bulletin*, 54, 297–312.

Chiappori, Pierre-Andre, Steven D. Levitt and Timothy Groseclose (2002) 'Testing Mixed-Strategy Equilibria When Players Are Heterogenous: The Case of Penalty Kicks in Soccer', *American Economic Review*, 92, 1138–1151.

Cohen, Stanley (1985) *Visions of Social Control* (Cambridge, Oxford, New York: Polity Press, Blackwell).

Cook, Philip J. (1980) 'Research in Criminal Deterrence: Laying the Groundwork for the Second Decade', *Crime and Justice: An Annual Review of Research*, 2.

Cronshaw, Mark B. and James Alm (1995) 'Tax-Compliance with Two-Sided Uncertainty', *Public Finance Quarterly*, 23, 139–66.

Diekmann, Andreas (2003) 'The Power of Reciprocity. Fairness, Reciprocity and Stakes in Variants of the Dictator Game', *Journal of Conflict Resolution*, 48, 487–505.

Doob, Anthony N. and Cheryl M. Webster (2003) 'Sentence Severity and Crime: Accepting the Null Hypothesis', *Crime and Justice. A Review of Research*, 28, 143–95.

Dreher, Günther and Thomas Feltes (1997) *Das Modell New York: Kriminalprävention durch Zero Tolerance?* (Empirische Polizeiforschung. Band 12. Holzkirchen: Felix Verlag).

Ehrlich, Isaac (1996) 'Crime, Punishment, and the Market for Offenses', *Journal of Economic Perspectives*, 10, 43–67.

Falk, Armin and Urs Fischbacher (2002) 'Crime in the Lab. Detecting Social Interaction', *European Economic Review*, 46, 859–69.

Fehr, Ernst and Herbert Gintis (2007) 'Human Motivation and Social Cooperation: Experimental and Analytical Foundations', *Annual Review of Sociology*, 33, 43–64.

Fischbacher, Urs (2007) 'Z-Tree. Zurich Toolbox for Ready-made Economic Experiments', *Experimental Economics*, 10, 171–178.

Foucault, Michel (1977) *Discipline and Punish: The Birth of the Prison* (New York: Pantheon Books).

Friedman, David (1995) 'Rational Criminals and Profit–maximizing Police. The Economic Analysis of Law and Law Enforcement' in Mariano Tommasi and Kathryn Ierulli (eds.) *The new Economics of Behavior* (Cambridge: Cambridge University Press).

Friedman, Daniel and Alessandra Cassar (2004) *Economics Lab: An Intensive Course in Experimental Economics*, 1st edition, (London: Routledge).

Fukuyama, Francis (1999) *The Great Disruption: Human Nature and the Reconstitution of Social Order* (New York: Free Press).

Gächter, Simon and Arno Riedl (2005) 'Moral Property Rights in Bargaining with Infeasible Claims', *Management Science*, 51, 249–63.

Garland, David (2001) *The Culture of Control: Crime and Social Order in Late Modernity* (Oxford: Clarendon).

Gibbs, Jack P. (1968) 'Crime, Punishment and Deterrence', *Social Science Quarterly*, 58, 15–28.

Gigerenzer, Gerd and Ulrich Hoffrage (1995) 'How to Improve Bayesian Reasoning Without Instruction: Frequency Formats', *Psychological Review*, 102, 684–704.

Guala, Francesco (2005) *The Methodology of Experimental Economics*, (Cambridge University Press).

Güth, Werner and Hartmut Kliemt (2003) 'Experimentelle Ökonomik, Modell-Platonismus in neuem Gewande?' in: Martin Held, Gisela Kubon-Gilke, and

Richard Sturm (eds.): *Experimentelle Ökonomik. Jahrbuch Normative und institutionelle Grundfragen der Ökonomik. Band 2.* (Marburg: Metropolis).

Henrich, Joseph, Steven J. Heine and Ara Norenzayan (2010) 'Beyond WEIRD: Towards a Broad-based Behavioral Science', *Behavioral and Brain Sciences*, 33, 111–35.

Hoffrage, Ulrich, Samuel Lindsey, Ralph Hertwig and Gerd Gigerenzer (2000) 'Communicating Statistical Information', *Science*, 290, 2261–2.

Horne, Christine and Anna Cutlip (2002) 'Sanctioning Costs and Norm Enforcement. An Experimental Test', *Rationality and Society*, 14, 285–307.

Horne, Christine and Michael J. Lovaglia (2008) *Experiments in Criminology and Law* (Lanham, MD: Rowman & Littlefield).

Hudson, Barbara (2002) 'Punishment and Control' in Mike Maguire, Rod Morgan, and Robert Reiner (eds.) *The Oxford Handbook of Criminology* (Oxford University Press).

Kagel, John Henry and Alvin E. Roth (1995) *The Handbook of Experimental Economics* (Princeton, NJ: Princeton University Press).

Levitt, Steven D. (2002) 'Deterrence' in James Q Wilson and Joan Petersilia (eds.) *Crime: Public Policies for Crime Control* (Oakland, CA: Institute for Contemporary Studies Press).

Levitt, Steven D. and John A List (2007) 'What Do Laboratory Experiments Measuring Social Preferences Reveal about the Real World?' *Journal of Economic Perspectives*, 21, 153–74.

Lewis, David (1973) 'Causation', *The Journal of Philosophy*, 70, 556–567.

Lewis, David (2000) 'Causation as Influence', *The Journal of Philosophy*, 97, 182–197.

List, John A. (2006) 'The Behavioralist Meets the Market: Measuring Social Preferences and Reputation Effects in Actual Transactions' *Journal of Political Economy*, 114, 1–37.

Morgan, Stephen L. and Christopher Winship (2007) *Counterfactuals and Causal Interference. Methods and Principles for Social Research* (New York: Cambridge University Press).

Morton, Rebecca B. and Kenneth C. Williams (2010) *Experimental Political Science and the Study of Causality: From Nature to the lab* (Cambridge: Cambridge University Press).

Moschini, Gian C. (2004) 'Nash Equilibrium in Strictly Competitive Games: Live Play in Soccer', *Economic Letters*, 85, 365–71.

Nagin, Daniel S. (1998) 'Criminal Deterrence Research at the Outset of the Twenty-First Century', *Crime and Justice. A Review of Research*, 23, 1–42.

Ostrom, Elinor, James Walker and Roy Gardner (1992) 'Covenants With and Without a Sword: Self-Governance is Possible', *American Political Science Review*, 86, 404–17.

Palacios-Huerta, Ignacio (2003) 'Professionals Play Minimax', *Review of Economic Studies*, 70, 395–415.

Pierce, A. H. (1908) "The Subconscious Again." *Journal of Philosophy, Psychology, & Scientific Methods*, 5, 264–71.

Plott, Charles R. and Vernon L. Smith (2008) *Handbook of Experimental Economics Results, Volume 1* (Amsterdam: North-Holland).

Rabe-Hesketh, Sophia and Anders Skrondal (2005) *Multilevel and Longitudinal Modeling Using Stata* (College Park: Stata Press).

Rauhut, Heiko (2008) 'Höhere Strafen zur Herstellung sozialer Ordnung?' in Karl-Siegbert Rehberg (ed.) *Die Natur der Gesellschaft. Verhandlungsband des 33. Kongresses der Deutschen Gesellschaft für Soziologie in Kassel 2006* (Frankfurt/M.: Campus).

Rauhut, Heiko (2009) 'Higher Punishment, Less Control? Experimental Evidence on the Inspection Game', *Rationality and Society*, 21, 359–92.

Rauhut, Heiko and Marcel Junker (2009) 'Punishment Deters Crime Because Humans are Bounded in their Strategic Decision-making', *Journal of Artificial Social Systems and Societies*, 12 (http://jasss.soc.surrey.ac.uk/12/3/1.html).

Rauhut, Heiko and Fabian Winter (2010) 'A Sociological Perspective on Measuring Social Norms by Means of Strategy Method Experiments', *Social Science Research*, 39, 1181–1194.

Ross, H. Laurence (1973) 'Law, Science, and Accidents: The British Road Safety Act of 1967', *Journal of Legal Studies*, 2, 1–78.

Ross, H. Laurence (1975) 'The Scandinavian Myth: The Effectiveness of Drinking and Driving Legislation in Sweden and Norway', *Journal of Legal Studies*, 4, 285–310.

Sellin, Thorsten (1961) 'Capital punishment', *Federal Probation*, 25, 3–10.

Selten, Reinhard (1967) 'Die Strategiemethode zur Erforschung des eingeschränkt rationalen Verhaltens im Rahmen eines Oligopolexperiments' in Heinz Sauermann (ed.) *Beiträge zur experimentellen Wirtschaftsforschung* (Tübingen: Paul Siebeck, JCB Mohr).

Shadish, William R., Thomas D. Cook and Donald Thomas Campbell (2002) *Experimental and Quasi-experimental Designs for Generalized Causal Inference* (Boston: Houghton Mifflin).

Shefrin, Hersh M. and Richard H. Thaler (1992) *Choice over Time* (New York: Russel Sage).

Sherman, Lawrence (1990) 'Police Crackdowns: Initial and Residual Deterrence', in Michael Tonry and Norval Morris (eds.) *Crime and Justice: A Review of Research, Volume 12.*

Tittle, Charles R. (1969) 'Crime Rates and Legal Sanctions', *Social Problems*, 16, 409–23.

Tsebelis, George (1989) 'The Abuse of Probability in Political Analysis: The Robinson Crusoe Fallacy', *American Political Science Review*, 1, 77–91.

Tsebelis, George (1990) 'Penalty Has No Impact on Crime. A Game Theoretic Analysis', *Rationality and Society*, 2, 255–86.

Von Hirsch, Andrew, Anthony E. Bottoms, Elizabeth Burney and Wikstrom Per-Olof (1999) *Criminal Deterrence and Sentence Severity – An Analysis of Recent Research* (Oxford: Hart Publishing).

Webster, Murray Jr. and Jane Sell (2007) *Theory and Experimentation in the Social Sciences* (London: Sage).

Willer, David and Henry A. Walker (2007) *Building Experiments – Testing Social Theory* (Stanford, CA: Stanford University Press).

Winship, Christopher and Stephen L. Morgan (1999) 'The Estimation of Causal Effects from Observational Data', *Annual Review Of Sociology*, 25, 659–706.

Winter, Fabian, Heiko Rauhut and Dirk Helbing (forthcoming) 'How Norms can Generate Conflict: An Experiment on the Failure of Cooperative Micro-motives on the Macro-level', *Social Forces.*

Yamagishi, Toshio (1986) 'The Provision of a Sanctioning System as a Public Good', *Journal of Personality and Social Psychology*, 51, 110–6.

Yitzhaki, S. (1974) 'Income Tax Evasion: A Theoretical Analysis', *Journal of Public Economics*, 3, 201–2.

Zimring, Franklin E. (2001) 'Imprisonment Rates and the New Politics of Criminal Punishment', *Punishment Society*, 3, 161–6.

# 11
## Gathering Counter-Factual Evidence: An Experimental Study on Voters' Responses to Pre-Electoral Coalitions

*Marc Hooghe, Sofie Marien and Thomas Gschwend*

### 11.1 Introduction

One of the main advantages of experimental research in the social sciences is that this method allows us to develop counter-factual evidence. While traditional research methods are dependent on real-life circumstances, experimental research in principle allows for a maximum of variance with regard to theoretically relevant variables. Research questions that normally cannot be addressed using traditional techniques can be handled in this manner. An obvious example might be the research of the consequences of pre-electoral coalitions (PECs) between two or more political parties. While this phenomenon is quite widespread (Golder, 2006), empirical research tends to be scarce. Most of the research is focused on coalition formation after the elections, and only few studies investigate coalition formation prior to elections. In particular, empirical research on voters' reactions to such pre-electoral coalitions is lacking. One of the reasons for this lack of knowledge might be that these reactions are difficult to assess in a valid manner. Ideally, we would have to know how voters would vote if the parties entering the cartel were to run independently from one another. Obviously, this is impossible to realize in real-life conditions and therefore we have to resort to experimental research. In this chapter, we report on experimental research, trying to achieve a better understanding of the factors that determine the success or the failure of pre-electoral cartels.

In 2003, Belgium introduced an electoral threshold for the first time, threatening the further existence of various small parties. As a reaction, some of these minor parties entered a pre-electoral cartel with some of the major parties. While apparently some of these PECs succeeded, others did not seem to lead to any electoral gain (Hooghe, Maddens and Noppe, 2006).

233

The determinants of voting for pre-electoral coalitions were investigated in an experimental manner by Gschwend and Hooghe (2008). The aim of that article was to investigate how voters decide whether or not to follow their initially preferred party into a pre-electoral coalition. This kind of question almost inevitably calls for experimental research, since at the election ballot voters only receive one opportunity to express their electoral preference. In this chapter, we will focus on the way an experimental design can be used to develop this kind of study. Before going into a number of (methodological) decisions that have been made when designing and implementing the experiment, we will briefly summarize the theoretical model underlying this research.

## 11.2   Pre-electoral coalitions

The formation of pre-electoral coalitions (PEC) is widespread. Golder (2005) lists a total of 134 elections in advanced industrial democracies, held between 1946 and 1998, in which at least one pre-electoral coalition participated. The formation of a pre-electoral coalition is found to be fostered by several institutional incentives (Golder, 2006). A disproportional electoral system provides a strong incentive to political parties to join hands. Parties are also more likely to cooperate if the party system is ideologically polarized, when the expected governing coalition is large and when the potential coalition partner is of a similar size. Finally, a PEC is generally formed between ideologically compatible political parties (Golder, 2006; Allern and Aylott, 2009).

While there is some research available on why parties enter a preelectoral coalition, less is known about whether and when these coalitions are electorally successful. It is possible that the coalition partners would have gained the same number of votes if they had contested the election independently. It is also possible that the coalition attracts fewer votes, as potential voters desert the coalition given that they feel that their interests are not sufficiently represented by the new coalition. Theoretical expectations on voters' behavior in case of the establishment of a PEC are scarce. In line with the logic put forward by Cox (1997: 272) it can be hypothesized that voters follow a seat-maximizing logic, and therefore, that they remain loyal to the initially preferred party. In addition, it can be assumed that most voters should be seen as cognitive misers with regard to politics, that they will not re-evaluate the new choice-set of options available to them and that they will remain loyal to the coalition. In sum, it is often assumed that voters will generally follow their preferred party into the pre-electoral coalition (Popkin, 1991).

Nevertheless, Gschwend and Hooghe (2008) identify five conditions under which voters will be more likely to deviate from this baseline prediction. The first hypothesis states that if the ideological distance between the preferred party and its coalition partner is too large, voters are likely to desert the PEC. Given that a lack of ideological congruence is likely to result in many policy concessions, voters tend to desert and to support a third political party.

The second hypothesis states that voters of smaller parties are more likely to opt out than voters of large coalition partners. In line with Martin and Vanberg (2003), the authors expect that the smaller political party will have to make more concessions than the larger partner. Smaller parties will experience an uphill struggle if they want to incorporate their views into the joint platform, and therefore small-party supporters will feel less represented and they are more likely to opt out of the PEC.

Third, in line with low information rationality models, the authors hypothesize that the likeability heuristic plays a role in the decision to follow the preferred party into the PEC. The more the voter dislikes the coalition partner, the more likely he/she is to opt out of the PEC. While dislike can be related to ideological position, this is not necessarily the case. The personality of major candidates or their historical experiences might also be a reason for disliking a political party, even if the party is ideologically related (Lavine and Gschwend, 2007).

Fourth, the effect of candidates is taken into account (Wattenberg, 1991). If a voter's most-liked candidate belongs to the preferred party or its coalition partner, the voter is likely to stay loyal, while this is not the case if the most-liked candidate belongs to a different party that is not involved in the pre-electoral coalition.

Finally, it is argued that voters need to 're-adjust their mental map of the political space' after the establishment of a PEC. This leads to the fifth hypothesis stating that the longer a pre-electoral coalition exists, the smaller the likelihood voters will desert their preferred party.

## 11.3 Research on voter reactions to pre-electoral coalitions

Since pre-electoral coalitions have emerged in several countries, researchers can tackle the research question by means of observational data. This dependence on real-life observations, however, limits the possibility of testing the predictive power of the theoretically relevant independent variables. In practice, most PECs are formed between ideologically related political parties, and therefore it is rendered impossible to test whether ideological congruence is indeed crucial to understand voters' reactions, since ideological distance basically will be a constant factor.

An additional problem with observational data is that voters cannot cast two votes simultaneously; they cannot vote on their initially preferred party and on the PEC at the same time. There is no possibility to ascertain what would have been the election result if the parties had not joined forces. One could compare the election results of the parties at the previous election with the results of the PEC at the next election, but inevitably there is a time lag. In the context of high voter volatility, it is not unlikely that one or both parties would have gained or lost seats anyhow without the PEC. Finally, it is also difficult to obtain reliable information on the reasons for following or deserting the PEC, as voters do not motivate their vote.

Therefore, a web-based survey-experiment was designed to tackle the main research question of how voters react to the presence of a pre-electoral coalition. Participants in the experiment were presented with two election ballots: one with all political parties individually listed (party vote condition), and one with the pre-electoral coalitions and other parties (coalition vote condition) that appeared on the ballots in the 2004 regional elections in Belgium. These two questions were embedded in a broader survey. Among the other questions asked were questions on the ideological position of the different political parties, likes and dislikes of the different political parties, the party of one's favorite candidate and so on.

The advantage of the experiment is that more information is available on the covariates (reasons to follow or desert the PEC) than in observational data. Moreover, there is no need to wait for observational opportunities and all kinds of combinations of political parties in a pre-electoral coalition can be presented to the participants. The experimental design allows us to develop a whole range of likely and unlikely coalitions, thus building stronger support for the theoretical model that predicts the likelihood that one will follow one's initial preferred party into a coalition. Variance in the independent variable can be expanded, thus allowing for a more reliable estimate.

This experiment was embedded in a larger web-based survey. In principle, surveys can also be conducted face-to-face, by telephone or by post. Web-based formats, however, have one major advantage given the current research question: Participants cannot refer back to their initial vote. Participants were confronted with separate screens for every question, with a sufficient number of questions between the first (party vote condition) and the second ballot (coalition vote condition). When confronted with the second ballot, there was no possibility of returning to the previous question. This is a crucial advantage if we ask participants to make two independent judgments: If they have an opportunity to check their initial choice (which is inevitable in postal surveys, and which cannot always be prevented in face-to-face circumstances), it is more likely that they will present a coherent choice in the two options that are presented.

Furthermore, survey experiments can be conducted both in a laboratory setting as in real life conditions. The advantage of laboratory conditions is that it allows for a full control of all relevant variables. A major disadvantage, however, is that most social science departments normally will not have access to laboratories that are fully equipped for this kind of research, as they are usually only present in psychology departments. In some way, this can be seen mainly as a start-up problem. As experimental research is rapidly gaining ground in some of the social sciences, it is quite likely that in the future, social science departments, too, will invest in the presence of a fully equipped laboratory setting. As long as this is not present, however, it limits the opportunities available for social scientists to use fully all the possibilities for experimental research. In this case, laboratory settings would have other disadvantages, as circumstances could be seen as artificial, and as participants might worry about the anonymity of their voting preference. Therefore, we opted for an experimental study in which participants could simply answer the survey wherever they had a computer available.

## 11.4 Recruitment of participants:
## Students as a convenience sample

The experiment was conducted with first-year university students in Belgium, shortly after the introduction of the PECs in the country. The experiment was conducted during the first weeks the students were enrolled at the university. While it is customary to recruit freshmen at the university for all kinds of experiments, the Belgian setting offers some specific characteristics. By law, Belgian universities are generally not allowed to conduct entrance exams, resulting in a broader recruitment pattern compared to universities in other industrialized countries. While this in itself does not offer any guarantee of the possibility for generalizing any research findings, it does mean that Belgian university students will be less remote from the population average than it is the case in other countries with a more selective university system. A test with political knowledge questions, for example, shows that first-year students in general do not have all that much information about the Belgian or international political system. Evidently, students were not taught about electoral behavior before the experiment was conducted, and they received all necessary information about this experiment after they had participated in it.

Within political science, it is not customary that students receive credits for participating in this kind of research, as it is the case in most psychology departments. Participation is thus voluntary, although it has to be acknowledged that professors have some leverage they can use to convince students to participate. The fact that participation is not compulsory means that the experiment itself cannot be too long or cumbersome, and that the questions have to be related in some way or another to the interest of the students. In practice, the most motivating factor is that students know the results of the experiments will also be used in the course, and that, as a result of this, the quality of the course can be further improved. There was also no subject pool available from which students could be recruited, as experimental research is still less common in political science. The advantage of this situation is that in contrast to economics and psychology students, political science students are less familiar with experimental research, so the risk that their answers would be biased or affected by repeated measurements was less. It has to be noted, however, that political science researchers will be confronted here with a disadvantage, compared with psychology or social psychology departments, where students and administrations are much more familiar with this kind of research design.

Every student enrolled in an introductory course on political science received an email with the request to participate in the study. Only about a quarter of all these students actually were pursuing a degree in political science, since most of them were enrolled in other programmes (communication science, law, sociology, philosophy, area studies and so on). The email also contained a unique access code that could only be used once. All questions had to be answered in a correct manner before the survey was labelled 'completed'. Students whose access code had not been used received a reminder after a week.

This unique identification code allowed us to track whether or not the participant had already taken part. The use of such a code has a drawback, since in principle the participant could be identified, and it is in principle possible to track his or her answering pattern. This dilemma, however, is not unique to web-based surveys. In any other form of survey in which reminders are being used (and in practice these are always necessary to ensure a sufficiently high response rate), some form of coded information has to be kept about who has already participated and who has not. This information, however, also endangers the anonymity of the answers. In practice, however, this possibility did not receive all that much attention from the potential participants, and no questions or remarks on this topic were received. All information that could potentially be used to identify the answers was of course deleted from the final dataset, which thus rendered them fully anonymous.

Recruiting university students for a web-based survey might entail a heightened risk of social desirability, as they know that in principle the professor responsible for their course might gain access to their answers. There is no empirical evidence, however, that this risk might lead to strong effects. Before 2004, this annual survey was conducted with a traditional pencil and paper form, and students could simply drop their ballot paper in a large box. This kind of survey was completely anonymous, and even for technically nonsophisticated participants, it was completely clear that nobody could ever gain access to their personal vote. When switching from the paper to the web method, there was no change at all for the score for the extreme right party 'Vlaams Belang'. From general population surveys we know that it is extremely difficult to arrive at a reliable estimate of the number of extreme right voters, as voters for this party are either less likely to respond to population surveys or fail to divulge their electoral preference in a sincere manner. The fact that the percentage of Vlaams Belang voters did not decline when the procedure was switched from paper to web-based, therefore allows us to assume that the use of web surveys does not entail any special risk with regard to social desirability of answers.

In practice, response rates were very high and more than 90% of all first-year students participated in the experiment. During three subsequent academic years, the same recruitment procedure was used. In the end, a total of 1255 students participated in three consecutive academic years from 2003 to 2005. These were different groups of students, except perhaps for a very limited number of unsuccessful students that took the same introductory course twice. The various waves of this experiment allowed us to study the dynamics of the entire process of PEC acceptance over time.

## 11.5  Limitations of a student sample

Since this study is based on an experiment with a very specific student sample, the figures reported in this article are not meant to be representative. While student samples are convenient, it is also clear that findings from this specific group cannot be generalized toward the general population. Students are younger and often have higher levels of political interest, knowledge and skills, especially if they are enrolled in social science courses. The experiment was only conceived to demonstrate causal processes that might occur among voters in response to the formation of pre-electoral coalitions at the polls. Given this exploratory character and the demands imposed on the participants, an experiment among undergraduate students was the most obvious (and in any case the only feasible) option for this research question.

Nevertheless, it is obvious that one has to be extremely careful if one wants to generalize findings from student samples towards the general population, and this care is not always sufficiently present in the studies that are available for the moment. Kam, Wilking and Zechmeister (2007) have already hinted at the fact that student samples might have such specific characteristics that they respond in a different manner to experimental conditions than the general population. As such, the use of student samples for the generalization of conclusions should be avoided, they suggest. Empirical proof for this caution was recently provided by a study conducted by Hooghe, Stolle, Mahéo and Vissers (2010). They investigated the differences in mobilization potential of face-to-face and online campaigns between students and citizens with little education. Approximately 400 participants between 18 and 25 years old participated in the experiments and they were exposed to the same mobilization content. The authors found that face-to-face mobilization has a larger effect on participants with a lower socio-economic background than on students. Web-based mobilization, on the other hand, was found to be more effective for the students who had a higher socio-economic background. Also with regard to the long-term behavioral effects, the authors found clear differences between the students and the less-educated participants. As such, it can be argued that findings among a student population should not be generalized towards the general population. Student samples, clearly, are not always the ideal population if one wants to arrive at general conclusions.

However, broadening the experimental population entails additional methodological challenges. Hooghe et al. (2010) describe the problems they faced with recruiting and motivating students with a lower socioeconomic status (SES) students to participate in their experiments. Due to the distance to and unfamiliarity with the university campus and a general lack of academic orientation, a substantial number of scheduled lower-SES students simply did not show up for the experiment. Moreover, the authors wanted to investigate the long-term effect of the mobilization of the experiment. Extensive efforts had to be made to motivate the lower-SES groups to return an additional questionnaire. Despite all the efforts made, attrition was significantly higher among the lower-SES groups.

From these experiences, the authors formulate some advice for scholars who want to set up experiments beyond the usual student sample. Doing the experiments 'on location' proved to be a fruitful approach. It was easier to convince lower-SES groups to participate if the experiments took place in a setting they were more familiar with than on the university campus. Further, the authors advise the experiment to be short, 'hands on' and explained in a suitable language. Therefore, the experiment needs to be adapted to the target group. However, when one wants to compare different groups (for example, low-SES and high-SES groups), this entails a difficult exercise.

In sum, it is important to be aware of the characteristics of the participants in the experiment. In principle, the experiment on pre-electoral coalitions could have been included in a web-based general population survey, too, but this entails other important disadvantages. Participation in web-based surveys, however, usually is heavily biased towards the higher educated and those with high levels of political interest (Sparrow, 2007). Although in some recent studies, improvements have been suggested to arrive at more representative internet panels, thus far it remains far from clear whether internet panels indeed can be used to conduct representative population studies. The main advantage of relying on a student sample in these circumstances is that we know internet coverage among this group is 100%, so there are no drop outs for technical reasons. The fact that we have direct access to them in a face-to-face manner also allows us to boost response rates among this group. In sum, for this experiment we opted for a highly representative sample of a specific subgroup of society, rather than for a nonrepresentative sample of the entire population.

## 11.6 Within-subject design: Problem of repeated measurement

A within-subject design was chosen for this experiment. The (same) participants were presented with two different electoral ballots, one with all political parties listed and one with the PECs. Therefore, we had information on the participants in two different 'states of the world', one in which all parties compete individually, and one in which some pre-electoral coalitions were formed. The advantage of this design is that the characteristics of the participants remain the same for both observations. In a between-subject design, it is possible that some third unobserved variable is responsible for the difference between the two questions, and even when one limits oneself to a very narrowly circumscribed sample like first-year students, it is very difficult to make sure that all possible confounding factors are controlled.

A within-subject design, on the other hand, also entails some risks. A first, obvious risk is that repeated measurements by themselves might have an effect on the answers of the participants. If, for example, one wants to compare the effects of two different election campaign video clips, one cannot ask the same respondents to watch two identical clips, and to pretend that they had not seen the first clip when expressing an electoral preference after the second clip. This kind of influence cannot be 'undone', and in these cases a between-subject design is to be recommended.

The fact that this experiment was conducted for three consecutive years also allowed us to refine the research design over the various waves. The initial idea was that the party condition always had to be offered first, and subsequently the coalition condition. The idea was that the image of a political party in some way or another could be contaminated by the knowledge that this party could also be associated with another political party in a pre-electoral coalition. Therefore, it was decided that participants would first reply to the ballot with individual political parties, and subsequently to the ballot with the coalitions. During some preliminary presentations of the results of this experiment, however, it became clear that not everyone was fully convinced of this logic. The basic criticism was that the assumed logic (coalition condition will contaminate party condition, but not the other way around) could be assumed, but that it at least should be proven. Therefore, in the third wave, a new additional test was included in the experiment. Half of the participants received first the party condition, and subsequently the coalition condition; and another half received the questions in reverse order. Participants were randomly assigned to one of the two orders. A simple test was sufficient to ascertain that there were no significant differences between the two split samples. Question order, therefore, apparently did not have an effect on the outcome of the current experiment. The lesson to be gained from this step, however, is that it is extremely difficult to conceive of all possible control variables prior to the experiment. If one is limited to a single-shot experiment (for example, because of funding or because one is dependent on real-life events), this kind of omission might invalidate the entire research design. In this case, we were lucky that the experiment could be repeated, and that therefore adding further controls was still possible during the process.

## 11.7   Results of the experiment

Obviously, the outcome of this kind of experimental research is unpredictable. A somewhat naïve prediction would be that all voters would simply follow their initially preferred party into a coalition. While this kind of observation might be interesting, this would lead to zero variance in our dependent variable, so there would be nothing to explain. The results of the experiment (Table 11.1) – fortunately – confirm the expectation that there is quite some variation on the dependent variable: While apparently a majority of voters follow their party in the pre-electoral coalition, we still find sufficient participants who do not, and who spread out to the other parties. For the analysis, this means we have access both to voters who remain loyal, and to those who opt out of the coalition.

*Table 11.1*   Results of Party and Coalition Vote Conditions (2003–2005 joint sample)

| Party Vote Condition | VLD/ Vivant | SP.A/ Spirit | CD&V/ N-VA | Groen! | Vlaams Blok | Others | N |
|---|---|---|---|---|---|---|---|
| VLD | 195 | 11 | 9 | 4 | 2 | 3 | 224 |
| Vivant | 8 | 5 | 1 | 1 | 0 | 5 | 20 |
| SPA | 3 | 308 | 9 | 11 | 1 | 2 | 334 |
| Spirit | 3 | 52 | 4 | 0 | 0 | 0 | 59 |
| CD&V | 4 | 21 | 227 | 6 | 0 | 0 | 258 |
| N-VA | 12 | 2 | 71 | 2 | 2 | 2 | 91 |
| Groen! | 3 | 13 | 5 | 178 | 0 | 1 | 200 |
| Vlaams Blok | 1 | 3 | 6 | 0 | 35 | 0 | 45 |
| Others | 3 | 3 | 6 | 1 | 0 | 15 | 28 |
| N | 232 | 418 | 332 | 203 | 40 | 28 | 1255 |
| Percentage | 18.5 | 33.3 | 25.7 | 16.2 | 3.2 | 2.2 | 99.1 |

The header "Coalition Vote Condition" spans the columns VLD/Vivant, SP.A/Spirit, CD&V/N-VA, Groen!, Vlaams Blok, Others.

Results of the experiments; entries are the number of respondents voting for that party, resp. in the party vote condition (rows) and the coalition vote condition (columns). VLD and Vivant: Conservative Liberals; SP.A and Spirit: progressive socialists; CD&V: Christian Democrats; N-VA: Flemish Nationalists; Groen!: Greens; Vlaams Blok: Extreme Right Wing.

With regard to the study of voters' reactions to pre-electoral coalitions, researchers usually have to rely on the real-life presence of these coalitions. The theoretical model, however, allows us to predict under what circumstances pre-electoral coalitions will be more or less successful. The problem is that political party elites most likely will only opt for a pre-electoral coalition if they assume that this coalition will be accepted by the potential voters. If one is dependent on real-life conditions, therefore, in practice, voters will only have access to likely coalitions, and not to unlikely coalitions. The experimental design allows us to develop a whole range of likely (and unlikely) coalitions, thus building stronger support for the theoretical model that predicts the likelihood that one will follow one's initially preferred party into a coalition.

The article reports on the 'real-life' cases that were presented to the participants, that is, the three pre-electoral coalitions that were formed: Christian-Democrats and conservative nationalists; Socialists and 'progressive liberals' and Conservative Liberals and a small tax reform party. The analyses showed that most party supporters followed the party cues and followed their initially preferred party in the coalition. It was possible to predict quite accurately which voters were more likely to opt out of the coalition. First of all, smaller party supporters were more likely to desert the coalition. Since it can be assumed that the common platform of the coalition will be dominated mainly by the senior coalition partner, it is indeed quite reasonable to assume that supporters of small parties will feel less fully represented in such a pre-electoral coalition. Second, disliking the coalition partner strongly encourages voters to desert the PECs. It has to be noted that 'disliking' in this case cannot be equated with ideological position. To provide just one obvious example: The Christian-Democratic party in Belgium historically has been the dominant political party, providing most of the country's prime ministers since World War II. The dislike thermometer question showed that there was quite some resentment against this party, purely because of its alleged close affiliation with 'the powers that be'. Even among participants that were ideologically quite close to the Christian-Democrats, this form of resentment was still present. Third, the smaller the ideological distance between the initially preferred party and the coalition partner, the more likely voters would stay loyal. The advantage of this experiment is that we could design pre-electoral coalitions that were ideologically quite distant from one another, and these 'unlikely coalitions' indeed did behave as predicted by the theory. This kind of counter-factual evidence, therefore, strengthens the theoretical status of our observations. Fourth, candidates also matter, and if participants preferred an electoral candidate from outside the PEC, this has a negative impact on their loyalty to the coalition. Finally, the likelihood that voters deserted the coalition decreased every year, and it can be assumed that if pre-electoral coalition becomes more familiar, it becomes easier for voters to remain loyal to them.

It can be argued that first-year students (who are typically age 18 in Belgium) offer an ideal sample to test this kind of time effect. It has been shown that voters are highly volatile during the first couple of times they participate in elections. Older voters might have developed more of a habit to vote for a specific party, and therefore they might be more difficult to persuade to vote for a different party.

At the age of 18, political socialization occurs very rapidly. It has to be remembered that those who participated in the third wave of the experiment were still 16 (10th grade of secondary school) when the first wave was conducted, and most likely they were not exposed regularly to political information at that age. Given this lack of experience, they can be influenced quite directly and rapidly by new information.

## 11.8    Expanding the available options

The experimental design enables us to look at various likely or unlikely pre-electoral coalitions that do not exist in reality and maybe this is the most important added value of this experimental design. First, in the case of unlikely coalitions, this is theoretically relevant. By offering the option to vote for a party in which the two partners have strong ideological differences, we extend the range of the independent variable, thus strengthening our models. Second, the likely coalitions have strong policy relevance. For quite some years, for example, there have been intensive debates about the possibility that Green and Socialist parties would join forces. From an ideological point of view, the distance between both parties is indeed very small, so that, according to the theory, they would be perfect partners to join forces in a cartel. Mostly for strategic and personal reasons, however, such a green/ red coalition has never emerged, although there are various examples of successful cooperation at the local level. The experimental approach, here too, allows us to test the occurrence.

During the academic year 2007–2008 ($n$ = 643) we tested these different coalitions, and indeed this kind of test proved to be crucial for our purpose. First of all, the results of this wave show that the major political parties are indeed well represented in this student sample. Although the electoral strength of the parties in this sample cannot always be directly compared to their electoral results, it is important to note that for all the major parties there are sufficient respondents in the sample to conduct valid tests. First, if we want to test the hypothesis of ideological distance, we need a valid assessment of the left-right placement of the parties. Two methods were applied to arrive at such an assessment. First, we asked students themselves to rate all the parties on such a scale, and second, an expert rating was used. Both measurements, however, correlated very strongly, not only validating the insights gained from the student sample, but also providing us with more confidence in the measurement. As can be observed in Table 11.2,

*Table 11.2* Voter Reactions to Likely and Unlikely Coalitions

| First Vote | Socialists | Greens | Right Wing Populists | Nationalists | Christian-Democrats |
|---|---|---|---|---|---|
| n | 128 | 61 | 33 | 45 | 187 |
| Average Ideology Party (Left-Right) | 3.04 | 2.60 | 6.20 | 6.01 | 5.04 |
| **Coalition Vote Condition: Follows Party in Cartel (proportions)** | | | | | |
| Socialists/Greens | 0.922 | 0.852 | | | |
| CD/Nationalist | | | | 0.933 | 0.882 |
| Greens/Nationalists | | 0.295 | | 0.400 | |
| Socialists/Populists | 0.266 | | 0.212 | | |

Results of likely and unlikely coalition, in the experiment of 2007. N = number of voters in the party vote condition; average score of party on a 0 to 10 left-right scale, and proportion of voters who remain loyal to the coalition for four different coalition conditions.

Socialists and Greens are situated on the left side of the political spectrum, the Christian Democrats are right in the middle, and the Nationalists and Populists are towards the right.

In a first coalition condition, we presented participants with the option to vote for a Green/Socialist cartel. This option was considered as quite realistic, as there indeed had been an intense debate about the strategic (dis-) advantages offered by such a coalition. As can be observed, there is indeed some reason to be optimistic about the chances of such a coalition as 92 per cent of the Socialist voters and 85 per cent of the Green voters would follow in the coalition. As predicted, the loyalty is slightly higher among the senior coalition partner (that is, the Socialist) than among the junior partner (the Greens). Since participants were also asked about their 'disliked' party, we had sufficient information to assess that there was not all that much historical animosity between the electorate of the two parties. In general, and only with regard to predictable voter reaction, our conclusion was that a Socialist/Green coalition could make sense after all.

Second, we presented an existing coalition between Christian-Democrats and Nationalists. Ideological distance between both parties remained limited (.97 on a 0 to 10 scale), and here, too, loyalty is quite high. In contrast to expectations, loyalty was lower (88 per cent) among the senior coalition partner than among the junior coalition partner (93 per cent). Although this runs counter to theoretical expectations, it can be related to the fact that the smaller Flemish Nationalist party acquired a very active and visible role in the coalition, while this was less the case for the more moderate Christian-Democrats. As such, we might hypothesize that the Flemish Nationalists felt more strongly that they could dominate the coalition than just by reading their electoral strength. In fact, since the June 2010 elections, the Flemish

Nationalists in Flanders are indeed the major party, outnumbering the Christian Democrats by more than 11 per cent of the vote.

The third option was the Greens and Nationalists coalition, and only 30 per cent of Green voters and 40 per cent of Nationalist voters would follow their party in such a coalition. The idea that voters are just cognitive misers with regard to politics, as they would simply follow the clues provided by party elites clearly is not supported by these results. In a fourth coalition, we also allow for a coalition between the Socialists and the right wing populist of the List Dedecker. Here loyalty is only 27 per cent for Socialists and 21 per cent for populists. Ideological distance clearly plays a major role in this decision: The difference between both parties is 3.16 on a 0 to 10 left-right scale. The impact of ideological distance is even further confirmed if we do not just look at the aggregate measurement (the average of the scores of all students assigned to the parties), but also at the individual measurement. Among the voters who remain loyal to the cartel, the perceived ideological distance between Socialists and populists was significantly smaller than among those who deserted this coalition. A second element (and in line with the hypotheses) is that nonideological dislikes also play an important role in the decision to abandon the coalition or to stay loyal to it. The populist party 'List Dedecker' mainly evolved around one person, the former sports coach Jean-Marie Dedecker. His style and personality attracted quite some media attention, but it also generated quite strong feelings among a major part of public opinion. The List Dedecker obtains quite high scores on the 'dislike' scale, especially among voters for the Socialists or the Greens. This personal dislike, too, plays a major role in the decision to abandon an unlikely pre-electoral coalition between Socialists and populists.

What can be learned from this manipulation is that the level of ideological and cognitive sophistication among participants is quite high. As we already discussed, this might be an artifact of the fact that all participants were first-year university students, but even for this group, their level of sophistication is quite remarkable. It would be highly interesting to investigate what kind of reactions we would obtain if the same experiment were conducted among less well educated participants. But in this experiment, participants not only correctly assigned a left-right position that is very much in line with the position assigned by experts, they also actively used this left-right scale in their decision making process about whether or not to stay loyal to a pre-electoral coalition. The idea that voters decide on various capricious grounds to vote for a specific political party is certainly not supported by these data.

The experimental data, therefore, allowed the authors to develop a comprehensive explanation about the likelihood of remaining loyal to a pre-electoral coalition. Coalitions should also be formed between two parties that are ideologically close to one another. They also should be 'direct neighbors' on a left-right scale, as the presence of a third party right between coalition partners (but not joining the coalition itself) only distracts voters. The process is smoother if coalition partners are roughly of similar size (or at least if the junior partner does not feel minimized in the coalition). Arriving at these conclusions would have been impossible without the counter-factual evidence provided by the experimental design of this study.

## 11.9 Conclusion

Using experimental methods in political science allows for a significant expansion of the kind of research questions that we can tackle successfully. Without experiments, the counter-factual evidence that was discussed in this chapter could never have been assembled. As always, one's research question determines the research method that will have to be used, although it also should be noted that a whole new array of research questions becomes accessible if one can use various research methods and designs. In this case, the participants in the experimental condition showed remarkably high levels of cognitive-based political decision making, and this kind of evidence does not emerge from other forms of political science research. Future research will have to determine whether this is just an effect of the fact that this study was conducted among university students, or whether the same behavioral pattern is also found among other groups of the population.

Two ethical considerations, however, are still in order. First, in this study we relied on first-year students. This practice, of course, is very common in psychology, and in that discipline, it is even considered a very good method of introducing new students to scientific thinking. In political science, this kind of practice is less common. For researchers, this means that start-up costs are higher, as new routines have to be developed. But the practice also raises ethical concerns. Although participation is voluntary, it could be argued that especially first-year students will feel somewhat obligated to participate if their professor asks them to do so. It has to be noted that response rates are usually somewhere between 90 per cent and 95 per cent, so at least a part of the students does not feel that obligated to participate. It is also important to take extreme care that the results of the study are indeed beneficial for the students themselves. In this case, the students did receive an introduction into the analysis of their results a month later, providing them with new insights into the study of electoral behavior. Students can also be motivated to consider participation as a fun experience, and in this case, the student newspaper even devoted an article to the results of these mock elections (including a list of the most disliked politicians). A formal evaluation of the students is also necessary, and the results of this evaluation showed that a vast majority considered the experiment a worthwhile and pleasant experience.

Second, from a strictly ethical point of view, it could be argued that the students involved in the experiment were the victims of deception, since

248 *Hooghe et al.*

in reality there is of course no cartel between Socialists and Populists. However, students were completely debriefed about the experiment and they received full reports about its results. Furthermore, the question can be posed whether this really should be seen as a form of deception, given the fact that students well knew that such a coalition did not exist. For all the students involved, it was very clear that this was an invitation to respond to a hypothetical situation, and they clearly responded to it in that manner.

## References

Allern, Elin H. and Nicholas Aylott (2009) 'Overcoming the Fear of Commitment: Pre-electoral Coalitions in Norway and Sweden', *Acta Politica*, 44, 259–85.

Cox, Gary (1997) *Making Votes Count: Strategic Coordination in the World's Electoral Systems* (Cambridge: Cambridge University Press).

Golder, Sona N. (2005) 'Pre-electoral Coalitions in Comparative Perspective: A Test of Existing Hypotheses', *Electoral Studies*, 24, 643–64.

Golder, Sona N. (2006) 'Pre-electoral Coalition Formation in Parliamentary Democracies', *British Journal of Political Science*, 36, 193–212.

Gschwend, Thomas and Marc Hooghe (2008) 'Should I Stay or Should I Go? An Experimental Study on Voter Responses to Pre-electoral Coalitions', *European Journal of Political Research*, 47, 556–77.

Hooghe, Marc, Bart Maddens and Jo Noppe (2006) 'Why Parties Adapt: Electoral Reform, Party Finance and Party Strategy in Belgium', *Electoral Studies*, 25, 351–368.

Hooghe, Marc, Dietlind Stolle, Valérie-Anne Mahéo and Sara Vissers (2010) 'Why Can't a Student Be More Like an Average Person? Sampling and Attrition Effects in Social Science Field and Laboratory Experiments', *Annals of the American Academy of Political and Social Science*, 628, 85–96.

Kam, Cindy D., Jennifer R. Wilking and Elizabeth J. Zechmeister (2007) 'Beyond the "Narrow Data Base": Another Convenience Sample for Experimental Research', *Political Behavior*, 29, 415–40.

Lavine, Howard and Thomas Gschwend (2007) 'Issues, Party and Character. The Moderating Role of Ideological Thinking on Candidate Evaluation', *British Journal of Political Science*, 37, 139–63.

Martin, Lanny W. and Georg Vanberg (2003) 'Wasting time? The Impact of Ideology and Size on Delay in Coalition Formation', *British Journal of Political Science*, 33, 323–32.

Popkin, Samuel L. (1991) *The Reasoning Voter* (Chicago: University of Chicago Press).

Sparrow, Nick (2007) 'Quality Issues in Online Research', *Journal of Advertising Research*, 47(2), 179–82.

Wattenberg, Martin P. (1991) *The Rise of Candidate-centered Politics* (Cambridge, MA: Harvard University Press).

# 12
# Using Time in the Laboratory

*Rebecca B. Morton*

## 12.1 Introduction

In many political science laboratory experiments, subjects participate in the same treatment over time, participate in multiple treatments over time or make choices sequentially. The subjects may engage in these tasks either within the same session or in sessions that are separated by days, weeks or even months. In this chapter, I discuss the reasons that experiments are designed to involve such multiple experiences over time, I point out the advantages and disadvantages and I provide recommendations on ways to minimize the problems. I illustrate how such experiments are conducted using some examples from my own research and those of other experimentalists.

## 12.2 Why have subjects participate in manipulations over time?

There are three basic reasons why researchers have subjects participate in manipulations over time: (1) to facilitate within-subject comparisons of treatment effects in order to better make causal inferences; (2) to better evaluate the predictions of game-theoretic models and (3) to consider particular hypotheses that require subjects to have experience with a previous treatment or treatments. I explain each of these motivations below.

### 12.2.1 Within-subjects designs and causal inferences

One of the main reasons researchers turn to experiments is the advantage that experiments provide in making causal inferences. Specifically, when researchers make causal inferences with observational data, they assume that counter-factual worlds are possible, that we can imagine individuals making choices in a world in which the treatments they experience and we observe them experiencing are different. The causal effect we wish to investigate is the difference between the behavior of the individuals in the counter-factual world and the world we observe. Typically, with observational data, researchers compare subjects who are arguably similar on observable variables available using, for example, regression or matching techniques (see for example, Ho et al., 2007), as a proxy for the true causal effect, which cannot be measured. Such analyses use what is called a *between-subjects* research design. Researchers must assume that there are no unobservable or unmatched variables which confound the comparison, and that the comparison provides an unbiased estimate of the causal effect of the treatment considered.

Within-subjects designs allow researchers to observe the same subject in multiple treatments or states of the world. Because the subjects still can typically only act in one treatment or state of the world at one time, most within-subjects designs involve subjects making choices in multiple treatments or states of the world over time. Experimentalists then can compare the same subjects in these alternative treatments in order to determine causal effects. If we assume that there are no changes in subject-specific characteristics over time, within-subjects designs conducted over time allow researchers to avoid comparing subjects who might differ on some observable or unmeasured variable that affects their responses to treatments. Thus, within-subjects designs theoretically hold these unobservable and unmeasurable subject-specific variables constant while considering the effects of treatment differences.

How do within-subjects designs conducted over time work in the laboratory? Consider an experiment conducted by Battaglini et al. (2010). In the experiment, seven subjects were told that there were two jars: a red jar with six white balls and two red balls, and a yellow jar with six white balls and two yellow balls. One of the jars was chosen randomly using a die roll by one subject chosen before the experiment began as a monitor. The probability that the jar was red was equal to one-half in some treatments and 5/9 in other treatments, which was common knowledge. Each subject privately drew a ball, with replacement, from the jar without being able to observe the jar color or any other balls in the jar. If a subject drew a red or yellow ball, then the subject was informed about the color of the chosen jar. If a subject drew a white ball, then he or she was not informed about the color of the chosen jar. After observing his or her private signal, each subject could either vote for the correct jar (red or yellow), or abstain.

The red jar automatically received a fixed number of votes – 0, 2, or 4 – depending on the treatment. The automatic votes simulated partisans in an election who always vote for a particular candidate. The voters in the experiment portray "swing" voters, who might vote for either party, depending on the information they receive. The jar which received the majority of votes was declared the winner. If the winner was the correct jar, each subject received 80 cents. If the winner was the incorrect jar, each subject received only 5 cents.

The experiment was designed to test the Swing Voter's Curse Theory proposed by Feddersen and Pesendorfer (1996). In the context of Battaglini et al. (2010), the theory predicts that when the red jar receives zero automatic voters, uninformed voters will abstain, delegating the choice to informed voters. In the case of two or four automatic votes, uninformed voters will randomize between abstaining and voting for the yellow jar, in order to offset the partisan bias received by the red jar so that informed swing voters can determine the outcome. The prediction of such offsetting votes by uninformed voters also holds even when the ex-ante probability that the correct jar is red is 5/9.

In order to evaluate the Feddersen and Pesendorfer (1996) theoretical predictions, Battaglini et al. compared the effects of several alternative treatment configurations: (1) how voters behave when informed as compared to uninformed, (2) how uninformed voters behave when the number of automatic votes vary and (3) how uninformed voters behave as the ex-ante probability that the correct jar changes. They used a within-subjects design for (1) and (2) by having subjects participate in the game repeatedly, with a new random draw of the jar for each voting period. In each period, each voter privately and randomly chose a ball from the correct jar. Subjects participated for a total of 30 periods with 10 periods for each possible number of automatic votes. Thus, the researchers were able to compare an individual subject's choices both when informed and uninformed and, when uninformed, how the individual's choices changed as the automatic votes received by the red jar changes.

Battaglini et al. demonstrate that the same subject's voting behavior is significantly different, and that it varies as theoretically predicted, depending on whether the subject is informed or not and the size of the automatic red votes. They are able to show these causal predictions of the theory are supported while maintaining as constant unobservable and unmeasureable differences between subjects. Thus, the use of the within-subjects design allows Battaglini et al. to make better causal inferences about the effects of information and biases on voter behavior from their laboratory experiment.

### 12.2.2 Repetition and evaluations of game theoretic predictions

Battaglini et al.'s experiment is also an example of how experimentalists might use subjects' choices over time as a method to improve their evaluation of game theoretic predictions. Experiments, which evaluate game theoretic predictions, as in Battaglini et al., often have subjects participate in the same game repeatedly. As discussed above, the researchers had subjects play the voting game for a given number of automatic votes and ex-ante probability that the jar is red for 10 periods at a time. What is the advantage of this repeated interaction setting? Equilibrium predictions are generally thought of by game theorists as choices that have evolved over repeated experiences playing the same game or similar games, either personally or through the experience of others. For example, Osborne (2004: 25) remarks: 'The notion of Nash equilibrium models action profiles compatible with steady states. Thus to study the theory experimentally we need to collect observations of subjects' behavior when they have experience playing the game.' Similarly, Fudenberg (2006: 700) argues: 'Game theorists have long understood that equilibrium analysis is unlikely to be a good predictor of the outcome the first time people play an unfamiliar game (...).' Hence, if an experimentalist had subjects participate in a game only once and arguably the game is unfamiliar to the subjects, the theorist who devised that game is unlikely to view the experiment as a true evaluation of the theoretical predictions since the theorist generally would not expect individuals to behave according to the game theoretic predictions the first time they are confronted with the situation modeled.

Battaglini et al. believed that their voting game was so abstract that one single run of the game would not have been sufficient to evaluate whether the predictions of the theory are supported. Hence, they had subjects play the same game under the same treatment repeatedly. Their results indicate that subjects were more likely to choose according to the equilibrium predictions in later periods of the same treatment than in earlier periods.

### 12.2.3   Evaluating hypotheses which involve choices over time

The game evaluated by Battaglini et al. has a time dimension as well: Subjects privately chose a ball from the correct jar (their signals), followed by their vote. Yet, subjects vote simultaneously, without any information about other subjects' choices, previous to the vote. In contrast, in a different experiment, Battaglini et al. (2007) consider sequential voting with a fixed voting order. Voters are informed about the previous votes before they choose how and whether to vote. They evaluate the theoretical predictions of Battaglini (2005) applied to a three-person sequential voting game. There are many theories that predict behavior of subjects in situations in which they make sequential choices, and experimentalists often use subjects making choices over time to evaluate these theories.

Sometimes, the theories make predictions about how subjects choose when they play the same game repeatedly. For example, Dal Bo (2005) conducted a laboratory experiment to investigate the degree of cooperation in repeated prisoner's dilemma games. In the prisoner dilemma, two players simultaneously choose whether to cooperate or defect. In the one-shot version of the game, the dominant strategy is for both players to defect. As a consequence, the Nash equilibrium of the one-shot game is for both players to defect. However, a repeated setting theory predicts that cooperation can be sustained. Furthermore, if the last iteration of the game is unknown, such cooperation can be maintained indefinitely. In order to evaluate whether cooperation can be sustained in the repeated prisoner's dilemma, Dal Bo had subjects play the game repeatedly in pairs, both with a known finite end to the repetition and with an unknown end to the repetition. As in Battaglini et al. (2010), subjects could gain experience from previous plays of the repeated game and his experiments to foster a more accurate evaluation of the game theoretic predictions which assume such experience.

A particular class of theories seems perfect for study through repetition in an experiment or so-called "learning theories" In a seminal paper, Erev and Roth (1998) analyzed learning in a large number of experiments in which subjects played a game for 100 or more periods with a unique equilibrium prediction that involved using randomized strategies (randomized strategies are typically more difficult for subjects to understand and use). They investigate the predictive power of a number of learning models. There is mixed evidence on the advantages of repetition in experiments to study learning. Salmon (2001) finds that experimental data have little power in discriminating between alternative learning models, and Wilcox (2006) finds that the assumption of a representative agent may drive some of the conclusions of the literature on this issue.

In all of the above examples, subjects participated in choices over time within one session. But in some cases, the hypotheses to be evaluated required a longer time span than could be implemented in one single laboratory session. For instance, Druckman and Nelson (2003) and Chong and Druckman (2007, 2009) considered whether framing effects, which have been found in single session experiments, are long-lasting by having the subjects return for a second experiment to evaluate the extent that the framing effects were still in evidence. They found that, indeed, for particular types of subjects, the framing effects were long lasting. Similarly, Casari, Ham and Kagel (2007) examined the effects of experience in a previous session on subject behavior in a particular game theoretic experiment. Thus, they invited experienced subjects to return for a second experiment in which the subjects played the same game. Another example is presented in Jamison, Karlan and Schechter (2008), who studied the effects of exposing subjects to deception in an experiment on their willingness to participate in a subsequent experiment, as well as their choices in that experiment. They conducted two virtually identical first experiments, one with deception and one without (revealing the deception to those deceived after the experiment), and then invited both types of subjects for a second experiment. By comparing the response rates of the deceived subjects with the undeceived and the behavior of the two groups, they were able to determine how deception affected subjects' willingness to participate in experiments and their behavior subsequently.

The subsequent sessions may take place many months after the original experiment. In many experiments, subjects are given a fixed sum of money, which they then use during the experiment. Bosch-Domènech and Silvestre (2006) study whether subjects' use of allocated money is influenced by the time of possession previous to the experiment. In a first experiment, subjects earned cash based on their answers to a basic knowledge quiz. Subjects were told that they would be expected to return for a second session some months later in which they may lose the money they had earned. Subjects were then invited to return four months later. The researchers found that almost all subjects returned for the second experiment and reported that they considered the money their own. However, the researchers found little difference between the choices of the subjects in the subsequent experiment and those of subjects who played with money they earned only immediately prior to the second experiment. These results suggest that concerns that subjects view the money they may lose in an experiment as 'unreal' are not supported.

### 12.2.4   Is repetition desirable to increase the number of observations?

A number of researchers believe that the main reason for allowing subjects to engage in repetition is to increase the number of observations per subject. Certainly, repetition within a single session does increase the number of observations, and to the extent that we can believe that the subjects' choices in each period are independent of their choices in other periods and the choices of other subjects in other periods, then arguably the power of the results at the individual level is increased. However, if subjects are learning through repetition and reacting to other subjects' choices over time, then the assumption of independence is likely violated. In fact, as noted above, many of the reasons for using repetition assume such learning and interdependence.

## 12.3   Disadvantages of manipulations over time

I have pointed out a number of advantages to manipulations over time, both within a session and across sessions. However, this practice does not come without costs. There are four main problems: (1) selection effects; (2) sequencing effects; (3) repeated game effects and (4) wealth effects.

### 12.3.1   Selection effects

Selection effects can be of two types; one type occurs when subjects make choices sequentially in a session, and the other type occurs when subjects are asked to return for a subsequent session. I begin with the problems that can happen when subjects make choices sequentially in a session. First, in an experiment in which subjects make choices sequentially, the experimentalist may not observe subjects in all the possible states of the world if subjects who choose early do not choose the full range of choices. For example, consider an experiment on the ultimatum game. In the ultimatum game, one subject is designated the proposer or first mover, and a second subject is designated the receiver or second mover. The proposer chooses how much of a fixed sum to offer to the receiver and how much to keep for himself or herself. The receiver can accept or reject the offer. In case of acceptance, the proposed allocation is implemented. In case of rejection, both the proposer and the receiver are allocated some reversion level. Note that the subgame perfect equilibrium prediction is that the receiver will accept any offer greater than the reversion level (and it will be indifferent between accepting and rejecting the reversion level).

Suppose the experimentalist wishes to observe the effects of different offers on receiver behavior to determine how variations in the amount the receiver is offered affect the receiver's tendency to accept or reject offers. However, each receiver can react to at most one possible choice. Furthermore, it may be rare that the first mover would offer the second mover amounts greater than half of the endowment, yet the researcher may wish to measure the likelihood that receivers care about fairness to such an extent that they might reject a too-generous offer.

Second, even if early subjects do choose the full range of choices, the experimentalist is no longer able to assign randomly to later subjects the desired manipulation, and the manipulation received by a later subject may be affected by the anticipation of what the later subject will choose by the subject who is acting earlier. That is, suppose that the proposer in the ultimatum game choice depends on receiver characteristics or choices made by the receiver in an earlier game the proposer has played with the receiver. As a consequence, the proposals the receivers face are no longer randomly assigned, but dependent on either their characteristics or previous choices.

How can a researcher deal with these selection effects? One possibility is the use of the 'strategy method', in which subjects make conditional choices for all the possible choices of the previous players. Bahry and Wilson (2006) use the strategy method in an ultimatum game. That is, before learning how much they are being offered, a receiver is given a list of the possible offers, and for each possible offer, the receiver designates whether he or she will accept or reject the offer. Then the receiver learns the actual offer made by the proposer, and his or her conditional choice is enacted. This way, a researcher gains observations in multiple states of the world simultaneously. This approach is the method Bahry and Wilson use in their experiment to determine how receivers respond to different offers.

Another concern might be that individuals' conditional choices would not accurately reflect their actual choices when confronted with the actual proposal. It might be the case that a receiver is willing to say he or she will accept an offer of only 20 per cent of the endowment in principle when the researcher uses the strategy method, but when actually told a proposer has offered him or her only 20 per cent, the receiver may experience anger that he or she did not anticipate, and reject the offer if the researcher had used the decision method. Proposers may also alter their behavior. One solution is to have subjects make choices using both methods, and randomize which method determines subjects' payoffs. However, the researcher loses some of the advantages of the within-subjects comparison afforded by the strategy method. Fortunately, a recent survey that compares the use of the strategy and decision methods suggests that concerns about differences in choices between the two methods are not supported (see Brandts and Charness, 2011).

The second type of selection problem occurs in multiple sessions over time. For example, if in Druckman and Nelson's and Chong and Druckman's experiments on framing, those subjects who were least likely to experience long-lasting effects from the framing are also least likely to return for a follow-up session, then the long-lasting effects from framing will be overstated. Similarly, in Bosch-Domènech and Silvestre's experiment, if those who most viewed the money earned in the first session as their own are the least likely to return for the second experiment, then the results from the second experiment may be biased as well.

How can researchers address these types of selection biases? In Casari et al., the researchers consider two ways to deal with such selection biases in multiple session experiments: through incentives and through post-experimental statistical analysis. They demonstrate that varying the incentives for returning subjects can provide a measure of the extent that there are selection effects in later sessions, which can then be used in the data analysis. Moreover, incentive schemes implemented in the design stage of the experiment provide a better method of dealing with these selection effects than statistical methods employed in the analysis stage of the experiment devised to deal with similar problems with observational data. The reason that incentives in the design stage works better is that the statistical measures were devised for much larger data sets than are generally produced in a typical experiment, and thus they are not as efficient when dealing with experimental data. That is, the theory that the statistical methods identify selection effects is based on asymptotic properties of these methods, which are questionable when the number of observations is small, as Casari et al. demonstrate.

### 12.3.2   Sequencing effects

As discussed above, Battaglini et al. (2009) used a within-subjects design to measure the causal effect of automatic votes (partisan biases) on uninformed swing voters' choices. By comparing the voting behavior of the same subjects as the number of automatic votes increases, the experimentalists control for unobservable or unmeasurable subject-specific variables that might affect their behavior. However, it might be the case that the sequence in which subjects participate in the manipulations affects their choices. That is, suppose that subjects first chose with the case in which the automatic votes were zero, then two, and then four. Suppose further that subjects were confused in the early periods of the experiment about the game, but in the later periods understood the game fully. Then there may be more error in the early periods, which affects the comparison between zero and the other values. Specifically, if subjects' choices are a function of their understanding of the game as well as the parameters of the experiment, and if the manipulations are correlated with how much subjects understood the game, then an experimentalist's ability to make accurate inferences is impaired.

There are two possible solutions for this problem: (1) have subjects make choices simultaneously for all possible manipulations, as we discussed above in the ultimatum game, or sequentially but without feedback from previous choices or (2) randomly vary the sequences in which subjects are exposed to the manipulations. Neither option is without drawbacks. The first option reduces the ability of subjects to gain experience through playing the same game repeatedly. Thus, subjects' behavior is likely to be noisier than with experience and it is more difficult to argue that the experimentalist is evaluating the equilibrium predictions of the theory. However, the second option requires that the experimentalist use a between-subjects comparison in order to evaluate whether there are sequencing effects, so the researcher loses some of the advantages gained from the within-subjects design. That is, the researcher now cannot control individual subjects' differences by observing the same subject in all possible manipulations and sequences. Battaglini, et al. chose the second option because of their desire to evaluate game theoretic predictions. In contrast, Costa-Gomes and Crawford (2006) wished to investigate subjects' choices when initially confronted with a situation and there is no learning, rather than an equilibrium game theoretic prediction, so they chose the first option.

### 12.3.3  Repeated game effects

The third problem that can occur when subjects participate in manipulations over time, either through repetition of the same game or engaging in multiple manipulations in the same session, is when subjects' behavior in one period is affected by their behavior in an earlier period (or the anticipation of a later period affects behavior in an earlier period) and such effects are not desired by the experimentalist. For example, suppose that subjects play the ultimatum game twice, but in the second period they reverse their roles and subjects know that such a role reversal will occur. Subjects might view the two games as part of a larger, super game, and the proposer in the first period, knowing he or she will be the receiver in the second period, might arguably make a fairer offer in the first period than he or she would if he or she believed the game was only a one-period game. Such effects can occur even when subjects play the same game with the same role repeatedly or when subjects play extremely different games but with the same partners over time.

Recall that we quoted Osborne (2004) as noting the importance that subjects have experience with a game in order to properly consider the experiment as an evaluation of a game theoretic equilibrium prediction. But Osborne (2004: 25, italics in the original) also notes the pitfalls of experience through repetition:

> But they [subjects] should not have obtained the experience while knowingly facing the same opponents repeatedly, for the theory assumes that the players consider each play of the game in isolation, not as part of an ongoing relationship. One option is to have each subject play the game against many different opponents, gaining experience about how the other subjects on average play the game, but not about the choices of any other given player. Another option is to describe the game in terms that relate to a situation in which the subjects already have experience. A difficulty with this second approach is that the description we give may connote more than simply the payoff numbers of our game. If we describe the *Prisoner's Dilemma* in terms of cooperation on a joint project, for example, a subject may be biased toward choosing the action she has found appropriate when involved in joint projects, even if the structures of those interactions were significantly different from that of the *Prisoner's Dilemma*. As she plays the experimental game repeatedly, she may come to appreciate how it differs from the games in which she has been involved previously, but her biases may disappear only slowly.

Because of the problems inherent in framing that Osborne describes above in the second option, most experimentalists choose Osborne's first option; they have subjects participate repeatedly, but randomize who they are matched with each period, unless the research question specifically focuses on repeated play as in Dal Bo's experiment on the repeated Prisoner's Dilemma, discussed above. Such random assignment to new partners is generally called *strangers matching*. When subjects are repeatedly matched to the same partner, it is called *partners matching* (Andreoni 1988). Sometimes researchers attempt to minimize all possible repeated game effects through a procedure called *perfect strangers matching*, in which in each period subjects are matched with a new partner who has not played a partner previously played by that subject. As noted above, Dal Bo also had his subjects play the repeated games with repetition, matching to new partners, using the perfect strangers matching procedure.

### 12.3.4   Wealth effects

The final problem that can occur when subjects participate in multiple manipulations in a session or the same manipulation repeatedly occurs when subjects are paid for each period and build up earnings through the experiment, leading to an increase in wealth as the experiment progresses. Such a payment procedure is called an *accumulated payoff mechanism* or

APM. If a subject's wealth changes during an experiment, the subject's risk preferences might also change during the experiment. Risk preferences may affect subjects' choices when they face uncertain options or uncertain actions by other players. Indeed, Lee (2008) finds that when experimentalists use APM, then there are wealth effects on subjects' choices suggesting the subjects are more risk neutral as their wealth increases.

Unlike the other problems we have discussed above, wealth effects can be relatively easy to solve by using a *random round payoff mechanism*, in which one or a few periods are randomly chosen as the basis for subjects' payments (Grether and Plott, 1979). Evidence suggests that this procedure works to separate the tasks for subjects and by suggestion eliminates wealth effects (see Lee, 2008 for a review). Interestingly, this mechanism can also help mitigate the repeated game effects discussed to the extent that it separates out the tasks in a subject's mind.

### 12.3.5 Conclusions

In this chapter, I have reviewed the many ways that laboratory experimentalists use the dimension of time within their experimental designs. Allowing subjects to engage in repetition or sequential choices provides opportunities for experimentalists to make within-subjects comparisons, to better evaluate game theoretic predictions and to consider hypotheses that require choices to be made either sequentially or repeatedly. Yet, there are pitfalls that experimentalists should consider carefully in their designs – in particular, experimentalists should be aware of the possibilities that sequences of manipulations, selection biases, repeated game effects and wealth increases can lead to biased inferences and they should attempt to control for these possibilities when using time in an experiment. Experimentalists should think of time and how choices are structured over time as aspects of an experiment that they can both manipulate and control, rather than as aspects exogenously determined constraints on their design. From this perspective, then, choosing how to structure the time of an experiment and the timing of choices can be viewed as an opportunity for yielding a better understanding of human behavior in an experiment.

### References

Andreoni, James (1988) 'Why Free Ride – Strategies and Learning in Public-goods Experiments', *Journal of Public Economics*, 37, 291–304.

Bahry, Donna L. and Rick K. Wilson (2006) 'Confusion or Fairness in the Field? Rejections in the Ultimatum Game Under the Strategy Method', *Journal of Economic Behavior & Organization*, 60, 37–54.

Battaglini, Marco (2005) 'Sequential Voting with Abstention', *Games and Economic Behavior*, 51, 445–463.

Battaglini, Marco, Rebecca Morton and Thomas Palfrey (2010) 'The Swing Voter's Curse in the Laboratory', *Review of Economic Studies*, 77, 61–89.

Battaglini, Marco, Rebecca Morton and Thomas Palfrey (2007) 'Efficiency, Equity, and Timing of Voting Mechanisms', *American Political Science Review*, 101, 409–424.

Bosch-Domenech, Antoni and Joaquim Silvestre (2010) 'Averting Risk in the Face of Large Losses: Bernouli vs. Tversky and Kahneman', *Economic Letters*, 107, 180–182.

Brandts, Jodi and Gary Charness (2011) 'The Strategy Versus the Direct-response Method: A First Survey of Experimental Comparisons'. *Experimental Economics*, 14, 375–398.

Casari, Marco, John C. Ham and John H. Kagel (2007) 'Selection Bias, Demographic Effects, and Ability Effects in Common Value Auction Experiments', *American Economic Review*, 97, 1278–1304.

Costa-Gomes, Miguel A. and Vincent P. Crawford (2006) 'Cognition and Behavior in Two-person Guessing Games: An Experimental Study', *American Economic Review*, 96, 1737–1768.

Dal Bo, Pedro (2005) 'Cooperation Under the Shadow of the Future: Experimental Evidence from Infinitely Repeated Games', *American Economic Review*, 95, 1591–1604.

Druckman, James N. and Dennis Chong (2007) 'Framing Public Opinion in Competitive Democracies', *American Political Science Review* 101, 637–655.

Druckman, James N. and Dennis Chong (2010) 'Dynamic Public Opinion: Communication Effects Over Time', *American Political Science Review*, 104, 663–680.

Druckman, James N. and Kjersten R. Nelson (2003) 'Framing and Deliberation: How Citizens' Conversations Limit Elite Influence', *American Journal of Political Science*, 47, 729–745.

Erev, Ido and Alvin E. Roth (1998) 'Predicting How People Play Games: Reinforcement Learning in Games With Unique Strategy Equilibrium', *American Economic Review*, 88, 848–881.

Feddersen, Timothy J. and Wolfgang Pesendorfer (1996) 'The Swing Voter's Curse. *The American Economic Review*, 86, 408–424.

Fudenberg, Drew (2006) 'Advancing Beyond Advances in Behavioral Economics', *Journal of Economic Literature*, 44, 694–711.

Grether, David and Charles Plott (1979) 'Economic Theory of Choice and the Preference Reversal Phenomenon', *American Economic Review*, 69, 623–638.

Ho, Daniel E., Kosuke Imai and Gary King (2007) 'Matching as Nonparametric Preprocessing for Reducing Model Dependence in Parametric Causal Inference', *Political Analysis*, 15, 199–236.

Jamison, Julian, Dean Karlan and Laura Schechter (2008) 'To Deceive or Not to Deceive: The Effect of Deception on Behavior in Future Laboratory Experiments', *Journal of Economic Behavior & Organization*, 68, 477–488.

Lee, Jinkwon (2008) 'The Effect of the Background Risk in a Simple Chance Improving Decision Model', *Journal of Risk and Uncertainty*, 36, 19–41.

Osborne, Martin J. (2004) *An Introduction to Game Theory* (Oxford: Oxford University Press).

Salmon, Timothy C. (2001) 'An Evaluation of Econometric Models of Adaptive Learning', *Econometrica*, 69, 1597–1628.

Wilcox Nathaniel T. (2006) 'Theories of Learning in Games and Heterogeneity Bias', *Econometrica*, 74, 1271–92.

# Part V
# Conclusion

# 13
## Conclusion: Ways Ahead in Experimental Political Science

*Bernhard Kittel and Wolfgang J. Luhan*

We conclude this volume by taking up a few recurrent themes that were advanced by the chapters. In the first section, we trace the aims that the chapter authors associate with experimental work. In the second section, we discuss the limitations of experimental work that are noted in the chapters. The third section summarizes the chapter authors' reflections on principles of good experimentation and the possibilities to adhere to these principles in practical work. Finally, we point to a few challenges ahead in the further development of experimental political science.

### 13.1 Aims and potentials: Reflections on experimental political science

Experimental research is changing the discipline of political science in a variety of ways. It has turned ontological debates about the fundamental roots of politics from ideology to science by making testable the assumptions on which theoretical edifices rest. With regard to measurement, it has replaced the analysis of attitudes and stated intentions expressed as survey responses by behavior observed in highly – though not fully – controlled environments. With regard to empirically testing causal theories, it has replaced speculations about the signs of coefficients in the context of linear additive model specifications resulting from shopping lists of variables by empirical assessments of point or range predictions from formal models. While testing causal theories is certainly the predominant objective in political experiments, experiments are used in a wider variety of applications. Generally, three motivations for experimental studies have been distinguished (Roth 1995): 'Speaking to Theorists', 'Searching for Facts' and 'Whispering in the Ears of Princes' (see also Davis and Holt, 1993; Morton and Williams, 2010; Myerson, 1992; Smith, 1994).

'Speaking to Theorists' summarizes experiments that intend to test model predictions and to record regularities in deviations from these predictions.

This is framed as a dialogue, as the next step would be an alteration/improvement of the theory in response to these empirical regularities. Currently, the majority of experimental research falls into this class, which is mirrored in this book: Perhaps except for Chapter 9 by Kalwitzki et al., and some examples in Chapter 2, all authors test predictions from formal theoretical models. While most chapters present various methodological points of view on the task of theory testing (see especially Chapters 3 and 7), Jens Großer explicitly describes the feedback from experimental results to theoretical models in Section 3 of Chapter 4.

The label 'Searching for Facts' is given to experiments examining the effects of variables without prior hypotheses from existing theories. In contrast to the deductive nature of theory testing, this approach follows an inductive research agenda. Observed regularities from previous experiments or the real world can be the motivation for these studies, sometimes triggering a scientific 'dialogue that experimenters carry on with one another' (Roth, 1995: 22). The prevalent paradigm of empirical – and therefore also experimental – political research is, however, deductive critical rationalism. Therefore, none of our contributing authors adheres to an inductive research agenda. When it comes to explaining unexpected behavioral patterns, however, many researchers do indeed resort to inductive reasoning (see, e.g., Chapters 4 and 5 in this volume). Finally, Kalwitzki et al. propose an inductive qualitative analysis of experimental chats as a complement to the classical deductive, quantitative analysis.

'Whispering in the Ears of Princes' signifies the dialogue between experimental researchers and real world decision makers or policymakers. Political consulting using experimental research usually takes the form of 'wind tunnel testing' for new policy measures or designing and testing certain institutions. Jens Großer describes the design and testing of voting mechanisms in Chapter 4. The scarcity of research in this field appears surprising given his praise of the benefits of experimental work: '[...] this way, political engineers can produce observations relatively quickly and cheaply to gain an initial understanding of decision behavior and outcomes in unexplored institutions and procedures' (Großer, this volume p. 74).

This availability of data is – according to our contributors – one of the biggest advantages of political experiments. In Chapter 5, Sauger et al. emphasize that the data necessary for testing the assumptions underlying theoretical models remain unobserved in common empirical studies. As Woon underlines in Chapter 3, when testing the predictions of a theory, the researcher is concurrently testing the auxiliary assumptions underlying this theory. The empirical rejection or confirmation of the theory is therefore only valid under the assumption that all auxiliary assumptions are valid. One of the building blocks of modern political theory, individual preferences, cannot be recorded using individual surveys. Any rejection of a theory might therefore be the result of incorrect assumptions about the preferences of the observed subject. In experimental studies, it is possible to control for preference structures by inducing preferences.

Hooghe et al., in Chapter 11, as well as Meffert and Gschwend in Chapter 7, describe the problem of examining explanatory factors that lack variance in field data. On the one hand, many variables of interest for researchers in political science do not vary at all or only very rarely in the course of decades or centuries. Examples of such variables are the type of government, the number of parties in parliament, the interval of elections, the number of neighboring countries or the pension system. On the other hand, combinations of certain variables that might never occur in reality could nevertheless be of theoretical interest. In an experimental design, it is easy to observe the implications of such counter-factual settings which allow testing any number of alternative realities in a controlled laboratory environment.

Control is, of course, the classical argument in favor of experimental research. In Chapter 3, Jonathan Woon describes the necessity of control to facilitate behavioral inference. When the researcher gains control over the data-generating process, this eliminates spurious correlations and unobservable factors of influence, a point also highlighted by Shikano et al. in Chapter 8. They argue that statistical procedures designed to control for problems with confounding factors in field data can also be used to improve inferences in controlled laboratory experiments. Kalwitzki et al., in Chapter 9, as well as Rauhut and Winter in Chapter 10, describe this control as the key for maximizing the internal validity of experimental results.

## 13.2   Doubts and criticism: Limits of experimentation

All contributors to this volume are rather critical regarding their research designs. Each chapter highlights certain limitations of the experimental approach, mostly in combination with a proposal to tackle these limitations.

One of the most prominent criticisms concerning experimental research is ecological validity of experimental results (Guala, 2005; Morton and Williams, 2010: Ch. 7). This term refers to whether causal relationships that have been identified in the lab remain valid in the real world. Basically, the question is whether the lab situation resembles the real world situation that initially triggered the research question.

As the first step in implementing a real-world situation in the experimental laboratory is the abstraction in the form of a theoretical model, a possible lack in ecological validity might stem from this model abstraction. Woon (Chapter 3) as well as Kalwitzki et al. (Chapter 9) acknowledge that it is exactly the high level of abstraction and the isolation from confounding factors which are a few of the main advantages in experimental research as they foster internal validity (see above). At the same time, they identify them as one of the reasons for a possible lack in ecological validity. Abstraction allows isolating the mechanisms driving the observed phenomena. In the real world, however, a multitude of mechanisms interacts, thereby jeopardizing the results from the highly artificial laboratory situation. This, however, is not different from other experimental sciences. Few physical laws can be directly observed but need a high degree of isolation from confounding factors in order to be proven. Just throw a paper plane from the Leaning Tower of Pisa and try to infer the law of gravitation from your observations. Equally, social regularities are typically hidden behind the disorder of reality.

In the same vein, in Chapter 7 Meffert and Gschwendt describe how the simple manipulation of singular variables can never represent everyday life in its complexity and plethora of changes. Yet, as we discussed earlier, the aim of the experiment is rarely to test the full richness of real-world situations but rather the very restricted focus of theoretical predictions. Similarly, Woon (this volume, p. 69) concludes that 'The real-world validity of the artificial environment is therefore an important concern common to both laboratory experiments and formal theories. Laboratory experiments are best viewed as complements rather than substitutes for field and observational data.'

Another prominent argument against the validity of experimental results is forwarded by Brader and Tucker (Chapter 6). The subject populations of students as experimental participants can never resemble the reference population of the research question and thus statistical validity is at stake, a viewpoint that is shared by Hooghe et al. in Chapter 11. Rauhut and Winter add the problem of ecological validity in Chapter 10: The convention of conducting experiments in one specific location (one university or even one specific country) might influence the results as cultural or social norms might constitute a considerable influence on the observed behavioral patterns. While the whole of Chapter 10 is devoted to questions of validity, the authors specifically deal with questions of ecological validity in sections 2 and 3.

Sauger et al. (Chapter 5), in turn, stress possible violations of the internal validity of experimental results that is caused by the administration of an experiment in different subject pools. This validity of causal inference might be jeopardized by a lack of control over all factors influencing the behavior of the experimental subjects. Minor variations in the experimental protocol unrelated to the research question can cause unexpected variations in the experimental results. The gender of the experimenter, the season, the day of the week or even the time the experiment takes place are some examples out of an almost endless list of uncontrolled and nonrandomized variations in parameters. Woon picks up a prominent example, the framing of the experiment. On the one hand, realistic terms in the instructions, e.g., 'candidate', 'voter' or 'party', can foster the participants' comprehension of the experimental protocol. On the other hand, such framed instructions may trigger behavioral associations that lie beyond the control and observation of the experimenter.

The methods of testing theoretical predictions are critically observed in Chapters 3 and 9. Jonathan Woon produces the argument of indeterminacy in Chapter 3: As every model is a set of assumptions, a rejection of the model's predictions constitutes a failure in one or more of these assumptions. The critical challenge is to identify the incorrect assumptions. In Woon's opinion, one of the most severe limitations to laboratory experiments is that they cannot test a theory's assumptions of the game form or the preferences. The game form is the direct correspondence of the model and the real world. By implementing this model abstraction in the lab, one can certainly not test whether this model was a good description of a real-world situation in the first place. Preferences are typically implemented and controlled by the experimenter, as they are formed as a cognitive process and remain largely unobservable to social sciences. Research on preference structures is almost exclusively conducted by inferring preferences from observed behavioral patterns which, in turn, rely on further behavioral assumptions.

This argument is the foundation of the critique by Kalwitzki et al. in Chapter 9. They claim that the purely outcome-oriented agenda is restricting experimental research to a very narrow set on research questions. Establishing a causal relationship between variation in single variables and the observed behavioral changes is only one step in establishing empirical regularities. In their view, the next missing step is to examine the causal path via which the treatment is linked to the outcome. After identifying factor A as a cause of outcome B, the logical questions to follow should be 'why' and 'how'.

## 13.3   Principles and practices: Compromises in research

Recently, experimental economists have started to reconsider thoroughly their practices and to revise standards of good practice (e.g., Bardsley, et al. 2010). In a similar vein, the chapters in this volume discuss principles of experimental research and introduce the reader to latent tensions between these principles and practices of actual experimentation.

One of the observations Kittel and Marcinkiewicz make in their overview of theoretical work guiding political science experiments (Chapter 2) is that the principle of cumulation is difficult to maintain in practical work. While a set of general established stylized facts is gradually evolving, the multitude of parameters changing across experiments makes direct linkages of different results ambiguous.

This issue is more specifically addressed by Woon in Chapter 3. Of all the advantages of experimental research as compared to observational studies, the possibility of disentangling different parts of a model to address each part in an individual treatment is perhaps the most far-reaching aspect.

Whereas observational studies often have to strike a compromise between the precision of the concepts used in a theory and the practical possibilities to measure these concepts, and they are often unable to differentiate empirically between different assumptions of the model, the assumptions going into the different parts of the model can be explicitly tested in an experiment. The tension between principles and practices turns up in two different meanings. On the one hand, he shows that the perfect Bayesian equilibrium is a bad predictor of the outcome, thus suggesting that actual practices of subjects do not follow a game theoretic solution principle. On the other hand, he also briefly describes the search process induced by this finding which is based on ad-hoc intuitions about possible reasons for this outcome, thereby violating the principle of theory-guided experimentation.

In Chapter 4, Großer gives the tension between principles and practices a different twist. He shows how experiments can be used to test the design of institutions before they are put into practice. By exploring the responses of subjects in the laboratory, expensive and consequential design errors can be identified and avoided in the actual implementation of a rule system. Laboratory experiments can thus be considered as a first test in a process of evidence-based institution-building and policy evaluation.

An important principle of experimentation is to ensure that effects can exclusively be attributed to treatment variables instead of uncontrolled factors. Random assignment of subjects to different treatments is a core requirement in this respect, but there are still factors that, while they can be randomized in principle, are difficult to randomize in practice. These conditions, such as the situation in the laboratory and the composition of the subject pool, should be kept constant for all treatments in an experiment. In practice, however, as Sauger et al. highlight in Chapter 5, this principle may be difficult to sustain. For example, the limited size of the subject pool sometimes necessitates cooperation between different institutions, sometimes even across countries. A second-best option then is to administer all treatments in all locations but to reduce the number of replications of the same treatment per laboratory and then control for the location in the analysis. Sauger et al. discuss an even more problematic situation, in which location and treatment cannot be fully separated because some treatments have only been administered to a subset of pools. They argue, however, that the impact on outcomes attributable to uncontrolled factors is fairly limited in many research situations. One reasonable principle might be to evaluate the extent to which such factors may have an impact on the treatment effect. The less a studied model is dependent on culture-specific conditions, the less likely the result will be disturbed by uncontrolled factors.

Two different perspectives on the tensions between principles and practices arise in Chapter 6 by Brader and Tucker. They discuss the problem of experimentally testing a theoretical argument that was originally developed for two-party systems in the multi-party setting. In practice, the challenge is not only to find a salient issue for which clear partisan positions can be distinguished, but also to make sure that there are either no pre-existing party positions or their positions on the issue are not widely known in order not to interfere with the experimental treatment. Thus, a compromise must be struck between issue salience, party attribution and treatment isolation which either undermines the expectable size of effects or the precision of estimates. A second, ethical, challenge is the need to use deception when stating invented positions in a survey. This move is necessary in order to obtain a clear treatment effect, but it clashes with the ban on deception in economic, though not psychological, experiments. Political science still has to find a consensus in this debate.

The tension between principles and practices is also faced by Meffert and Gschwend in Chapter 7 when they present their attempt to triangulate different experiments. Although the experiments are designed to test the same research question, the differences in the experimental procedures are large and hence it is unclear which part of the variation in results must be attributed to pure randomness and which part is a design effect. Hence, the principle of replication underlying triangulation is difficult to meet and evaluate in practice.

In their approach to deal with insufficient control in experimental designs through statistical means in Chapter 8, Shikano et al. argue that current practices in the statistical analysis of experimental data can be substantively improved by using more sophisticated tools such as the multi-level framework, which is well suited to capture random variation at the subject level.

Similarly, in Chapter 9, Kalwitzki et al. suggest that current practices in the analysis of data from group experiments fall short of the potential contained in the data. Thus, there is still room to improve practices with regard to meeting the principle of maximizing inferential leverage through intensive data exploration.

In Chapter 10, Rauhut and Winter self-critically assess their attempts to implement principles of validity in practical experimental research. In the discussion of the problems they encountered, they reveal some compromises which they had to make in order to proceed. Similarly, Hooghe et al., in Chapter 11, reflect on two practical challenges to principles. The principle of independent observations is often broken by consecutively assigning different treatments to the same subjects. While in some instances learning effects are explicitly required by the research question, for other problems this may invalidate inferences. However, one has to weigh the costs of inviting subjects to a one-shot game against the losses in inferential leverage incurred by repeated measurement. The second issue routinely ignored by laboratory experiments is the generalizability principle. Hence, the authors discuss the limitations incurred by this restriction in practice.

Finally, Morton elaborates on the issues arising when subjects participate repeatedly in Chapter 12. The causality claim in experiments is stronger

than in observation studies because subjects can be exposed systematically to different treatments, thereby holding constant any unobservable or
unmatched variables. But because repetition engenders learning effects, it
depends on the research question whether repetition is innocuous or even
necessary for the interesting effect to accrue. The researcher thus has to
weigh advantages against disadvantages of repetition and carefully deal
with unintended side effects of designs that involve a time dimension.

The chapters thus provide different insights into the compromises struck
in practical research with regard to the obedience to highly valued principles of research. While research seldom fully conforms to the requirements,
experimental research scores higher than observational research in many
dimensions.

## 13.4   Ways ahead: Challenges for experimental research in political science

The power of experimental research to test theories and their underlying
assumptions has also laid bare the troubles of formal theories relying on
the rational choice assumption, thereby replacing the sweeping founda-
tional critique still raging in the early 1990s (Green and Shapiro, 1994) by a
productive cooperation (Druckman et al., 2006). Similar to the revolution in
microeconomics set in motion by behavioral economics and experimental
economics (Camerer, 2003; Smith, 2008), experimental work has provided
crucial evidence against the empirical salience of predictions based on the
assumption that individuals maximize subjective expected utility. Some are
reluctant to conclude from this state of affairs that the premises of formal
work should be revised (Ferejohn, 2002). While one can argue that rational
choice theory provides counter-facts that serve as conceptual anchors for
empirical work as various discussants of the rational choice approach have
suggested (Pettit, 1996; Scharpf, 2000), the findings may also be taken as
an indicator of the need to put formal theory on a different fundament to
be able to proceed. For example, probabilistic behavior, social reactions and
other-regarding preferences can be taken into account in models that also
encompass the classical model as a special case (Frohlich and Oppenheimer,
2006; Oppenheimer, Wendel and Frohlich, 2011). It has even become acceptable to assume and model preference change that is not induced by informational learning (Dietrich and List, 2011). The same individual's behavior
may at one moment be predictable from the rational choice assumption,
and at another moment follow a different logic. While the development of
these models has been motivated by experimental work, these theoretical
developments seem to have outpaced experimental work and testing the
empirical implications is still a challenge for the future.

As another example, the importance of reconsidering the fundaments of
our theoretical models is accentuated by a finding that stands out in the

overview of topics covered by experimental research (this volume, Chapter 2): the crucial role of information and communication for individual behavior and collective outcomes in experimental studies. There is now ample evidence that formal models are better in predicting voting behavior, the less information is available to voters and the more this information is structured by the experimental design. In contrast, the more communication is allowed, and the less structure is imposed on the mode of communication, the more subjects depart from induced preferences in favor of social considerations and norms such as equality or reciprocity. This points to the extreme importance of context and past experience for the mode of interaction chosen by subjects and undermines the hope for simple models. Norm-driven and utility-maximizing voter models may coexist because both tendencies are observable in experiments. Results indicate more or less clear tendencies pointing to one or the other model, but neither model satisfactorily explains the results.

These observations, however, suggest that we may currently be witnessing a sequence of scientific revolutions in political science triggered by the growing apprehension of experimental results. Such processes are nothing specific and have been observed repeatedly in other disciplines (Kuhn, 1962). The question thus is how we can give these revolutions additional momentum. At this level of abstraction, we believe that there are at least four challenges ahead.

First, we have to continue building an analytical behavioral framework that takes into account the persistent findings from experimental work, and we have to work hard in finding a consensus about adequate experimental designs for particular research questions that improve our ability to compare and combine results from different studies. Game theory and evolutionary theory are promising candidates as a backbone for these integrative endeavors (Gintis, 2007). Although such a request might be considered a hindrance to creativity, including a treatment that explicitly replicates one particular and crucial aspect of a previous study might be sufficient to provide the necessary link.

Second, as a community, experimental political science has not yet developed a standard of publication of experimental protocols (Leeper, 2011), and neither is a repository of data for replication studies available that meets the currently proposed standards (King, 1995; 2011). If the aim of cumulative scientific progress is taken seriously, the use of others' protocols and replication of analyses must be made easier in order to encourage a step-by-step procedure of hypothesis testing. While some, or even many, may worry about illicit competition and data theft, available empirical evidence on citation frequencies tends to support the proposition that actually full availability of data is positively correlated with the citation index of authors (Piwowar, Day and Fridsma, 2007). Still, unfortunately, such concerns have a reasonable core and have to be taken seriously. It might be a challenging field experiment to explore the design of institutions that simultaneously foster replication and ban the risk of intellectual theft in the experimental political science community.

Third, at the infrastructural level, we believe that one more factor slowing down progress is the uniform orientation toward a few large ('A-level') scientific journals publishing lengthy, landmark articles that dominate political science. While formal theoretical and experimental work is quite successful in gaining access to these journals, their publication criteria – new theory, new methods and new data – are too demanding for 'normal science' to be publishable. Every single contribution has to be revolutionary. However, progress with experimental work relies on replication and limited variation. If a premium is put on grand new paradigms in the most respected journals, and academic careers have to be built on publishing strategies targeted at these journals, then the work necessary to overcome the 'dappled world' (Cartwright, 1999) stage will be avoided. What is hence needed is a set of peer-reviewed journals specifically inviting short, three- to four-page research notes in which the newest twists to streams of experimental work can be reported at a fast rate. What we call for, therefore, is a social science equivalent to the format of journals like *Nature*, *Science* or the *Proceedings of the National Academy of Sciences* (PNAS). It should be noted, however, that in recent years, an increasing number of contributions from the social sciences have been published in these journals, among which a substantial number is based on formal theory and experimental in design.

Fourth, instead of bemoaning the increasing sophistication of mathematical modeling involved in theoretical work as a mystification that makes top-level work in political science inaccessible to the modal political scientist, we should reconsider the curricula that we offer to the next generation. As long as only a few political science programs worldwide include a mandatory section on mathematics, formal modeling and game theory, political science as a discipline will not gain the capacity to catch up with its own scientific frontier, let alone be able to productively integrate, and take issue with, the invasion by economists into its core topics.

This is not to say that all political science must embark on formal modeling and experimentation. The social sciences, in contrast to the natural sciences, are concerned with the interaction of meaning-producing subjects, and thus there is much to gain from the in-depth, interpretive study of individual and collective practices (Yanow and Schwartz-Shea, 2006). There is also, we submit, much to gain from integrating experimental and interpretive perspectives. Whereas theoretical models and experimental studies aim for general patterns, understanding individual behavior – that may deviate from those general patterns – involves more than its mere categorization. Understanding the diversity of motives and aims of individuals helps build more appropriate models, as models help us understand individual behavior. In the concert of approaches, methodologies and methods, experiments have now been established as a respected approach in political science, and contribute to the advancement of understanding politics.

## References

Bardsley, Nicholas, Robin Cubitt, Graham Loomes, Peter Moffatt, Chris Starmer and Robert Sugden (2010) *Experimental Economics. Rethinking the Rules* (Princeton: Princeton University Press).

Camerer, Colin F. (2003) *Behavioral Game Theory. Experiments in Strategic Interaction* (Princeton: Princeton University Press).

Cartwright, Nancy (1999) *The Dappled World. A Study of the Boundaries of Science* (Cambridge: Cambridge University Press).

Davis, Douglas D. and Charles A. Holt (1993) *Experimental Economics* (Princeton: Princeton University Press).

Dietrich, Franz and Christian List (2011) 'A Model of Non-Informational Preference Change', *Journal of Theoretical Politics*, 23, 145–164.

Druckman, James N., Donald P. Green, James H. Kuklinski and Arthur Lupia (2006) 'The Growth and Development of Experimental Research in Political Science', *American Political Science Review*, 100, 627–635.

Ferejohn, John A. (2002) 'Rational Choice Theory and Social Explanation', *Economics and Philosophy*, 18, 211–235.

Frohlich, Norman and Joe Oppenheimer (2006) 'Skating on Thin Ice. Cracks in the Public Choice Foundation', *Journal of Theoretical Politics*, 18, 235–66.

Gintis, Herbert (2007) 'A Framework for the Unification of the Behavioral Sciences', *Behavioral and Brain Sciences*, 30, 1–61.

Green, Donald P. and Ian Shapiro (1994) *Pathologies of Rational Choice Theory. A Critique of Applications in Political Science* (New Haven: Yale University Press).

Guala, Francesco (2005) *The Methodology of Experimental Economics* (Cambridge: Cambridge University Press).

King, Gary (1995) 'Replication, Replication', *PS: Political Science & Politics*, 28, 443–99.

King, Gary (2011) 'Ensuring the Data Rich Future of the Social Sciences', *Science*, 331, 719–721.

Kuhn, Thomas S. (1962) *The Structure of Scientific Revolutions* (Chicago: University of Chicago Press).

Leeper, Thomas J. (2011) 'The Role of Protocols in the Design and Reporting of Experiments', *The Experimental Political Scientist. Newsletter of the APSA Experimental Section*, 2, 6–10.

Morton, Rebecca B. and Kenneth Williams (2010) *Experimental Political Science and the Study of Causality. From Nature to the Lab* (Cambridge: Cambridge University Press).

Myerson, Roger B. (1992) 'On the Value of Game Theory in Social Science', *Rationality and Society*, 4, 62–73.

Oppenheimer, Joe, Stephen Wendel and Norman Frohlich (2011) 'Paradox Lost: Explaining and Modeling Seemingly Random Individual Behavior in Social Dilemmas', *Journal of Theoretical Politics*, 23, 165–87.

Pettit, Philip (1996) *The Common Mind. An Essay on Psychology, Society, and Politics* (Oxford: Oxford University Press).

Piwowar, Heather A., Roger S. Day and Douglas B. Fridsma (2007) 'Sharing Detailed Research Data is Associated with Increased Citation Rate', *PLoS ONE* 2, e308.

Roth, Alvin E. (1995) 'Introduction to Experimental Economics', in John H. Kagel and Alvin E. Roth (eds.) *The Handbook of Experimental Economics* (Princeton: Princeton University Press).

Scharpf, Fritz W. (2000) 'Institutions in Comparative Policy Research', *Comparative Political Studies* 33, 762–790.

Smith, Vernon (1994) 'Economics in the Laboratory', *Journal of Economic Perspectives* 8, 113–131.

Smith, Vernon (2008) *Rationality in Economics. Constructivist and Ecological Forms* (Cambridge: Cambridge University Press).

Yanow, Dvora and Peregrine Schwartz-Shea (2006) *Interpretation and Method. Empirical Research Methods and the Interpretive Turn* (Armonk, NY: M.E. Sharpe).

# Appendix
## Resources for Experimental
## Research in the Social Sciences

*Jana Keller, Bernhard Kittel and Wolfgang Luhan*

There are abundant resources available for experimental political science, but for the novice it seems difficult to identify the best resource to turn to for the solution of particular problems. In this appendix, we present a few currently available resources and give hints for places to start further explorations.

## 1. Web resources

Several experimental laboratories have developed ready-made experiments that can be used for both educational and research purposes. They are easy to use and do not require any programming knowledge.

Veconlab (http://veconlab.econ.virginia.edu/admin.htm)
Veconlab has been developed by Charles Holt at the University of Virginia and contains most of the experiments discussed in his textbook (Holt, 2007) as modules. The page offers a variety of games ranging from abstract games via two-player market games and bargaining games, to N-player public goods and voting games. Each game can be played in several variants, with varying numbers of participants, rounds and payoff parameters. The results are provided automatically in diagrams and tables. The experiments are run online and no software needs to be downloaded. Most experiments focus on micro- and macroeconomic problems, but political scientists can build on the bargaining, public goods and voting games.

EconPort (http://www.econport.org/)
EconPort is an online archive of experiments in economics that is currently located at the Georgia State University and which is coordinated by James C. Cox and J. Todd Swarthout (Cox and Swarthout, 2006). It contains ready-made online experiments, teaching modules and further links to online resources in experimental economics. Among the available experiments are

simple and more complex two-player and N-player games, auction games, public finance games and public goods games. The experiments are rather flexible and adjustable und allow users to develop more complex experiments without the need to program them.

ComLabGames (http://www.comlabgames.com/)

ComLabGames has been developed by a research team directed by Robert A. Miller at the Carnegie Mellon University, Pittsburgh (Miller and Prasnikar, forthcoming). The software for online experiments is used at high schools and colleges to teach students strategic behavior through personal experience and data analysis. The software can be downloaded and it is easy to install and use. ComLabGames offers various functions to conceptualize and describe games and to analyze the data.

## 2. Software

For many research questions in political science, the ready-made online modules do not provide adequate designs because they are targeted at the needs of economists. Still today, many experimentalists design their own experiments in some programming language. But before evading to all-purpose programming environments, the use of software packages developed for experimental research should be considered. This experimental software is usually developed for economic applications as well, but offers enough possibilities to develop new experiments that model political interaction situations. The list of software below is not exhaustive and varies in terms of ease-of-use, available functions and complexity of the programming language. However, it contains the most common packages that may be useful for topics in political science.

z-Tree (http://www.iew.uzh.ch/ztree/index.php)

z-Tree (Zurich Toolbox for Readymade Economic Experiments) has been developed at the University of Zurich by Urs Fischbacher (Fischbacher, 2007) and it offers a simple programming environment with functions that allow the development of most constellations encountered in experimental research in the social sciences. The license is free of charge.

Multistage (http://software.ssel.caltech.edu/)

Multistage, developed jointly at the California Institute of Technology (Caltech) and UCLA by a team headed by Thomas Palfrey, is a programming environment for social science and economic experiments based on Java. In contrast to other experimental software, users have full access to the source code to adjust the experimental design to their specific needs. Many prebuilt modules and functions can be selected and adjusted to the researcher's specification of the experiment.

PEET (http://econlab.uaa.alaska.edu/software.htm)

Modeled after Multistage, PEET (Python Experimental Economics Toolkit) has been developed at the University of Alaska at Anchorage Experimental Economics Laboratory by Ben Saylor in the programming language Python. The program can be downloaded free of charge and requires prior installation of Python.

JMarkets (http://jmarkets.ssel.caltech.edu/)

Initiated by Charles Plott, among others at Caltech, JMarkets is a Java-based programming environment which supports the development and running of large-scale experiments. Its main field of application is interwoven financial and monetary systems.

## 3. Recruitment of participants

In order to avoid costly and error-prone procedures for inviting experimental subjects, programs for the administration of social science experiments have been developed which facilitates the organization of the subject pool and the coordination of experiments. Typically, these environments allow for the definition of characteristics of invited subjects, and they collect statistics on the subject pool, such as who has participated in which experiment.

ORSEE (http://www.orsee.org/), Online Recruitment System for Economic Experiments, has been developed by Ben Greiner (Greiner, 2004) as a multipurpose platform which manages the basic functions necessary for running experiments.

MooreRecruiting (http://moorerecruiting.ssel.caltech.edu/) has been developed at Caltech as platform for social science experiments, which, in addition to the basic functions, also includes the possibility of administering questionnaires, the responses on which can be used as a filter for invitations to experimental sessions. Also, payment functions have been amended by a PayPal facility.

## 4. Laboratories and online research links

A list of operating laboratories for experimental research in economics and the social sciences is being maintained at Laboratoire Montpelliérain d´Economie Théorique et Appliquée (LAMETA) at the Université de Montpellier (http://leem.lameta.univ-montp1.fr/index.php?page=liste_labos&lang=eng*).

Links are maintained at:

- California Social Science Experimental Laboratory (http://www.ssel.caltech.edu/info/index.php?option=com_weblinks&view=category&id=10&Itemid=13)

- Università Pompeu Fabra in Barcelona (http://www.upf.edu/leex/links/)
- University of Tasmania (http://www.economicexperiments.com/).

## 5. Associations

APSA Organized Section on Experimental Research
American Political Science Associationhttp://www.apsanet.org/content_70629.cfm
 Newsletter: The Experimental Political Scientist, since 2010
 Economic Science Association
 http://www.economicscience.org
 Journal: Experimental Economics

## References

Cox, James C. and J. Todd Swarthout (2006) 'EconPort: Creating and Maintaining a Knowledge Commons', in Charlotte Hess and Elinor Ostrom (eds.) *Understanding Knowledge as a Commons: From Theory to Practice* (Cambridge: MIT-Press).

Fischbacher, Urs (2007) 'z-Tree: Zurich Toolbox for Ready-Made Economic Experiments', *Experimental Economics*, 10, 171–178.

Greiner, Ben (2004) 'An Online Recruitment System for Economic Experiments', in Kurt Kremer and Volker Macho (eds.) *GWDG Bericht 63* (Göttingen: Gesellschaft für wissenschaftliche Datenverarbeitung).

Holt, Charles A. (2007) *Markets, Games, & Strategic Behavior* (Boston: Pearson).

Miller, Robert A. and Vesna Prasnikar (forthcoming) *Strategic Play* (Stanford: Stanford University Press).

# Index

Univ.-Bibl.
Bamberg
UB Bamberg
ausgeschieden